Discourse, Media, and Conflict

Bringing together contributions from a team of international scholars, this pioneering book applies theories and approaches from linguistics, such as discourse analysis and pragmatics, to analyze the media and online political discourses of both conflict and peace processes. By analyzing case studies as globally diverse as Germany, the USA, Nigeria, Iraq, Korea, and Libya, and across a range of genres such as TV news channels, online reporting, and traditional newspapers, the chapters collectively show how news discourse can be powerful in mobilizing public support for war or violence, or for conflict resolution, through the linguistic representation of certain groups. It explores the consequences of this "framing" effect, and shows how peace journalism can be achieved through a non-violent approach to reporting conflict. It will therefore serve as an essential resource for students, scholars, and experts in media and communication studies, conflict and peace studies, international relations, linguistics, and political science.

INNOCENT CHILUWA is Professor of English Linguistics (Discourse Analysis) and Media/Digital Communications in the Department of Languages & General Studies, Covenant University, Ota (Nigeria). His recent publications include *Discourse and Conflict* (Palgrave Macmillan, 2021), and *Activism, Campaigning and Political Discourse on Twitter* (Nova Science, 2019).

Discourse, Media, and Conflict
Examining War and Resolution in the News

Edited by
Innocent Chiluwa
Covenant University, Nigeria

CAMBRIDGE
UNIVERSITY PRESS

Shaftesbury Road, Cambridge CB2 8EA, United Kingdom

One Liberty Plaza, 20th Floor, New York, NY 10006, USA

477 Williamstown Road, Port Melbourne, NY 3207, Australia

314–321, 3rd Floor, Plot 3, Splendor Forum, Jasola District Centre, New Delhi – 110025, India

103 Penang Road, #05–06/07, Visioncrest Commercial, Singapore 238467

Cambridge University Press is part of Cambridge University Press & Assessment, a department of the University of Cambridge.

We share the University's mission to contribute to society through the pursuit of education, learning and research at the highest international levels of excellence.

www.cambridge.org
Information on this title: www.cambridge.org/9781009073684

DOI: 10.1017/9781009064057

© Innocent Chiluwa 2022

This publication is in copyright. Subject to statutory exception and to the provisions of relevant collective licensing agreements, no reproduction of any part may take place without the written permission of Cambridge University Press & Assessment.

First published 2022
First paperback edition 2025

A catalogue record for this publication is available from the British Library

ISBN 978-1-316-51340-8   Hardback
ISBN 978-1-009-07368-4   Paperback

Cambridge University Press & Assessment has no responsibility for the persistence or accuracy of URLs for external or third-party internet websites referred to in this publication and does not guarantee that any content on such websites is, or will remain, accurate or appropriate.

Contents

List of Figures	*page* viii
List of Tables	ix
About the Authors	x
Foreword	xv
OLIVER RAMSBOTHAM	
Introduction: Media, Conflict, and Peace-Building	1
INNOCENT CHILUWA	

Part I   Conflict Discourse in Newspaper Reporting   17

1 Elián González in the *New York Times:* Media Roles in the
   Trajectories of International Conflict   19
   MARK FINNEY AND SARAH FISHER

2 The Construction of Threat of "Islamist Terrorism" in German
   Newspapers   47
   ENIS BICER, LINA BRINK, AND ALEJANDRA NIEVES CAMACHO

3 "Herdsmen Are Terrorists": Analyzing News Headlines on the
   Herder–Farmer Conflict in the Nigerian Press   69
   INNOCENT CHILUWA, ISIOMA M. CHILUWA, AND ANGIE O. IGBINOBA

4 Covering the War on Iraq: The Pragmatics of Framing and Visual
   Rhetoric   93
   AHMED SAHLANE

Part II   Electronic Media and Online Discourses of Conflict   117

5 Making a Case for War: CNN and the Representations of
   Humanitarianism, Gadhafi, and NATO in the 2011 Bombing of
   Libya   119
   ADA PETER AND INNOCENT CHILUWA

6 "The Situation on the Korean Peninsula": *Voice of America* and *China Radio International* on China and the USA about the North Korean Conflict 140
VALERIE A. COOPER

7 Against a Hard-Earned Peace: (De)legitimation Discourses of Political Violence in Online Press Statements of Dissident Republicans in Post-Conflict Northern Ireland 162
STEPHEN GOULDING

8 Ideological Exclusion: Defining the (Dis)believer in Extremist Muslim Periodicals – *Dabiq* and *Inspire* 194
TROY E. SPIER

9 Violence for Social Change: An Analysis of the *#FeesMustFall* Movement in South Africa 213
FIONA CHAWANA AND UFUOMA AKPOJIVI

Part III Media Discourse and Conflict Resolution 233

10 The Language of Peace in Conflict Transformation: A Critical Analysis of the *New York Times*' Coverage of the Israeli–Palestinian Peace Agreement and Its Role in the Discursive Context of the Oslo Negotiations 235
GIULIANA TIRIPELLI

11 The Historical Context in Media Narratives in Search of Peaceful Resolution to the Israel–Palestine Conflict: A Comparative Study of BBC and Al Jazeera 257
JELENA TIMOTIJEVIC

12 From Peace Talks to Military Operation: Pakistani Newspapers' Representation of the TTP Conflict 278
LUBNA SHAHEEN AND MUHAMMAD TARIQUE

13 From Collision to Diplomatic Compromise: "We are very sorry" – One Official Utterance, Different Interpretations in the Chinese and US Mainstream News Coverage of the 2001 Mid-Air Collision 300
LUTGARD LAMS

14 Constructing Identities in Crisis Situations: A Study of the
    "Volunteer" in the Spanish and English Press   324
    MARÍA DEL MAR SÁNCHEZ RAMOS

    Conclusion   339
    INNOCENT CHILUWA

Index   344

Figures

1.1	Favorability towards Castro's control of Cuban politics	page 30
1.2	Favorability towards Castro's control of the Cuban people	30
1.3	Favorability towards Castro's control of the Cuban economy	31
1.4	Favorability towards Castro's control of Cuban culture	31
1.5	Favorability towards Cuba's economic system	32
1.6	Favorability towards Cuba's political system	32
1.7	Favorability towards Cuba's rights	33
1.8	Favorability towards military intervention	34
1.9	Favorability towards economic intervention	34
1.10	Favorability towards diplomatic intervention	35
1.11	Favorability towards keeping González in the US	35
1.12	Favorability towards sending González back to Cuba	36
3.1	Concordance of "Fulani herdsmen" in the headlines corpus	79
3.2	Concordance of "farmers" in the headlines corpus	82
5.1	Libya 2011: The semantics of CNN headlines on the civil war	126
5.2	CNN news frequency of key narratives	131
5.3	Categorization of key pragmatic actors and analysis	134
7.1a	(Anti-)state actors and (alleged) operational links	168
7.1b	Timeline of events and statements	169
7.2	Matrices of legitimation (adapted from Van Leeuwen 2008)	177

Tables

1.1	Cooperation	*page* 29
2.1	Distribution of topic assignments to articles	54
3.1	Newspapers and the number of words in the headlines	75
3.2	Wordlist from the corpus of headlines showing the most frequent lexical words	77
3.3	Killings and attacks attributed to the Fulani herdsmen by the *Daily Post* newspaper	81
3.4	Distribution of actions attributed to the actors in the conflict in the headlines	84
4.1	Iraq War media frames	109
5.1	Monitoring the trends and mentions of key actors	126
5.2	Pragmatic acts	133
5.3	The rate at which each actor performed each act	134
6.1a	Country mentions in CRI	148
6.1b	Country mentions in VOA	148
7.1	Discourse historical approach strategies (adapted from Reisigl and Wodak 2016)	178
7.2	Legitimation strategies	178
7.3	Discourse topic coding results	179
7.4	Statement AS2 legitimation diagram	181
8.1	Derived lexemes of $\sqrt{SLM}$	197
8.2	Corpora of *Da'esh* and *al-Qaida* extremist periodicals	200
8.3	Derived lexemes and statistics	201
13.1	Units of analysis	302
14.1	VOLUNTEER-COR: A comparable corpus of volunteering in crisis situations	331
14.2	Most frequent collocates for the lemma "volunteer" (The Guardian_EN)	333
14.3	Most frequent collocates for the lemma "volunteer" (ElPais_ES)	334

About the Authors

Ufuoma Akpojivi is Associate Professor at the Department of Media Studies, University of the Witwatersrand, South Africa. He holds a Ph.D. in Communication Studies from the University of Leeds, United Kingdom and Postgraduate Diploma in Higher Education from the University of the Witwatersrand. His research interests include citizenship and activism, new media, media policy and democratization, and language politics. He is Fellow of the African Humanities Programme and a recipient of the Vice-Chancellor and Faculty of Humanities individual teaching and learning award (2017), and the Friedel Sellschop Research Award (2021).

Enis Bicer is a postdoctoral researcher at the Akkon University of Applied Sciences, Berlin, Germany. His research interests are in racism and discrimination, immigration societies, media and discourse research, intergroup conflict and social networks. He completed his Ph.D. at the University of Bremen, exploring intergroup boundaries in school class social networks. Since 2018 he has been working on the funded research project "The Threat Scenario of 'Islamist Terrorism' from the Perspectives of Politics, Media and Muslim Communities."

Lina Brink is a postdoctoral researcher at the University of Augsburg, Germany. She wrote her Ph.D. on media representations of protests in Egypt 2011–2014 at Eberhard Karls University, Tübingen, as a member of the junior research group (transcultural public spheres and solidarity). Her research fields are discourse research, critical media studies, social movement studies, cultural studies, gender studies, and postcolonial studies.

Fiona Chawana holds a Master's degree in Media Studies from the University of the Witwatersrand, South Africa. She is an aspiring academic who is passionate about researching social justice issues, social movements, and digital activism. She is currently working at The Global Data Barometer as a Communications Intern.

Innocent Chiluwa is Professor of English Linguistics (Discourse Analysis) and Media/Digital Communications in the Department of Languages & General Studies, Covenant University, Ota, Nigeria. He is a Humboldt scholar and visiting professor in the Department of English, University of Freiburg, Germany. His research interests include discourse studies and pragmatics; discourse and conflict and peace studies; social movement studies; social media and society; deception, fake news and disinformation, cyber civic engagement, online activism, terrorism and political violence. He is on the Editorial Boards of *Discourse & Society* (SAGE), *Journal of Multicultural Discourses* (Routledge) and the *Journal of International and Intercultural Communication* (Taylor & Francis).

Isioma M. Chiluwa is Assistant Lecturer in the Department of Languages & General Studies, Covenant University, Ota, Nigeria. Her research interests are multimodal discourse analysis, online/social media communications, and deception studies.

Valerie A. Cooper is Lecturer in Media and Communication at Victoria University of Wellington | Te Herenga Waka in New Zealand. Her research includes global power dynamics in communication, especially in the areas of communication for development, public diplomacy, and media representations. She has previously lectured in Mozambique, Hong Kong, and China.

Mark Finney is Associate Professor of Mass Communications at Emory & Henry College in Virginia, USA. His research strives to combine the insights and methodologies of conflict theory and mass communication theories into a broad approach for understanding international conflict and the relationship between conflict and media.

Sarah Fisher is Assistant Professor of Politics at Emory & Henry College in Virginia, USA. She teaches a range of courses from Statistics for the Social Sciences to Women and Politics to National and International Security. Her research focuses on conflict broadly defined and college pedagogy. Her most recent published work is on a survey in Belize and research methods pedagogy.

Stephen Goulding is a final-year Ph.D. Researcher at the Centre for Media Research at Ulster University, Northern Ireland, where he is also a teaching assistant in the School of Communication and

Media. Goulding's research focuses on the discursive construction of Irish republicanism through mainstream, alternative, and social media, with a specific focus on the movement's discursive modernization and mainstreaming from a grassroots perspective. His research has appeared in *Critical Discourse Studies*.

Angie O. Igbinoba is a doctoral candidate in the Department of Mass Communication, Covenant University, Ota, Nigeria. Her research interests include risk communication, public health education, development studies, media studies, science communication, management, and leadership studies.

Lutgard Lams is Professor of Pragmatics, Media Discourse Analysis and Intercultural Communication at the Faculty of Arts at the KU Leuven Campus, Brussels, Belgium. Her research interests relate to authoritarian discourses, political communication in China/Taiwan, media framing practices, European media narratives about the Chinese region, Othering in the Chinese official media, ideology in the Taiwanese media, and memes on Chinese social media. Recent publications include "Ideological patterns in Chinese state media narratives concerning issues of security and sovereignty," in C. Shei (ed.), *Routledge Handbook of Chinese Discourse Analysis* (2019) and "Examining strategic narratives in Chinese official discourse under Xi Jinping," *Journal of Chinese Political Science* (2018).

Alejandra Nieves Camacho is an M.A. student in International Relations at Freie Universität Berlin, Humboldt-Universität zu Berlin, and the University of Potsdam, Germany. She researches on migration and gender studies and is a staff member at the German Center for Integration and Migration Research (DeZIM) in the Migration Department.

Ada Peter is Assistant Professor, Digital Media, and International Security, Covenant University, Ota, Nigeria. She explores the processes of cyber weaponization, terrorism, and conflict to help governments make informed decisions about warfare in the fifth domain. She has received several regional and international awards for her research. The most recent was from the US Department of State, recognizing Dr. Peter as SUSI Scholar on US National Security and Policymaking. Her current research focuses on how US national cyber strategies undermine critical infrastructures' protection against previous and potential cyber weapons.

About the Authors

Ahmed Sahlane is Assistant Professor of English at the University of Jeddah, Saudi Arabia (the English Language Institute, Jeddah). He has published extensively in the area of mediated political argumentation and critical linguistics, with particular reference to the coverage of the 2003 Iraq War in Western opinion-editorial press. Dr. Sahlane's current research is concerned with the role played by media in bearing witness to the Iraqi conflict.

María del Mar Sánchez Ramos is Associate Professor in the Department of Modern Philology at the University of Alcalá, Madrid, Spain, where she teaches localization and specialized translation. She holds a Ph.D. in Translation and Interpreting Studies from the Universitat Jaume I, Castellón, Spain. Her research is focused on translation and technology, corpus linguistics, and discourse analysis. She is also an active member of different research projects related to the specific (technological) needs of non-governmental organizations in multilingual settings, and the European Parliament's representation of the refugee crisis.

Lubna Shaheen, Assistant Professor in the Higher Education Department of the Government of Punjab, Pakistan, completed her Ph.D. in Communication Studies. She was awarded a merit scholarship to do postdoctoral research on media and conflict studies at Utrecht University, the Netherlands. She has served as a postdoctoral fellow and faculty at the Institute of Media and Cultural Inquiry (ICON), Utrecht. Currently, Dr. Shaheen is engaged in a project on "the presentation of conflicts in films." She has authored several publications.

Troy E. Spier is a full-time professor of English and Linguistics at Universidad San Francisco de Quito, Ecuador. He earned his Ph.D. and M.A. in Linguistics at Tulane University, his B.S.Ed. in English/Secondary Education at Kutztown University, and his A.A. in General Studies at Reading Area Community College. His research interests include language documentation and description, discourse analysis, corpus linguistics, and linguistic landscapes.

Muhammad Tarique is Postdoctoral Researcher and faculty at the Institute of Media and Cultural Inquiry (ICON), Utrecht University, the Netherlands. He previously served as Assistant Professor at the Bahau din Zakaria University Lahore, Pakistan. He is currently working on his postdoctoral project: *Digital Media as Conflicts*

(De)escalation Platform. He is also involved in a project entitled "Introduction of Peace Paths in Computational Journalism."

Jelena Timotijevic is Principal Lecturer at the University of Brighton, UK. Her research centers around the discourse of political protest, nationalism, conflict; migration and marginalities. She situates analyses of discourse within a historical materialist tradition, following Marx and Voloshinov, as well as applying Vygotskian concepts in the context of language teacher education. Dr. Timotijevic is on the editorial board of the *Journal of Language & Communication* and *International Journal of English and Cultural Studies*. Her monograph entitled *Protest on Trial: A Critical Communication Analysis of the Attempted Criminalisation of the UK Student Demonstrations* is in preparation with Rowman & Littlefield.

Giuliana Tiripelli is Senior Lecturer in Digital Journalism and Media Discourse at De Montfort University, UK. Her research focuses on the role of mediated information in sociopolitical processes of change, and normative media approaches for the promotion of fair and peaceful societies. She was Lecturer in Digital Media and Methods (Sociological Studies) and Research Associate on Digital Communication in Crisis Situations (Information School), at the University of Sheffield, UK. She has a Ph.D. in Media Studies (Sociology) from the Glasgow University Media Group, University of Glasgow, 2013.

Foreword

Oliver Ramsbotham, University of Bradford

This book addresses a critical issue in the contemporary world. How does the communications revolution affect conflict and conflict resolution? And what is the role of the mass media in this? What needs to happen for "media and online political discourses" to contribute to peacemaking, peace-building and reconciliation rather than to the opposite? The chapters that follow apply discourse analytic approaches in order to explore these questions.

The extraordinary rapidity and scale of the spread of information and communications technology (ICT) in recent years, together with all the attendant forms of digital connectivity (Internet, social media, cell phones), have profoundly affected both the manifestation of conflict at all levels, and the way it is analysed/reported/framed and responded to worldwide. This has had a major impact on the way conflicts are instigated and conducted, on how conflict is understood (data, interpretation), and on efforts to prevent, mitigate, end and ensure a non-recurrence of its worst aspects. In all of this the media play a crucial role.

We know that the impact of communications technology on conflict in general is not as new as is sometimes made out. On the widest historical scale, we can think of the advent of writing itself at the time of the first states and empires; printing by moveable type at the time of the reformation and the wars of religion in Europe; the creation of the mass media and the rise of nationalism in the nineteenth century; the invention of the telephone, radio, film and TV in relation to the world wars and subsequent cold war and decolonisation wars of the twentieth century. In the worst genocide of the late twentieth century in Rwanda in April–July 1994, the most potent media role in instigating the massacre was played by a private radio station, Radio Television Mille Collines (RTMC), broadcasting to a largely illiterate audience between 8 July 1993 and 31 July 1994. And the main weapons used in the massacre were machetes. Nevertheless, it seems hard to overestimate the significance of the onset of the digital age – young though it still is – so far in the twenty-first century.

For one thing, the field of conflict analysis and conflict resolution has been radically affected by the impact of ICT in such a way that traditional distinctions between international, national and local levels of human conflict are being eroded. And – in line with what I understand to be the theme and hopes of this book – perhaps the basis for a future global partnership for peace is being constructed.

But the analysis in these chapters emphasises the deep ambivalence of the role of the media and online political discourse in all this. On the one hand, in relation to the cyberworld, both Norbert Wiener (creator of cybernetics) and Tim Berners-Lee (creator of the World Wide Web) in their different ways hoped that the new capacity would be a powerful instrument for peace – in Berners-Lee's words "to empower humanity by launching transformative programs that build local capacity to leverage the Web as a medium for positive change". This accords with the aspiration of the *World Summit on the Information Society* in 2003 in its "Tunis Commitment" that the new technology would be used to promote "a people-centred, inclusive and development-oriented Information Society" premised on the purposes and principles of the Charter of the UN, international law, multilateralism, and the Universal Declaration of Human Rights.

These hopes and aspirations remain vibrant and inspire many of the younger generation all over the world. But we hardly need to be reminded of the close relationship that has existed historically between technology and militarism, or the manifest danger of the opposite happening as underlying and mounting global problems impact on young, urbanised and increasingly informed populations outside the former monopolists of power, as well as on those "left behind" within them. A new digitalised worldwide field of contestation is opened up where mass media are co-opted and exploited by unscrupulous populist commercial and political forces, including the leaderships of the most powerful countries currently engaged in geopolitical struggles in what has recently become a multi-polar world.

Mass communications and the role of the media have always been a two-edged sword. They can inform, educate, empower, emancipate, and enable forms of cooperation. But they can also manipulate, polarise, escalate, exacerbate division, and enhance hegemonic control. The militarisation of new technology is an old story – in recent years connected to the Revolution in Military Affairs (RMA). The Internet itself was born as the ARPANET funded through a US Department of Defense project in 1969. And we still hear more about cyber war, cyber warriors, cyber-attacks etc. than about the possibilities for cyber peace. Something comparable occurs in relation to commercialisation. The jury is out on whether the new digitalised mass media overall increases democratisation or its Orwellian opposite; whether it opens communication or results in the creation of isolated "information bubbles"; whether it promotes more mutual understanding through mutual exposure (the contact hypothesis) or leads to a break-up of the mass media itself into ghettoised "echo chambers" where those inside only hear what they want to hear and divergent messages from outside are dismissed as "fake news".

These are portentous issues in which the role of the media is central. Behind them lies the question: how can standards of "ethical or accountable journalism" or "responsible reporting" be redefined in the digital age? Attempts have been made in recent years to set out applicable criteria (Lynch and Galtung 2010; Hoffmann and Hawkins 2015; Lynch 2015) as also to warn against an overly "top down" imposition of interpretation (Sutherlin 2013). There has been advocacy for a concerted international effort at the "pacification of cyberspace" (Woodhouse 2014), and an attempt to grapple with the very idea of "neutral", "impartial" or "disinterested" reporting in areas of intense linguistic intractability and "radical disagreement" (Ramsbotham 2010, 2017).

These are some of the larger themes explored in this book. The authors' contributions offer analysis of this complex field across different sectors, in relation to different topics, at different levels, and with reference to case studies from many different parts of the world. Discourse analysis techniques are applied. The result is a study that contributes valuable information about the interplay between mass media/online political discourse and human conflict, and thereby casts light on what needs to happen if future development is to be in the direction that the authors hope to see.

References

Hoffmann, Julia and Virgil Hawkins, eds. 2015. *Communication and Peace: Mapping an Emerging Field*. London: Routledge.
Lynch, Jake. 2015. "Media in Peace and Conflict Resolution." In Hoffmann and Hawkins, 16–33.
Lynch, Jake and Johan Galtung. 2010. *Reporting Conflict: New Directions in Peace Research Journalism*. Brisbane: University of Queensland Press.
Ramsbotham, Oliver. 2010. *Transforming Violent Conflict: Radical Disagreement, Dialogue and Survival*. London: Routledge.
Ramsbotham, Oliver. 2017. *When Conflict Resolution Fails: Engaging Radical Disagreement*. Cambridge: Polity Press.
Sutherlin, Gwyneth. 2013. "A Voice in the Crowd: Broader Implications for Crowdsourcing Translation During Crisis." *Journal of Information Science* 29 (3), 397–409.
Woodhouse, Tom. 2014. "Pacifying Cyberspace in the Age of the Zettabyte." *Journal of Conflictology* 29(3), 23–30.

Introduction
Media, Conflict, and Peace-Building

Innocent Chiluwa

1 Introduction

The media not only play vital roles in the mediation of conflicts and wars, they also are involved in discursive practices and cultural politics that predict the possibilities of social transformation and peace-building (Ivie 2016). The study of these roles in the context of local and global conflicts and peace-building efforts becomes more crucial in terms of how the professional practices of a journalist are defined. According to Carpentier and Terzis (2005), a journalist has the responsibility to adopt a particular model of war or peace reporting, such as those proposed by Galtung (1998) (i.e., peace-oriented journalism, which is generally perceived as people- and solution-oriented, or conflict/war journalism, which is violence-oriented, and tends towards propaganda). Citing Galtung (2000; Galtung and Fischer 2013), Nijenhuis (2014) argues that the media in the practice of war journalism are capable of exacerbating the conflict by:

> focusing on violence, highlighting the differences between groups, and presenting conflict as a zero-sum game, while ignoring the broad range of causes and outcomes of conflict ... Audiences reading war journalism are served a simplified black and white image, which makes them more likely to support violent "solutions" to the conflict. (65)

This suggests that the media, unfortunately, appears to prefer war journalism to peace journalism, and what is eminently perceived as "news" is when violent conflict is involved (Shinar 2013). To explain this phenomenon, Griffin (2010), notes that this is due to the fact that reports or images associated with violent conflicts reflect matters of life and death and generally attract more intense public attention and potentially influence public opinion. However, Galtung (1987) advocates peace journalism, where journalists take a non-violent perspective when reporting conflict. This will involve taking a proactive approach, framing stories in a way that focuses on peace, minimizing cultural differences, promoting conflict resolution, and espousing the culture of peace and reconciliation (Gouse et al. 2019, 437).

Contributions to this book apply theories and approaches in linguistics (mainly discourse analysis and pragmatics) to examine and analyze media and online political discourses that exemplify conflict and peace journalism. While some of the chapters examine the implications and consequences of some particular worrisome representations of past conflicts and wars in their cultural and historical contexts, some others raise the alarm about possible future conflicts within the purview of war reporting. The keyword in most of the contributions, and especially in Parts I and II of the book, is "representation" or "framing," which highlight particular evaluations and perspectives about persons and events in the conflict stories.

Part III of this book comprises critical analyses of journalism peace efforts and practical examples of the roles of media in the search for a peaceful resolution to some major ethnic and global conflicts. In the next subsections of this introductory chapter, I examine conceptual and theoretical issues on discourse and representation. I then go on to explain the logic of media representation, highlighting empirical studies about media construction of particular conflict situations, as well as roles played by the media in the practice of peace journalism. I conclude with a summary of each of the chapters.

2 "Discourse" as Used in This Book

In the context of this book, "discourse" is simply defined as language use in the news – particularly highlighting language choices, which, according to Fowler (1991), are far from being neutral. In other words, the choice of one word over another by a journalist or the use of a particular grammatical structure rather than other available options is significant – especially because of their power not only to shape public opinion about a topic in the news but also to mobilize mass actions.

Because journalists often function as mediators between political actors and the public, they have the ability to "process," "select," or "sort systematically" what should be considered as news (Fowler 1991). This suggests that news is not simply a value-free accurate report of what happened. Hence, in manipulating the news, a journalist produces a new media reality – ultimately to achieve the purpose of the report. This way, the journalist becomes not only a news-maker, but also a meaning-maker (Broersma 2008).

In terms of theory, the approach to discourse analysis in this book draws from the post-structuralist position that the knowledge of the world should not be treated as objective truth. This means that discourse (or language use) constructs the social world in meaning (Laclau and Mouffe 1985); and because meaning cannot be fixed, discourse is constantly being transformed, and different discourses are always representing particular ways of talking about and understanding the social world (cited in Jorgensen and Phillips 2002, 5).

According to Suurmond (2005), the way we talk (or write) does not neutrally reflect the world of identities and relations, but rather plays an active role in creating and changing them. Therefore, the struggle between what we claim to know about the world, also represents a discourse struggle – the struggle between different discourses showing different ways of understanding aspects of the world and constructing different realities and identities for speakers (see Jorgensen and Phillips 2002, 6).

Although linguistic and discourse analytic approaches have not been popular in studying conflict, especially in the context of media, certain definitions of conflict have always associated conflict with talk or human conversations. For instance, interpersonal and group conflicts have been viewed as any type of verbal or nonverbal opposition, ranging from disagreement to disputes, mostly in social interaction (Kakava 2001). Thus, the understanding of discourse as social interaction and the analysis of the structural properties of conflict talk become a matter of theory and method in discourse analysis – where studies of conflict have shown that opinions, roles, identities, and ideologies, for example, are constructed and supported through conflict talk (see Billig 1989; Kakava 2001). Individuals' utterances follow different patterns and discourse analysis provides the framework for the analysis of these patterns, whether in social or cultural discourse, political discourse or institutional discourse, and these have their huge implications for conflict as well as for the peaceful co-existence of people in a society (Kakava 2001).

Going by the discourse theory of Laclau and Mouffe, I will agree with Suurmond (2005) that discourse analysis is not just another method of data analysis, rather it is a whole package of philosophical views on the role of language in human social life, integrating theoretical paradigms, methodological tools, and specific research techniques, although with its own weaknesses and strengths. "Among the strengths of qualitative and critical approaches (of discourse analysis) are the rich and informative results, the emphasis on dynamics instead of statics, and the primacy of the subject matter instead of the method" (19); hence, discourse analysis may be applied as a methodology for the study of national identities, for example – which is one of the potential causes of conflict. Such critical analysis can provide insights on how cultural or religious tensions may cause conflict through the analysis of the manner in which people speak about others or construct "other(s)" (21). The chapters in this collection, by adopting the various methods of analysis in the contemporary discourse research schools (e.g., Frame Analysis, Narrative Analysis, Conversation Analysis, Critical Discourse Analysis) and applying the same to media discourse, contributes to insights to the significant place of discourse analysis both in theory and practice.

3   Conceptualization of Discourse and Representation

In linguistics or discourse analysis, representation refers to the use of language in a text (written or spoken) to assign meaning to persons or groups and their social practices – to events, to social and ecological conditions, and to objects (Fairclough 1989; van Dijk 2002; Wenden 2005). As highlighted above, this definition is influenced by the social constructionist view of the role of language in social life, which posits that meaning is not embedded in reality but is construed and constructed through linguistic representation.

Since discourse is a form of social action that plays a part in reproducing the social world – including knowledge, identities and social relations, different social understandings of the world lead to different social actions, and it becomes clear that social construction of knowledge and truth has social consequences (Jorgensen and Phillips 2002). Fairclough (1989) has also argued that discourse is a social practice and, as one of other social practices, plays a fundamental role in constructing the social world. The relation between discourse and society is dialectical, whereby one influences the other and vice versa.

Although representations vary depending on the perspective from which they are constructed, Wenden (2005) argues that there is still the "politics of representation," which is a discursive struggle for the "preferred" way of constructing reality, either by groups, politicians, or the news media. For instance, while the Iraq war was constructed in Canadian media as the "war on Iraq" (Härmänmaa 2014), various Arab media outlets framed it as an "invasion" or "occupation," and North American media referred to it as "operation free Iraqi" (Kellner 2004) or the "war on terror" (Barrett 2007) (see Chiluwa and Chiluwa 2020). Thus, representations comprising the production of versions of reality are often reflected in the choice of vocabulary and grammatical processes that are used to express individual or group opinions and evaluations. In other words, discourse or language use in everyday life, as in the media, is always reflective of different representations of life, expressing viewpoints and perspectives that may have huge implications for social security and peace.

4   Media and Representations of Conflict

Much of everyday conversations and public opinion about conflict or war is inspired by the mass media. Speakers and writers often refer to the television or the newspaper as their source of information and authority of knowledge or opinions about ethnic or national conflicts (van Dijk 2008). News reports and images of war are widely presumed to influence public opinion, perceptions and attitudes, potentially reinforcing or eroding public support for war policy, which is why governments and political interest groups are interested in the content of the news, including photographs of particular conflicts (Griffin 2010). In many cases, governments have therefore worked hard to control, limit or delay some particular content from production and circulation. "Such efforts are aimed not only at shielding particular images from public view but at promoting and facilitating the distribution of preferred types of images (or news) and establishing an approved universe of imagery as accepted public record" (Griffin 2010, 8).

Much of the literature on the representation of war and conflict in the media has documented "a long-standing preference for war" by journalists who manipulated their reports in favor of a certain ideology of war (Shinar 2013, 1).

Citing the conflict in the former Yugoslavia, which was of an ethnic and religious nature, Shinar (2013) argues that "nationalist propaganda disseminated by major media channels sponsored by the Milosevic regime in Serbia, enhanced violent attitudes and behaviours on the part of civilians against rival minorities" (1). This suggests media messages didn't further peaceful solutions to the conflict, but rather may have inspired hatred and division. This was an unfortunate instance of how media channels contributed to the destruction of Yugoslavia, and to an increase in extreme nationalism and division between groups who had hitherto lived alongside each other in a peaceful manner. Puddephatt (2006) notes that "It was a frightening example of how a society can disintegrate, how fear can be exploited by the power of media in the hands of those unscrupulous enough to wield it as a weapon" (2). In a similar case, Croatian journalists drew on global discourses of violence to justify and legitimize war crimes in the coverage of the war in Serbia, Croatia, and Bosnia (Erjavec and Volcic 2007; Kurspahic 2003, cited in Shinar, 2013). In Africa, the Rwandan genocide of the 1990s was attributable significantly to hate speech disseminated by the media (Viljoen 2005). Commenting on the genocide, Yanagizawa-Drott (2014) concludes that "access to such broadcasts served to increase organized and civilian violence; that they caused approximately 10% of the participation in genocidal violence." In all of these cases, the media presented the conflicts as irresolvable, making war inevitable. In the Yugoslavian case, "war was neither inevitable nor the only means of resolving the conflicts that lay behind the break-up of Yugoslavia, and the local media played an important role in preparing the ground for war, by ensuring public opinion was mobilised behind the different participants. Media campaigns between rival media outlets prefigured the war itself" (Puddephatt, 2006, 8). As regards the Vietnam War, Cihankova (2014) blames the American media for "inconsistency" in their accounts of the conflict. Newspapers reported statements from government officials, not minding to what extent they were lied to, and correspondents were witnessing a different course of events than what they were told by the government.

Public perceptions of war or conflict are often the reflections of media framing and representations of the conflicts. Saramifar (2019) argues that framing political actors in a particular way, either through photographs or news content, generally persuades viewers or the general public to align with propagated narratives and frames. In the case of the Iran–Iraq war, viewers remained committed to the rigid categories created in the news, such as martyrdom and sacrifice being the common frames of dying in the war.

Unfortunately, living with certain ideological and sometimes dangerous perceptions of conflict/war may be far-reaching: people who have lived through conflicts may continue to relive the horrors of war, as well as remain in fear of resurgences. For instance, Abdulbaqi and Ariemu (2017) fear that reports of the herder–farmer conflict in Nigeria by the Nigerian media are typical of war journalism, which is likely to spur greater conflict. The study argues that the choice of words in the representation of the conflict is "divisive, stereotypic and conflict inciting" (78). Therefore, rather than mending division in the society, the media may be perpetuating it.

However, in spite of war journalism, there is also peace journalism that proposes a more positive outcome of media roles in the mediation of conflict and peace-building.

5 Media and Peace Discourses

Some studies (e.g., Puddephatt 2006) have argued that for a sustained media involvement in peace processes, the constitutional rights of the media/press must be respected by various governments and law enforcement agencies. Such a media environment must be empowering, being built on the recognition that the freedom of expression and the right to receive and exchange opinions, as well as ideas and information, are among the virtues of true democracy (Puddephatt 2006). The media have long been regarded as having a particular role to play in guaranteeing the individual right to free expression, as it is through the media that this individual right takes public form. Therefore, "in any peace negotiations, the role of the media should form a part of the agreement – all parties should be asked to agree to respect the independence of the media and to refrain from either using media for propaganda purposes or to resist from any attempt to intimidate, threaten or abuse media independence" (9). Puddephatt (2006) further identifies a fundamental limitation in the discussion of media roles in "peace journalism," which arises from the confusion on the different roles of the mass media in conflict situations. For instance:

In addition to the representation of the groups they are reporting on – in this case parties to the conflict – journalists also present their own views and interests. In this respect the media itself becomes an actor in the conflict, for example when it takes an editorial position or when the media focus on certain issues or aspects of the conflict leads to the exclusion of others. The idea that the journalist sits outside of the events they are covering, whatever their perspective on "peace journalism" is misleading. The media, in this sense, are themselves actors or agents in the conflict and their behaviour will have an effect on the way the conflict develops. Policy makers therefore need to focus on the media's role in constituting the public sphere of society – how that can be fostered and nurtured in such a way as to allow non-violent resolution of conflict. (10)

Puddephatt's position clearly highlights the precarious position of the journalist both as a professional and as an individual member of the society who has the right to subjective construction of reality, even in peace mediation. This brings to the fore the importance of the choices a journalist makes (including language choices), such as the choice of what to report and what not to report. This choice can either promote violence or contribute to mitigating it. Hence, Lynch (2015) defines peace journalism as "whenever editors and reporters make choices about what stories to report and how to report them – which create opportunities for the audience to consider and to value nonviolent responses to conflict" (193). And it is not just about the pursuit of violent conflict, rather it is for readers and audience to "consider the value of non-violent responses – it situates peace journalism in the realm of professional journalism, committed to factual reporting" (193).

Ahlsen (2013) adds that besides trying to explain the causes of conflicts, peace journalists "give voice to all perspectives – including nongovernmental organisations and people from all parts of civil society. They report on different efforts made to resolve the conflict, look closely at all sides, and choose their words carefully. In return, they are able to produce a more comprehensive report, and contribute to a more developed democracy where well-informed citizens can make well thought out decisions – that could possibly bring about peace" (4). Similarly, Gouse et al. (2019) view a "peace journalist" as someone that "proactively reports on the causes of and solutions to a conflict, giving voice to all parties through responsible, empathetic journalism" (436).

Literature abounds with scholarly research on peace journalism. Gouse et al. (2019) chronicle scholarly articles that investigate the attributes of peace and war journalism in newspaper, television and radio reports. Results suggest that most peace journalism studies examine media in the frontline – within direct violence as it is happening – and assess conflict most often by using the war/peace indicator of elite-oriented versus people-oriented. Mandelzis (2007) explores the positive impact of three Israeli newspapers in the aftermath of the Oslo accord of 1993 – how they "demonstrated a dramatic change in attitude and terminology: The familiar war discourse was rapidly being replaced by peace representations and peace images" (1). In a similar study, Gavriely-Nuri (2010) applies a cultural approach to Critical Discourse Analysis (CCDA) to analyze the Israeli political peace discourse and finds that the use of the term "peace" fosters the construction of the Israeli speaker's positive self-image as peace-seeker together with the delegitimation of rivals; and also facilitates public acceptance of strategically problematic actions, primarily the use of military violence, by their presentation as part of the peace discourse.

It is therefore clear that scholarly conversation on conflict and war cannot be complete or lead to any significant conclusion without an equal and fruitful discourse on peace-building and peace processes. In the past, war and conflict have received more attention in scholarly literature than conflict resolution. The current volume contributes to scholarly intervention in research on media efforts towards peace-building and conflict resolution.

6 Summary of Chapters

The current volume is divided into three parts: Part I and Part II examine the constructions of conflicts in the media and analyze media representations of specific conflicts. While Part I focuses on the print media of newspapers and magazines, Part II pays attention to electronic and digital media. Part III, which is made up of five chapters and the concluding chapter, analyses "media discourse and conflict resolution." In this part, the contributors provide in-depth analyses of media (positive) roles in the processes of peaceful resolution to a number of regional and global conflicts.

The analyses presented here further shed some light on the useful methodological synergy between linguistics, media studies and conflict studies. In the past, media representations of people and situations, for instance racism, asylum seekers, immigrants, Muslims, and ethnic minorities among others, have been extensively researched by linguistics and media scholars – applying methods in corpus linguistics, discourse/linguistic pragmatics and Critical Discourse Analysis (CDA) (see van Dijk 1991; Baker 2010; Baker & McEnery 2005; Chiluwa 2011; Ahmed and Matthes 2017; Cap 2018). In the current book, the authors have applied mainly linguistic and discourse analytical approaches to examine topics on media representations of violence, conflict and war. The insights from these studies and the methodological approaches adopted by the contributors to this book, I believe, will open up stronger interest and research collaborations among language and media scholars and researchers.

In chapter 1, Mark Finney and Sarah Fisher examine the *New York Times*'s representation of the Elián González custody case of 1999, and argue that discourses used by the *New York Times* in its coverage of the González case corresponded with the themes of the broader conflict between the United States and Cuba, and that American sources represented in the coverage exemplified predictable attitudes about Cuba and Communism. By applying a discourse analytical framework, the study shows that conflict trajectories in democratic societies are influenced by news representations in so much that news is both influenced by context and also influences public knowledge and opinion.

In chapter 2, Enis Bicer, Lina Brink, and Alejandra Nieves Camacho explore the different meanings of Islamist terrorism and terrorist threats in four popular German newspapers, namely *Die Welt*, *Der Spiegel*, *Die Zeit*, and *Die Tageszeitung*. The study applying the sociology of knowledge approach to discourse (SKAD) finds that three interpretive schemes about threats associated with Islamist terrorism can be found – namely Islam and Muslims represented as antagonists to the Western "Us," the erosion of state order and public security, and risks to the preservation of the current "open society" in countries that experience Islamist terror attacks. They argue for their different references to anti-Muslim stereotypes and racism.

In chapter 3, Innocent Chiluwa, Isioma Chiluwa, and Angie O. Igbinoba apply a combination of CDA and corpus linguistics to investigate the representations of the herder–farmer conflict in news headlines of seven broadsheet newspapers in Nigeria. The study argues that the frequent representation of the herder–farmer conflict as domestic terrorism, and the description of the herdsmen as terrorists, prognosticates more serious violent conflicts in Nigeria. The study further argues that the whole truth about the conflict is not yet told by titling news analysis of the situation in favor of one party in the conflict. Furthermore, due to the prevalence of violence attributed to Muslims following domestic and international acts of terrorism, much of the world seems occupied with the views and actions of Muslims, calling particular attention to the Salafi sect.

In chapter 4, Ahmed Sahlane analyses how the Iraqi war was covered in Western media through the use of "pragmatic framing and visual rhetoric." The study argues that the coalition mainstream media erroneously painted the picture of the US so-called sophisticated weaponry, chivalrous heroism and militarist humanitarianism, rather than reporting the true images of suffering, destruction, dissent and diplomacy. By muting dissenting voices, the pro-war coalition media frames manufactured an "interpretive dominance that was inextricably structured in hegemony and social control."

Chapters 5 to 9 cover accounts and analyses of media representations of violent conflicts and wars focusing on electronic media and the Internet. In Chapter 5, Ada Peter and Innocent Chiluwa examine the criticisms of NATO's involvement in the Libyan crisis of 2011, concentrating on the textual structures and discourse strategies in the CNN reports that could have contributed to the transformation of the so-called "uprising" to a civil war (see also Bouvier 2014). Applying discourse pragmatic methodology, the authors propose new questions that may inspire arguments on whether semantic, narrative and pragmatic acts impacted attitudes that might have validated and propagated the war in Libya.

In Chapter 6, Valerie A. Cooper applies quantitative content analysis and corpus linguistics and CDA to analyze the *Voice of America* and *China Radio International*'s thematic and linguistic deconstruction of North Korea's threats of a nuclear strike and subsequent test-firing of missiles in March 2016. The results show that these government-sponsored media outlets used similar linguistic techniques to assign or avoid blame in reference to North Korea, as well as to China and the United States.

In a report written by Alan Cowell entitled "50 years later, troubles still cast 'huge shadow' over Northern Ireland," and published in the *New York Times* of October 4, 2018, the author lamented that the constant asymmetric conflicts in Northern Ireland – "the troubles would not go away." The author cited a former civil rights Protestant and peace activist as lamenting that the Troubles "are so burned into our lives that they are part of our DNA ... They are with us every day – especially those of us who were bereaved. It's a festering sore, because it's never been dealt with." Stephen Goulding (in Chapter 7 of this volume) continues this conversation and reveals how the media supports the legitimation of conflicts being promoted by "dissident republican organizations." Applying discourse analytical methods, the chapter demonstrates how the investigation of discourse strategies, topics and micro-linguistic features can provide insights into the framing and justification of the conflict. The study suggests that the dissident actors devote much of their communication to threatening the peace and acting as the mouthpiece for the legitimation of conflict in Northern Ireland.

In Chapter 8, Troy E. Spier applies Critical Discourse Analysis to engage with questions of ideology relating to the question of who a "believer" and an "unbeliever" is following the Arabic triliteral root word (i.e. $\sqrt{KFR}$) referring to disbelievers and states of disbelief. His data were obtained from the publications of two extremist Muslim online English magazines – *Dabiq* and *Inspire*. The findings of the study show that members of al-Qa'ida and Da'esh do not strictly consult the religious denotations of the triliteral root. Instead, they establish the "Self" and the "Other" dichotomy on pseudo-religious grounds and perpetuate stereotypes and contemporary prejudices that misrepresent those who adhere to the Islamic faith.

Fiona Chawana and Ufuoma Akpojivi question the feasibility of achieving social change through violence via the study of the *#FeesMustFall* social movement protests of 2015 and 2016 at the University of Witwatersrand in South Africa. The study shows that the movement used "systematic violence" to disrupt the state apparatus and also disturbed the university activity system that had hindered students' socioeconomic and cultural development.

Introduction 11

As highlighted above, the media have long been considered as having significant roles in the process of peace-building, which is founded within the principles of peace journalism. Part III of this book is focused on specific cases of media efforts in achieving world peace. The Israeli–Palestinian conflict and peace negotiations are a well-known intractable case that has almost defied international peace efforts. In Chapter 10, Giuliana Tiripelli carries out a Critical Discourse Analysis of the *New York Times*'s coverage of the Israeli–Palestinian peace agreement in the discursive context of the Oslo negotiations. The study argues that by promoting a peace focused on separation instead of investing in commonality, the *Declaration of Principles* prevented these transformative discourses from entering the new debate on peace-building in Israel and Palestine. In a similar study, Jelena Timotijevic (Chapter 11) supplies additional theoretical rigor by engaging with discourse analysis as a form of "history writing." Drawing from the tradition of cultural-historical and activity theory, the study offers a critical examination of the language of the Western actors and media outlets to assess whether such narrative impacts on prospects for a peaceful resolution of the Israel–Palestine conflict.

Another well-known peace process that has engaged the world is the proposal and negotiation to end the ongoing war in Afghanistan. Since the war began in 2001, ongoing negotiation and the peace movement have made considerable progress, especially in 2018 when peace talks between the Taliban and the Afghan government began in earnest. Also, there were (failed) peace talks between the Pakistani government and the TTP (Tehrik-i-Taliban Pakistan) after the 2014 "Operation Zarb-e-Azb" – a joint military offensive conducted by the Pakistan armed forces against all militant groups in North Waziristan. This operation wiped out all local and national militant groups in Waziristan and improved the security situation, as well as reducing terrorist attacks in Pakistan to a six-year low since 2008.[1] In Chapter 12, Lubna Shaheen and Muhammad Tarique analyze news discourses covering the peace talks between the Pakistan government and the TTP, and the culmination of these peace talks to the military operation Zarb-e-Azb. The research argues that the overall stance of the *Dawn* and *The Nation* (two popular Pakistani English newspapers) is condescending, contemptuous and demonizing – thus demoralizing the TTP instead of being conciliatory.

In Chapter 13, Lutgard Lams applies speech act theory to examine the constitutive role of the media in influencing and interpreting official apologies in the realm of international conflict resolution. The study investigates the Sino–US diplomatic row after a midair plane collision over the South China

---

[1] "Pakistan Launches Offensive against Militants near Afghan Border," *Huffington Post*, June 15, 2014. "Militant Attacks Declined after Zarb-E-Azb Operation: Report," *The Nation*, June 17, 2015. Archived from the original on June 17, 2015.

Sea on April 1, 2001. The study argues that the Chinese requests for a formal US apology and the latter's expressions of regret were discursive issues of contention and subject to different media interpretations. The results show that the US and Chinese media participated in negotiating an American expression of "apology/regret," disseminating the message through skillful translation techniques, and metapragmatically interpreting its significance.

The study of the construction of conflict and peace-building processes in the media has not focused much on volunteerism and volunteers as salient actors in peace-building. Yet, according to UNESCO, the work carried out by volunteers is very important in peace-building initiatives and dates back as far as the 1920s, after World War I. Since then, volunteerism has been involved in promoting social cohesion and reconciliation and helping to develop nation civilian capacities, all of which make a critical positive difference to peace-building processes and initiatives. Voluntary movements have been involved in postwar reconstruction, solidarity and the reconciliation of people from different backgrounds through collective voluntary engagement as a way of recreating interpersonal linkages. After World War II, various international networks were set up based on the renewed realization that sustainable peace relies on solid connections and trust among people, which can be fostered through concrete joint actions for the common good.[2] In Chapter 14, María del Mar Sánchez Ramos applies a corpus-assisted discourse analytical approach to examine the representation of volunteer identity in the English and Spanish newspapers. The study finds that "volunteering is constructed as a helping activity – a more politicized discourse focused on the volunteer as an activist and actor of social change."

This volume contributes essentially to our understanding of our past and present (as well as, possibly, our predictable future) when it comes to how the media engages in the processes of conflict and conflict resolution. It will therefore serve as an essential resource for students, scholars and experts in media and communication studies, conflict and peace studies, international relations, linguistics and political science.

References

Abdulbaqi, Saudat and Ariemu, Ogaga. 2017. "Newspapers Framing of Herdsmen–Farmers' Conflicts in Nigeria and Its Implication on Peace-Oriented Journalism." *Creative Artist: A Journal of Theatre and Media Studies* 11(2): 1–29.

Ahlsen, Pernilla. 2013. *Peace Journalism: How Media Reporting Affects Wars and Conflict.* https://kvinnatillkvinna.org/wp-content/uploads/2018/10/11-Peace-journalism-ENG.pdf.

---

[2] UNV Issue Brief, January 2014. https://sustainabledevelopment.un.org/content/documents/119 020443_UN%20Volunteers%20POST-2015%20Brief%20-%20Peacebuilding%20and%20Volu nteerism%20WEB.pdf.

Ahmed, Saifuddin and Matthes, Jorg. 2017. "Media Representation of Muslims and Islam from 2000 to 2015: A Meta-Analysis." *International Communication Gazette* 79(3): 219–244.

Baker, Paul. 2010. "Representations of Islam in British Broadsheet and Tabloid Newspapers 1999–2005." *Journal of Language and Politics* 9(2): 310–338.

Baker, Paul and McEnery, Tony. 2005. "A Corpus-Based Approach to Discourses of Refugees and Asylum Seekers in UN and Newspaper Texts." *Journal of Language and Politics* 4(2): 197–226.

Barrett, Del. 2007. "'War on Terror': An Intentional Choice of Words? A Corpus Analysis of *War on* and *War against*." In *Proceedings of the Corpus Linguistics Conference, CL2007*, University of Birmingham, July 27–30. https://pdfs.semanticscholar.org/7830/751168d5f212b4e1624c6a1b4dd04b92e7af.pdf.

Billig, Michael. 1989. "The Argumentative Nature of Holding Strong Views: A Case Study." *European Journal of Social Psychology* 19, 203–223.

Bouvier, Gwen. 2014. "British Press Photographs and the Misrepresentation of the 2011 'Uprising' in Libya: A Content Analysis." In D. Machin (Ed.), *Visual Communication*. Berlin: De Gruyter Mouton, 281–299.

Broersma, Marcel. 2008. "The Discursive Strategy of a Subversive Genre: The Introduction of the Interview in US and European Journalism." In H.W. Hoen and M.G. Kemperink (Eds.), *Vision in Text and Image*. Leuven: Peeters, 143–158.

Cap, Piotr. 2018. "From 'Cultural Unbelonging' to 'Terrorist risk': Communicating Threat in the Polish Anti-Immigration Discourse." *Critical Discourse Studies* 15 (3): 285–302.

Carpentier, Nico and Terzis, George, Eds. 2005. *Media Representations of War and Conflict*. A workshop organized on March 18, 2005 by the KUB-Center Communication for Social Change, the Communications Department of the Vesalius College (VUB), Brussels and the Pascal Decroos Fund for Investigative Journalism. http://nicocarpentier.net/war&media_finalreport.pdf.

Chiluwa, Innocent. 2011. *Labeling and Ideology in the Press: A Critical Discourse Study of the Niger Delta Crisis*. Frankfurt: Peter Lang.

Chiluwa, Innocent and Chiluwa, Isioma Maureen. 2020. "'Deadlier Than Boko Haram': Representations of the Herder–Farmer Conflict in the Local and Foreign Press. *Media, War & Conflict* February 2020 (online) https://doi.org/10.1177/1750635220902490.

Cihankova, Hana. 2014. "Influence of Media on Vietnam War." Bachelor thesis, Palacky University, Olomouc. https://theses.cz/id/h0uo3z/Bachelor_Thesis_Hana_Cihankova.pdf.

Erjavec, Karmen and Volcic, Zala. 2007. "Recontextualizing Traumatic Pasts: Croatian Justification of War Crimes in Bosnia-Herzegovina." *Global Media Journal Mediterranean Edition* 2(1): 10–22.

Fairclough, Norman. 1989. *Language and Power*. London: Longman.

Fowler, Roger. 1991. *Language in the News: Discourse and Ideology in the Press*. London: Routledge.

Galtung, Johan. 1987. "Language and War: Is There a Connection?" *Current Research on Peace and Violence* 10: 2–6.

Galtung, Johan. 2000. "The Task of Peace Journalism." *Ethical Perspectives* 7(2–3): 162–167.

Galtung, Johan and Fischer, Dietrich 2013. "High Road, Low Road: Charting the Course for Peace Journalism." In Johan Galtung, *SpringerBriefs on Pioneers in Science and Practice*, vol 5. Berlin: Springer, 95–102.

Gavriely-Nuri, Dalia. 2010. "The Idiosyncratic Language of Israeli 'Peace': A Cultural Approach to Critical Discourse Analysis." *Discourse & Society* 21(5): 565–585.

Gouse, Valerie, Valentin-Llopis, Mariely, Perry, Stephen, and Nyamwange, Beryl. 2019. "An Investigation of the Conceptualization of Peace and War in Peace Journalism Studies of Media Coverage of National and International Conflicts." *Media, War & Conflict* 12(4): 435–449.

Griffin, Michael. 2010. "Media Images of War." *Media, War & Conflict* 3(1): 7–41.

Härmänmaa, Marja. 2014. "Gruesome Entertainment: The Representation of the Iraq War in the Italian Press." In Aki-Mauri Huhtinen, Noora Kotilainen, and Marja Vuorinen (Eds.), *Binaries in Battle: Representations of Division and Conflict*. Newcastle upon Tyne: Cambridge Scholars.

Ivie, Robert L. 2016. "Hegemony, Instabilities and Interventions: A Special Issue on Discourses of War and Peace." *Journal of Multicultural Discourses* 11(2): 124–134.

Jorgensen, Marianne and Phillips, Louise J. 2002. *Discourse as Theory and Method*. London: Sage.

Kakava, Christina. 2001. "Discourse and Conflict." In Deborah Schiffrin, Deborah Tannen, and Heidi E. Hamilton (Eds.), *The Handbook of Discourse Analysis*. Malden, MA: Blackwell Publishing, 650–670.

Kellner, Douglas. 2004. "Preemptive Strikes and the War on Iraq: A Critique of the Bush Administration's Unilateralism and Militarism." *New Political Science* 26(3): 417–440.

Kurspahic, Kemal. 2003. *Balkan Media in War and Peace*. Washington DC: USIP Press.

Laclau, Ernesto and Mouffe, Chantal. 1985. *Hegemony and Socialist Strategy: Towards a Radical Democratic Politics*. London: Verso.

Lynch, Jake. 2015. "Peace Journalism: Theoretical and Methodological Developments." *Global Media and Communication* 11(3): 193–199.

Mandelzis, Lea. 2007. "Representations of Peace in News Discourse: Viewpoint and Opportunity for Peace Journalism." *Conflict & Communication Online* 6(1): 1–10.

Nijenhuis, Judith. 2014. *Peace and War Frames in the Media Representations of the Libyan Civil War*. Nijmegen: Radboud University. https://theses.ubn.ru.nl/bitstream/handle/123456789/2783/Nijenhuis%2C_Judith_1.pdf?sequence=1.

Puddephatt, Andrew. 2006. "Voice of War: Conflict and the Role of the Media." *International Media Support*. www.mediasupport.org/publication/voices-of-war-conflict-and-the-role-of-the-media/.

Saramifar, Younes. 2019. "Framing the War in the Post War Era: Exploring the Counter-Narratives in Frames of an Iranian war Photographer Thirty Years after the Ceasefire with Iraq." *Media, War & Conflict* 12(4): 392–410.

Shinar, Dov. 2013. "Reflections on Media War Coverage: Dissonance, Dilemmas, and the Need for Improvement." *Conflict & Communication Online* 12(2): 1–13.

Suurmond, Jeannine. 2005. *Our Talk and Walk: Discourse Analysis and Conflict Studies*. Working Paper No. 35, Netherland Institute of International Relations (Clingendael), Conflict Research Unit. https://slidelegend.com/our-talk-and-walk-clingendael-institute_5a075d561723dd5fba211873.html.

van Dijk, Teun. 1991. "The Interdisciplinary Study of News as Discourse." In K. Bruhn-Jensen and N. Jankowksi (Eds.), *Handbook of Qualitative Methods in Mass Communication Research*. London: Routledge, 108–120.

van Dijk, Teun. 2008. *Discourse and Power*. Basingstoke: Palgrave Macmillan.

van Dijk, Teun. 2002. "Political Discourse and Political Cognition." In Paul Chilton and Christina Schaffner (Eds.), *Politics as Text and Talk: Analytic Approaches to Political Discourse*. Amsterdam: John Benjamins, 203–237.

Viljoen, Frans. 2005. "Hate Speech in Rwanda as a Test Case for International Human Rights Law." *The Comparative and International Law Journal of Southern Africa*, 38(1): 1–14.

Wenden, Anita. 2005. "The Politics of Representation: A Critical Discourse Analysis of an Aljazeera Special Report." *International Journal of Peace Studies* 10(2): 89–110.

Yanagizawa-Drott, David. 2014. "Propaganda and Conflict: Evidence from the Rwandan Genocide." *The Quarterly Journal of Economics* 129(4): 1947–1994. doi:10.1093/qje/qju020.

Part I

Conflict Discourse in Newspaper Reporting

1 Elián González in the *New York Times*
Media Roles in the Trajectories of International Conflict

Mark Finney and Sarah Fisher

1.1 Introduction

On Thanksgiving Day in 1999, fishermen off the coast of Florida intercepted a young child, floating among the debris of a wrecked boat, which his family had used to flee Cuba and immigrate illegally to the United States. Elián González – 6 years old at the time – was the sole survivor of their flight from Cuba, and over the next seven months, his presence in the United States became international news. What role do mainstream news accounts have in the trajectories of international conflict? This complex question vexes both scholars and practitioners of conflict and communication, perhaps now more than ever, in the digital age.

From a normative conflict studies perspective, there is value in studying the role of news accounts, towards developing a more comprehensive understanding of the spread of information and information literacy, the development of attitudes about self and other, the issues underlying a conflict, its likely outcomes and proposals for its resolution. Previously conducted studies, for example Brenner and Castro (2009), Blight and Brenner (2002), Bender (1975), Erisman and Kirk (2006), Lakoff (1991) and Perez (1999), have shown how US coverage of flash points has moved US audiences' perceptions of Cuba, Cuban people and Cuban leadership. These perceptual shifts have contributed to shifts in US policy towards Cuba, such as the dramatic shift in policy during the Obama presidency and the just as dramatic retrenchment of the Trump administration. In this chapter, we apply a media studies framework and employ discourse analysis techniques in order to examine the news coverage of a flash point (the Elián González custody dispute) within the context of the ongoing conflict between the United States and Cuba. This scholarship contributes to the study of conflict by focusing on the discourses that underpin it: the ways that news reflects, informs and alters prevalent ideas about the conflict, and is ultimately aimed towards making positive contributions to understanding the issues and parties and the ways that the conflict could ultimately be resolved.

1.2   Literature Review

News coverage and the other communicative features of the conflict between the United States and Cuba were the subject of considerable scholarly thought in the twentieth century. In much the same way that Cuba and the Cuban revolution captured the American imagination, the academic community also, for a time, shared this fascination with the study of Cuba and the Cuban–American conflict. Tension between the United States and Cuba had been a constant feature since before the Spanish–American War in 1898, as popular myths about the importance of Cuba in American newspapers attest, and since the end of the nineteenth century, scholars have argued that the news coverage has fed both Cubans and Americans a steady diet of coverage about the other. A lull in both the academic coverage and the news coverage appears to have emerged around the end of the Soviet Union's involvement in Cuba, an era which in Cuba is called the "Special Period in Time of Peace" that began in 1989.

In academic literature on this subject, the parent/child relationship metaphor has been used over time to construct the relationship between Cuba and the United States. For instance, Brenner and Castro (2009) argue that such metaphors lie at the heart of messaging about the conflict.

In the early days of the twentieth century, according to Brenner and Castro, "[despite the] devious purpose of the Platt Amendment, the metaphor that American officials deployed at the time was one that flourished for the next sixty years, with remnants evident even today: parent and child" (239). The metaphor of parent and child enabled US policymakers to simultaneously convey to American audiences the supposed inferiority of their Latin American neighbors while providing a seemingly natural route to intervention: In much the same way that a parent is expected to intervene to correct the behavior of the child, the United States has an obligation to intercede in the immature decision making of its smaller neighbor and help them to become more mature. But Brenner and Castro argue that while the United States viewed itself through the lens of parent/child, that was not the predominant metaphor used to explain the conflict from the Cuban point of view. In fact, the title of the piece "David and Gulliver" refers to just two of the competing metaphors that have been employed by the United States and Cuba to understand themselves in conflict with one another.

"David," a reference to the David and Goliath story from the Bible, is also a predominant theme in Cuban discourse about the conflict. Brenner and Castro argue that José Martí, Cuba's national poet and moral touchstone, first employed it "when he wrote that 'my sling is David's'" (2009, 238). "The comparison is obvious," write Brenner and Castro, "and even though David takes Goliath's life, sympathy is usually reserved for him because he was both the underdog and defender of those whom Goliath would have oppressed" (239). In the predominant metaphor in the United States, however,

> Gulliver is a gentle giant who intends no harm and who warrants the reader's sympathy. Gulliver is well-aware that the Lilliputians are no match for him: "while I had my liberty," he recounts, "the whole strength of that empire could hardly subdue me, and I might easily with stones pelt the metropolis to pieces." But he restrains himself, out of a sense of "honour." The Lilliputians are not children in his eyes; he recognizes that they have developed a complex and technically advanced society, even as Gulliver comes to abhor their king's values and thwart his plans for conquering the people on the neighbouring island of Blefuscu. His intention is to help them, not kill them. (240)

While both Cubans and Americans viewed themselves through metaphors that represent the asymmetry of their relationship, they do so through metaphors with starkly different roles for themselves, the other and the trajectories in their narrative journeys. The predictable outcomes of such narrative cohesion in the minds of American and Cuban leaders were to ignore counterevidence and question the motivations of the others when they did not conform to existing schemas. This was the case, for instance, in 2001, when "the head of the U.S. Interests Section in Havana asserted that Cuba 'missed the opportunity to join the international coalition against terrorism' in the immediate aftermath of the 9/11 attacks" (248). Instead, as Brenner and Castro argue, "The Cuban government officially condemned the terrorist attacks on the afternoon of 11 September 2001. It then offered to provide the United States with all the medical and humanitarian aid it could muster, and to allow Cuban airspace for United States aircraft" (248). Relying on metaphors to understand themselves caused both states to consistently ignore counterevidence, question the motivations of the other and inappropriately extoll their own virtues.

In much the same way, Brenner and Castro also argue that the parent/child metaphor explains, for American audiences and policymakers alike, the sense of obligation on the part of the United States that compels intervention in Cuba. Quoting Louis Perez, they note:

> The metaphor of Cuban as children drew upon the dense web of reciprocities commonly understood to regulate the parent–child relationship as model for governance: the parent to supervise, the child to submit; the parent to discipline, the child to obey ... the Cubans as children were expected ... to be heedful and compliant and always properly appreciative and grateful. (240)

Throughout this analysis, though, Brenner and Castro note the inadequacy of metaphors for explaining reality. Their narrative thread and moral duality contribute more to misunderstanding than understanding, making policymaking more difficult and less appropriate. This idea is reaffirmed by Brenner in a chapter for the book *Redefining Cuban Foreign Policy: The Impact of the Special Period*, edited by Erisman and Kirk (2006). Referring again to the metaphors which he argues drive public knowledge about the Cuban–American conflict, Brenner suggests that an important consequence is to artificially alter the importance of asymmetry in the relationship, which he argues is "a real conflict of interests" (281). Whether the metaphor is parent/child, Gulliver, or David, the superimposition of the metaphor obscures the consequences and motivations of actual behavioral and policy choices.

Louis Perez' book *Cuba in the American Imagination* (2008) again interrogates the use of metaphors to describe the conflict and inform policymakers. Perez begins his book by drawing attention to the long history of Cuba's centrality to the American mission, arguing that from the start "Cuba occupies a special place in the history of American imperialism" (1). But just as importantly, Perez finds that Cuba represents a special notion in the American imagination. Due to its proximity, its perceived inferiority, its otherness, and the centrality of imperialism to the American ethos, Perez argues that Cuba represents an idea that is "indispensable to the 'actual existence' of the United States" (2). Instead of viewing American incursions in Cuba as examples of imperialism or as an extension of American might, the metaphors provide cover for American policymakers. "Cuba entered the American imagination early in the nineteenth century principally by way of metaphor: depictions fashioned as a function of self-interest, almost always in the form of moral imperatives in which the exercise of power was represented as the performance of beneficence" (2–3). Metaphors enabled American legislators and the public to view US activity abroad through a lens that favored the humanitarian potential of intervention. American involvement in the Spanish–American War, for instance, was represented "as an undertaking for humanity that served to fix the moral calculus by which the American thereafter imagined the purpose of their power and celebrated the virtue of their motives" (6).

Perez distinguishes between the use of metaphors as a model for conduct and a mode of knowledge. "That this process was at the same time a source of knowledge further invites attention to the role played by metaphor in the maintenance of systems of domination and more" (6). Perez argues that the metaphor provides both explanatory power, in terms of helping parties understand the contexts within which activity takes place, as well as prescriptive power, in the sense of providing a way of understanding how to shape future behavior and policy. But, as Perez argues, doing so is really a manipulation of emotions that fosters "predisposition toward some matters and prejudice to others" (6).

How, then, is it possible to distinguish between metaphorical and factual representations of the conflict? This question, though implied in the preceding works, is more explicitly considered by Phillip Brenner and James Blight in their book *Sad and Luminous Days: Cuba's Struggle with the Superpowers after the Missile Crisis* (2002). Blight and Brenner consider whether there is any air between the interpretations of the Cuban state and Cuban media (23). Instead, they find the two institutions are largely synonymous, and that the perspective represented in Cuban media is heavily influenced, if not completely controlled, by the interpretations of the state. They find a perspective on the conflict in Cuba's coverage that is strongly oriented at reminding Cuban audiences of the asymmetry that exists between the United States and Cuba. As the bigger, more powerful party, the United States is represented as having some obligation to act first towards ending hostility (xxvi). Blight and Brenner also note that from the Cuban perspective, little has been done on the part of the US to positively change relations. They note the Cuban belief that since the revolution, there have been "5,700 acts of terrorism, sabotage and murder" perpetrated by the US in Cuba (17).

Blight and Brenner's book makes two additional contributions to the study of the conflict process. First, they argue that the Cuban Missile Crisis, despite being concluded bloodlessly and without war, was a resolution without content from the Cuban perspective. Cuba was not merely the site of Soviet missiles aimed at the United States. Cuba had invited the Soviets to aid in their defense against the United States, but because of the global scope and potentially devastating consequences of a hot entanglement between the United States and the Soviet Union, the matter was ultimately decided between those two parties – leaving Cuba out. Blight and Brenner argue that the Soviets and Americans, negotiating with each other, excluded Cuba and did not take adequate account of Cuban needs in their ultimate resolution (27).

A second process-oriented point is emphasized in their development of an argument about how Cuba attempts to exert power in the conflict with the United States, when in a practical sense its relative power is considerably less. They describe what they call "the Cuban style of deterrence," a method of engagement in which "a relatively less powerful country tries to deter aggression by raising the costs for the aggressor to an unacceptable level in terms of both blood and treasure" (87). Blight and Brenner provide a clever phrase to help understand the Cuban strategy that aims, not at victory in a traditional sense, but in terms of exerting pain on the other and through moral battles won on the international stage.

Written long before Blight and Brenner's text, Lynn Darrell Bender's *The Politics of Hostility: Castro's Revolution and United States Policy* (1975) also explores the Cuban style of deterrence, through her examination of what she considers to be the self-perpetuating hostility between the United States and Cuba, which preceded the Cuban revolution. What Bender's text provides in terms of this study is a way of understanding how both the United States and

Cuba use the representation of each other to deflect responsibility for unpopular or negative domestic policy choices. In post-revolution Cuba, corruption is blamed on the United States embargo (7). It isn't that Cuba's communist system of redistributive resources is an inadequate way to sustain a population; rather it is that the United States' embargo prevents Cuba from being able to achieve the true potential of their innovative system. The fact of the United States' long history of intervention in Cuba only supports claims like this with the Cuban people. She writes, "Anti-Americanism conditioned Cuban attitudes" (14) and continues to do so today.

Bender argues that "this self-perpetuating hostile orientation, based largely now on fixed threat-images, has produced a foreign policy context in which doctrinaire rigidity tends to replace a more rational framework for effective policy formulation" (75). She writes that policymakers in the United States have long assumed that a hostile Cuba would pose a strategic naval threat in the Caribbean, thus making control over Cuba a strategic goal (3). At the same time, Bender notes that the United States sees this conflict at least in part as a proxy for a larger, ideological, conflict: that between not just the United States and Cuba, but between democratic and totalitarian ideals and between capitalist and communist economies. "The continuation of the containment policy framework seems not to further progress toward attaining desired goals, but to articulate and defend a set of retaliatory principles – notably 1) to punish Cuba for its anti-U.S. belligerency and 2) to denigrate the Cuban example in the eyes of the world" (127).

It makes narrative and ideological sense, therefore, that when Elián González was saved by US fishermen off the coast of Florida on Thanksgiving Day, 1999, that his presence and the ensuing conflict over his custody and rights was viewed by many both within and outside of government (on both sides of the Florida Straits) as more than merely a custody battle or a question of immigration. Instead, it became a high-stakes flash point in the longstanding international conflict. As Sarah Banet-Weiser explores in her article "Elián González and 'The Purpose of America': Nation, Family, and the Child-Citizen," the representations of Elián González in US media accounts reflected "hyperbolic proportions" (2003, 151), composed of religious and nationalistic symbolism, in which partial evidence was used to draw up stark contrasts between the Land of the Free and "barren and lifeless Castro-led Communist Cuba" (153).

Though Banet-Weiser's article is not a content study in a strict sense, she uses US media coverage of the conflict to explore its cultural implications. She finds that the coverage of Elián González existed in contrast to typical immigration and illegal immigration stories at the time. Elián González' journey is, in no small sense, a minor's illegal immigration from Cuba to the United States. But Banet-Weiser finds that González was treated differently by media than other child refugees (157). This was due, at least in part, to the skepticism that was cast on the custody claims of Elián's father, Juan, as "a dubious alibi for Castro's scheme – and thus a particular kind of threat to American democracy" (157).

Banet-Weiser finds that the information and ideas presented in the media were conveyed inconsistently and in such a way as to support the dominant ideas about Communism and Castro in the United States. Casting Castro as a sort of deadbeat dad (163), Elián was cast as the innocent victim of Castro's abuse or negligence, and the United States was cast as his savior. González' flight from Cuba was represented not as a choice to immigrate, but as a necessity to escape the bonds of the oppressive communist regime (165). The implications of this narrative for the United States paint its obligation in terms of "establishing the United States as a political savior" (174).

Another reason why the coverage of Cuban immigration may be different than other cases has to do with the prominent and atypically wealthy Cuban immigrant community, which resides principally in Miami, Florida. As Guillermo J. Greiner and Max Castro explain in their chapter "Blacks and Cubans in Miami: The Negative Consequences of the Cuban Enclave on Ethnic Relations" (2001), the Cuban exile community is compositionally distinct from other exile communities in the United States, in part because the first wave of Cuban exiles were what have become known as "Golden Exiles," who immigrated to escape the Cuban revolution between 1959 and 1961 (139). These exiles were the wealthiest and most entrepreneurial; they had the most to lose from the communist revolution (140).

The exiles' entrepreneurialism and political activism translated easily in their new American context, which meant that they developed wealth and political power, especially when they obtained citizenship over time and embraced the anti-communist politics of Republican political leaders such as Ronald Reagan (144). Greiner and Castro describe the Cuban American community in Miami as politically engaged, economically dominant, tightly knit and well organized. This conception of the Cuban immigrant community is supported by Daniel Erikson, who wrote about the influence of the Cuban community on national politics for the neoconservative magazine, *The National Interest*. Arguing that "for most of the embargo's existence, the issue of U.S. Cuba policy has been a primary motivator for only one constituency: the exiled Cuban-American community, located predominantly in south Florida" (2002, 66). Erikson suggests that the Cuban exile community's oversized influence on Florida and American politics is due to the effective organizing of the Cuban American National Foundation (CANF) and the coincidence of Florida's being considered a presidential swing state, "a development that has magnified the influence of the Cuban-American constituency still further" (67).

Despite this oversized antipathy to Castro in Miami and on the plane of national politics, William G. Mayer's analysis of polling data in 2001 suggests that the US population does not regard Cuba as a "constant, serious threat to their survival" (585). Instead, "public opinion about Cuba often seems to fluctuate in reaction to the immediate events and crises of American foreign policy" (586). While noting that polling data about Cuba during the revolutionary period was thin, Mayer's article for *Public Opinion Quarterly* is an aggregation of their findings, in which he argues that though attitudes towards Castro are consistently negative (1% viewed Castro as positive and 92% viewed him as negative in 1964), attitudes about the country of Cuba are much less strident (586).

Not until the early 1990s did the public's hostility toward Cuba and its leader soften somewhat. In a question asked by the Roper Poll, for example, between 1982 and 1984 about 45 percent of Americans called Cuba an "enemy of the state." This declined to 34 percent in 1993 and then to 30 percent in 1998. In a quadrennial series of polls sponsored by the Chicago Council on Foreign Relations, respondents were asked to rate Cuba on a 0–100 "feeling thermometer". The mean rating for the Caribbean nation was 32 in 1978, fell to 25 in 1982, then rose to 37 in 1994 and 38 in 1998. (587)

Mayer finds that "though most Americans have held decidedly negative views of both Castro and Cuba, they have not regarded Cuba as an especially serious threat" (587). Instead, and especially following the end of Soviet support for Cuba, the "perceived threat from Cuba declined" over time (590).

1.3 Method

The research presented above suggests a significance to the study of how news covers conflict. Discourse analysis provides a conceptual link, suggesting that conflict trajectories in democratic societies are influenced by news representations, in so much that news is both influenced by context and also influences public knowledge and opinion. But while the study of conflict representation in news is a worthwhile endeavor, its effective implementation is hampered by significant methodological challenges. Content analysis, designed to study texts, frequently leaves out visual and aural content. Qualitative textual analysis lacks representativeness. Discourse analysis can provide a way through these methodological challenges, by focusing on the contextual and constructive use of language.

This particular research project, aimed at exploring the news coverage of the Elián González case in the context of the ongoing US–Cuba conflict, is especially problematic, because the previous literature suggests that the coverage of the conflict is heavily influenced by metaphors or figures of speech, defined by the *Merriam-Webster Dictionary* as "literally denoting one kind of object or idea is used in place of another" (ND). How does one assert with methodological certainty that the presence of one idea in the coverage is actually being used to denote or stand in for some other idea? Another methodological difficulty is found in the affirmative nature of existing scholarship on metaphors, i.e., the scholarly representation of metaphors as simultaneously present, accepted and behaviorally meaningful. There were few attempts, in the scholarship presented in the previous section, to distinguish between the attitudes of news subjects, news content and audiences' perceptions. This is not to say that they are not connected, rather that further study is warranted to understand how news content incorporates metaphors and how audiences learn about and adopt metaphorical representations. This too falls outside the scope of this project.

Instead, this project aims to empirically study the *New York Times* representation of the Elián González custody case, within the broader context of the conflict between the United States and Cuba. The scope of this project is purposely limited and points to the need for further research. The central question that frames this work is the extent to which ideas about the conflict between the United States and Cuba can be shown to influence the coverage of this specific episode, and vice versa: the extent to which the episode is represented as having influence on the broader conflict. To this end, a mixed-methodological content study was developed, focused on the examination of four hypotheses, derived from a review of the literature:

H1: Coverage of the Elián González case will serve as proxy for the larger conflict between the United States and Cuba;

H2: American sources' attitudes about Cuba that are represented in the coverage of the González case will reflect attitudinal trends from the broader conflict;

H3: Cuban sources' attitudes about the United States that are represented in the coverage of the González case will reflect attitudinal trends from the broader conflict;

H4: The coverage of the González case will reflect the longstanding trend of using economic sanctions for dealing with the conflict with Cuba.

These four hypotheses were operationalized into a code book, designed to collect quantitative data and qualitative notations on a census of stories about the case in the *New York Times*. Tone; the presence, absence and qualification of sources; the presence of metaphors and representations of conflict themes (the issues, trajectories and avenues for resolution); the representations of the countries and their relative merits; immigration; and blame were all coded and the data was used to test the hypotheses (further explication of the codes and their application will be presented in the quantitative findings section).

The code book was refined and tested on an independent sample of stories about the case from the *Washington Post* with the help of an undergraduate honors student. The code book was then applied to a census of *Times* stories (n=149), using stories containing the word "Cuba" as the unit of analysis, for eleven months following the discovery of Elián González in the Florida Straits on Thanksgiving Day, 1999. The eleven-month period was selected in order to capture stories about the González case, up until the presidential election, in November 2000.

As noted, the scope of this research is limited and is not broad enough to be representative of all-American news sources. Instead, it borrows heavily from both media studies and discourse analysis to develop an analysis focused on the ways that news content is both influenced by and influences the context of the conflicts it covers. As John Collins and Ross Glover point out in the introduction to their edited book *Collateral Language* (2002), "Language, like terrorism, targets civilians and generates fear in order to effect political change. When our political leaders and our media outlets use terms like Anthrax, terrorist threat, madmen, and biological weapons, a specific type of fearfulness emerges, both intentionally and unintentionally. We are all targets for this type of language, and we are all affected by it as well" (2). Much like Collins and Glover explore how language represents particular ideas and ways of knowing in the Global War on Terror, this study seeks to address similar concerns about the language choices and implications of such language, with regard to the conflict between the United States and Cuba.

1.4   Quantitative Findings

In many ways, the *New York Times* coverage of the González case can be seen to support H1, that the case coverage would serve as a proxy for the larger conflict between the United States and Cuba. The hypothesis was operationalized into a Likert scale, positive/negative coding questions about the attitudes of the sources that were present in the coverage and proposals that were presented for resolving the González case. Language that connected attitudes about the González case and the broader conflict was also noted, as were instances when the outcome of the González case was presented as having implications for the broader conflict and how it would affect the relative standing of the two states towards one another.

Polarization, or representations that identified Cuba and the United States as opposed to one another, was an important feature of the coverage. This finding is reflected in several data points. For instance, when comparing references to Cuban–American cooperation, the significant majority of references in the coverage reflect an attitude of either non-cooperation or neutrality, but only one suggested cooperation between the two countries: an article from December 1999, describing a very successful trip to Cuba made by the Milwaukee Symphony. Sixty-four percent of the stories conveyed non-cooperation between the two countries (see Table 1.1).

Table 1.1 *Cooperation*

Cooperation	Freq.	Percent	Cumulative%
Non-cooperation	87	63.97	63.97
Neutral	48	35.29	99.26
Cooperation	1	0.74	100.00
Total	136	100.00	

The *Times* contextualized the Elián González case in terms of Cuba's economy and the political system. In so doing, the coverage represented Cuba's economy in 45 percent of their stories, and of those, 80 percent were negative. Similarly, Cuba's political system was represented in 41 percent of stories, 47 percent of which were negative. Cubans' rights were represented in 45 percent of stories, of which 80 percent were negative. When the *New York Times* represented President Fidel Castro's control over the Cuban people, economy, culture and politics, the coverage was similarly negative. Of the 40 percent of stories (n=60) about Castro's power over the Cuban people, only 15 percent were neutral/positive. Castro's control over the economy was represented in 33 percent (n=50) of stories, 86 percent of which were negative; his control over Cuban culture was represented in 28 percent of stories (n=41) and as negative in 68 percent of those. While Castro's control over politics was only present in thirty-one stories (n=46) it was cast as negative in 83 percent of them. The *Times* also represented the human rights abuses of the Cuban government twice as frequently as those of the United States (n=63 and 31, respectively) and though neither state's human rights abuses were especially prevalent in the coverage, 51 percent of stories containing Cuban human rights abuses did so prominently, while only thirty-five covered US human rights abuses prominently (see Figures 1.1–1.7).

The United States was covered at a much lower rate during the period under study, and was generally covered more favorably. The US economy was only represented in 22 percent of the stories, and only 2 percent of those were negative; Americans' rights were also represented in 22 percent of stories, but were represented negatively only 21 percent of the time. The American political system was represented in 38 percent of stories, but at a much lower rate of favorability (12.5 percent positive, 46 percent negative).

Polarization and conflict attitudes can also be seen in the coverage in terms of the disparity in the representation of sources from Cuba and the United States. Twenty-two Cuban sources were present in the coverage, while 122 US sources were represented. There were ten sources that were neither American nor Cuban present in the coverage.

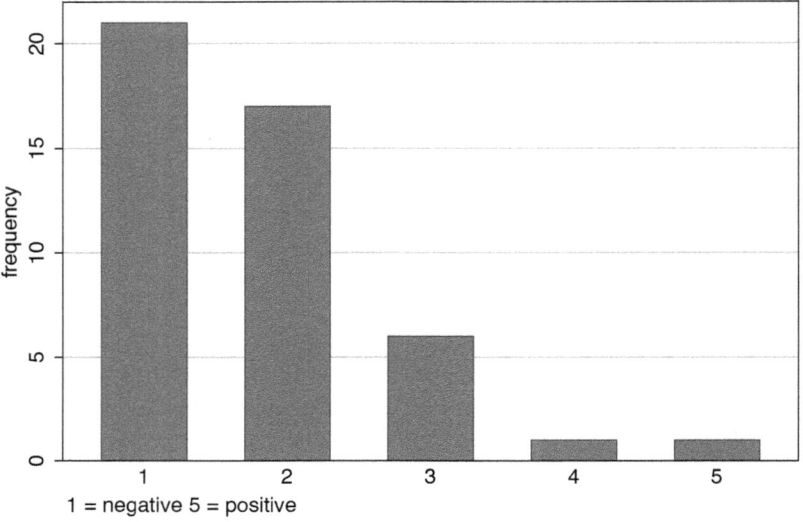

Figure 1.1 Favorability towards Castro's control of Cuban politics

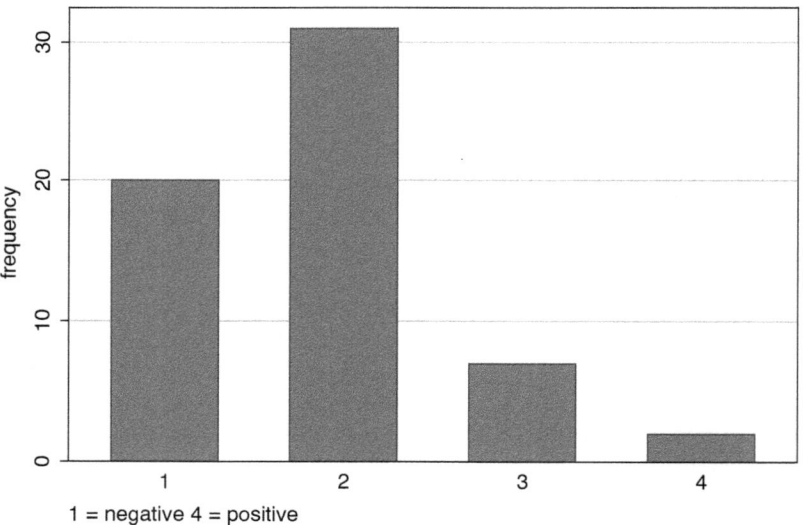

Figure 1.2 Favorability towards Castro's control of the Cuban people

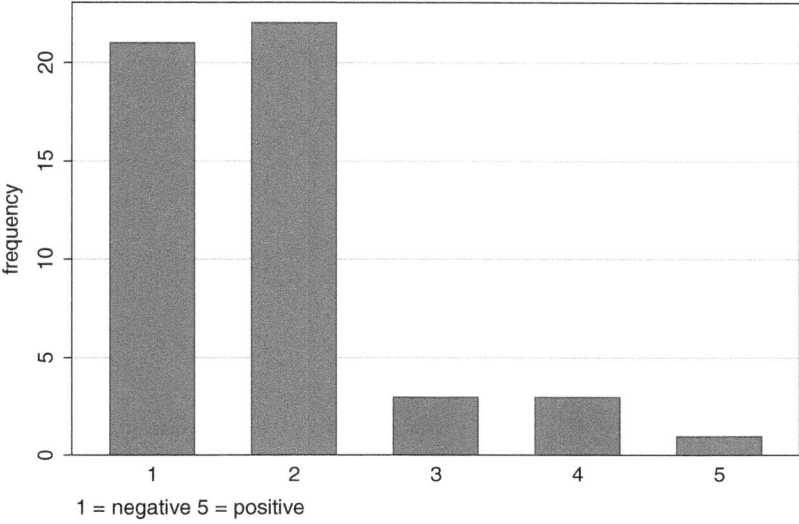

Figure 1.3 Favorability towards Castro's control of the Cuban economy

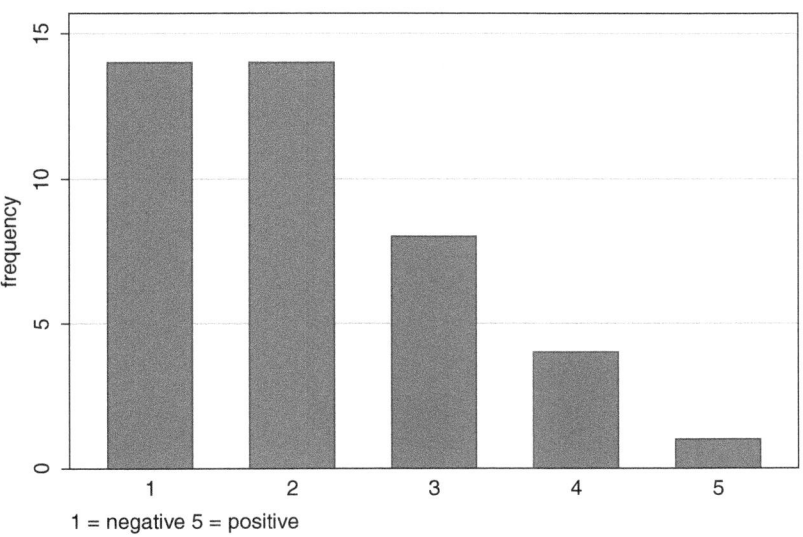

Figure 1.4 Favorability towards Castro's control of Cuban culture

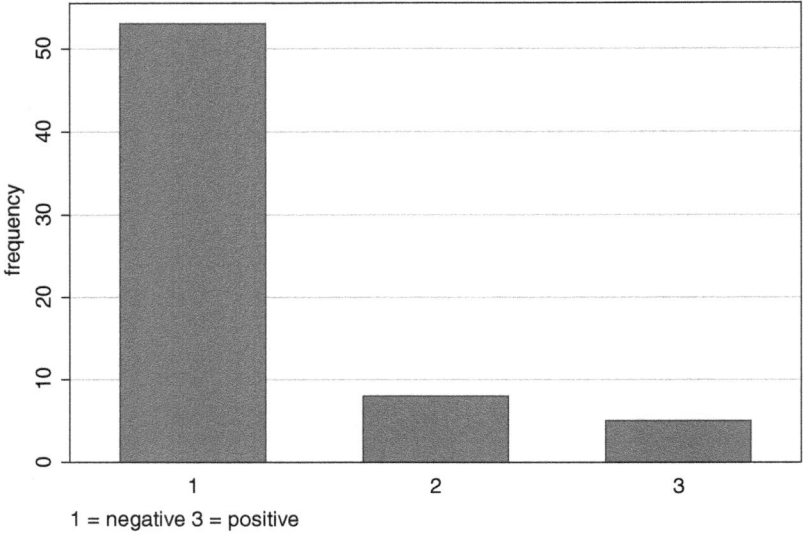

Figure 1.5 Favorability towards Cuba's economic system

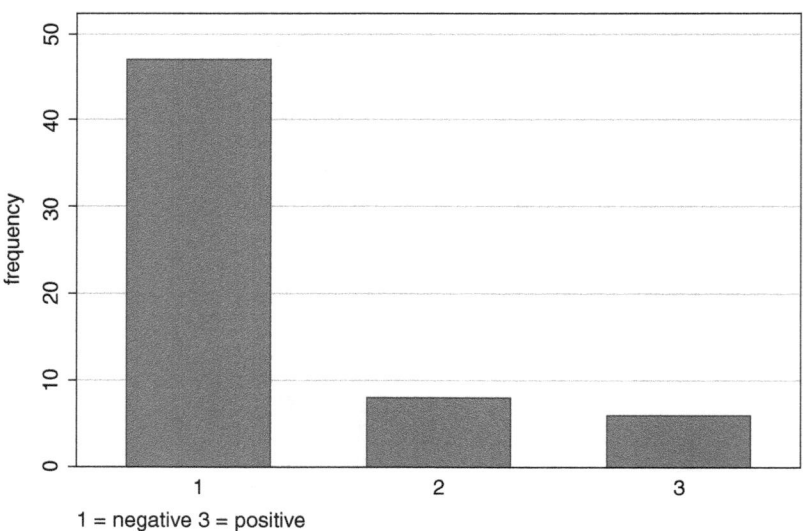

Figure 1.6 Favorability towards Cuba's political system

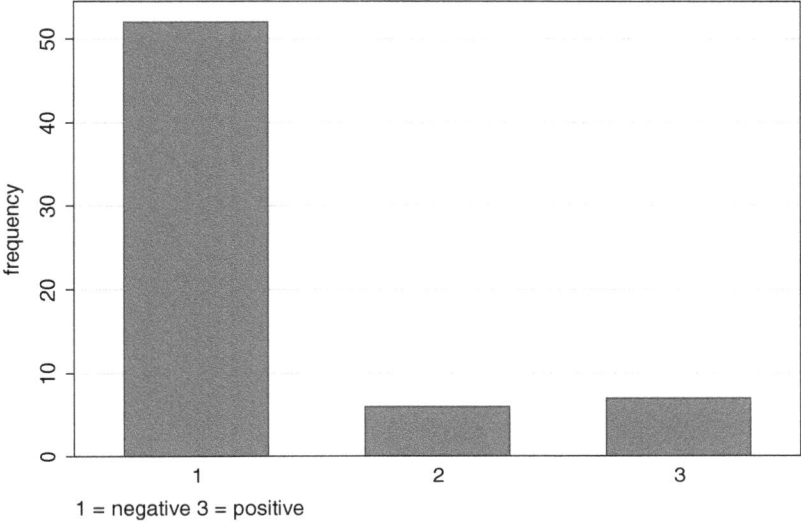

Figure 1.7 Favorability towards Cuba's rights

There was also evidence that the outcome of the González case itself would have implications for the broader conflict. Alongside representations for resolving the Elián González case were representations for resolving the broader conflict between the United States and Cuba, such as in 58 (39 percent) of stories that contained references to the embargo and its potential for favorably resolving the conflict between the two countries. In those fifty-eight stories, 31 percent were negative; 41 percent were positive. At the same time, there were references to diplomatic resolutions, via negotiation or the United Nations (n=43), and far fewer references to military intervention (n=6) (see Figures 1.8–1.10).

Though not prevalent, the *New York Times* reflected a preference for González to be allowed to remain in the United States. This was measured in two ways: through explicit mentions (34) of whether he should be allowed to stay as well as mentions of whether he should be returned to Cuba (38). While expressions that González be returned to Cuba were principally neutral, expressions that he should be allowed to stay were more strongly stated; 88 percent of them were positive (see Figures 1.11 and 1.12).

In some instances, the way that the González case should be resolved was represented as having explicit implications for Cuba and the United States. Though not prevalent in the coverage (n=27), when this connection was made, it principally suggested that how the case was resolved would have little to no

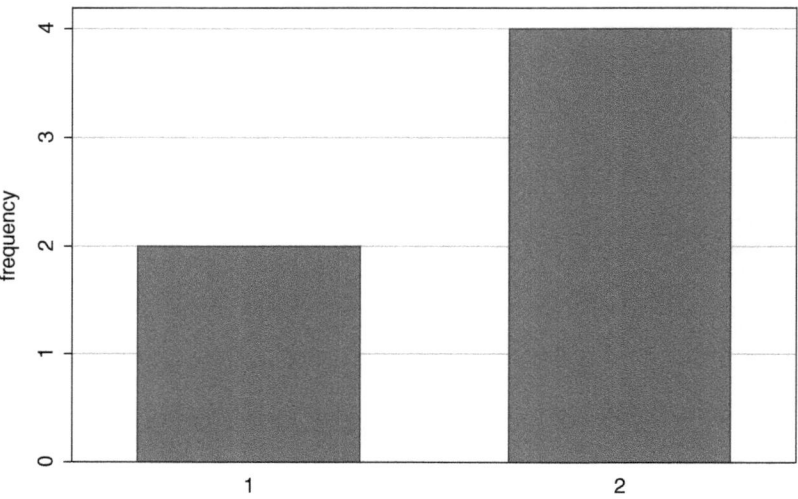

Figure 1.8 Favorability towards military intervention

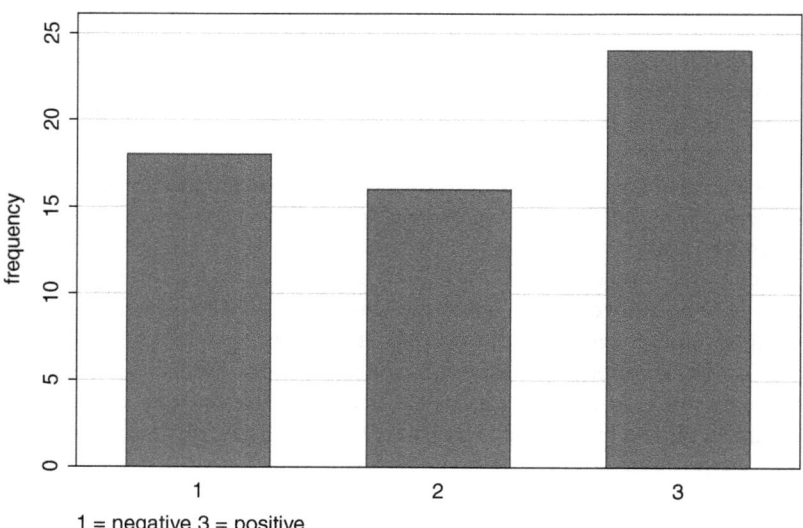

Figure 1.9 Favorability towards economic intervention

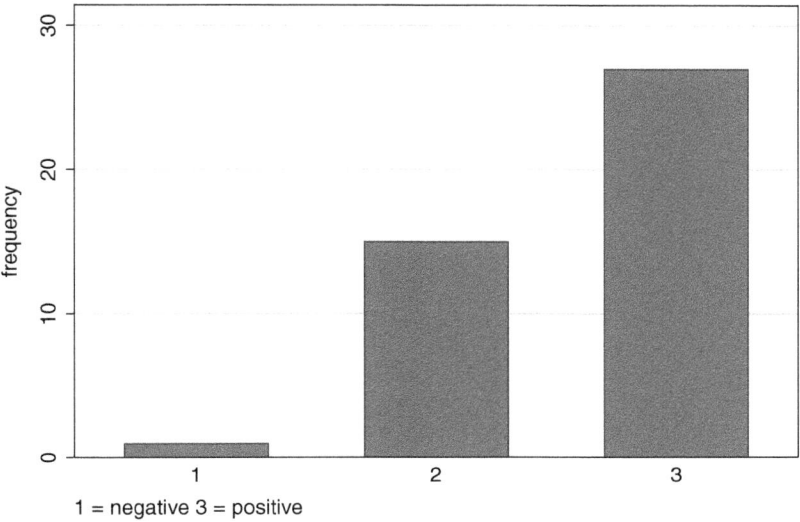

Figure 1.10 Favorability towards diplomatic intervention

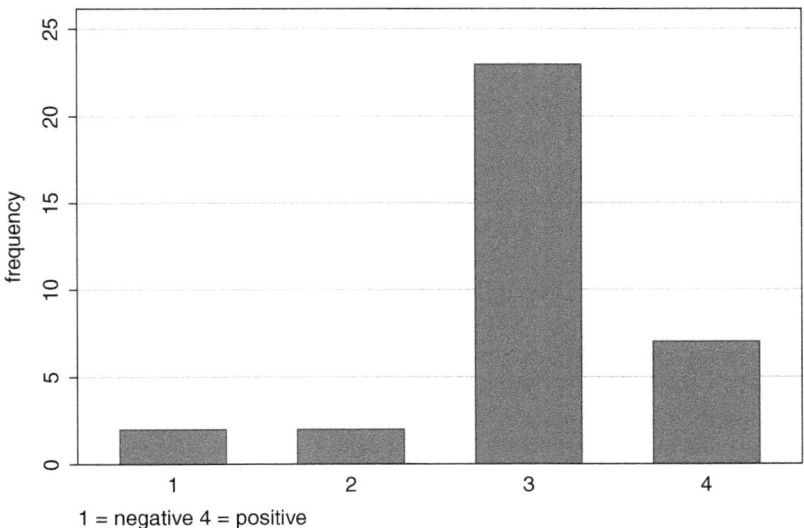

Figure 1.11 Favorability towards keeping González in the US

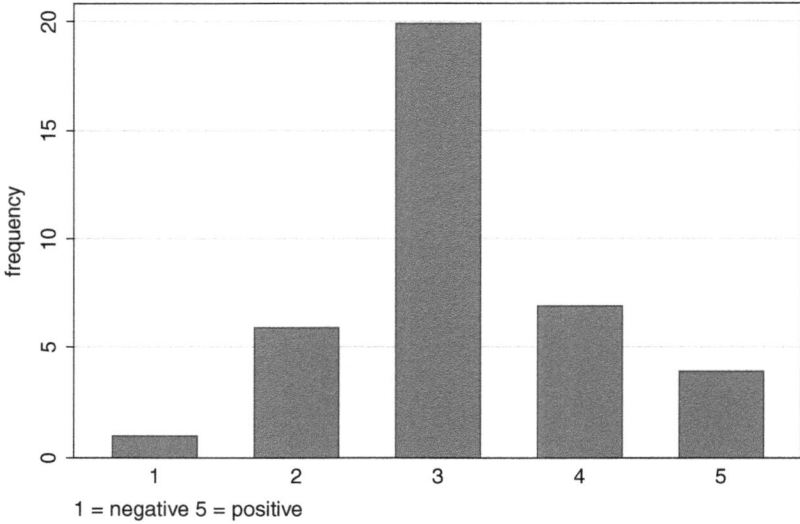

Figure 1.12 Favorability towards sending González back to Cuba

consequence for the US (96 percent neutral, if González remains in the United States, 84 percent neutral if he were returned to Cuba). But when the question was the effect on Cuba, the data was somewhat different: Keeping González in the US was still principally represented as neutrally meaningful for Cuba (85 percent), but sending him home was represented as having a positive effect on Cuba in 38 percent of cases.

While most data suggested the correctness of H1, there was some contradictory and complicating data. Cuban sources were present in only twenty-two total stories, compared to ninety stories containing sources from the US, though some of those (n=16) were Cuban exiles. In addition, the threat of Cuba to the United States was only present in eleven stories, and in most of those cases (n=7) the threat was either verbal or non-immediate. By contrast, the United States was represented as threatening to Cuba in fifty-four instances, 46 percent of which were merely verbal, but 29 percent were serious and immediate. While the *New York Times* coverage did contain references to how the long-standing conflict between the United States and Cuba should be resolved, they were not statistically significantly correlated to representations for how the Elián González case should be resolved.

Hypothesis 2 was also supported in the coverage. H2 suggests that the attitudes about Cuba that were represented in the *Times* would reflect attitudinal trends from the conflict. This idea was operationalized into the examination of attitudes towards Cuban President Fidel Castro, Cuba's communist-style economy, and the Cuban people. In addition, this hypothesis suggests that the coverage would interrogate or question the motivation of sources from Cuba and the United States.

As stated previously, and anticipated in H1 and H2, attitudes towards Cuba's president, Fidel Castro, were prevalent and uniformly negative. Castro was represented in the coverage as exerting negative control over Cuba's economy, political system, the rights of citizens and Cuban culture. In all instances, his influence was presented negatively (86, 83, 85, and 86 percent, respectively). While, as noted above, Cuba was not represented as threatening to the United States, it was framed as provocative in 29 percent of stories.

Cuba's communist economy was also represented as having negative consequences for the people and conditions in Cuba. Across fifty-nine stories in which sources from the US mentioned poverty in Cuba, 69 percent blamed Cuba for that poverty, as opposed to 14 percent that recognized the role of the US embargo. Cuban sources were more likely to implicate the United States' embargo in causing Cuban poverty (72 percent), but were only present in half as many stories (n=25). When the Cuban economy was mentioned in the coverage (n=66), it was presented negatively 80 percent of the time.

The idea that Cubans want to immigrate from Cuba was present in forty-two stories (29 percent). In thirty-four of those (81 percent) the topic of Cuban immigration was framed in terms of illegal immigration. In only thirteen stories (31 percent) was legal immigration also represented.

Contrasting with H2, was the level of questioning of the Cuban and American sources present in the coverage. While Cuban sources were present in twenty-two stories, when Cubans were present, they were mostly Cuban government sources (50 percent). Unaffiliated Cuban citizens were present in seven stories and members of identifiable Cuban groups were represented in four stories. Sixty percent of Cuban sources were questioned or challenged by other sources or the reporter. Seventy-three percent of US sources' perspectives were challenged (n=122).

H3 suggested that attitudes represented in the *New York Times* towards the US will reflect attitudinal trends from the conflict, namely that the United States would be presented positively, benevolently, and responsibly, that US motivations would be represented as positive, and that Cuban citizens' attitudes towards the US would either be positive and benevolent, while Cuban government sources would be represented as having polarized and negative views of the US, while questioning the motives of the US. The data, much of which has already been represented above, is mixed for this hypothesis, leading to the conclusion that it is not supported. The *New York Times* was complex in its reporting of the US as an actor in the González case and the conflict with Cuba. Twenty-seven stories (18 percent) mentioned US attempts to use sabotage in

Cuba and sixteen stories (10 percent) mentioned US propaganda efforts in Cuba. The US was variously framed as actor and responder in the conflict, and in a plurality of instances (42 percent) was represented with complexity in this regard, as doing things that were both provocative and responsive.

H4 proposed that the coverage would reflect the longstanding trend of using economic sanctions for dealing with the conflict with Cuba. Violence and diplomacy were not expected to be prevalent proposals for dealing with the case or the longstanding conflict. Instead, economic means were presumed to be presented as the primary way of resolving this and other conflicts between the United States and Cuba.

This hypothesis was partially supported. As mentioned previously, the prevalence of the idea that either country was threatening to the other was low. There were few references to overt violence as a means for resolving the conflict (n=6) and none of those favored military intervention. However, diplomacy was prevalent (n=43) and more favored at a rate of 63 percent. Economic intervention, though most prevalent of the three strategies (n=58), was presented in a more balanced way than diplomacy. Thirty-one percent of the stories presented economic interventions negatively, 41 percent presented economic interventions positively, and 28 percent did so either neutrally or through the presentation of multiple perspectives.

1.5 Qualitative Findings

Qualitative data was collected alongside the quantitative; notes were made on the *New York Times* use of language as reflective and constitutive of the context of the conflict between the two countries. In addition, notes were made on modality expressions in the coverage, especially the forcefulness and certainty of assertions that were made by sources and others, the expression of attitudes and beliefs, when assertions were made but not supported by evidence, and other expressive language in the coverage that caught coders' attention.

Given the reputation of the *New York Times*, there were a surprising number (n=20) of assertions about both Cuba and the United States, made throughout the coverage, that were either unsupported or improperly sourced. For instance, throughout the period that Elián González was in the United States, Cuban people at various times took to the streets to demonstrate their support for reuniting Elián and his Cuban father and bringing them both home (Juan Miguel also spent several months in the United States, awaiting the return of Elián). A feature of the coverage of this phenomenon was the repeated yet unsupported assertion that these demonstrations were not organized by Cuban people but staged by the Castro government, as a form of propaganda. For instance, a letter to the editor by Paul Hollander, from December 11, 1999, stated that

The highly organized demonstrations are a textbook example of the demagogic reflexes of a totalitarian regime. The dutiful crowds provide a wonderful diversion from a chronically mismanaged economy, endemic, shortages, corruption and the capriciousness of President Fidel Castro, whose policies generated the desperate escapes of the putative beneficiaries of his system in the first place. (A18)

On one hand, it is easy to discount the words of a letter-writer as extraneous to the coverage, but the *New York Times* chose to run the letter, implicating its editorial control. Another example from a Reuters news story from January 4, 2000 states, "Tens of thousands of Cubans marched this afternoon past a monument to Argentine-born guerrilla legend Ernesto Guevara, known as Che, in the latest of daily protests organized by Cuba's governing Communist Party" (A8). It is not insignificant that the *New York Times* repeatedly printed unsupported assertions about Cuban protests. However, the assertions themselves are also worthy of mention. To assert that protests are staged or state organized is to challenge the genuineness of protesters' motivations and discount their meaning. A staged protest is not a protest at all, and to question them, as the *New York Times* does, is to call into question by implication Cubans' freedom and government control as well as Cubans' commitment to their country and their country's international engagements.

An illustrative article by Rick Bragg on December 9, 1999 began by highlighting the care that González was receiving from his Miami relatives. "'He's happy here,' said his 21-year-old cousin, Marisleysis González. 'Let's not turn this into a political thing'" (A1). Later in the story, Bragg asserts that "the Cuban government has trucked in thousands of marchers, waving signs that read, 'We want Elián back home'" (A1). Bragg uses people "in Miami's exile neighborhoods" to source this assertion, but they are poor sources, given their overt distaste for Castro and lack of proximity and access to the demonstrations. As with the previous example, the discourse presented here implies incapacity on the part of the Cuban people to control themselves or hold ideas on political issues. In addition, this particular anecdote sets up a false equivalency between Cubans in the United States and those who are in Cuba, in terms of their authoritativeness with regard to contemporary events in Cuba, further undermining the idea that Cubans are valid sources on their own lives and positions.

Cuban exiles were central to the coverage and were used to describe Cuba, its leaders, economy, and state of affairs. For instance, in a story by Lizette Alvarez on April 9, 2000:

Here, politicians are judged first and foremost by how much they despise Fidel and Communism, not by where they stand on education and Social Security. You grow up meeting former political prisoners who spent 15 years in Cuban jails for showing their disillusionment with the revolution, and thousands of others who broke Cuban law and jumped on teeny, tottering rafts just to get away. You know lots of cousins here who hate cousins there because they are Communist believers, and you hear endless sorrowful tales from mothers who can't get their children out of Cuba ... To them, Fidel Castro is not an irrelevant dictator. He is not a curious relic (4,7).

This kind of vitriol for Castro was not limited to the Cuban exiles, though. The *New York Times* also published a letter by Barry Farber, a conservative talk-show host, on June 18, 2000, in which the author compares the Castro regime's youth programming to the Hitler Youth paramilitary program (4,14).

While the *Times* coverage of Castro and his regime was vitriolic and based largely on the opinions of those outside of Cuba, it was also remarkably critical of US efforts to depose him and to exert what some might consider undue influence in another country's affairs. And at the same time, the *New York Times* also pushed back on anti-Castro claims. In a story by David González on December 30, 1999, the author interviews Cubans who challenge the assertions that Elián's life would be better in the US: "The neighbors say they cannot understand why Elián's relatives in Miami are so intent on keeping the boy, and they dismiss any suggestion that he could have a better life there" (A12).

While much vitriol was levied against Castro, the coverage reflected a nostalgia about Cuba and Cuban people, akin to Edward Said's (1979) conception of Orientalism (1). Throughout the period there were stories by professional and amateur authors who described Cuba as a strange and wonderful place with a thriving black market, in which Cubans make very little money but make do, and where foreign tourists can live like kings. An essay by Kirk Kraeutler describes an anecdote about buying gas, in which a station attendant implied that he should pull his car around to the back of the shop, because they could not legally sell to him. Kraeutler also describes "a golden-haired green-eyed young mother named Paula, who quickly offered her address and, only half in jest it seemed, the baby suckling at her breast" (5,31). Similarly, Lizette Alvarez uses the recollections of Cuban exiles to paint Cuba as a place of "sand on the beaches ... as fine and as white as sugar and where everyone lived in perfect harmony" (4,7).

Carey Goldberg also exemplifies this kind of Orientalist nostalgia in her piece, "Exploring Two Sides of Cuba's West." She describes locals shouting "No," when she made a wrong turn (because her Cuban map was unreliable) and a nice hotel room at the beach, for which they paid "just $40 a night" (5,9). The focus of Goldberg's story is a scuba diving trip in which she and her companion, "total neophytes" and without certification, were trained by a dive guide and allowed to dive numerous times. "Thank goodness, is all I can say, that Cuba goes its own way in some things, and is not yet afflicted by that wet-blanket word, 'liability'" (5,9). But at the same time that Goldberg describes the bizarre world of Cuba for tourists, she also touches on what she calls "a kind of tourism apartheid," in which Cubans are barred from visiting some tourist locations and, even if they were allowed, could probably not afford to do so.

The contrasts between stories that are critical of Cuba's government and leadership and stories that are nostalgic about Cuban people reflect linkages between the case and the broader conflict, such as were demonstrated in the quantitative findings section, while conforming well with the metaphorical conceptions presented in the literature review and the idea that the United States views itself as a beneficent Gulliver or the protector of a child against a deadbeat dad. Stated more concretely, as the protector of the Cuban people against the ruinous terribleness of Castro's Communism.

In the quantitative section, the data presented suggests that the coverage of the Elián González case and the conflict overall was fairly even-handed; but in one important way it was not. Letters to the editor were not infrequent features of the coverage and many authors expressed strong antipathy towards both Cuba and the United States, and especially the embargo.

David Hayden, a letter-writer from Wilton, Connecticut, writes:

The contemptible exploitation of 6-year-old Elián González by both the Cuban government and the Cuban exile community in Florida ... is a sad reminder of the fact that children are charming in part because they are largely ignorant of the adult world ... Both factions in this case are coldly trying to turn Elián's tragedy to their own political advantage; both sides understand that an innocent child who is the victim of a tragedy has a sympathetic charisma that can never be attained by mere political leaders ... Elián's mother made a desperate attempt to flee Cuba apparently because Fidel Castro's dictatorship has turned daily life into a humiliating struggle with deprivation and repression. (A26)

Other letter writers were equally vitriolic in opposition to the United States. For instance, Esther B. Siegel, from Southampton, New York, writes, "Isn't it time we recognized Cuba, a small nation with which we could trade, and perhaps improve the lives of the people there, or don't we have the courage?" (A16). Referring to a trade bill that was passed in the US during the period under study, David Wald of Santa Clara, California, writes:

The terms of the bill forbid financing by private and government sources in the United States, and Cuba is denied the right to export any commodities here as a form of payment for its purchases. Fidel Castro has deemed the bill 'humiliating' and has announced that Cuba will make no purchases under the act ... The anti-Castro members of Congress and the Cuban American National Foundation are gleeful about the bill, which they regard as a victory over those who would genuinely seek to ease the embargo. The main victims, aside from the people of Cuba, are the American voters, who have once again been told that this odious 40-year embargo is being eased while, in reality, it is being tightened. (A24)

In these and other letters like them, we see authors asserting facts without evidence and making forceful expressions of belief that the *New York Times* presents without caveat or correction. In short, the letters to the editor are textual representations that enable the *Times* to interject emotional, passionate and emotive values into the discourse.

1.6 Discussion

The *New York Times* coverage of the Elián González case and the conflict between the United States and Cuba was complex and varied, a remarkable finding, given the conclusions presented in the literature review. While there were data supporting all four hypotheses, there were also contraindicating data. Most strongly supported were hypotheses 1 and 2. Hypotheses 3 and 4 were not well supported.

However, there may be some rationale to consider H3 as a null hypothesis, especially because doing so may actually lead to a way to understand data about H4. The ideas supporting H3 are in the literature on the Cuba–US conflict and in conflict studies generally: that in times of international conflict, coverage from within a country tends to bolster its position, show support for its leaders and in other ways establish national support for the country's conflict goals. H3 therefore anticipated that the coverage would support the US position on both the González case and the longstanding conflict, that it would be presented as benevolent and responsible and that US motivations would be represented as positive.

Instead, the coverage reflected a myriad of perspectives about the United States as an actor in this case and the broader conflict, the embargo as a strategic policy and its effects on human rights, and how the González case was playing out in the legal system and in the media. There was no consistency in the *Times* coverage of the United States. But perhaps that lack of consistency helps explain the support in the coverage for H4, having to do with the economic embargo. By the time that the Elián González case occurred, the embargo had been in place for nearly forty years. During that time it had not achieved the goals of ousting President Castro, ending Cuban communism or destroying the Cuban government. Yet despite its apparent failure, it continued to be the law of the land (even, as discussed earlier, after legislation was passed that was initially designed to undercut it). How does a policy with such a poor track record continue to receive support, especially in a situation of such intractability?

These findings from the *New York Times* suggest a much more complex relationship between self and other in this conflict than is typical in international conflict. Surely complicated by the geographic proximity between the United States and Cuba and the clear geographic, economic, and political disparity of power between the countries, in this conflict the presence of the Cuban exile community contributed greatly to discord and therefore also to the challenge of crafting policy.

In fact, this sense of complexity can be seen in all the factors typically at play in conflict: parties, interests and outcomes. Parties, explicated above, were especially complex, as the Cuban exile community played an outsized role in the shaping of US national leadership. Interests, or issues that are viewed as pertinent to a conflict, were complex due to the long-term nature of this conflict, the changing shape of global politics over time, the fact of Soviet withdrawal from Cuba in the early 1990s, and the obvious failure over time of the embargo to produce its political aims. In addition, readers were well aware of the humanitarian consequences of the embargo. Outcomes, too, were muddled in the *Times* coverage. While the longstanding goal of defeating both Castro and Communism were always present, the presence of Cubans and Cuban exiles in the coverage demonstrated to readers how complex the outcomes of international conflict can be.

In terms of testing or affirming the validity of previous research, the findings of this project are mixed. As noted previously, the coverage was not overtly composed of metaphors or expressive of metaphorical concepts, nor was it especially hyperbolic. At the same time, though, the qualitative findings highlight that Cuba – its leaders, people and the cores of their beliefs (about themselves and the conflict) – were treated with a rhetorical disdain that could not but influence readers' perceptions. While quantitative data suggest that the *Times* coverage was even-handed, well grounded in evidence and appropriately mixed ethos and logos, there were numerous instances of unsupported assertions, especially when it came to explaining what Cubans believed and wanted, and why.

In terms of metaphors, there are two important limitations that must be detailed. First, authors like Perez, Blight and Brenner are not media scholars, and their work was not focused on parsing the differences between news production, content and audience (the typical media studies trifecta). Their examinations of metaphors for understanding the conflict between the United States and Cuba seem to be focused not on their presence in news coverage per se, but rather on their use by news makers, who are then represented in news coverage. As noted in the methods section, how does one examine the presence or absence of metaphors in news coverage or their effective transmission? This research appears to make no meaningful contribution to resolving this question, except to point out its value and the extent that metaphors were not prevalent in the coverage, which suggests that if they are predominant, they are being developed through other means.

Second, another prominent conclusion of the literature is the predominance of what Banet-Weiser called the "hyperbolic proportions" (151), of the case, in which coverage of González case was bereft of substance, except in the pursuit of ideological gains. Again, this conclusion is not supported in the findings of this project. However, just as with metaphors, it is probable that the juxtaposition of findings suggests a limitation of the research. In many ways, the González case was played out for US audiences on television screens instead of news pages, and when one thinks of the case, it is probably the visual image – the Pulitzer Prize-winning photo by Alan Diaz of an armed federal agent seizing Elián from inside a closet in his uncle's home – that comes to mind. Even in 1999, there was an increasing gulf between how American audiences were receiving their news and, by limiting this research to the most staid of news media, print, it is necessarily limited. There were few "talking heads" in the *New York Times* coverage. When they were present, they tended to be former federal officials, whose words were written out, considered and edited.

In comparing the evidence from this project to the literature, one of the most interesting findings is that the González case seems to conform well with what Blight and Brenner call the "Cuban style of deterrence." Framed as a method of engagement in which "a relatively less powerful country tries to deter aggression by raising the costs for the aggressor to an unacceptable level in terms of both blood and treasure" (87), the González case seems to be a clear victory for Cuba, because not only was Elián returned to Cuba over the objections of Cuban exiles and other prominent voices in the United States (and US public opinion generally), it was done in a way that seemed also to undermine the international leadership of the United States, pointed to disunity in the US population, and provided another way for Castro to highlight the value of his country and their way of doing things. Despite stories that pointed out the economic depravity of Cubans and the disparity between the rights of tourists and citizens in Cuba, the nostalgic Orientalism of the coverage suggested that Cuba is a place and that Cubans are a people with value and worthy of regard. In stark contrast to typical stories about the conflict other, Cubans were not subject to degeneration in this coverage (though Castro certainly was).

All of this leads to the need for further research on the topic of the conflict between the United States and Cuba through a media studies lens. Other cases (the so-called Havana Syndrome of 2016–2017, President Obama's trip to Cuba in 2014, the Bay of Pigs, the Cuban Missile Crisis, and the reimposition of sanctions by the Trump administration) are opportunities to study the representation of flash points in news coverage in a conflict that, to this day, continues to not get hot. More research, on news coverage in different media that are oriented toward different populations, is needed for the sake of comparison and in order to develop a fuller sense of the shape of the coverage of flash points and the longstanding conflict. The media studies lens, though implicated in much previous literature on the topic, has not yet been fully explored. In addition, the methodologies of media studies have not yet been employed to understand the content in a way that would enable representative analysis. As mentioned previously, much research has implicated the media without attempting to apply rigorous media studies methodologies. This project, through the imposition of a quantitative/qualitative content study that has been heavily influenced by discourse analysis, has made a step towards appropriate media studies methods but, as is evident in the findings, needs refinement. Quantitative content analysis, as it turns out, is a poor choice for the explication of metaphors; story-level analysis, though useful in many ways, leads to a good deal of contradictory findings due to the variety of perspectives and ideas that were sometimes present in a single story.

References

Anderson, John Ward. 2000. "Viva Elián! Hero of the Revolution!" *Washington Post*, April 18.
Bamrud, Joachim. 1987. "Cuba's Media: Interview with Lazaro Barredo." *Index on Censorship* 16(3): 15.
Banet-Weiser, Sarah. 2003. "Elián González and 'The Purpose of America': Nation, Family, and the Child-Citizen." *American Quarterly* 55(2): 149–178.
Bender, Lynn Darrell. 1975. *The Politics of Hostility: Castro's Revolution and United States Policy*. San Juan: Inter-American University Press.
Bennett, W. Lance. 2011. *News: The Politics of Illusion* (9th ed). New York: Pearson.
Blight, James and Brenner, Phillip. 2002. *Sad and Luminous Days: Cuba's Struggle with the Superpowers after the Missile Crisis*. Washington DC: Rowman & Littlefield.
Brenner, Phillip and Castro, Soraya. 2009. "David and Gulliver: Fifty Years of Competing Metaphors in the Cuban-United States Relationship." *Diplomacy & Statecraft* 20: 236–257.
Central Intelligence Agency. 1979. *Official History of the Bay of Pigs Operation*. Washington DC: Central Intelligence Agency.
Collins, John and Glover, Ross, Eds. 2002. *Collateral Language: A User's Guide to America's New War*. New York: New York University Press.
Demo, Anne Teresa. 2007. "The Afterimage: Immigration Policy after Elián." *Rhetoric & Public Affairs* 10(1): 27–50.
Erikson, Daniel P. 2002. "The New Cuba Divide." *The National Interest* 67(Spring): 65–71.
Erisman, Michael and Kirk, John. Eds. 2006. *Redefining Cuban Foreign Policy: The Impact of the Special Period*. Gainsville, FL: University Press of Florida.
Fiore, Faye and Baum, Geraldine. 2000. "Many Find Video of Boy Disturbing." *Los Angeles Times*, April 14.
Fox, Jan. 2017. "Shot in Havana." *Index on Censorship* 46(2): 58–61.
Garthoff, Raymond. 1985/1986." American-Soviet Relations in Perspective." *Political Science Quarterly* 100 (4)Winter: 451.
González, Edward. 1972. "The United States and Castro: Breaking Deadlock." *Foreign Affairs* 50(4): 722–737.
Greiner, Guillermo and Castro, Max. 2001. "Blacks and Cubans in Miami: The Negative Consequences of the Cuban Enclave on Ethnic Relations." In Michael Jones-Correa (Ed.), *Governing American Cities: Inter-Ethnic*

Coalitions, Competition, and Conflict. New York: Russell Sage Foundation, 137–157.

Hall, Stuart. 1973. *Encoding and Decoding in the Television Discourse.* Paper for the Council of Europe Colloquy on "Training in the Critical Reading of Television Language."

Hall, Stuart, Critcher, Chas, Jefferson, Tony, Clarke, John and Roberts, Brian. 1978. *Policing the Crisis: Mugging, the State, and Law and Order.* London: Palgrave.

Iyengar, Kavitha. 2015. "The Venceremos Brigade: North Americans in Cuba since 1969." *International Journal of Cuban Studies* 7(2): 236–264.

Johnson, David. 2000. "The Elián González Case: The Overview; U.S. Gathers Officers, Preparing to Take Cuban from Miami Kin." *New York Times*, April 21: 1.

Kuusisto, Riikka. 2009. "Comic Plots as Conflict Resolution Strategy. "*European Journal of International Relations* 15(4): 601–626.

Lakoff, George. 1991. *Metaphor and War: The Metaphor System Used to Justify War in the Gulf.* Presented to the Alumni House, University of California at Berkeley, January 30.

Landau, Saul. 2003. *The Pre-Emptive Empire: A Guide to Bush's Kingdom.* London: Pluto Press.

Lohmeier, Christine and Pentzold, Christian. 2014. "Making Mediated Memory Work: Cuban-Americans, Miami Media and the Doings of Diaspora Memories." *Media, Culture & Society* 23(6): 776–789.

Mayer, William G. 2001. "Trends: American Attitudes toward Cuba." *American Association for Public Opinion Research* 65(4): 585–606.

Montgomery, Louise. 1988. "Images of the United States in the Latin American Press." *Journalism Quarterly* 65(3): 656–660.

Nixon, Richard. 1959. *Rough Draft of Summary of Conversation Between the Vice President and Fidel Castro.* The National Security Archive, The George Washington University. https://nsarchive2.gwu.edu/bayofpigs/19590425.pdf.

Perez, Louis. 1999. *On Becoming Cuban: Identity, Nationality & Culture.* Chapel Hill, NC: The University of North Carolina Press.

Perez, Louis. 2008. *Cuba in the American Imagination: Metaphor and the Imperial Ethos.* The Chapel Hill, NC: University of North Carolina Press.

Pertierra, Anna Cristina. 2012. "If They Show Prison Break in the United States on a Wednesday, by Thursday It Is Here: Mobile Media Networks in Twenty-First-Century Cuba." *Television & New Media* 13(5): 399–414.

Said, Edward. 1979. *Orientalism.* New York: Vintage Books.

Tamayo, Juan. 2014. *Thick Flies and a Long Memory.* Nieman Reports: Summer.

Venegas, Christina. 2010. *Digital Dilemmas (New Directions in International Studies).* New Brunswick, NJ: Rutgers University Press.

Vicari, Stefania. 2014. "Blogging Politics in Cuba: The Framing of Political Discourse in the Cuban Blogosphere." *Media, Culture & Society* 36(7): 998–1015.

2 The Construction of Threat of "Islamist Terrorism" in German Newspapers

Enis Bicer, Lina Brink, and Alejandra Nieves Camacho

2.1 Introduction

For the vast majority of people in Western countries, the immediate physical threat posed by terrorism is not experienced directly, but rather indirectly through mass media coverage. What exactly we know (or think we know) about Islamist terrorism has usually been mediated through the specific depictions the media provide us with about that topic (Trautmann 2006: 141). Especially when we lack direct experience, media discourse becomes crucially important as our sole source of information and will influence our social construction of meaning and reality (Adoni and Mane 1984). Consequently, in the case of Islamist terrorism, we consider media discourses as important processes of meaning-construction and reality formation (Tuman 2010).

Even though Islamist terrorism poses an actual life-threatening risk, on a quantitative scale it is still quite negligible compared to other risks of mortality. Nevertheless, media attention and public threat perception often disproportionately emphasize topics connected to terrorism (Bock 2017; Jirschitzka et al. 2010). This is generally explained by pointing towards specific journalistic practices that consider terrorism to have a higher news value and newsworthy factors (Chermak and Gruenewald 2006; Galtung and Ruge 1965). Thus, this large amount of media attention towards terrorism and terrorist events facilitates a "threat- and violence-based communication process," which outlines one crucial defining characteristic of terrorism (Schmid 2011, 61).

Furthermore, regarding the structure of media coverage about terrorism, studies show that terrorist events with a Muslim perpetrator get relatively

This study is based on a project funded by the German Federal Ministry of Education and Research (Project Code: 01UG1830AX) and was conducted at Akkon University of Applied Sciences, Berlin. We especially want to thank Felicitas Qualmann and Aron Trieb for supporting us in realizing this project.

more media attention compared to terrorist acts from non-Muslim perpetrators (Kearns et al. 2019). A biased and unbalanced media representation of Muslims, bringing them into excessive association with terrorism or/and representing them disproportionally as terrorist subjects, is likely to facilitate anti-Muslim attitudes, Islamophobia and threat perceptions towards them (Cinnirella 2012; Jaspal and Cinnirella 2010).

In the following analysis, we look at the media discourse on three major terrorist events that happened in France and Germany in the years 2015 and 2016. The aim of this study is to answer the following questions: What kind of different meanings of threat regarding Islamist terrorism are constituted and can be found in the examined media discourse? How are anti-Muslim stereotypes and racism applied in producing meaning and knowledge about the societal phenomena of Islamist terrorism and associated threats? To provide answers to these questions, this study applies the Sociology of Knowledge Approach to Discourse (SKAD) (Keller 2011, 2012, 2018). In the findings section we identify and describe three dominant interpretive schemes of threats associated with Islamist terrorism in the media discourse. In the conclusions, we sum up the findings and outline the specific role of anti-Muslim stereotypes and racism within the identified interpretive schemes.

2.2 Islam and Terrorism in the Media

Studies constantly show a negatively biased picture and overly homogenizing media representation of Muslims and Islam (e.g., El-Menouar 2019; Poole 2002). A recent meta-analytical study by Ahmed and Matthes (2017) validates a general negative representation of Muslims in the media and, as a consequence, contributes to a specific negatively connoted construction of Muslim subjects in the Western imagination. The findings of this analysis show that Muslims are often represented in a way that underlines their potential threatening influence on Western societies. According to this study, media representations of Muslims and Islam often appear alongside topics of migration, terrorism and war, whereas Islam is predominately depicted in association with violence and referring to cultural otherness (Ahmed and Matthes 2017).

Although this study emphasizes the specific role of the terrorist attacks of 9/11 in promoting this media coverage, the particular image of Muslims and Islam in the sense of cultural "Others" and as antagonistic subjects towards the Western world is not as completely new a phenomenon as might appear. From a historical point of view, the current negative image of Muslims and Islam find its predecessor in historical sources of common knowledge about the Muslim world as an antagonist and hostile force against the Christian West. This dates back to common beliefs about Islam in medieval times which were instituted for the purposes of medieval crusades against the imaginary "barbaric" and "faithless" occupying alien force of the so-called Holy Land in the East (Benz 2017: 513ff.). This process of cultural "Othering" and alienation is also apparent in how the Christian forces of Reconquista promoted their battle to gain control over Muslim-ruled Al-Andalus up to the early seventeenth century (Soyer 2013). In his classical work, Edward Said shows how the historically based images of the cultural "Other," represented as the "Oriental," serves as a negative background against which to construct a positive and superior colonial Western in-group identity (Said 1985, 2003). In his follow-up work he also shows how Western media coverage contributes to solidifying and (re)constructing a specific negative and homogenized representation of the Islamic "Other" (Said 1981).

Taken together, in the media representations of Muslims and Islam, one can observe some major patterns. Muslims and Islam are often represented as a threatening factor to Western societies, either directly to security, by referring them to Islamist terrorism and/or migration (Trautmann 2006), or more as a cultural threat, by highlighting fundamental cultural differences and contradictions between the Islamic and Western cultures (Soyer 2013). Western culture and values appear to be at stake because of the presence of Muslims in Western societies (Poole 2002). While Muslims and the Muslim world most often represent conflict, war and cultural and societal underdevelopment, the Western world, in contrast, most often represents superiority and advancement in terms of culture, civilization and freedom (Ates 2006; Poole 2002).

This hegemonic discursive practice of constructing an essentialist dichotomy between a positively characterized in-group and a negatively contrasted culturally defined out-group (Hall 1992) strengthens boundaries, rejection and hostility towards the minority group of Muslims in Western societies, and can contribute to group-level stigmatization, discrimination and hate towards the so constructed out-group (Benz 2012, 2017). Recent extremist right-wing and supremacist attacks, like the tragic Christchurch mosque shootings in early 2019,[1] indicate that the discursive practice of constructing an imagined out-group enemy can end up being, in some extreme cases, a factor promoting hate crimes.

Anti-Muslim sentiments, Islamophobia[2] and anti-Muslim racism[3] are common phenomena in Germany and other countries in the West (Attia et al. 2014; Bayrakli and Hafez 2019; Hafez 2012; Hafez and Schmidt 2015; Helbling 2012). The concept of anti-Muslim racism reflects and manifests the structure of power relations and a culture of dominance within societies (Attia et al.

---

[1] While this chapter was under review, in February 2020, another severe racist attack happened, this time in Hanau, Germany, targeting and killing nine People of Color.
[2] There are different academic perceptions about the term Islamophobia and its conceptual and analytical relation to racism (see, e.g., Allen 2010; Hafez 2019).
[3] By relying on the foundations of postcolonial theory and by referring to cultural racism, Iman Attia established the concept of anti-Muslim racism in German academic research on racism (Attia 1994, 2009).

2015; Rommelspacher 1995). In her study about anti-Muslim narratives and topoi, Shooman (2014) emphasizes several key defining aspects about the racialization of Muslims. The discursive racialized construction of Muslims emanates from a dominant societal position. It creates a homogenized and essentialist perception and image of Muslims as "Others" in contrast to the White Christian/atheist society. Thus, racialization creates and contributes to distinct collective knowledge and meanings about that constructed group, so that they clearly are identifiable as such (Shooman 2014: 64f.). This form of racialization affects almost all aspects of social life. For example, Fekete (2009) demonstrates in her work how consequential anti-Muslim racism works when it comes to practices of the security state towards what is socially perceived as threatening, just because of an ascribed group affiliation as a Muslim.

2.3 SKAD as Theoretical and Methodical Frame for Analyzing the Discursive Construction of Threat

The Sociology of Knowledge Approach to Discourse (SKAD) (Keller 2011, 2018) combines the Foucauldian approach to discourse[4] with the sociology of knowledge tradition of Berger and Luckmann (1967) (Keller 2011, 48). Proceeding from this, it aims "to examine the *discursive construction* of symbolic orders which occurs in the form of conflicting social knowledge relationships and competing politics of knowledge" (Keller 2011, 48, emphasis in original). It conceives discourse in terms of social practice and seeks to explore the processes it entails. Therefore it "looks for fixed and fluid rules of interpretation practices and takes an interest in the participating actors' part in conflicts on collective levels of 'definition of the (collective's) situations' (W. I. Thomas and D. Thomas)" (Keller 2011, 49). Hence, based on collectively shared stocks of knowledge and signs, social actors are interpretatively involved in meaning-construction of social situations and phenomena, and by doing so, they are (re)constructing and (re)producing social definitions and meanings of reality. This process of interpretative construction of reality shows itself in discourse and in discursive battles over societal phenomena and matters (Keller 2018, 16f.). Or as Keller states: "In discourses, the use of language or symbols by social actors constitutes the sociocultural facticity of physical and social realities" (Keller 2011, 51). By referring to Foucault, discourses are seen as regulated and structured social practices of sign usage, for example (but not solely) by language, which SKAD aims to analytically unfold (Keller 2011, 53).

---

[4] A more in-depth view on SKAD's reference to the Foucauldian notion on discourse can be found in Keller (2012: 52ff).

For example, Foucault's study on the so-called Rivière case (Foucault 1982) marks discourse as a power-related struggle over the legitimate social definitions of events, and thus affirms a close theoretical relation between the aforementioned concept of the sociology of knowledge and the symbolic interactionist tradition (Keller 2012, 53).

SKAD offers a useful analytical and methodological framework in which to analyze discourses of social conflict (see, e.g., Ide 2018). (Islamist) terrorism represents a conflictual societal phenomenon that undergoes permanent processes of social definition through discourse in various arenas, and its common meanings rest upon socio-historical stocks and social relations of common knowledge production (Brunner 2011).[5] This is actually what SKAD, as a research agenda, aims to investigate.

To conduct this investigation about which meanings of threat are discursively negotiated in association with Islamist terrorist events, we draw upon the convenient analytical tools offered by SKAD (Keller 2011, 57ff.). Our focus lies upon the specific knowledge configuration to understand the typology of meaning-construction of our discursive content. In this empirical study, we consider interpretive schemes of threats as a suitable analytical dimension. As regards our focus on threat construction, interpretive schemes show what kinds of meanings of threat have been discursively addressed in association with Islamist terroristic events. We therefore concentrate on some convenient dimensions of meaning-construction, as, for example, subject positions, explanatory causes, responsibilities, solutions and evaluations.

2.4 Data and Analytical Procedure

The data for this study consist of German newspaper and news magazine articles, all relating to the topic of Islamist terrorism. At the very beginnings of the project (from spring 2018 onwards), we conducted a steady review of online and hard-copy news media publications of articles in relation to the topics of interest, namely publications connected to (Islamist) terrorism, incidents of Islamist violence/crime and general media discussions relating to Muslims in Western societies. The aim was to establish a first overview and to get a feeling of the basic characteristics of media discourse about Muslims and Islamist terrorism in the field. Based on this initial field exploration, we acquired several keywords,

---

[5] "Social relations of knowledge are complex socio-historical constellations of production, stabilization, structuration and transformation of symbolic orders that link agency, practices and objects within a variety of social arenas. These constellations imply hierarchies, domination, exclusion, compliance, conflict, resistance and competing ways of accounting for what is 'real': a concern, a problem, the right way to evaluate factual and moral evidence and how to act" (Keller 2018: 18).

such as "Islamist terrorism," "Terrorist," "Islamist violence," which we subsequently used in the search and collection of relevant published articles on a database application for journalistic products.[6]

Before performing this search, we decided to confine our search only to editorials and journalistic commentaries from four well-known German daily and weekly newspapers and news magazines. We restricted the data corpus specifically to editorials and commentaries, because the interest and focus of this study lies in opinions and journalistic positions regarding the topic of Islamist terrorism and its importance in discourse and public opinion (see, e.g., Pfetsch et al. 2004). With the aim of covering a wide range of political orientations, the selected newspapers/magazines were: *Die Welt*, *Der Spiegel*, *Die Zeit* and *Die Tageszeitung* (taz). Finally, we confined our data sample to three relevant timeframes in which major terrorist attacks took place in France and Germany. The first period covers November to December 2015, comprising the terrorist attacks in Paris, where about 130 people were murdered by a concerted action of persons loyal to the terror organization ISIS. The second period in the dataset covers the months of July and August 2016, when a couple of terrorist acts occurred in Germany and France. The most significant attack took place again in France (in the city of Nice), where a single perpetrator conducted an assault on civilians, using a truck as a weapon. More than eighty people lost their lives in this attack. Compared to this, two minor Islamist-related attacks happened in two towns in Bavaria, Germany (Würzburg and Ansbach), in July 2016. Two single asylum seekers conducted both of these attacks in Germany. For the third and last period included in the dataset, we concentrated on the timeframe from December 2016 to January 2017, where again a truck-based terror attack took place. This time the Christmas market of Berlin was the aim of the perpetrator, who murdered more than ten people in his attack. Up to that point, this was the most severe Islamist terror attack carried out in Germany.

Conducting the database-provided search for articles within these three time spans, we managed to find a total of 189 published articles (including only editorials and commentaries). To narrow the selection, we followed Keller's suggestions for performing structured discourse research, which proposes a two-level procedure starting from a macro analysis and moving towards a micro/in-depth analytical procedure (Keller 2013, 98ff.). Thus, the first step of this study's analytical approach was to conduct a macro-analytical examination of the overall structure of the entire corpus and to classify the articles according to the main topics they refer to. In this step, we identified ten thematic classifications to which the articles of the full

---

[6] We used the database of journalistic articles provided by the application LexisNexis.

corpus could be assigned.[7] Furthermore, we identified a number of articles that could be shortlisted for being especially insightful in reconstructing the characteristic features of the discourse. These articles were then potential candidates on which to perform a subsequent fine analysis.

Following the guidelines of SKAD regarding the selection procedure for articles to be fine-analyzed (see Keller 2013, 99f.), we conducted a strategy in accordance with the ideas of theoretical sampling derived from Grounded Theory (Corbin and Strauss 2015; Strauss and Corbin 1996) and thus applied the principle of minimal and maximal contrast. Our sampling thus consisted of a successive procedure of choices of articles to be analyzed. For each main topic, we started by open coding one article that we had marked as relevant. From this starting point, we made further choices of articles to be analyzed, with the specific aim of finding and including articles that substantially differed in statements and meanings from the previous article(s) (max. contrasting). At the same time, we successively also looked out for and included those articles in our analyzing sample that were similar to already analyzed articles and thus particularly suitable to further deepen already encountered meanings and discursive statements (min. contrasting). This applied procedure ensured that we were able to analytically identify and account for the breadth as well the depth of the relevant discourse. By applying this principle, in the end, we came to analyze fifty-nine articles in detail. Table 2.1 provides an overview of the distribution of assigned thematic fields to articles, differentiated for the full sample and the fine-analyzed sample of articles. Furthermore, the analytical tools of Grounded Theory, especially coding, memos and commentaries, as useful techniques for the specific purposes of discourse analysis (Keller 2013, 109), were used as the basis for the practical approach to our fine analysis. We made use of memos and commentaries to successively evolve our textual interpretation and theoretical ideas regarding the reconstruction of the discourse. The coding procedure was designed as open and consensual within the researching team. The entire qualitative analysis was performed using the MAXQDA software (VERBI Software 2017).

2.5 Findings

Our analysis revealed several dominant interpretive schemes. All of them do contain particular patterns of interpretation about the specific characteristic of threats, accounting for different causes and responsibilities, including different subject positions and differentiations, for example

---

[7] These classifications comprise the following thematic fields: security state; war on terror; integration; perceived security; refugee flight; reflections on societal discourses; identity attributions and conflict; prevention; right-wing populism; perpetrator profile.

Table 2.1 *Distribution of topic assignments to articles*[1]

Thematic classifications	Number of topics assigned to articles (full sample)	Number of topics assigned to articles (fine-analyzed sample)
Security state	62	16
War on terror	14	9
Integration	15	8
Perceived security	24	12
Refugee flight	24	9
Reflections on societal discourses	48	18
Identity attributions and conflict	17	9
Prevention	7	3
Right-wing populism	4	3
Perpetrator profile	24	9
In total	*239*	*96*

[1] Note that multiple assignments to each article were possible.

between "Us" and "Them," and proposing a variety of solutions. In the following, we present three of these interpretive schemes in their fundamental structure.[8]

2.5.1 Islam and Muslims as Antagonists to the Western "Us"

In this interpretive scheme, the phenomenon of terrorism and terrorist violence is explained by taking up the perceptions on Muslims and Islam as a culturally different antagonistic subject to the Western "Us." This happens by constituting Muslims and Islam in association with a foreign and opposing cultural value system, which due to its specific essential characteristics, finds itself in fundamental confrontation with the Western world. Thus, in this interpretive scheme, responsibilities and causal explanations regarding terrorism are clearly located towards both Islam as an antagonist value system and Muslims as personified representatives of this antagonism. Following this, the emphasis on a causal connection between being a Muslim and an associated potential threat to security constitutes a central element of this scheme. Sometimes this

[8] Please note that even though we actually were able to derive more interpretive schemes of threat out of the analyzed data than we actually describe in our findings sections, we chose these three schemes as they exhibit relevance regarding to our question about the role of anti-Muslim racism within the discourse.

association is even quite explicitly depicted, as the following exemplary quotation from our data proves:

The practiced wisdom that not all Muslims are terrorists, but most of today's terrorists are Muslims, statistically also means that the risk of terrorism in Europe increases the more Muslims live here. (*Weihnachtsmarkt_Die Zeit* – 29.12.2016: Das Gegenteil von Dankbarkeit; own translation)

In this example, the argumentative attribution and classification of Muslims in reference to terrorism is directly assigned to a potential threat scenario to Western, and more precisely European, societies, and is causally encouraged by the sheer presence of Muslims in those societies.

Another argumentative figure locates the explanatory causes of terrorist violence and Islamist radicalization in characteristic inherent elements of the religion itself, which is interpreted as an expression of a fundamental value-related and cultural "Otherness" to one's own cultural model/self-identity. The following example from a newspaper illustrates this, by pointing towards cultural specifics of Islam that make it prone to radicalization:

Unfortunately, these symptoms cumulate, and they are not harmless. The quite "ordinary" or "traditional" understanding of Islam, as we encounter it hundreds of thousands of times in Europe today, certainly has something to do with the extreme image of Islam that the fundamentalists claim for themselves, such as Salafists, Wahhabis or the so-called Islamic State.

The everyday, traditional Islam contains many seedlings, from which an extreme interpretation can blossom as soon as the appropriate greenhouse is available. (*Würzburg/Nizza_Die Welt* – 25.07.2016: Im Gewächshaus einer Religion; own translation).

Islam, understood here as a culturally and traditionally definable entity, is addressed in this quote by referring to nature-related metaphors. The elements leading to terrorist radicalization seem to be naturally and essentially inscribed in it (the traditional Islam), and all that it needs to unfold terrorism out of it is an appropriate "botanical" promotion. While this is particularly explicit regarding the argumentative figure about the causal responsibility of Islam for terrorism, the other textual representations in this scheme nonetheless all have in common that the foundation of terrorism is to be identified in the cultural and value-related peculiarities and strangeness of Islam.

Alongside the above-described patterns of problem definition in relation to the causes of terrorism, the discussed solutions in this interpretive scheme are also mainly located at the level of a cultural and value-related confrontation with Islam and Muslims. Two related aspects are especially prominent here. First, the Western world has to become (re)aware of and perform a severe (re)orientation towards its own cultural values. In order to be successful in a cultural and value-related confrontation with Islam, an effort to return to one's own values and traditions becomes necessary. Since the Western self-identity seems to be potentially at stake because of the "Otherness" of Islam and Muslims, a revitalization and restoration of one's own cultural identity and values should work as a counterculture to Islam. Thus, according to this interpretive scheme, a possible solution to a potential cultural threat posed by Islam would involve utilizing a strengthened cultural and value-based self-identity. Secondly, based on a (re)orientation to one's own cultural identity, cultural assimilation and adaption to Western standards has to be actively demanded from Muslims. Thereby, a successful ideological and cultural confrontation with the Islamist terrorist threat does not only require a (re)strengthening and self-assurance of one's own identity, but also requires an active enforcement on those subjects who potentially deviate from "Us" on cultural and value-related aspects. The following passage gives an illustration of this:

It is also necessary to take a fresh look at the integration results of Muslims in Europe. Despite many recent efforts, many immigrants and their children ... still do not wish to be integrated into a society whose cultural traditions they do not appreciate, whose way of life they find repugnant, and whose democratic values they oppose as signs of weakness. They need pressure. Stronger than ever. From their ranks the radicals become recruited and become terrorists. (Paris_Die Welt – 17.11.2015: Einsichten im Terrorkampf; own translation)

The positions of three subjects become apparent. These are the subjectification of Muslims and terrorists, as well as the self-subjectification in sharp contrast to the "Others."

As described above, Muslims are constituted with regard to their value-based and cultural "Otherness." Thus, as bearers of the Islam trait, they are represented as subjects who are culturally outside of the Western liberal society and in some cases even positioned as subjects hostile to it. In this respect, not only does an externalization of Muslims from Western societies become apparent, but also a confrontational situation between a liberal Western "Us" versus an antagonistically positioned "Them" is constituted. Consequently, the so constituted subject "Muslim" represents a negative counter-image to the Western "Self."

The subject positions of terrorists within this interpretive scheme often negotiate the terrorist's affinity to Islam and the significance of an individual religiosity. Furthermore, the religiousness of the perpetrators' family members is discussed in quite a similar way. Surprisingly, a large number of text passages do not attest a strong Islamic religiosity on the part of the perpetrators and/or their families. Nevertheless, the ascertained common discursive practice of categorization and judgments about the religiosity of a perpetrator and their family reveals that, even in the case of lacking a strong affinity to the religion, the symbolic attribute of Islam still plays an important role when it comes to the subjectification of terrorists.

By contrast, the representation of an "Us" or "We" finds itself in sharp opposition and contrast to the subject positions of the "Others." At the center of the subject position regarding one's own identity, we find positively value-based characterizing concepts such as freedom, liberality, openness/tolerance, civilization and humanity. These characteristics are usually attributed to self-subjectivity and lead to a demarcation and differentiation from non-belonging subjects such as Islam and/or Muslims. While the "Own" is marked and evaluated in a particularly positive way, the "Other" only becomes apparent as an opposite negative counter-example on the dimensions of freedom, tolerance, civilization and so forth. Furthermore, under the conditions of experienced terrorism, the liberal "Us" appears to be under fundamental attack by its antagonist. This becomes apparent in numerous passages, where the concrete terrorist act and/or terrorism as a whole, is interpreted as an attack on one's own cultural way of life and identity. Thus, the terrorist threat is seen as a challenge on a cultural-identity dimension. Consequently, in order to counter the phenomenon successfully, the appropriate responses to this threat have to be located on the dimensions of culture and identity.

2.5.2 The Liberal and Open Society at Stake

In this interpretive scheme, threat is related to a particular domestic development, which highlights risks regarding the preservation of the current "open society" in countries who experience Islamist terror attacks. Two lines of argumentation are dominant here: On the one hand, there is a threat of a severe change of the society towards an authoritarian (security) state, leading to associated restrictions to fundamental freedoms of the people. On the other hand, threats to developments in the aftermath of a terrorist event are referred to as the danger of strengthening right-wing political parties and movements in the society, which potentially give rise to anti-Muslim racism and contribute to a severe division within societies.

The threat towards open society posed by an authoritarian state primarily arises from reactions and actions by (authoritarian) political actors and their political objectives. Strategically they exploit the spread of fear in the society induced by terroristic events, in order to implement particular measures, which are legitimized as necessary to preserve national security. The central threat here is associated with a possible establishment of an authoritarian state, in which the people's rights are severely restricted for security reasons. This is perceived as fundamentally antagonistic towards a liberal, open society, as it is (still) present today and represents a serious threat towards it:

But when even the French in Paris, the metropolis of freedom, when the Belgians in the EU metropolis of Brussels, need to switch to the most serious emergency mode; when the majority of European leaders openly talk about "war," then it looks grim for the liberal, open and laissez-faire society we have all been accustomed to. (*Paris_Die Welt* – 24.11.2015: Demokratie und Notstand; own translation)

While the existence of a liberal constituted and open society is seen here as a given fact, its preservation is at stake by the political declarations of a state of emergency (seen here as necessary) within European countries.

The second line of argumentation highlights the danger of an increasing differentiation between "Us" and the Muslim "Other" and the potential risk of the social exclusion of Muslims, which constitutes a threat for an open and tolerant society. In particular, the negative construction of Muslims in general and/or specifically Muslim refugees as a threat to inner security, which is often highlighted by right-wing populist actors, is problematized and is regarded as a danger in terms of social cohesion. The issue of rising anti-Muslim racism in Western societies is critically addressed here as being a problematic social construction, especially when it comes in the form of homogenization and externalization. In some cases, there is also an explicit criticism about establishing a direct (causal) association between Islam and Islamism, as, for example, in this fragment: "The short circuits are just as irresponsible in the general accusations when, for example, radical Islamism and Islam are frivolously lumped together" (*Paris_Taz* – 30.11.2015: Was machte sie zu Massenmördern; own translation). In this scheme, the problematic consequences of homogenization of Muslims, such as discrimination, restrictions in fundamental human rights and critical divisions within society, are pointed out. Furthermore, we can find explicit warnings about a general suspicion of Muslims, like, for example, this one: "However, much more of importance is, that Europe does not draw the consequence of a general fear against Muslims out of the attacks, that they do not get excluded and stigmatized" (*Paris_Taz* – 23.11.2015: Die Normalität verteidigen; own translation).

In terms of relevant subject positions, the interpretation of a liberal "Us" that is situated in contrast to an authoritarian/right-wing populist "Them" is substantial here. This, for example, becomes clear when considering the following quote: "The sorrow that filled the continent after the mass murders is now followed by an armed defensive regime, of which nobody knows how long it will last – and can last without permanently destroying our free way of life" (*Paris_Die Welt* – 24.11.2015: Demokratie und Notstand; own translation). Similar to the interpretive scheme of antagonist Muslims and Islam, the self-positioning here is represented by values like freedom, plurality, tolerance, and the liberal openness of society. While this self-identity is at stake because of the cultural "Otherness" and antagonism of Muslims in the aforementioned scheme, exactly this subject position of the "We" is endangered here by the political elite and right-wing political powers from within. They not only threaten the liberal foundations of the society, but also are responsible for splitting society apart. Central social divisions constituted by right-wing populists are located between the majority of the society and the Muslims (or refugees) on the one hand, and between migration advocates and opponents on the other. The following quote defines the "scaremongers" as the real threat to European societies:

This is precisely where the challenge will lie in the future, for France and for other societies that see themselves as democratic. The threat is not coming from the outside, it is not about barbaric hordes, camping in front of the gates of Europe. The real struggle will take place elsewhere, within, whether the scaremongers will triumph or whether Europe will be ready to continue defending that diversity that makes it strong and vulnerable at the same time. (*Paris_Taz* – 19.11.2015: Krieg gegen Lebensformen; own translation)

In addition to the subject position of right-wing populists, there are also some subject positions of politicians and media actors located as antagonists to open society. Politicians are accused of exploiting terrorist events in order to successfully implement their own political agenda:

Those who are attacked often times do not react rationally. That is also understandable. But it is disgusting when, immediately after a terrible act, politicians take their table templates out of the drawer in order to benefit from an act of violence. (*Weihnachtsmarkt_Taz* – 21.12.2016: Mit Bedrohungen müssen wir leben; own translation).

Lastly, in this scheme, the main cause for terrorist radicalization can be traced back to ongoing discrimination and marginalization of Muslims in Western societies, both in social and economic ways. Consequently, a possible solution to prevent this radicalization and terrorism lies upon a restructured relationship between the West and Muslims, by providing support to Muslims, both domestically and abroad.

2.5.3 The Erosion of Order and Security

In this interpretive scheme, threat is located towards a supposed erosion of public security and state order. In particular, this interpretive scheme of threat is discursively attributed to the incidents with regard to the migration of refugees in 2015 and its allegedly causal connection with Islamist terroristic events throughout Europe in the following years.

In this respect, the causes of experienced terrorism are localized in certain mistakes in security policy as well as in governmental malfunctions and failures with reference to a convenient political handling of the challenges posed by the refugee situation and the potential risks of Islamist terrorism. These shortcomings are seen as a sign and expression of an inherent existing weakness on the part of the responsible government actors/system and the security apparatus as a whole. Especially the political approach and decisions taken concerning the refugee-question of 2015 play a crucial role within this scheme. A consistent critical attitude towards the refugee situation and the related political and official decisions and actions becomes evident here. The immigration of refugees is mainly addressed in terms of a potential terrorist risk to public safety. Referring to a temporarily uncontrolled and unrestricted influx of refugees for which politicians and security authorities are responsible, the causes of the terrorist threat to Europe and Germany are traced back to a planned infiltration of terrorists by ISIS, taking strategic advantage of this situation:

There is a whole department existing at ISIS which is responsible for planning attacks outside the Middle East. Absurdly it's called "external security." They probably also gave rise to the idea of mixing potential assassins into a stream of refugees. Investigators know of six to seven of those suspected cases. (*Würzburg/Nizza_Die Zeit* – 21.07.2016: Als der Wolf verrückt wurde; own translation)

With reference to the political handling of the refugee situation and the terrorist violence associated with it, the inadequacies of the immigration and asylum policy are identified as the central and initial causes of the terrorist threat. The specific points of criticism are attributed to the shortcomings of respective laws and restricted regulatory capabilities. Criticism is also directed towards responsible political actors in terms of their deficient decisions and incapacities, and partly also in their supposed unwillingness to counter the problem by means of implementing fortified security state measures:

What if: Terrorists trained in Syria mingle with innocent migrants. They are known as potentially dangerous, but uncontrolledly travel through Europe. … You can delete this subjunctive, as this was exactly how the scenario happened. On the 13th of November 2015, the assassins of Paris cold-bloodedly took benefit out of Europe's defenselessness, which the German government deliberately accepted. (*Weihnachtsmarkt_Die Welt* – 10.01.2017: Sicherheit ist keine Fußnote; own translation)

This gives an example of this criticism, highlighting the causal connection of refugees, the inability and failure of political actors and state representatives to face the situation in terms of enforcing regulatory power towards asylum seekers, and the consequential terrorist threat.

Besides direct references to the shortcomings regarding the refugee and security policy, responsibilities for terrorist threats are more generally located in a fundamental failure of the security state authorities with respect to the surveillance of terrorist subjects and thus their failing to ensure security for the public. Regarding this, an overstraining and overload of the security authorities serves as a further possible explanation for the inability to prevent terrorist acts of violence. This becomes apparent, for example, in the inadequate regulation and monitoring of the (internet) communication of active terrorist subjects and organizations or in the deficiencies of cross-national cooperation between different security authorities in European countries.

In order to be able to successfully counter the threat of potential terrorists through a robust state response, the interpretive scheme here argues for an expansion of regulatory competences and a more consistent enforcement of state power options. Thus, while the explanatory cause of the terrorist threat is attributed to a supposed weakness of the state and its representatives, the proposed convenient solution lies in a resurgence of state power and regulatory force. Three main argumentative figures can be identified in the proposed solutions.

Firstly, as already mentioned, refugees are causally associated with the terrorist threat to Western societies, so the problem-solving approaches proposed within this scheme deal to a large extent with the question of a harder and more assertive handling of refugees. Thus, the solutions include more robust asylum policy measures that need either to be tightened up or newly introduced. The predominant argumentative figure lies on preserving security for the host societies from potentially terrorist and violent refugees. These measures include reintroducing border control and consistent identity verification, and deportation for those whose identity cannot be verified. Refugees whose identities are not clarified seem to pose a central threat to Western European societies. The example below reflects the dominant idea to enforce robust regulatory mechanisms towards asylum seekers:

To close this flank, Europe must do two things, among others: it must reliably know who is staying within its borders. And it must be able to expel those who are not allowed to live within its borders. This requires border controls where the identity of people is clarified. No longer is it acceptable for a person to be without a passport, without an identity – and thus to be able to easily evade the monopoly on legitimate use of force. (*Weihnachtsmarkt_Die Welt* – 23.12.2016: Zum Narren gehalten; own translation)

Secondly, at the center of the measures regarding the expansion of the competencies and practices of the security state is the recommendation for intensified surveillance of potential terrorist perpetrators. The following excerpt illustrates the necessity for intensified surveillance on those subjects being suspects of terrorism:

In the case of the ISIS perpetrators, a pattern becomes noticeable, that they have been mentally disoriented for a long time, known to the police, and being Muslims. The authorities know of the criminal record and the religion, they must also know about the lability. It must be possible to monitor such people. This is a sensitive topic, affecting medical confidentiality, the prohibition of ethnic-religious dragnet controls and much more. However, we cannot go on as before, that is not possible. (*Würzburg/Nizza_Die Welt* – 26.07.2016: Mitten in Deutschland; own translation)

This example shows that the terrorist threat is mainly attributed to a certain group of people with certain characteristics, namely being a Muslim, showing psychological peculiarities and being on the police record. If all three criteria apply to an individual, then the terrorist threat emanating from that person appears to be maximized, and accordingly, the authorities have to exhaust all possibilities of surveillance regarding this group of people. Principles of a liberal state order, such as medical confidentiality or even the prohibition of racist police practices, are considered here rather as obstructive and counter-productive with regard to an effective security state confrontation with Islamist terrorism. It seems to become necessary to restrict freedoms, especially for the group of people who are constructed to be potentially threatening. Thus, the last sentence, "However, we cannot go on as before, that is not possible," refers to the urgency of a change in the direction of expanding security state competences, even at the expense of possible restrictions on freedom.

Lastly, the expansion of security state competencies is also legitimized by referring to the symbolic dimension for the state's own population. Under the given conditions of general uncertainty and loss of confidence amongst the population, it is only by exhibiting strong and robust security behavior that the state and politicians can succeed in regaining confidence and delivering a sense of security:

It is about people's belief that our open, freedom-loving and tolerant society can also defend itself, that it not only wants to establish rules, but also wants to enforce them, that in general the principle applies that the more diverse a community is, the more unequivocal the rules are. (*Weihnachtsmarkt_Die Zeit* – 29.12.2016: Es ist eine nationale Aufgabe)

Central to this is to symbolically convey to its own population the state's determination and preparedness to successfully fight terrorism. In addition to this, in this scheme the representations often refer to a free, open and liberal society, which can only be maintained if the state and responsible politicians are determined to demonstratively and actually implement a fortified state and thus protect their citizens from the potential security threat which terrorism poses.

In the following, we will briefly describe the characteristics of the central subject positions we were able to identify throughout our analysis. The subject position of "Us" serves the narrative of weakness, failure and incompetency. This negative frame is especially directed towards security authorities, politicians and the current security and asylum policy. Under the circumstances of state-level disorder and insecurity, within this interpretive scheme, society is addressed in terms of experiencing a severe erosion in trust regarding the functioning of the state in ensuring the safety of its citizens. Thus, (re)establishing the security state's defensiveness and assertiveness not only plays a role in actively combating the threats stemming from terrorists and potential violent refugees, but also is important as an inward-directed symbol of strength. Its aim is to regain self-confidence, trust and certainty about the competent protecting and guarding role of the state, by robustly taking up the challenges of terrorism and migration. Consequently, the following textual example supporting the deployment of military units inside the country (which is exceptional in Germany) describes the positive symbolic outcome for the society as follows:

However, when visibly and effectively armed security forces demonstratively protect the citizens and preserve their right to integrity and freedom of movement in public space, this is not a symbol of militarization nor the renunciation of the peaceful basic constitution of an open society. On the contrary, it restores civil society's self-confidence and dignity, which have been violated in their innermost core by the bloody acts of the terrorist murderers. It makes clear that free societies are not defenseless and that their citizens are not helplessly at the mercy of the arbitrary murderous lust of unleashed fanatics – thus expressing the pathos of the will for freedom. (*Würzburg/Nizza_Die Welt* – 09.08.2016: Freiheit muss bewaffnet sein; own translation)

This reveals the symbolic relevance of enforcing power and strength by state authorities. Its aim is primarily oriented inwards and intends to restore its own citizens' faith and trust in the fortified and defensible state.

In stark contrast to this, the subject positions of those social actors who are advocates of maintaining an open and liberal society and do not welcome an expansion of security state competences and measures are characterized as naïve and ideologically driven subjects, failing to adequately be positioned against the threat and challenges of terrorism. Taken together, the subject positions of some politicians, advocates of refugee migration and opponents of an extensive expansion of the security state embody the weakness and disorder of the state and its institutions.

Lastly, in this interpretive scheme the subject positions of refugees almost consistently are associated with a potential terrorist threat delivered by them through their unregistered and uncontrolled immigration.

2.6   Conclusion

As one of the founding fathers of postcolonial theory, Edward Said traced how the construction of a negatively connoted "Oriental" serves as an opportunity to solidify a positive and superior Western in-group identity (Said 2003). A hegemonic discursive practice of cultural racism, whereby an essentialist dichotomy is built up between a positively characterized in-group and a stereotypically contrasted cultural "Other" (Hall 1992), can be identified in some of the interpretive schemes that we were able to find in the examined discourse about Islamist terrorism. In particular, the interpretive scheme of the culturally *antagonist Islam and Muslims* most obviously demonstrates this practice of constructing the "Other" in contrast (and confrontation) to "Us." The homogenized "Otherness" of Muslims and Islam in a cultural and value-based dimension accordingly poses a threat to current European societies in several aspects. Firstly, as a direct threat to security, as Islam's and Muslims' cultural peculiarities and "Otherness" are primarily made responsible for Islamist radicalization and terrorism. In addition, the threat constituted in this scheme also relates to the dimension of self-identity. The presence of a cultural "Other" causes the certitude of one's own identity to be challenged. Therefore, the mental and collective return to one's own cultural traditions and values seems to be a remedy in the confrontation with the terrorist threats mediated through Islam and Muslims. The (re)consolidation of a self-identity seems to be the main goal and desired cure for the terrorist threat. Thus, while the "Self" is mainly seen in terms of freedom, liberty and as highly civilized, the supposed opponent does not match these attributes and cultural standards at all, but indeed represents the contrary, a negative reflection of one's own. This confrontational duality contributes to manifesting a self-identity that exactly requires this differentiation from the "Other" in order to establish a positive and superior imagination of the "Self" (Hall 1992).

With regard to the remaining two interpretive schemes described in the findings section, the process of cultural "Othering" towards Muslims does not take place that blatantly. Nevertheless, similar to the aforementioned scheme, the emphasis on the subject position of the "Self" is central in both schemes. The self-identities represent a notion of the "Self" that also is in close association with value-laden concepts such as freedom, liberty, tolerance and democracy. Whereas this self-identity concept is at stake because of the cultural *antagonism of Muslims and Islam* in the first interpretive scheme, different allocations of the causal sources on supposed threats towards one's own identity are addressed in the other schemes. Within the scheme *liberal and open society at stake*, a strong and similar self-concept is effective, which considers itself as under attack by certain political powers and movements who oppose the liberal constitution of the state and the society. Right-wing political forces especially, who benefit from the terrorist events by spreading uncertainty and aim to divide society along racial, ethnic or religious categories, are made responsible for threats towards the liberal "Us." Thus, in this scheme, the anti-Muslim racist agenda of those political parties and movements is identified as particularly harmful regarding social cohesiveness and the preservation of a self-identity associated with the concepts of tolerance, openness and liberality. Furthermore, these societal divisions in the form of stigmatization and discrimination towards Muslims are made responsible for their Islamist radicalization and devotion to terrorism. Nevertheless, while anti-Muslim racism is seen critically as a temporary and undesirable phenomenon, its structural and historical foundations are not the focus of this interpretive scheme. Lastly, in the interpretive scheme that highlights an *erosion of order and security* in the society and the state, self-identity is also seen as being at stake. In contrast to the aforementioned schemes, here the state's and politicians' incapacity, as well as the failure to assure people's safety in the face of an imminent danger of terrorism, primarily delivered through the unregulated influx of refugees, are made responsible for making people progressively lose their confidence and affinity towards the democratic political system and shared values. Thus, to be able to conserve a self-identity associated with democratic and liberal values, this interpretive scheme pleads for an administrative and political crackdown, either factually or just symbolically. While the scheme *Islam and Muslims as antagonists* attributes the origin of terrorist threat to Islam and Muslims in general, in the interpretive scheme *erosion of order and security*, the origins of terroristic threat are founded in the group of refugee migrants. Refugees are consistently represented here in association with their harmful role in committing crimes and terrorist acts. Given that in this context, almost all addressed refugees originate from Muslim countries, even without explicitly referring to it, it becomes clear that threatening refugees are implicitly associated as Muslims (or at least come from Muslim countries). Consequently, within this interpretive scheme some patterns of anti-Muslim racism also indirectly become served.

The aim of this study was to investigate what different meanings of threat are prominent within the discourse of Islamist terrorism. Therefore, we conducted a discourse analysis based on the principles of the SKAD and looked at different interpretive schemes within the discourse. This study describes three different interpretations of terrorist threat. All of them offer different and unique meanings of threats associated with Islamist terrorism, differing in attributed causes, possible solutions and subject positions. Nonetheless, what they all have in common is a sense of threatened self-identity. As our findings show, anti-Muslim stereotypes and attributions play an important role, either by directly or indirectly reproducing them within the discourse, or by addressing them as a negative and harmful societal outcome of Islamist terrorism. In the light of the findings in this study, the question arises about what media coverage of Islamist terrorism should look like in order not to reproduce historically inscribed imaginings of a conflictual situation, represented by culturally (pre)defined opponents. With regard to occurrences of racist and anti-Muslim terrorist attacks in the Western world, an appropriate answer to this question remains one of the most pressing tasks the media and society have to address in these current times, and for the future.

References

Adoni, Hanna, and Mane, Sherrill. 1984. "Media and the Social Construction of Reality: Toward an Integration of Theory and Research." *Communication Research* 11(3): 323–340. DOI: 10.1177/009365084011003001.

Ahmed, Saifuddin, and Matthes, Jörg. 2017. "Media representation of Muslims and Islam from 2000 to 2015: A Meta-Analysis." *International Communication Gazette* 79(3): 219–244.

Allen, Christopher. 2010. *Islamophobia*. Farnham: Ashgate.

Ates, Seref. 2006. "Das Islambild in den Medien nach dem 11. September 2001." In *Massenmedien, Migration und Integration. Herausforderungen für Journalismus und politische Bildung*, ed. by Christoph Butterwegge and Gudrun Hentges, 153–172. Wiesbaden: VS Verlag für Sozialwissenschaften.

Attia, Iman. 1994. "Antiislamischer Rassismus: Stereotypen – Erfahrungen – Machverhältnisse." In *Aus der Werkstatt: Anti-rassistische Praxen. Konzepte, Erfahrungen, Forschung*, ed. by Siegfried Jäger, 210–228. Duisburg: DISS.

Attia, Iman. 2009. *Die "westliche Kultur" und ihr Anderes*. Bielefeld: Transcript.

Attia, Iman, Häusler, Alexander, and Shooman, Yasemin. 2014. *Antimuslimischer Rassismus am rechten Rand*. Münster: Unrast-Verlag.

Attia, Iman, Köbsell, Swantje, and Prasad, Nivedita (eds.). 2015. *Dominanzkultur Reloaded. Neue Texte zu gesellschaftlichen Machtverhältnissen und ihren Wechselwirkungen*. Bielefeld: Transcript (Sozialtheorie).

Bayrakli, Enes, and Hafez, Farid (eds.). 2019. *European Islamophobia Report 2018*. Available online at www.islamophobiaeurope.com/wp-content/uploads/2019/09/EIR_2018.pdf.

Benz, Wolfgang. 2012. "Vorurteile gegen Muslime – Feindbild Islam." In *Vorurteile: Ursprünge, Formen, Bedeutung*, ed. by Anton Pelinka, 205–220. Berlin: de Gruyter.

Benz, Wolfgang. 2017. "Antiislamische Diskriminierung." In *Handbuch Diskriminierung*, ed. by Albert Scherr, El-Mafaalani, Aladin, and Gökçen Yüksel, 511–527. Wiesbaden: Springer Fachmedien Wiesbaden.

Berger, Peter L., and Luckmann, Thomas. 1967. *The Social Construction of Reality. A Treatise in the Sociology of Knowledge*. New York: Anchor Books.

Bock, Andreas M. 2017. "Islamistischer Terrorismus. Die konstruierte Bedrohung." *Zeitschrift für Außen- und Sicherheitspolitik* 10(2): 245–265.

Brunner, Claudia. 2011. *Wissensobjekt Selbstmordattentat. Epistemische Gewalt und okzidentalistische Selbstvergewisserung in der Terrorismusforschung*. Wiesbaden: VS Verlag für Sozialwissenschaften.

Chermak, Steven M., and Gruenewald, Jeffrey. 2006. "The Media's Coverage of Domestic Terrorism." *Justice Quarterly* 23(4): 428–461. DOI: 10.1080/07418820600985305.

Cinnirella, Marco. 2012. "Think 'Terrorist', Think 'Muslim'? Social-Psychological Mechanisms Explaining Anti-Islamic Prejudice." In *Islamophobia in the West. Measuring and Explaining Individual Attitudes*, ed. by Marc Helbling, 179–189. London: Routledge.

Corbin, Juliet M., and Strauss, Anselm. 2015. *Basics of Qualitative Research: Techniques and Procedures for Developing Grounded Theory*, 4th ed. Los Angeles, CA: Sage.

El-Menouar, Yasemin. 2019. "Der Islam im Diskurs der Massenmedien in Deutschland." In *Antimuslimischer Rassismus und Islamfeindlichkeit*, ed. by Bülent Uçar and Wassilis Kassis, 169–184. Göttingen: Vandenhoeck & Ruprecht.
Fekete, Liz. 2009. *A Suitable Enemy. Racism, Migration and Islamophobia in Europe*. London: Pluto.
Foucault, Michel (ed.). 1982. *I, Pierre Rivière, Having Slaughtered My Mother, My Sister, and My Brother. a Case of Parricide in the 19th Century*. Reprint New York 1975. Lincoln, NE : University of Nebraska Press.
Galtung, Johan, and Ruge, Mari Holmboe. 1965. "The Structure of Foreign News." *Journal of Peace Research* 2(1): 64–91.
Hafez, Farid. 2012. "Islamophobie und die deutschen Bundestagsparteien: Eine Analyse vom 27. Oktober 2009 bis 9. Juni 2011." In *Verhärtete Fronten: Der schwere Weg zu einer vernünftigen Islamkritik*, ed. by Thorsten Gerald Schneiders, 57–67. Wiesbaden: VS Verlag für Sozialwissenschaften.
Hafez, Farid. 2019. "Antimuslimischer Rassismus und Islamophobie: Worüber sprechen wir?" In *Antimuslimischer Rassismus und Islamfeindlichkeit*, ed. by Bülent Uçar, and Wassilis Kassis, 57–76. Göttingen: Vandenhoeck & Ruprecht.
Hafez, Kai, and Schmidt, Sabrina. 2015. *Die Wahrnehmung des Islams in Deutschland*. Gütersloh: Bertelsmann Stiftung.
Hall, Stuart. 1992. "The West and the Rest: Discourse and Power." In *Formations of Modernity*, ed. by Stuart Hall and Bram Gieben, 275–320. Cambridge: Polity Press.
Helbling, Marc (ed.). 2012. *Islamophobia in the West. Measuring and Explaining Individual Attitudes*. London: Routledge.
Ide, Tobias. 2018. "Using SKAD to Investigate Cooperation and Conflict over Water Resources." In *The Sociology of Knowledge Approach to Discourse. Investigating the Politics of Knowledge and Meaning-Making*, ed. by Reiner Keller, Anna-Katharina Hornidge, and Wolf J. Schünemann, 237–253. Abingdon: Routledge.
Jaspal, Rusi, and Cinnirella, Marco. 2010. "Media Representations of British Muslims and Hybridised Threats to Identity." *Contemporary Islam* 4(3): 289–310. DOI: 10.1007/s11562-010-0126-7.
Jirschitzka, Jens, Haußecker, Nicole, and Frindte, Wolfgang. 2010. "IV Mediale Konstruktion II: Die Konstruktion des Terrorismus im deutschen Fernsehen – Ergebnisdarstellung und Interpretation." In *Inszenierter Terrorismus*, ed. by Wolfgang Frindte and Nicole Haußecker, 81–119. Wiesbaden: VS Verlag für Sozialwissenschaften.
Kearns, Erin, Betus, Allison, and Lemieux, Anthony. 2019. "Why Do Some Terrorist Attacks Receive More Media Attention Than Others?" *Justice Quarterly* 36(6): 985–1022.
Keller, Reiner. 2011. "The Sociology of Knowledge Approach to Discourse (SKAD)." *Human Studies* 34(1): 43–65.
Keller, Reiner. 2012. "Entering Discourses: A New Agenda for Qualitative Research and Sociology of Knowledge." *Qualitative Sociology Review* 8(2): 46–75.
Keller, Reiner. 2013. *Doing Discourse Research. An Introduction for Social Scientists*. Los Angeles, CA: Sage.
Keller, Reiner. 2018. "The Sociology of Knowledge Approach to Discourse. An Introduction." In *The Sociology of Knowledge Approach to Discourse: Investigating*

the Politics of Knowledge and Meaning-Making, ed. by Reiner Keller, Anna-Katharina Hornidge, and Wolf J. Schünemann, 16–47. Abingdon: Routledge.

Pfetsch, Barbara, Eilders, Christiane, Neidhardt, Friedhelm, and Grübl, Stephanie. 2004. "Das 'Kommentariat': Rolle und Status einer Öffentlichkeitselite." In *Die Stimme der Medien. Pressekommentare und politische Öffentlichkeit in der Bundesrepublik*, ed. by Christiane Eilders, Friedhelm Neidhardt, and Barbara Pfetsch, 39–73. Wiesbaden: VS Verlag für Sozialwissenschaften.

Poole, Elizabeth. 2002. *Reporting Islam. Media Representations of British Muslims*. London: Tauris.

Rommelspacher, Birgit. 1995. *Dominanzkultur: Texte zu Fremdheit und Macht*. Berlin: Orlanda.

Said, Edward W. 1981. *Covering Islam. How the Media and the Experts Determine How We See the Rest of the World*, 1st ed. New York: Pantheon Books.

Said, Edward W. 1985. "Orientalism Reconsidered." *Cultural Critique* 1: 89–107. DOI: 10.2307/1354282.

Said, Edward W. 2003. *Orientalism*. Reprinted with a new Preface. London: Penguin.

Schmid, Alex P. 2011. "The definition of terrorism." In *The Routledge Handbook of Terrorism Research*, ed. by Alex P. Schmid, 39–98. London: Routledge.

Shooman, Yasemin. 2014. "...weil ihre Kultur so ist". *Narrative des antimuslimischen Rassismus*. Bielefeld: Transcript.

Soyer, François. 2013. "Faith, Culture and Fear. Comparing Islamophobia in Early Modern Spain and Twenty-First-Century Europe." *Ethnic and Racial Studies* 36 (3): 399–416. DOI: 10.1080/01419870.2013.734383.

Strauss, Anselm, and Corbin, Juliet. 1996. *Grounded Theory: Grundlagen qualitativer Sozialforschung*. Weinheim: Beltz.

Trautmann, Sebastian. 2006. "'Terrorismus und Islamismus' als Medienthema. Neue Bedeutungslinien im öffentlichen Diskurs zur Politik der Inneren Sicherheit." In *Massenmedien, Migration und Integration. Herausforderungen für Journalismus und politische Bildung*, ed. by Christoph Butterwegge, and Gudrun Hentges, 141–151. Wiesbaden: VS Verlag für Sozialwissenschaften.

Tuman, Joseph S. 2010. *Communicating Terror. The Rhetorical Dimensions of Terrorism*, 2nd ed. Thousand Oaks, CA: Sage.

VERBI Software. 2019. *MAXQDA 2020 [computer software]*. Berlin, Germany: VERBI Software. Available from maxqda.com.

3 "Herdsmen Are Terrorists"
Analyzing News Headlines on the Herder–Farmer Conflict in the Nigerian Press

Innocent Chiluwa, Isioma M. Chiluwa, and Angie O. Igbinoba

3.1 Introduction

The mass media play a crucial role in times of violent or non-violent conflict, and they are unfortunately capable of turning a non-violent conflict into a violent one through discursive means. The media can achieve this through mobilizing mass support in favor of war or violence, and by shaping the conflict perceptions of large and diverse groups – interpreting conflict from a particular subjective perspective. Also, through consistent representation of certain group actors in a particular way, and through polarization strategies, the media can actually recommend violence as a means of resolving conflicts. Hence, some studies have questioned whether media are indeed an agent of conflict or conflict resolution (Rahman and Eijaz 2014). Maeseele (2015) argues that through discursive strategies and processes, media discourses do facilitate as well as impede democratic debate and citizenship. To facilitate democratic debate, the media can repeatedly challenge existing power relations "in terms of revealing competing sets of assumptions, values and interests underlying opposing responses to scientific uncertainty" (278). Citing Galtung (2000; Galtung and Fisher 2013), Nijenhuis (2014) further argues that the media in the practice of war journalism can indeed worsen a conflict by "focusing on violence, highlighting the differences between groups, and presenting conflict as a zero-sum game, while ignoring the broad range of causes and outcomes of conflict" (65).

However, Betz (2017) has argued that the media can also be an instrument of peace in conflict-prone areas by providing early warning of potential conflicts and possibly creating "pressure" to address the conflict, by bringing together different groups to discuss issues, by helping to improve governance, by providing the motivation for peace, and by increasing the knowledge of complex issues, among others (12–13).

This chapter examines the roles of the Nigerian press in the construction and representation of the perennial conflicts between farmers and herdsmen mostly in the northern region and Middle Belt of Nigeria, even though violent conflicts have now spread to the southern part of the country. The study examines some systematic constructions of actors and identities, as well as the conflict itself, in news headlines of selected local Nigerian newspapers and analyzes their implications and consequences. The study argues that news headlines are discursive and that systematic evaluative structures of headlines and their overlines are reflective of the mediatized influence of the press on society.

The research questions this study has attempted to answer are:

1. How are the main actors in the herdsmen–farmers conflicts represented in the Nigerian press news headlines?
2. What ideological positions are discernible in the actions attributed to actors in the headlines?
3. What are the consequences and implications of these particular evaluations for peace in Nigeria?

3.2   Herders and Farmers Conflict in Nigeria

Nigeria has a history of war and violence that has existed along ethnic, religious and political lines since independence from colonial rule in 1960. However, since 1999, violence related to the Fulani herdsmen and farmers has reached alarming levels, reportedly leading to the killings of thousands and displacing tens of thousands more. Besides the direct humanitarian crisis, the conflict has led to the proliferation of ethnic and vigilante militias and worsened intercommunal tension, and has also hindered the growth of the Nigerian agricultural sector (Baca 2015).

The Fulani group is part of a *Fula* ethnic group that span across West and Central Africa. They occupy an important position in Nigerian history as the fourth largest ethnic group in Nigeria. The Fula indigenes are predominantly nomads, earning them the name "Fulani herdsmen" (Onyema, Gideon and Ekwugha 2018). They occupy the northern part of the country. The herdsmen are known for moving their cattle across lands in search for green pastures, and the Middle Belt region, especially Benue state, provide the largest concentration of herders in Nigeria. The Fulani are the main producers of meat and milk in Nigeria and contribute up to 3.2 percent of Nigeria's GDP (Idowu and Okunola 2017).

Lands were allotted for ranching purposes during the pre-colonial era – a practice traced to the traditional grazing ground (or *Hurmi*) situated around northern Nigeria. These lands were restricted from other uses like crop production and habitation. Since there were no legal laws surrounding the restriction of such land use, increased population resulted in encroachment by farmers. Interestingly, the herdsmen surrounded by sedentary farmers in the northern part of Nigeria initially shared a harmonious relationship during this era. As farmers relied on the waste of the cattle to nourish their crops, the herdsmen enjoyed grazing rights and crop produce in exchange (Abdullahi, Daneyel and Aliyara 2015). However, as demand for land for other uses increased, tensions began to emerge between the farmers and the herdsmen. In order to reduce these tensions, the Nigerian government established a grazing reserve in northern Nigeria in the 1960s (Chukwuemeka, Aloysius and Eneh 2018). The failure of the project and continual open grazing system continued with cases of violence between the farmers and the pastoralists. According to Amnesty International (2018), cases of violence have occurred in at least twenty states across the Nigerian federation. Between 2016 and 2018, Amnesty International recorded 312 cases of attacks and reprisal attacks in twenty-two states in Nigeria, estimating loss of over 3,000 lives and displacement of over 180,000 people – suggesting that the Fulani herdsmen are the fourth deadliest terrorist group in the world (Amnesty International 2018, *Global Terrorism Index* cited in Buchanan 2015).

The farmer–herders crisis in Nigeria is a product of certain complex systems that are driven by competing interests (Onyema et al. 2018). Some observers argue that it is an extension of ethno-religious struggles that predate the colonial period, citing the Nigerian civil war as a factor. Other theories blame climate change that has resulted in environmental degradation across the Sahel region, increased cases of cattle rustling, expansion due to over-population and decline in traditional authority (Baca 2015). Some have attributed the conflicts to retaliatory attacks to ceaseless cases of cattle rustling. As livestock trade became very profitable in West African urban centers, criminals who rustle cattle for profit were attracted to the trade. Also, youth unemployment forced many youths into cattle rustling. In addition, more sophisticated groups of rustlers in the northwest began to take advantage of the Boko Haram violence and the general insecurity in the north to engage in widespread cattle robbery and violence. These criminal activities created constant fear and caused people to run from their homes, sometimes abandoning their cattle for the rustlers (Bagu and Smith 2017). In an interview with *The Punch* newspaper, the chairman of the Miyetti Allah cattle breeders association, Plateau state chapter, argued that the government had done nothing to protect herdsmen from rustlers and the group had no security backup in rural areas; hence, their resort to the use of arms was a self-defense strategy (Atoyebi et al. 2016).

According to Nnoko-Mewanu (2018), corporate mining activities and competitive overuse of forests, pastoral rangelands and water resources has exacerbated climate change. "Growing aridity in the Sahel and northern regions, advancing desertification, and heightened risk of extreme weather events have resulted in decreased availability of grazing land ... the Sahel is creeping southward by approximately 1,400 square miles a year, swallowing whole villages and reducing the land available for grazing" (2). The weak government regulation of pastoralism, poor land management, and inadequate policies on climate change adaptation in African countries have also worsened land-related tensions.

3.3　News Headlines

Headlines encapsulate the entire news on a particular subject matter and are generally written with the marketization of the newspaper in mind. Often written with particular stylistic and graphological features and preferences, headlines are believed to have emotive effects on the reader. They are said to be one of the "main visual entry points" to the news content and can be memorable to the reader, providing a "high-level overview" of the story without demanding much of the reader's time or attention (Piotrkowicz 2017, 20). Significantly, headlines are characteristically sensational, where words and expressions are often used with highly evaluative patterns and structures. Graphically, headlines often combine capital and small lettering, where the use of capitals is for emphasis. Exclamation marks are also often used unconventionally, sometimes combining both the double and the single marks (Conboy 2007).

The syntactic structures of headlines are unique. Sometimes, headlines are written as a one-line expression or may comprise two parts, the second part often performing a complementary function. Often, headlines are incomplete sentences, where articles and auxiliary verbs are deleted, leading to vagueness or ambiguity. And this is usually done on purpose in order for the headline to perform some important ideological functions, such as concealment of responsibility for an action (van Dijk 1991). News actors such as politicians, government officials, professionals, accused persons, criminals or terrorists are often placed first in headlines. "Syntactically news surrounding these persons becomes condensed to descriptive noun phrases ... where the description becomes a contributor to the 'script' of the newspaper ... Syntax and vocabulary are both compressed into an intense concentration of communicative form, with puns, alliteration, reference to proverbs and inversion so popular saying" (Conboy 2007, 15) featuring prominently in headlines. Sometimes, headlines feature humor, where humorous effects tend to override the intended meaning (16).

Headlines perform three basic functions; first, "they provide a brief summary of the main news; second, they attract attention, and third, they provide an initial indicator to the content and style of the news values of the newspaper. Thus, headlines are an important part of the way in which the newspaper appeals to its audience" with an "additional attraction of directly chiming with the speech patterns of its readership and enhances the familiar bond between medium and audience." Headlines can also "flatter the targeted reader's knowledge of literature or history, and can trigger or signal key political debates to informed readers" (Conboy 2007, 14). Hence, headlines are in themselves a distinctive contribution to the news values of a paper, which is evident in the ways in which their syntactic structures and stylistic patterns are framed.

In addition to their textual functions, headlines also perform cognitive and ideological functions. Since they are usually read first, the information contained in the headline is often used by the reader in the process of understanding, to construct the overall meaning of the text, and in some cases, readers read just the headline (van Dijk 1991). The headline information is "used to activate the relevant knowledge in memory the reader needs to understand the news report" (50). Thus, the word "herdsmen" or a phrase like "herdsmen kill . . . " will activate the relevant knowledge in the memory of the reader that they need to understand or interpret the entire story. Hence, the "herdsmen script" about what the reader already knows about herdsmen and their activities influences the interpretation of the details of the rest of the story. Thus, "headline information is used by the reader as an overall organizing principle for the representation of the news event in the memory, namely the so-called 'model of the situation'" (van Dijk 1991, 50). For instance, having read news reports about herdsmen attacks and killings in the Nigerian Middle Belt region, the reader having understood these reports must have built a personal memory representation or model of the events. This will generally guide the reader's interpretation of events around herdsmen even without reading full reports of the situation. In other words, the information contained in the headline signals to the reader how to define the situation or the event (van Dijk 1991).

As highlighted above, headlines do have ideological implications. Van Dijk (1991) argues that since headlines express the assumed most important information in the news report, "they may bias the understanding process " (51). The summary of the news contained in the headline generally contains value judgment or the journalist's own opinion of the situation in the news, and the journalist's perspective of the event may aim at upgrading a less important topic by including it in the headline, while actually downgrading the most important aspect of the event. So, headlines are often a subjective definition of the situation, which influence the reader's interpretation of the situation (ibid.). For instance, defining a clash between herdsmen and farmers as "carnage" or "killings" carried out by the herders may lead to a different interpretation of the news report and hence achieve a different model of the situation from where the event is defined as "aggression" or "terrorism" by the Fulani herdsmen. Interestingly, headlines are the part of the news story that is best recalled by the reader and are often not written by the reporters themselves but by special editors or headline experts, who not only think of the best summary for the news but also the most catchy and sensational title that will appeal to the reader. Sometimes, readers may decide to read a news report or not only on the basis of the information contained in the headline (van Dijk 1991).

Because of the importance of news headlines, Piotrkowicz (2017) argues that headline texts should be studied as a separate phenomenon. Chiluwa (2007) has argued that "news headlines are discourse units that are analyzable as independent texts ... as they are functional parts of news stories that are pragmatically encoded to underscore some special kinds of social meaning other than mere encapsulation of the body of news stories" (63).

A number of studies covering electronic media (Monsefi and Mahadi 2017; Rustam 2013; Al-Hindawi and Ali 2018), print media (Chiluwa 2009; Abba and Musa 2015), and social media (Piotrkowicz 2017) have been carried out on the structures and functions of news headlines. And many of these studies analyze the construction of actors and events in conflict and war situations. For instance, Al-Hindawi and Ali (2018), in their study of CNN and BBC news headlines on the Syrian conflict show that assertive and commissive speech acts in CNN news headlines make them much more influential on how the reader perceives the conflict. A similar study of news headlines on Boko Haram attacks in Nigeria suggests that assertive speech acts were mostly used in the headlines but were not used to instigate fear or threat; rather the headlines portray the ideological position of the newspapers (i.e., *Daily Trust* and *The Nation*) about the Boko Haram terrorism in Nigeria (Abba and Musa 2015). Rustam (2013) further finds that CNN news headlines covering the conflicts in Pakistan derive their illocutionary force from representative, directive and commissive acts, which give the headlines their sense of urgency, emphasis and emotional appeal in the news about Osama Bin Laden and the US war on terror. The current study differs from these studies in the way it examines the functions of headlines in the specific Nigerian conflict situation involving Fulani herdsmen and farmers; the study analyzes not only the lexical and grammatical structures of headlines but also their ideological implications, and how these portray the mediatized function of the press in the systematic manipulation of the reader's judgment and perspective on particular events and situations.

3.4 Methodology

The data for the study is made up of 175 news headlines consisting of 1,574 words, being the headlines of online reports of seven newspapers on the herdsmen–farmers conflict in Nigeria. The seven popular Nigerian broadsheet newspapers are *Vanguard, Daily Post, This Day, The Punch, The Nation, The Sun,* and *The Guardian*. The reports cover a period of four years beginning from February 24, 2016 to April 6, 2019. This was the period of intense violence and widespread reports of killings between the two groups. It was also the time that produced enhanced interest and sensational headlines in the local and global news media about the conflict. News reports of the conflict suggested that more coordinated attacks were carried out by the Fulani herdsmen. Table 3.1 shows the newspapers, the number of headlines being studied and the number of words in the twenty-five headlines of each newspaper. This selection does not suggest that all the seven newspapers released the exact same number of articles over the same period of time. Rather, to compile the corpus, the headlines that emphasized the herder–farmer conflict were searched on google.com; the timeframe of the study was also specified in the searches. The topics/search terms used are (i) herdsmen–farmers conflict 2016–2019, (ii) herdsmen attacks 2017–2019, (iii) herdsmen killings 2016–2019, (iv) herder–farmer conflict 2017–2019, and (v) farmer attacks 2016–2019. While most of the seven newspapers published more than twenty-five stories, some of them (e.g., *The Sun* and *Vanguard*) reported exactly twenty-five stories according to our searches. In order not to appear subjective in our selection and judgment, we decided to peg the number of headlines for each newspaper to twenty-five. A study of more than twenty-five stories from some newspapers may suggest bias in the results. If, for example, fifty stories from *The Guardian* and twenty-five stories from *Vanguard* construct the farmers as innocent, what is the likelihood that fifty stories from *Vanguard* will construct the farmers as innocent? That is the reason we decided to study twenty-five stories across the board.

Quantitative analysis of the data is carried out with the use of *AntConc 3.5.8* (Anthony 2019). AntConc, by Laurence Anthony, is a software tool for conducting corpus linguistic study. It provides a toolkit for the word frequency count and concordance program. It is used in this study to provide

Table 3.1 *Newspapers and the number of words in the headlines*

Newspaper	Headlines	Words
Daily Post	25	250
The Guardian	25	215
The Nation	25	208
The Punch	25	238
The Sun	25	196
This Day	25	221
Vanguard	25	234
TOTAL	**175**	**1574**

some basic quantitative analyses of the headlines, showing wordlists and concordances of the most significant words in the headlines. A combination of corpus/content analysis and critical discourse analysis carried out in this study assumes that frequency of occurrence of lexical and syntactic features of the content of a text is an important factor in the communication process (Richardson 2007). However, content analysis and word count like those carried out in corpus linguistics are not usually enough when doing discourse analysis, as they often tend to ignore the *intentions* of meanings in a text. Questions about implicit meaning and ideologies underlying certain actions attributed to some actors or the representation of certain identities can be better answered by approaches in discourse analysis or qualitative critical discourse analysis.

Critical Discourse Analysis (CDA) analyzes social problems by examining ideologies that institutionalize and sustain social inequalities, power asymmetry, prejudices and gender discriminations, among other things. According to Reisigl and Wodak (2009), CDA further includes the analysis of questions about persons, objects, events, processes and actions named linguistically in the text, as well as characteristics, qualities and features attributed to social actors, objects and events. Arguments and perspectives are also examined, as well as how nominalizations and attributions are used to assign actions to actors.

Hence, this study develops from *what* the newspapers write about (i.e., lexical/linguistic choices) in their news headlines about the Fulani herdsmen and farmers conflict, as well as the attribution of actions to the actors, to the analysis of *how* and why the newspapers write what they write about the conflict And it relates the representations of actors and events to the larger social and political context. Thus, the CDA carried out in this study examines the reasons underlying certain representations of the main actors and their actions in the texts and their ideological implications in relation to peace and security in Nigeria.

Table 3.2 shows the wordlist of the words that appeared most frequently in the headlines. "Most frequent words" are taken to be those that occurred at least three times in the corpus of the headlines of 1,574 words and that rank between 1 and 81 in order of importance.

Among the words in Table 3.2 with their frequencies are names of states and cities that are associated with the conflict. These include Benue (43), Anambra (11), Plateau (11), Kaduna (8), Taraba (8), Delta (7), Adamawa (6), Enugu (5), Kogi (5), Ekiti (3), and Zamfara (3). Significantly, nine out of the eleven states listed above are located in the Middle Belt region and southern states of Nigeria. Only Adamawa and Zamfara are northern states, which are supposed to be the original homeland of the Fulani herdsmen. This shows that the conflict and attacks of

Table 3.2 *Wordlist from the corpus of headlines showing the most frequent lexical words*

Rank[a]	Freq.	Word
1	155	herdsmen
3	50	attack
4	44	fulani
5	43	benue
6	41	kill
8	28	killed
10	23	attacks
11	23	suspected
12	22	community
13	22	killings
15	20	farmers
17	15	anambra
20	11	communities
22	11	plateau
23	10	again
25	9	buhari
26	9	clash
28	9	villages
29	8	fresh
30	8	kaduna
31	8	taraba
33	7	delta
36	6	adamawa
37	6	killing
38	6	people
39	6	police
41	5	enugu
42	5	haram
43	5	kogi
44	5	many
48	4	boko
49	4	death
52	4	government
54	4	group
55	4	houses
56	4	injured
57	4	killer
58	4	nigeria
59	4	reveals
62	3	amnesty
63	3	bloody
64	3	conflicts
65	3	ekiti
66	3	fields

Table 3.2 (cont.)

Rank	Freq.	Word
72	3	men
75	3	persons
76	3	policemen
77	3	scores
78	3	security
79	3	speaks
80	3	strike
81	3	zamfara

[a.] Since the study concentrates on lexical words, which have the capacity to express ideological meanings, we deleted all grammatical words (e.g., articles, prepositions) from the wordlist, leaving only the lexical items. Hence, the ranking in the wordlist is not serial. For example, "the," which ranks as number 2 – the next highest occurring word after "herdsmen" – is deleted. The same goes for rank 7 and others.

the herdsmen have concentrated in the southern and Middle Belt states, where the herders have migrated to. Benue state with the highest frequency in the corpus provides the highest concentration of herdsmen in Nigeria.

3.5 Analysis and Findings

Our analysis examines the significance of the most frequent words in the corpus. By analyzing the semantic content of words in the headlines through a concordance program, the meanings of the words with their collocational associations are highlighted, and their ideological implications are also analyzed. It is important to note that the choice of one word rather than another to express the same meaning is often not neutral, especially in the media. Lexicalization of semantic content generally expresses value judgments, opinions, emotions or the stance of the speaker. Hence, the words used in the headlines are important and powerful, not only in shaping public opinion, but also in that they mirror the position of the newspaper on the event in question. In other words, the choice of vocabulary in the headlines signals the social or political opinion of the newspaper about the events. In the analysis of the headlines, however, qualitative critical discourse analysis significantly draws from the main stories in the news (i.e., the textual content of the reports) and not just the headlines, in order to properly establish and explain the context and events in Nigeria that the headlines refer to.

3.5.1 Lexicalization in the Headlines

The eleven most frequently used lexical words in the headlines were selected for analysis. They are: herdsmen (155), attack (50), Fulani (44), Benue (43), Kill (41), Killed (28), attacks (23), suspected (23), community (22), Killings (22), farmers (29). In the headlines, "herdsmen" and "Fulani," which together occurred 199 times, are often used together as "Fulani herdsmen." In the analysis, they are examined as one discourse unit used in the headlines as a noun phrase (see Figure 3.1). The word "kill" and its variants "killed" and "killings" are also analyzed as one semantic unit. However, the various semantic and pragmatic contexts of their use in the headline corpus were examined. The three words altogether occur ninety-one times. The words attack (50) and attacks (23), altogether occurring seventy-three times, are also studied together. Hence, the lexical items analyzed are Fulani herdsmen, kill/killed/killings, attack/attacks, suspected, community, and farmers. The word "community" occurs in the corpus along with proper names such as Delta, Anambra, Enugu, Agatu, and they appear as "Delta community," "Enugu

1	herdsmen are killing people 10. Fulani Herdsmen: Again, 4 killed in fresh	headl
2	change and herdsmen crisis 13. Fulani herdsmen and farmers\x92 clash	headl
3	any sins of Fulani herdsmen 25. Fulani herdsmen and farmers\x92 clash	headl
4	om both sides of the mouth 10. Fulani herdsmen and the killing fields o	headl
5	on Fulani herdsmen killings 15. Fulani herdsmen and the killing fields o	headl
6	nd the killing fields of Benue 16. Fulani herdsmen and the killing fields o	headl
7	9. Governor Ishaku reveals why Fulani herdsmen are killing people 10. F	headl
8	ack Adamawa communities 22. Fulani herdsmen attack Taraba villages,	headl
9	nd the killing fields of Benue 11. Fulani herdsmen attack two Benue com	headl
10	ges 20. Taraba residents flee as Fulani herdsmen attack villages, kill sco	headl
11	cs 23. Scores killed in Taraba, as Fulani Herdsmen attack villages 24. Fay	headl
12	in 5. Plateau imposes curfew as Fulani herdsmen attack 11 villages 6. Pl	headl
13	es 6. Plateau imposes curfew as Fulani herdsmen attack 11 villages 7. He	headl
14	gs \x96 Nigerian government 8. Fulani herdsmen: CAN breaks silence or	headl
15	)2s attacks 24. The many sins of Fulani herdsmen 25. Fulani herdsmen a	headl
16	villages in Adamawa 19. Benue: Fulani herdsmen have killed over 500, 3	headl
17	five 23. Six Tiv farmers killed by Fulani herdsmen 24. Herdsmen attack: A	headl

Figure 3.1 Concordance of "Fulani herdsmen" in the headlines corpus

community," and "Agatu community," among others. These are the places where some specific attacks took place.

What is important in the concordance for "Fulani herdsmen" in Figure 3.1 is what it reveals about the associations or words that co-occur in the same linguistic context. This also highlights agency attribution or the actions that are associated with the main actors, namely the herdsmen and the farmers. For instance, Fulani herdsmen in the concordance are associated with words within the domain of violence/aggression (e.g. "kill," "killings" and "attack" or "attacks") (see Figure 3.1). The presence and actions of the herdsmen are the major subjects of the headlines. The negative actions attributed to the Fulani herdsmen are emphasized and nominalized in the headlines of all seven newspapers. Below are typical examples:

(1) 15 killed as herdsmen attack Benue community (*The Nation*, February 21, 2019)
(2) Herdsmen hit Benue again with fresh attack ... OPWS confirms 7 killed, LG boss 16 (*The Sun*, March 3, 2019)
(3) Herdsmen Kill 17 Persons in Benue (*This Day*, February 20, 2019)
(4) Herdsmen attacks: Police confirm 86 deaths, 6 injured in Plateau (*Daily Post*, June 25, 2018)
(5) Again, suspected herdsmen kill seven Tiv farmers in Nasarawa (*The Guardian*, April 26, 2018)
(6) Herdsmen attack 11 Plateau villages, kill 86, torch 50 houses (*The Punch*, June 25, 2018)
(7) Fresh alarm over killer-herdsmen in the South-South (*Vanguard*, June 11, 2017)

From the above examples, the lexical content of the headlines portrays Fulani herdsmen as aggressive, violent and terrorist. The *Vanguard* of June 11, 2017 specifically referred to them as "killer-herdsmen." Hence, the atmosphere attributed to them is that of war, tension, fear and alarm. The *Daily Post* newspaper released the statistics of casualties between January 2015 and May 2017, contained in a report released by the Benue state government showing the number of people allegedly killed by the herdsmen (see Table 3.3).

Table 3.3 represents a graphic record of the murderous activities of the herdsmen produced by the *Daily Post* newspaper. This type of report will generally produce fear and inspire a dire sense of insecurity among the Christian south, since the news is generally silent on the violent actions of the farmers. Moreover, according to *World Report* 2019, at least 1,600 people were killed and another 300,000 were displaced in 2018 alone, when violence

Table 3.3 *Killings and attacks attributed to the Fulani herdsmen by the* Daily Post *newspaper*

Date	No. of persons killed by herdsmen	Others	Location
January 27, 2015	17	-	Agatu LGA
January 30, 2015	9	-	Logo LGA
March 15, 2015	90	-	Egba village, Agatu
April 27, 2015	28	Houses and farmlands razed	Guma LGA
May 11, 2015	5	8 wounded	Turan, Kwande LGA
May 24, 2015	100	-	Logo LGA
July 7, 2015	1	Several injured	Kwande LGA
November 5, 2015	12	25 injured	Buruku LGA
February 8, 2016	10	300 displaced	Buruku LGA
February 21–24, 2016	500	7,000 displaced	Agatu LGA
February 29, 2016	11	-	Agatu LGA
March 5, 2016	-	Houses burnt	Agatu LGA
March 9, 2016	8	-	Logo LGA
March 10, 2016	2	-	Obagaji, Agatu
March 13, 2016	6	-	Tarka LGA
January 24, 2017	15	-	Ohimini LGA
March 2, 2017	10	-	Gwer East LGA
March 8, 2017	3	-	Logo LGA
March 11, 2017	7	-	Buruku
May 13, 2017	8	-	Logo LGA
TOTAL	**842**		

in the Middle Belt intensified and got worse.[1] Compared to the negative representation of the herders, the actions of the farmers are consciously and conspicuously minimized in the headlines. Farmers are largely constructed as victims. In Figure 3.2, the concordance of "farmers" shows that although the headlines construct the herdsmen and farmers as the main actors in the conflict, still in most of the newspapers, the actions of

---

[1] www.hrw.org/world-report/2019/country-chapters/nigeria.

1	3. 10 killed in Katsina herdsmen, farmers clash 24. Herdsmen at
2	ner 13. 4 injured as herdsmen, farmers clash in Anambra 14. S
3	iyemi decries bloody herdsmen- farmers clash in Ekiti 5. Buhari,
4	iyemi decries bloody herdsmen- farmers clash in Ekiti 25. 13 kill
5	Four feared killed as herdsmen, farmers clash in Ogun 22. Troo
6	unities 12. Politics of herdsmen/farmers conflict 13. Herdsmen-
7	/farmers conflict 13. Herdsmen- farmers conflicts becoming mo
8	ce, Nigeria\x92s Herdsmen and Farmers Form Unlikely Alliance
9	men Kill 16 People in Benue 24. Farmers, Herdsmen Clashes Nc
10	1 Ogun 8. AI: 3,641 Lives Lost to Farmers, Herdsmen Clashes 9.
11	gular migration - Think-tank 11. Farmers/herdsmen conflict, ecc
12	Benue Village 17. Arresting the Farmers-Herdsmen Conflicts in
13	ted\xA0herdsmen kill 6, behead farmers in Anambra 20. Halt es
14	spected herdsmen kill seven Tiv farmers in Nasarawa 10. Herds

Figure 3.2 Concordance of "farmers" in the headlines corpus

the farmers are completely minimized and the farmers are framed as non-violent, victim or innocent. In the examples below, most of the headlines show the killing of farmers by the herders and never the other way round:

(1) Suspected herdsmen kill six farmers, injure many in Anambra (*Daily Post*, April 8, 2019)
(2) Again, suspected herdsmen kill seven Tiv farmers in Nasarawa (*The Guardian*, April 26, 2018)
(3) Four farmers killed by suspected herdsmen in Benue (*The Nation*, December 22, 2018)
(4) Herdsmen kill seven villagers in Taraba, Anambra attacks (*The Punch*, February 24, 2016)
(5) Suspected herdsmen kill 6, behead farmers in Anambra (*The Sun*, April 7, 2019)

Actions attributed to the herders in all the above headlines are kill (or killed), attacks and injure. Over time, this pattern of action attribution has formed the general opinion of the southern general public about the herders, and forms the basis of the construction of the "killer-herdsmen" script. And unfortunately, this becomes what the average reader easily remembers about the conflict. Gradually, the conflict was systematically interpreted along ethnic and religious lines. Up till the time of this research, it appears that the average Nigerian southerner understands little or nothing about the conflict other than that the Fulani herdsmen are engaged in a Jihad either for total Islamization of the country or for "territorial control" of the southern region of Nigeria, or to possess "our land" (see *The Nation*, January 11, 2018)[2]. For instance, the governor of Taraba state was once quoted as saying that "his people" were attacked and killed without any cause: "they attacked and killed innocent people in Taraba without provocation." With this type of conclusion, no one seems to be certain about how many of the herdsmen and their cattle have been killed in the conflict, even after the General Secretary of the Christian Association of Nigeria (CAN) had advised Christians in the affected states to defend themselves. This call by the CAN president happened after the killings of Christians and attack on churches became more frequent. An example was the killing of two Catholic priests and seventeen worshippers by some herdsmen in Benue state in 2018 (*The Punch*, April 25, 2018)[3]. CAN had earlier attacked the Nigerian president for creating the impression that he was in power to serve the interest of his Fulani ethnic group and had "flagrantly violated the (Nigerian) Constitution and adopted Sharia ideology as operational standard" (Godwin 2018, 1). On May 18, 2019, a former Nigeria president in a keynote address at an Anglican church in Delta state publicly admitted that the Boko Haram terrorism and the herdsmen violence were deliberate acts in the process of "West African fulanisation, African islamisation and global organized crimes of human trafficking."[4] This controversial remark by former President Olusegun Obasanjo attracted national outcry and criticisms. His remarks appear to corroborate CAN's earlier claim.

3.5.2 Evaluative Patterns in the Semantic and Syntactic Structures of the Headlines

Positive and negative actions attributed to the main actors in the conflict follow the same pattern as the lexical choices expressed in the semantic and grammatical structures of the headlines. The questions here is, what actions are nominalized (or topicalized), and whose actions are highlighted or minimized. In this section of the analysis, attention is paid to individual newspapers and how their perspectives expressed in their choice of vocabulary also influenced the syntactic structures of their headlines. As already highlighted above, Fulani herdsmen (or simply "herdsmen") and farmers are the main agents of the actions in the headlines; they also appear as receivers of actions, as in the case of farmers, who are generally constructed as the victims of aggression. Here also, other agents (e.g., government, the police, CAN) are examined along with what positive or negative/neutral roles are ascribed to them. For instance, the government is typically represented as the responsible agent of neutral or negative actions.

---

[2] https://thenationonlineng.net/herdsmen-killing-people-governor/
[3] https://punchng.com/protests-in-benue-as-herdsmen-kill-two-catholic-priests-17-others-inside-church/
[4] www.vanguardngr.com/2019/05/mobilising-nigerias-human-and-natural-resources-for-national-development-and-stability-by-obasanjo/

Table 3.4 *Distribution of actions attributed to the actors in the conflict in the headlines*

Actor categories/relations	Daily Post	Guardian	The Nation	The Punch	The Sun	This Day	Vanguard
Herdsmen: positive action: (e.g., agree to expose sponsors; agree to end conflict)	01	01	-	-	-	01	01
Herdsmen: negative actions (e.g., kill, kidnap, attack, injure)	15	12	18	16	14	17	19
Farmers: as victims	01	01	02	-	01	-	0
Farmers: negative action	-	-	-	-	-	-	-
Police/military (PM): positive action (e.g., voluntary policing)	-	-	02	01	-	-	-
PM: negative action (e.g., late response, kill herdsmen)	-	-	-	-	-	01	-
PM: neutral actions (e.g., arrest)	02	01	-	02	-	01	-
Government(govt): positive action (e.g., mediation, strengthen security)	02	-	01	-	-	-	-
Govt: neutral action (e.g., silent; ban open grazing)	02	04	02	03	01	01	01
Others (e.g., Amnesty Intl.): positive action (e.g., report violence; indict the Nigerian government)	02	02	-	-	-	-	-
Neutral action (e.g., call for dialogue/peace)	01	04	01	03	09	04	04

In the quantitative analysis of the twenty-five headlines of each of the papers, the number of times some specific roles and relationships occurred for the major actors (i.e., herdsmen and farmers) and others (e.g. the government, military or the police) were manually counted and identified. This gives insight into the evaluative patterns of the different papers in relation to the actors in the conflict. The analysis also examines what positive, negative or neutral roles are assigned to the various actors (Table 3.4). This pattern of representation of the roles of the herdsmen as well as other actors in selected headlines of four of the newspapers is shown in the examples below.

Daily Post
(1) Suspected herdsmen kill six farmers, injure many in Anambra

(2) 3 policemen, locals killed as herdsmen attack Kogi community
(3) Military speaks on 'herdsmen attack' in Benue
(4) Amaechi reveals those behind herdsmen killings, speaks on plans to Islamize Nigeria
(5) Fulani herdsmen strike in Plateau, kill 8.

The Guardian
(1) Suspected Fulani herdsmen, others kill 32 in Kaduna, Sokoto
(2) Fayemi decries bloody herdsmen–farmers clash in Ekiti
(3) Buhari, IGP, urged to act on Fulani herdsmen killing in Delta
(4) NEC bans open grazing as herdsmen attacks persist
(5) Again, suspected herdsmen kill seven Tiv farmers in Nasarawa

The Nation
(1) 15 killed as herdsmen attack Benue community
(2) Herdsmen kill 48 in attack on Enugu community
(3) Police arrest eight herdsmen over attacks
(4) Fulani herdsmen attack two Benue communities
(5) Four farmers killed by suspected herdsmen in Benue

The Punch
(1) Herdsmen attack 11 Plateau villages, kill 86, torch 50 houses
(2) Herdsmen kill 19 in Plateau midnight attack
(3) Herdsmen kill 11, torch 50 houses in Plateau
(4) 14 die as suspected herdsmen attack Plateau again
(5) Plateau imposes curfew as Fulani herdsmen attack 11 villages

It is important to mention here that the syntactic structures of the headlines reflect the nominalization of the active agent, where the performer of an action is made explicit (e.g., "Fulani herdsmen kill 48 in attack on Enugu community") and the process of passivization, where the agent is deleted and the performer of an action is unknown (e.g. "15 killed as herdsmen attack Benue community"). In the first example, the action of the agent (Fulani herdsmen) is the killing of forty-eight victims. In the second example, the killers of fifteen people are not made explicit, although the killing was a sequel to herdsmen's attack. It could be assumed that the victims could come from both sides.

3.5.3   Ideological Evaluations of Main Actors and Actions

The logic of representation stems from the view of the role of language in social life that meaning is not necessarily embedded in reality as we perceive it, but is constructed through linguistic representation (see Wenden 2005). Thus, language use in texts (or talks) assigns meaning to persons and groups and their social practices, to objects, events and situations in a particular way that either promotes or demeans them. Although representations vary depending on the perspective from which they are constructed, there still could be a *preferred* way of perceiving or representing reality or persons and their actions. For instance, in the media, given the same condition (e.g., conflict, as in this study), some social actors and actions may commonly be constructed in a particular negative way.

Table 3.4 shows that the attribution of negative actions to the herdsmen is highest in the headlines, with the lowest score being 48 percent (i.e., 12 out of the 25 headlines) in *The Guardian* newspaper and the highest score 76 percent (19 out of the 25 headlines) in the *Vanguard*. Unlike the other actors that have no action attribution scores in some newspapers (e.g., farmers without any negative actions in all the newspapers), the herdsmen have negative scores in all the newspapers, ranging from 48 percent to 76 percent. The only positive actions attributed to the herdsmen in four newspapers are those that claim to expose their sponsors and those agreeing to end the conflict. *This Day* newspaper still refers to this agreement as an "unlikely alliance." On the one hand, the herdsmen are constructed both as active agents (i.e., in noun phrases with active verbs, e.g., "herdsmen kill 19 ... ") and also in passive constructions (e.g., "four farmers killed by suspected herdsmen"). On the other hand, the farmers are constructed as victims at least once in five of the seven newspapers under study. While it appears that the construction of the farmers as victims is low, the actual identity of those killed in most cases is not disclosed. In all the papers, neutral constructions such as "scores killed," "kill locals," "kill 5 villagers," "Kill 8," "kill 15" are used. The physical contexts of the reported killings (e.g., in villages and local government areas) suggest that they are farmers. Besides, it could be assumed that most of those referred to as "locals," "villagers" or "15" are actually farmers. Thus, the reports tend to attract more sympathy for the farmers. In all the 175 news headlines, only one headline by *The Punch* newspaper made reference to the killing of the Fulani herdsmen as follows:

"Troops killed 21 herdsmen in Benue." (*The Punch*, August 20, 2018)

The agent (troops) performs the negative action of killing the herdsmen, where the herders, for the first time, are constructed as the victims of an attack. Notice also that the agent (or the killers) in this case is not the farmers, rather "troops," who are either the police or the military. *The Punch*, although it reported the killing of the herdsmen, is still one of the papers with the highest (68%) instances of negative representation of the herdsmen in its headlines.

The ideological implications of the headlines' representation of the herdsmen solely as the aggressor, the killer, or the attacker and frequently associating them with actions such as terrorism, banditry, clash, menace, etc. falls short of reports that thoroughly investigate the real causes of the conflict, the casualties from both sides and the prospects of ending the conflict. *The Guardian* recorded the least negative evaluation of the herdsmen and appeared to adopt some form of neutral stance on the conflict. It was also the only newspaper that reported the killings of the herders by cattle rustlers. "Rustlers," as highlighted earlier, are armed bandits that had terrorized the herdsmen for a long time; their activities and stealing of cows and cattle were said to be the main cause of the armed resistance adopted by the herders to defend both themselves and their cattle. The use of arms by the herders was not originally intended for war against farmers. According to Baca (2015), cattle rustling became a big business following the rise of the meat market in West Africa's urban centers, and crime syndicates had increasingly targeted herds. For example, rustlers stole about 60,000 head of cattle in 2013 alone, forcing many herders to arm themselves with semi-automatic weapons. Victimized pastoralists would generally blame the agriculturalist population for their loss of livestock, even in cases where the actual culprits were their fellow Fulani kinsmen.

Understandably, the conflict with farmers began when farmers saw the herders as enemies who came to destroy (and actually destroyed) their farmland in order to feed their animals. And in most cases, when roaming cattle entered and destroyed farmland, there was no compensation. *The Guardian* reported actions by other actors in the conflict referred to in this study as "others" (e.g., government agencies, Amnesty International, the youth), such as the banning of open grazing by the government and the indictment of the Nigerian government by Amnesty International; however, their reports still betray ideological tilting of reports to favor popular positive feelings towards farmers, as many of the reports refer to "herdsmen attacks" or "herdsmen killings."

Significantly, in a report written by Dan Agbese entitled "Fulani herdsmen? Here are the grim statistics," the author argues that it is incorrect to describe the conflict as a "clash," rather it is "attacks" carried out by the herdsmen.

> A clash is a violent conflict between two groups of people and usually leaves casualties on both sides. From what I have read about these attacks and killings, the attackers suffer no casualties and there is no evidence that those attacked ever faced the attackers or that they had a chance to fight back. These attacks and killings are unprovoked and the attackers choose where and when to strike. They attack when their intended victims are most vulnerable. In several cases in Plateau State, for instance, the attackers came at night when the villagers were asleep and killed and sacked whole villages and disappeared before day break. They did the same thing several times in Agatu in Benue State. In no case was there any evidence that Agatu people provoked them or had a chance to engage them. (*The Guardian*, November 3, 2017, 2)

In his report, Agbese (a contributing editor for *The Guardian*) noted that in 2016 alone, 2,500 people were killed and 62,000 displaced; $13.7 billion were lost to the conflict and 47 percent of the internally generated revenue in the affected states was lost. In December 2015, the attacks in some parts of Kaduna state claimed the lives of 880 people. Fifty-three villages were destroyed, 1,422 houses were burnt and 18 churches and one elementary school were also burnt down. The author disagreed that the killers were Fulani herdsmen because the herders were incapable of the actions attributed to them. In his opinion, the rural herdsmen could not have armed themselves with AK-47 guns and they lacked the military training to use them. If indeed the herders recognized themselves as strangers in the areas they found suitable as grazing grounds for their animals, why would they periodically engage in "a killing spree"? They had also made efforts to broker peace with farmers through their umbrella body known as Miyetti Allah. So, what has happened? Dan Agbese believes that "Fulani herdsmen are now a franchise. People kill and do other dirty jobs and find it easy to conveniently blame Fulani herdsmen for them."

Indeed, Agbese's position represents the perspective of the average educated Nigerian about the conflict – the truth that we do not know who the Fulani herdsmen really are. The government has also been accused of complicity in the attacks, as it seemed that the president had been surprisingly silent or had not done enough in terms of military intervention. Like Dan Agbese's, many theories have emerged from individuals and institutions, including foreign media, about the identity of the herdsmen, their sponsors and collaborators. Some persons and groups in the media and on the Internet believe that the "herdsmen" are actually a faction of Boko Haram – "Jihadists masquerading as herdsmen" (*Daily Post*, May 9, 2018). If not, how come they operate in the same guerrilla fashion as Boko Haram? How come they attack churches and murder priests and worshippers? How come they attack schools? If they are mere herders, how are they highly trained in the use of sophisticated weapons, including grenades and machine guns? To lend credence to this argument, the Nigerian Army announced the arrest of a suspected Boko Haram member in Benue on April 27, 2018. The suspect, one Aminu Yaminu (aka Tashaku), was said to have masterminded most of the "recent" attacks in Benue state (*The Nation*, April 28, 2018).

Speculations from the Internet had also argued that there were possible links between Boko Haram and the herdsmen. For instance, a Fulani group had admitted that they were "committing Jihad in the name of Allah" (Stolicker 2018, 1). This, according to the online source, suggests that there was more to the herders' violence than mere attempts to gain pastoral lands. Even if the herders and Boko Haram were not the same people, it was clear that they shared some form of cooperation and ideology. Stolicker (2018) argues that there is evidence that the herders were assisted by Boko Haram, possibly through the provision of arms and logistics. After all, the herdsmen's tactics conformed to those of Boko Haram. In the past, the herders would attack and then escape, but now, they would attack villages and then set up camps; and like Boko Haram, they are beginning to take territories. In the villages and towns, they attack, and homes are burnt to the ground, while Muslim homes and mosques in the same area are untouched.[5]

Some social actors have further conjectured that the Fulani herders are returnee soldiers from Libya – among whom were recruits from Benin Republic and terrorists operating from Mali and around the Sahel region. Interestingly, this version of conjecture originated from the Nigerian president himself, who, speaking to the BBC in London in May 2016, claimed that the herdsmen were "non-Nigerians who came from Libya" (Odunsi 2016, 1).[6] In recent times, however, events in the country seem to have proved the president wrong; President Buhari also appeared to have contradicted himself when his government approved the establishment of "Ruga settlements" for Fulani herdsmen across the country. The question now is: if the Fulani herdsmen were non-Nigerians, why would the president establish settlements for them in the thirty-six states of the federation in spite of the huge financial and economic implications? According to Adeniyi (2019), the establishment of eight Ruga settlements in Taraba state was approved at the cost of over 166 million naira (i.e., over $461,000). "Ruga" is a Hausa word for "cattle colony."

This plan by the government was vehemently opposed by Nigerians, especially from the south, who feared that the project might spark off another civil war. While the government looked forward to rural settlements that would be "organised places with the provision of necessary and adequate basic amenities such as schools, hospitals, road networks, vet clinics, markets and manufacturing entities that will process and add value to meats and animal products" (Mudashir et al. 2019, 1), Ruga settlements in southern Nigeria were perceived as a ploy by the Muslim president to infiltrate southern Christian lands with Fulani/Islamic cultures. The project was suspended by the Buhari government due more to non-compliance with the terms of the National Livestock Transformation Plan developed by the National Executive Council and approved by the government in its implementation than to the strong opposition the plan received from southern state governments.[7]

3.6 Conclusion

By consistently attributing negative actions to Fulani herdsmen in the armed conflict, and constructing farmers as non-violent victims, the newspapers perform the following functions. (1) They establish the killer-herdsmen script with which herders are frequently evaluated, and this forms the general perception of the Fulani herdsmen, including those (herders) that may have been victimized.

---

[5] www.mnnonline.org/news/could-the-fulani-herdsmen-and-boko-haram-be-related/
[6] https://dailypost.ng/2016/05/14/herdsmen-killing-nigerians-are-from-libya-buhari/
[7] www.pmnewsnigeria.com/2019/07/05/inside-story-why-buhari-suspended-ruga-settlement/

The continual association of the herdsmen with lexical items like *kill, attack, terrorist, death* creates the general atmosphere of apprehension and tension in relations between herders and farmers. (2) The news further exacerbates suspicion and mistrust between herders and farmers; hence, the anticipated peace may never be realized. (3) The attribution of negative actions to the herdsmen and associating them with aggression and terrorism will always generate fear and insecurity. And if, indeed, the real herders are not the "killer-herdsmen," some innocent herdsmen might be the target of violent attacks or even silent killings. If the real identity of those involved in the brutal killings of farmers and villagers is unknown, who then were the twenty-one herders that were reportedly killed by troops in Benue in 2018? As some authors have suggested, it is possible that some Islamic militants were responsible for the attacks that were blamed on the herdsmen. The mass media only increases the chances of victimizing those who may not be directly involved in the killings, and in some cases, they have incited violent conflict against the herdsmen. As it now stands, it is impossible to accurately quantify the degree of deaths and human sufferings in the Nigerian conflicts. Unfortunately, the Nigerian conflict situation is fast becoming what is described as an "institutionalized war economy," where conflict becomes self-sustaining and peace is hard to determine, because there are significant vested interests (even at the national level) in continuing the conflict (Puddephatt 2006).

While global attention is drawn to the farmers–herders conflict in Nigeria, and the disturbing mass killings go on, this study argues that the whole truth is not told by the press by titling their news analysis of the situation in favor of one party in the conflict, while the root cause of the conflict and the identity of the main actors and vested interests remain unknown. Through its mediatized role, the Nigerian press is shaping perceptions of the conflict, not just those of ordinary people but also those of political institutions, security agents, leaders and politicians, and this influences practices and attitudes about the herders and farmers, who are increasingly dependent on the media and conforming to their principles of news production and consumption. Unless a balanced view of the conflict is constructed by the media for the Nigerian population, peace might remain elusive.

References

Abba, Tijani S. and Musa, Nasiru. 2015. "Speech Act Analysis of *Daily Trust* and *The Nation* Newspapers' Headline Reports on Boko Haram." *Journal of Communication and Culture* 6(1): 63–72.

Abdullahi, S., Daneyel, N. and Aliyara, Y. 2015. "Grazing Reserves and Pastoralism in Nigeria: A Review." *Vom Journal of Veterinary Science* 10, 137–142.

Adeniyi, Olusegun. 2019. "The Problem with Ruga Settlement." *This Day*, July 4. www.thisdaylive.com/index.php/2019/07/04/the-problem-with-ruga-settlement/.

Al-Hindawi, Fareed and Ali, Abid. 2018. "A Pragmatic Study of CNN and BBC News Headlines Covering the Syrian Conflict." *Advances in Language and Literary Studies* 9(3): 43–41.

Amnesty International. 2018. "Harvest of Death: Three Years of Bloody Clashes between Farmers and Herders in Nigeria." Abuja: Amnesty International. www.amnesty.org/en/documents/afr44/9503/2018/en/.

Anthony, Laurence. 2019. *AntConc* [computer software]. www.laurenceanthony.net/software/antconc/.

Atoyebi, Olufemi, Ogundele, Kamarudee, Awoyinfa, Samuel and Makinde, Femi. 2016. "Fulani Herdsmen-Farmers Amass Arms, Combat Killings." https://punchng.com/fulani-herdsmen-farmers-amass-arms-combat-killings/.

Baca, Michael. 2015. "Farmer–Herder Clashes Amplify Challenge for Beleaguered Nigerian Security." *IPI Global Observatory*. https://theglobalobservatory.org/2015/07/farmer-herder-nigeria-buhari-abuja-fulani/.

Bagu, Chom and Smith, Katie. 2017. "Criminality & Reprisal Attacks in Nigeria's Middle Belt." *Search for Common Grounds*. www.sfcg.org/wp-content/uploads/2017/04/Criminality-Reprisal-Attack_FINAL.pdf.

Betz, Michelle. 2017. "How Media Can Be an Instrument of Peace in Conflict-Prone Settings." Roundtable Background Paper for the UNDP Oslo Governance Centre. https://issat.dcaf.ch/Learn/Resource-Library2/Policy-and-Research-Papers/How-Media-can-be-an-Instrument-of-Peace-in-Conflict-prone-Settings.

Buchanan, Rose. 2015. "Global Terrorism Index: Nigerian Fulani Militants Named as Fourth Deadliest Terror Group in the World." *The Independent* (UK), November 18. www.independent.co.uk/news/world/africa/global-terrorism-index-nigerian-fulani-militants-named-fourth-deadliest-terror-group-world-a6739851.html.

Chiluwa, Innocent. 2007. "News Headlines as Pragmatic Strategy in Nigerian Press Discourse." *International Journal of Language, Society and Culture* 27: 63–71.

Chukwuemeka, Emma, Aduma, Aloysius and Eneh, Maximus. 2018. "The Logic of Open Grazing in Nigeria: Interrogating the Effect on Sustainable Development." *Family Business Management* 2(1): 1–17.

Conboy, Martin. 2007. *The Language of the News*. London: Routledge.

Galtung, Johan. 2000. "The Task of Peace Journalism." *Ethical Perspectives* 7(2–3): 162–167.

Galtung, Johan and Fischer, Dietrich 2013. "High Road, Low Road: Charting the Course for Peace Journalism." In Johan Galtung, *SpringerBriefs on Pioneers in Science and Practice*, vol 5. Berlin: Springer, 95–102.

Godwin, Ameh. 2018. "Fulani Herdsmen: CAN Breaks Silence on Killings in Nigeria, Blasts Buhari." *Daily Post*, January 16. https://dailypost.ng/2018/01/16/fulani-herdsmen-can-breaks-silence-killings-nigeria-blasts-buhari/.

Idowu, Adetayo and Okunola, Taofik. 2017. "Pastoralism as a New Phase of Terrorism in Nigeria." *Global Journal of Human Social Science* 17(4): 3–7.

Maeseele, Pieter. 2015. "Risk Conflicts, Critical Discourse Analysis and Media Discourses on GM Crops and Food." *Journalism* 16(2): 278–297.

Monsefi, Roya and Mahadi, Tengku. 2017. "The Rhetoric of Persian News Headlines: A Case Study of Euro News." *International Journal of Applied Linguistics & English Literature* 6(2): 36–45.

Mudashir, Ismail, Ogbonna, Nabob and Aliyu, Abdullateef. 2019. "Nigeria: Why Government Is Establishing Ruga Settlements – Presidency." *Daily Trust*, July 1. https://allafrica.com/stories/201907010050.html.

Nijenhuis, Judith. 2014. "Peace and War Frames in the Media Representations of the Libyan Civil War." Nijmegen: Radboud University. https://theses.ubn.ru.nl/bitstream/handle/123456789/2783/Nijenhuis%2C_Judith_1.pdf?sequence=1.

Nnoko-Mewanu, Juliana. 2018. "Farmer-Herder Conflicts on the Rise in Africa." *IPS*. www.ipsnews.net/2018/08/farmer-herder-conflicts-rise-africa/.

Odunsi, Wale. 2016. "Herdsmen Killing Nigerians Are from Libya – Buhari." *Daily Post*, May 14. https://dailypost.ng/2016/05/14/herdsmen-killing-nigerians-are-from-libya-buhari/.

Onyema, Mac-Anthony, Gideon, Idoreyin and Ekwugha, Ugochi. 2018. "The Onslaught of Farmer-Herdsmen Crises in Nigeria: Perspectives from Sociological Viewpoint." *Journal of African Interdisciplinary Studies* 2(9): 28–35.

Piotrkowicz, Alicja. 2017. *Modelling Social Media Popularity of News Articles Using Headline Texts*. Ph.D. Thesis, School of Computing, The University of Leeds, UK. http://etheses.whiterose.ac.uk/20430/.

Puddephatt, Andrew. 2006. "Voice of War: Conflict and the Role of the Media." *International Media Support*. www.mediasupport.org/publication/voices-of-war-conflict-and-the-role-of-the-media/.

Rahman, Bushra and Eijaz, Abida. 2014. "Pakistani Media as an Agent of Conflict or Conflict Resolution: A Case of *Lal Masjid* in Urdu and English Dailies." *Pakistan Vision* 15(2): 238–264.

Reisigl, Martin and Wodak, Ruth. 2009. "The Discourse-Historical Approach (DHA)." In *Methods of Critical Discourse Analysis*, ed. by Ruth Wodak and Michael Meyer (2nd ed.). London: Sage, 87–121.

Richardson, John. 2007. *Analysing Newspapers: An Approach from Critical Discourse Analysis*. Basingstoke: Palgrave Macmillan.

Rustam, Rabiah. 2013. *Pragmatic Analysis of CNN Headlines Representing Pakistan*. Ph.D. thesis, Higher Education Commission, Islamabad. http://prr.hec.gov.pk/jspui/handle/123456789/2732.

Stolicker, Beth. 2018. "Could the Fulani Herdsmen and Boko Haram Be Related?" *Mission News Network*, August 10. www.mnnonline.org/news/could-the-fulani-herdsmen-and-boko-haram-be-related/.

Van Dijk, Teun. 1991. "The Interdisciplinary Study of News as Discourse." In *A Handbook of Qualitative Methodologies in Mass Communication Research*, ed. by Klaus Bruhn-Jensen and Nicholas Jankowksi. London: Routledge, 108–120.

Wenden, Anita. 2005. "The Politics of Representation: A Critical Discourse Analysis of an Aljazeera Special Report." *International Journal of Peace Studies* 10(2): 89–110.

4 Covering the War on Iraq
The Pragmatics of Framing and Visual Rhetoric

Ahmed Sahlane

4.1 Introduction

In the build-up to the 2003 Iraq War, the US–British mainstream news/opinion–editorial media deployed an arsenal of prudential and "humanitarian" rhetoric to justify the invasion. For example, by allowing the pro-war official sources privileged access to media space while muffling the dissenting voices, the US–British mainstream media played a major role in instigating and propagating conflict (Sahlane 2012; Wilson et al. 2012). In this sense, media organizations discursively set the stage for the impending Iraq conflict by shaping public opinion, US policy, and the production of symbolic meanings by metaphorically normalizing the US threat to attack Iraq (Sahlane 2013) and by relegating anti-war dissent to a sphere of "deviance" (Sahlane 2015). The 2003 invasion of Iraq has generated extensive media frame analysis. These studies reveal that media subject agendas were in conspicuous congruence with the ideological perspectives of the countries they operated in, as the following section will illustrate.

4.2 Mediating Ideology in the Iraq War Discourse

Since media framing is generally defined as making salient certain aspects of "reality" in a way that primes social stereotypes, promotes a particular definition of a situation, shapes the way issues are perceived by target audiences and/or warrants a preferred course of action (Entman 1993, 52), it is expected that media frames presented in news/editorial coverage of the 2003 Iraq War would most likely exclude views that fall outside the US government's news management agenda. In other words, official sources play a vital role in the construction of news in a way that predisposes the news media to adopt certain news frames over others and to fail to give voice to any frame negotiation or contestation.

For example, in the context of investigating pre-Iraq War coverage, US newspaper opinion and editorial pieces (op/eds) marginalized "morality and legality" by restricting their discussion to the prudential concerns. About 60 percent of the op/eds endorsed the invasion of Iraq. In addition, 30 percent of the overall pro-war argument discussed the need to effect a regime change in Iraq, and only 15 percent of the op/eds were fully anti-war. More interestingly, only about 6 percent of the op/eds debated the Iraqi issue from a principled "moral" or "legal" angle. Such an "avoidance" strategy lent a fake legitimacy to the Bush administration's pro-war position (Nikolaev and Porpora 2007). "Moral muting" also took the form of "mitigation," "incompleteness," "strategic ambiguity" (fuzzy framing) and "enthymemic" reasoning (Porpora and Nikolaev 2008).

Similarly, Goddard et al. (2008) analyzed how news and editorials framed the 2003 Iraq War in its initial combat phase. The study revealed that British newspapers concentrated on the "battle/strategy" topic, which dominated 46 percent of their news stories. Only casualties (15%), media (12.5%) and diplomacy (11.8%) stepped beyond 10 percent of coverage. Other subjects such as domestic protest (4%) and the rationale for war (4.4%) were downplayed (ibid., 16). More interestingly, there was a remarkable congruence between newspapers' editorial perspectives and their subject agendas (ibid., 17). For example, *The Independent* contained the lowest "battle/strategy" stories (42.7%), compared to 53 percent in *The Daily Mail*. Likewise, more than 50 percent of *The Times* and *The Daily Telegraph*'s editorial content was pro-war. However, it is in the reporting of human suffering that a "substantial discrepancy" obtained, contingent upon the paper's editorial perspective. For example, while the anti-war *Daily Mirror* devoted 27.1 percent to the coverage of human suffering, the other papers did not exceed more than 12.6 percent. Absurdly, while the pro-war *Sun* suppressed the topic of "Iraqi civilian casualties" (2.0%), "coalition casualties" constituted 11.8% of its coverage (ibid.). Therefore, the low level of coverage of anti-war protest (7.6%) and the abundant use of official sources by most papers (87.3%) showed that the British media had to rally round the flag. However, it is the "tone" of reporting that made a significant divergence in approach. While *The Sun* was "reinforcing" towards the coalition actors and "deflating" towards their Iraqi counterparts, *The Daily Mirror* was the newspaper "most likely to deflate coalition actors," followed by *The Independent* (ibid., 20).[1]

---

[1] *The Mirror* tried to sympathize with Iraqi victims, but had to pay a dear cost: the paper lost circulation. Hence, the pressure from shareholders culminated in the sacking of the editor. Similarly, the BBC correspondent Rageh Omaar (who eventually joined the *Al-Jazeera* English TV channel), sympathized with Iraqi victims, and subsequently the British government intervened to get him fired, and the British government's pressure culminated in the resignation of senior BBC staff (Brown 2006, 102–103).

In the same vein, Barker (2012) investigated the coverage of the 2003 invasion of Iraq in US and Swedish television news programs (*CNN* and *Fox News* vs. SVT 2's *Aktuellt* and TV4's *Nyheterna*) and print news (*New York Times* (*NYT*) and *Washington Post* vs. *Dagens Nyheter* and *Svenska Dagbladet*) over the period from March 18 to April 15, 2003. The Swedish news delegitimized the war in its coverage. In contrast, the US media depicted the war within the "master frame" of "humanitarian" interventionism. Besides, while the US media predominantly used US official political and military sources (in addition to embedded reporters), the Swedish media used live reporting and more footage from Iraqi and Arab TV channels. The study concluded that while the Swedish media prioritized the coverage of human suffering and the damage inflicted upon the infrastructure of Iraq, their US counterparts focused on US war strategy and sophisticated weaponry. While the Swedish media represented the war as a failure of the United Nations (UN) and as an illegal US "messianic" militarist venture, the US media reframed the war as a "necessary" and "benign" war of "liberation" (Barker 2012).

Dimitrova and Strömbäck's (2005) study about the framing of the 2003 US-led invasion of Iraq in Sweden and the US further corroborated Barker's findings. The study investigated the news articles appearing in two leading agenda-setting newspapers, *Dagens Nyheter* and *NYT* over the period from March 20 to May 1, 2003. The study found that *NYT* depended more frequently on government officials (44%) and military sources (48%) than did *Dagens Nyheter* (28% and 12%, respectively). In addition, *Dagens Nyheter* contained more negative coverage of the war compared to *NYT*, reflecting the official political perspectives in each country. The coverage of "anti-war" protest and "responsibility issues" was almost absent in *NYT*, as a clear reflection of its endorsement of the US "war on terror" narrative. More interestingly, while *Dagens Nyheter* focused on worldwide anti-war protest and the US responsibility for the war (thematic frame), *NYT* regarded the "responsibility attribution" as a non-issue (Dimitrova and Strömbäck 2005, 410).[2] While the "human interest frames" in *NYT* mostly focused on American forces, *Dagens Nyheter* gave more attention to the suffering of Iraqi civilians (ibid.). *NYT prioritized* "military conflict" issues (e.g., "war strategies"). In this sense, the US media blinded its audience to other perspectives by restricting its coverage to "episodic frames" that were of a national manufactured consensus (ibid., 412).

---

[2] Likewise, while the Samarra shrine bombing "spurred [*NYT*] journalists to increasingly use the Danger of Civil War frame [despite little elite support]," "the Occupation Frame" of anti-war activists "rarely appeared in news coverage and, when it did, was always attributed to outside sources," but "was never used by journalists" (Speer 2017, 296–297). Conversely, "the Insurgency Frame" was "the most common way of presenting the war in *NYT* articles, both in statements attributed to outside sources and in statements by journalists themselves (without attribution)" (ibid., 297).

Likewise, Aday et al. (2005) investigated how TV news networks selectively featured stories that induced preferred frames (Aday et al. 2005, 10). The study found that while *Al Jazeera* devoted 6.7 percent of its stories to global political dissent, US TV media coverage of domestic and worldwide anti-war opposition was marginal (Aday et al. 2005, 11). Similarly, US news networks disregarded the UN's role, while 13 percent of the sampled stories from *Al Jazeera* were about international diplomacy. More interestingly, unlike *Fox News Channel (FNC)*(which was only 62.1% "neutral" and 37.9% pro-American), *Al Jazeera* demonstrated "neutral" reporting (90%), compared to the major US TV outlets. Besides, while US news channels exposed viewers to a portrait of a sanitized war, *Al Jazeera* focused more heavily on UN diplomacy and anti-war dissent, and less on battlefield operations and war strategy. However, though it did not air many stories of civilian casualties (4.5%), *Al Jazeera*'s tone failed to be "objective" (36%). But its coverage was largely balanced and displayed no sign of "anti-Americanism" (ibid.).

Reporting under titles such as "America at War" (*CBS*), "Strike on Iraq" (*CNN*), "Operation Iraqi Freedom" (*FNC, NBC* and *MSNBC*) (in addition to the use of the "American flag waving at the bottom of the screen during reports," Calabrese 2005, 168) showed that "US television coverage tended toward pro-military patriotism, propaganda, and technological fetishism, celebrating the weapons of war and military humanism, highlighting the achievements and heroism of the US military" (Kellner 2004a, 57). Conversely, international broadcasting networks were "highly critical of the US and UK military and often presented highly negative spectacles of the assault on Iraq and the shock and awe high-tech massacre" (ibid.). For example, the Canadian *CBC* used the logo "War on Iraq" while Arab networks framed the Anglo-American attacks as an illegal "invasion" and "occupation" (Kellner 2004a, 329).

Lee's (2004) study about the coverage of the 2003 Iraq War in *NYT, The Arab News*, and *The Middle East Times* further explored how the reinforcing relationship between government, news media and corporate interests helped to promote militarist "humanitarianism." Lee analyzed the content of 502 articles, editorials and opinion pages that covered from March 20 to May 1, 2003. The study revealed that *NYT* adopted a more pro-war perspective while Arab newspapers denounced the war. The "liberation" argument was more salient in *NYT* (56.4%) than in *The Arab News* and *The Middle East Times* (26.3% and 22.2%, respectively) (Lee 2004, 95). Besides, *NYT* depended heavily on US officials as sources of information while Arab newspapers cited more Arab sources (ibid., 107).

In a similar study, Dimitrova and Connolly-Ahern (2007) examined the representation of the war in *NYT* and *The Guardian* and *Al-Ahram* and *Al Jazeera* TV site. The coverage of war in Arab media websites focused heavily on the theme of "violence" of war and the "responsibility" frame (one-third of the Arab coverage consisted of "blame attribution") while the US–British media's websites gave more salience to the "reconstruction of Iraq"[3] frame (Dimitrova and Connolly-Ahern 2007, 161). Besides, while 97 percent of the sources used by *NYT* were government officials, *Al-Ahram*'s sourcing was 100 percent official. Conversely, *The Guardian* used government sources in only one-third of its online coverage. While Arab news relied on journalists as sources, the US–British media did not (ibid., 160). In addition, the coalition news outlets remained predominantly "neutral" in tone. In contrast, the Arab news media were often "critical" of the war and their tone was consequently "negative" as they cited Arab political leaders as their main official sources. In contrast, the reliance of the US–British media on coalition political and military sources resulted in their "objective" tone. Hence, while "the Arab online audience saw a war with high human cost and heavy military and civilian casualties," the US–British spectators viewed a "clean" war, "where efficient and precise Coalition weapons were used to help liberate the Iraqi people and open up possibilities for growth and national development" (Dimitrova and Connolly-Ahern 2007, 163).

Media coverage of the 2003 Iraq War seems to reflect narrative frameworks and patterns of discourse that resonate within different culture-specific journalistic ethical codes. For example, while *The Dawn* (Pakistan) and *The Times* (India) put more focus on the "harsh and cruel war," the US–British "quality" broadsheets (*Times, The Guardian* and *NYT*) considered the coverage of Iraqi civilian casualties ethically improper (Ravi 2005, 59). Besides, the need to support "our" troops during war became an unquestionable "value" (ibid.). While Pakistani and Indian newspapers stressed the human cost of the war, *NYT* focused on the "rapid advance of the American and British troops and the Iraqi army melting away without much of a fight" (ibid., 58). More significantly, only *The Dawn* gave some credence to the "tough Iraqi resistance" and "images of civilian deaths caused by the coalition attacks" (ibid.). On the other hand, *The Times* (London) fully supported the pro-war stance and fervently criticized anti-war political dissent in the British parliament in its editorials (see also Sahlane 2019). When the bombs started falling on Baghdad, *The Guardian*'s vehement anti-war tone faded away (ibid., 57). Only *The Dawn* quality newspaper spoke "in terms of America unleashing its terror on the Iraqi people in its editorial" (ibid.). *The Times* (India) seemed to have "no dog in the fight" and remained mostly "neutral."

This "culturalist" approach to media coverage of the 2003 US invasion of Iraq was also corroborated by Maslog et al.'s (2006) study. The authors investigated "442 stories from seven English-language Asian daily newspapers and one news agency from five countries" (Maslog et al. 2006, 26). The news media from the non-Muslim countries (India and Sri Lanka) showed

---

[3] The "rebuilding" of Iraq should be understood within the military-industrial complex context, which implies the "destruction" of Iraq's infrastructure to create jobs for US companies.

a significantly higher support for the invasion than did their Muslim counterparts (Pakistan and Indonesia, but not the Philippines). More significantly, while the foreign wire stories were clearly supportive of the war, the locally produced stories portrayed the Iraqis more favorably and were more critical of the war coalition.

Media echoing of official political perspectives was also revealed in Dimitrova et al.'s (2005) content analysis of how online media in 246 news websites (newspapers, TV/radio news stations) from 48 countries differentially covered the first night of the US 2003 War on Iraq. The study found that "[m]ore than 33 percent of the coverage in countries not supporting the war was negative as opposed to only 15 percent in countries officially supporting the war" (Dimitrova et al. 2005, 32). More interestingly, the US websites predominantly constructed war as mere *domesticated* stories about US soldiers' families, their frustration, and their prayers in church services for their relatives who were joining the war in Iraq (ibid., 35–37). This surreal *victim/perpetrator reversal* strategy was motivated by the need to put a local spin on news stories to be able to sell them well to the local audience. Similarly, Dimitrova's (2006) content analysis of *The Australian* (online edition) showed that there was "very little discussion about the reasons for [the 2003 Iraq] war" (Dimitrova 2006, 122). The paper also offered very little discussion of the "responsibility" attribution. The "antiwar protest" frame was muted despite the vocal anti-war sentiment that existed, particularly among students (ibid., 123). Therefore, "the reporting was in sync with the national foreign policy, celebrating victory and praising the success of allied troops on their mission in Iraq" (ibid., 123).

In the same vein, Kristensen and Ørsten (2007) conducted a seventeen-day content analysis of Danish media coverage of the 2003 Iraq War. The study concluded that despite the widespread public opposition to a war without UN mandate and the elite differences of opinion present in the Danish parliament, the Danish newspapers and electronic media often downplayed anti-war dissent, especially from the Franco-German side (Kristensen and Ørsten 2007, 333). Besides, at the beginning of the war, the Danish political opposition "swore a public oath of silence" and the war coalition gained the most access to the media (ibid., 334). The use of inexpert official sources by the Danish media contributed to the image of a "cleaner" war, wherein "neither the text nor the visuals told the story of the human casualties of the war" (ibid., 332).

Robertson's (2004) content analysis of *The Herald* and *The Scotsman* (and their Sunday sisters) lends further support to the argument that media were biased in their coverage of the 2003 Iraq War. The study revealed that most of the reporting was about the "military achievements or movements" of the US–British troops. The suffering of Iraqi people, caught amidst the massive "Shock and Awe" bombing campaign, received scant media attention. All the four newspapers "have failed in aspects of their watchdog role" (Robertson 2004,

475) because, compared to web-based news outlets and forums, "they did not report at a level commensurate with the massive 'collateral' damage to the Iraqi environment and its people" (ibid.).

Such biased coverage of the 2003 Iraq War seems to be partly the direct result of embedded reporting. While embedded journalists provided a major portion of Western media coverage of the war, they tended to be more likely to develop a "camaraderie" relationship with the US–British military in a way that discounted objective reporting (Kuypers and Cooper 2005; Haigh et al. 2006). Therefore, given the swell of "patriotism," the clear alignment of the media with political elite interests, and the "integration of the media into the military industrial complex" (Kumar 2006, 49–50), the American TV networks "presented exultant and triumphant accounts that trumped any paid propagandist. The embedded US network television reporters were gung-ho cheerleaders and spinners for the US and UK military and lost all veneer of objectivity" (Kellner 2004, 55). This war information management was also extended to the photographic representation of the Iraqi conflict, as shown in what follows.

4.3 Performative Media War Images and the Pragmatics of Visual Narrative

In today's highly mediatized conflicts, wars are no longer fought only on the battlefields; they are also waged and won through strategic narratives deployed in visual argumentation embedded in media rhetoric ("image warfare"). The ideological power of the visual image is very instrumental, in that graphic imagery can be strategically deployed to mobilize support for one's self-interest through engaging the emotions of the target audience. Hence, emotional appeal is increasingly visual because images are more credible, and thus can capture more attention and outlast the verbal argument. Besides, media effect studies credit news photographs with high memorability and impact on reader assessment of political conflicts (Pfau et al. 2008). In other words, the scholarship reviewed below indicates that visual narratives can be weaponized to gain a strategic advantage over the enemy. In what follows, the reviewed literature explores how graphic news framing can be rhetorical and action-oriented (performative) in that visual images constitute stances in arguments deployed to Orientalize the Iraqi/Muslim cultural "Others."

Fahmy (2005, 2010) content analyzed the photographic portrayal of the 9/11 attacks and the US retaliatory bombing of Afghanistan in the English-language newspaper *The International Herald Tribune* (*IHT*) and the Arabic-language newspaper *Al-Hayat*. The study showed that while *IHT* endorsed the pro-war frame through highlighting "guilt in the 9/11 attack by showing visual messages that humanized the victims" (images of mourning, funerals, mug shots of the deceased), it sanitized the bombing of Afghans by suppressing images of human suffering (not "a single image of casualty and loss of life" was published and focus was more on "humanitarian aid," "patriotism" and weaponry) (Fahmy 2005, 385; Fahmy 2010, 711). Similarly, *Al-Hayat* showed images of Afghan casualties, refugees, and humanitarian crisis while it only presented "fewer images of [US] people mourning" and focused more on "images of material destruction" of the 9/11 attacks (Fahmy 2010, 711). Hence, such contrasting visual narratives failed to (re)humanize the other. For example, while *IHT* published a photograph of a Palestinian guerrilla man and a few children from the Ain al-Hilweh refugee camp in Lebanon celebrating the 9/11 attacks (hence constructing Palestinians as unworthy of empathy), *Al-Hayat* newspaper showed photographs of Syrian women mourning at a church and Muslim Iranians holding candles memorializing the 9/11 victims. Therefore, though the editorial gatekeepers of the two papers used the same source (Reuters), they selected image representations that would perfectly serve their ideological stance (Fahmy 2005, 396; Fahmy 2010, 712).

Editorial "perspectivation" of news is more conspicuous in the case of the 2003 Iraq War. For example, in the lead-up to the 2003 Iraq War, *Delo* (the Slovenian daily newspaper) focused on the US–British military superiority, in sharp contrast to the scare images of Saddam's threatening "hordes." During the military assault on Iraq, *Delo*'s editors erased the graphic face of civilian casualties and only showed images of the "advancing troops, tanks and airplanes" (Trivundza 2004, 488). Images of larger groups of Iraqi civilians being captured and guarded by a small number of US soldiers invoked the Orientalist stereotype that Iraqi/Muslim bodies should constantly be stopped and searched to impede their propensity for "terrorism." With the capture of Baghdad (and in keeping with Orientalist frames), images of "looters" of the Iraqi archaeological museum and historical libraries served to reinforce these racialist anti-Muslim stereotypes. For example, "[p]hotographs depict an elderly woman carrying an office chair or a young boy pushing his booty in front of US tanks" (ibid., 489). Iraqi women (on behalf of whom the war was allegedly waged) were reduced to the snapshot of images of faceless, nameless, and burqa-clad nonentities. These "shapeless black silhouettes covered from head to toe" (ibid., 490) were portrayed as the gendered Iraqi Other in terms of their sexual availability, conquest, and dominance (Trivundza 2004, 492). Images of "self-torturing" (*Shi'i*) Iraqis, who were wearing "traditional" garb were portrayed as "passive subjects, demonstrating or performing religious rituals or mourning" (ibid., 491). The "desacralization of the regime's symbols" provided the climactic closure to the "Road to Baghdad" drama (ibid., 488), which also "dominated the British TV news for three weeks" (Lewis 2004, 307). Similarly, *The Australian* newspaper featured images of the Iraqi prisoners of war (POWs), guarded by "responsible" and "caring" US troops (who handed in bottles of water). Personalized Americans were also depicted as brave soldiers, in control of the situation (by showing them pointing guns at Iraqi POWs, who were kneeling or lying on the ground). The paper also ran the "staged" picture of the toppled Saddam statue (Dimitrova 2006, 116).

The Othering of Iraqi women is also manifest in the way visual depictions of emancipated women were totally absent in *Delo*'s visual depiction of Saddam's modern Iraq (Trivundza 2004). Such culturally bound images (considering the *veil/burqa* as a symbol of "backwardness") resonate with the US rhetoric of "liberating" Afghan women from the repressive Taliban regime. However, after the US removal of the Taliban, Afghan women continued to wear their burqas, a culturally rooted symbol of their identity (Fahmy 2004). Therefore, *Associated Press* wire photographs showed visual framing of imperiled Afghan women in less stereotypical roles through "visual cues of camera angles, focus, social distance and women's role" (Fahmy 2004: 106). Staged photographs of Afghani women casting off the burqa captured much Western media attention to justify the endless US unilateralist militarist intervention in the Muslim world (ibid., 108).

In the same vein, Brown (2006) found that "[t]he pro-war papers emphasised Iraqi barbarity" (Brown 2006, 104). While *The Sun* showed images of the US prisoners with a caption "at mercy of savages," *The Times* portrayed US forces as "brave" and "caring." Conversely, *The Times* depicted Iraqi soldiers as "disloyal" and "cowardly" as they allegedly used Iraqi civilians as "human shields" and attacked American forces "from behind" (ibid.). The implication is to justify "collateral" costs to Iraqi civilians. While *The Sun* showed no Iraqi civilians, *The Times* featured only one story of a Bedouin, who tried to "bribe" the coalition soldiers for water and food. He looked like a "suicide bomber" (ibid., 105). "This painted a picture of Iraqis as primitive, untrustworthy, and only interested in personal gain" (ibid.). Conversely, *The Guardian* had three main articles describing Iraqi civilian victims (ibid.). However, the paper that lengthily exposed the human suffering was *The Mirror*. It showed photographs of a "burned baby," "an Iraqi man carrying an unconscious girl with severe leg trauma," a "mother ... with her injured screaming baby," two "Iraqi soldiers' bodies ... in a trench with a white flag clearly visible," and "a blood-soaked Iraqi victim" (ibid., 105). However, *The Mirror* did not hide its "admiration for British troops," while portraying Iraqis as helpless victims (ibid.). *The Guardian* remained "the only newspaper that gave Iraqis a credible voice, although this emphasised Iraqi powerlessness" (ibid., 106). Therefore, "barbarity, incompetence, and weakness" were the main traits assigned to Iraqis by the British print media. This was achieved "as much by what was left out of stories as what was included" (ibid., 108).

Conversely, the 2003 Iraq War discourse portrayed US–British soldiers as professional "peacekeepers," and "humanitarian" aid workers who acted "more decently and humanely" (Machin 2007, 131) while patrolling the streets of Baghdad. They were also depicted as "caring" people, who wrote letters to their families back home. Unlike the Iraqi unruly militia/rebel groups (dressed in "Islamic" civilian clothes), the US–British armed forces were well equipped and well trained (ibid. 131). Iraqi "insurgents" seemed to fight for no real political cause; they were simply "enemies of freedom" (ibid., 132). More interestingly, Iraqi civilians were deagentivized (they were merely involved in praying, mourning, carrying coffins, protesting en masse or simply standing around and watching the US troops pass by). The only "individualized" Iraqis were mainly women and children (through close-up shots). These "suppressed" Iraqi women (wearing black "*abayas*") and the "neglected" Iraqi children were used as symbolic icons to show the corruption of the Iraqi regime (ibid., 130). Therefore, "[j]ust as we do not see middle class Iraqis, we do not really see Iraq" (ibid., 138). Unlike in Vietnam (where images of war atrocities were rendered public), the 2003 Iraq War battle scenes were reduced to mere decontextualized and blurred images of distant places inhabited by the "enemies of democracy" (Machin 2007, 138). These images were carved mainly to appeal to the viewers' emotions, rather than to inform or record historical events (ibid.).

More inconsistently, there was "a lack of fit between the verbal and the visual texts in both the CBS and BBC images, often a verbal text referring to corpses or the dead is accompanied by images of burning tanks" (Lipson 2009, 154). Images of coalition soldiers displayed "green night vision in which combat is surreal and the soldiers seem to be firing into green space, often against unseen targets" (ibid., 154–155). Hence, "[b]roadcasters found themselves irresistibly drawn into the action-packed drama of a war against a rarely seen enemy: if Iraqi civilians were enigmatic, the Iraqi soldiers were almost invisible – rarely seen or discussed, but generally assumed to be supportive of Saddam Hussein" (Lewis 2004, 305). Similarly, little visual coverage of the "actual combat activity of any kind" was displayed in *The Guardian* and *NYT* (Fahmy and Kim 2008, 454). In this sense, Abu Ghraib images "may be the only real imagery" (Machin 2007, 138) of the war that was leaked into the public sphere.[4]

Griffin's (2004) study of the photographic representation of the 1991 Iraq War, the 9/11 events and the 2003 US-led invasion of Iraq lends more credence to the news media bias. Griffin's investigation of an inventory of "photographs published in *Time*, *Newsweek*, and *US News* and *World Report*" (Griffin 2004,

---

[4] "The US media would be willing to show graphic images in cases where these images were deemed too newsworthy to ignore" (Johnson and Fahmy 2010, 47).

387) revealed that the US war photojournalism framed the 1991 Iraq War within the "American myth of providential supremacy" (ibid.). The US magazines also promoted "an impression of on-the-ground, first-hand recording of events" (ibid., 383), even though the coverage of real combat operations was marginalized (3% of published photographs) (ibid., 386). The "cataloguing" of the "US weapons arsenal" (23%) and US "troops in non-combat situations" (14%) were the major war images (ibid., 385). Similarly, the US-led 2003 invasion of Iraq provoked the same "dominant visual discourse," despite the presence of embedded reporters within the US military units: "we saw an overwhelming and unstoppable American military machine relentlessly roll across Iraq to Baghdad" (Griffin 2004, 397). The "Road to Baghdad" theme overshadowed all the other images of "collateral damage" and human suffering. Embedded reporting "further reinforced a purely American-centered perspective" (ibid.). On the other hand, the news coverage of the 9/11 attacks highlighted "the spectacle of explosions and fires and the scale of destruction and suffering" (Griffin 2004, 388). The heroic "rescue efforts," the mobilization of "aid efforts" gained more media salience through accounts of "volunteers," "aid campaigns" and "blood donations." Besides, "secondary effects" (e.g., "disruption of economic activity," "the suffering of the survivors, and the families of the victims") also gained some prominence. In contrast, "images of the destruction and human cost resulting from American military action [during the 1991 Iraq War] were largely absent" (ibid., 392). Most images of the military action were "canned" and were constructed outside Iraq. Hence, news media simply helped "advertise and celebrate the scope and reach of US military technology and power" (ibid., 385). These photographs served mainly "to prime viewers towards certain dominant discourse paradigms and frames of interpretation" (ibid., 399). They "more often reinforce preconceived notions and stereotypes than reveal new information or provide new perspectives" (ibid.).

Similarly, Wells (2007) found that during the 2003 invasion of Iraq, *The Guardian* displayed images of innocent "lone" Iraqi children "standing on an abandoned Iraqi tank" and "giving the victory salute" under the "protecting gaze of a soldier" (Wells 2007, 63). The images of "children taking food parcels from the back of a military truck" (ibid., 62) constructed coalition soldiers as "humanitarian" agents, despite their military uniforms. Conversely, Iraqi adults were constructed as "missing carers," whose role was taken by the British troops. More absurdly, the erasure of the historical and sociopolitical reality of the unfolding events rendered the Iraqi children's plight more attributable to parental neglect or to a "human condition" rather than being the direct result of the US invasion (ibid., 66). Conversely, *The Daily Mirror*'s iconography clearly confronted the readers with the "brutal realities of the invasion" (ibid., 69). Hence, "its narrative was one of *shame* about what was being done '*in our name*'" (ibid., 68; italics added). A story headlined "Images to explode myths of war" accompanying a photo of a burned baby, who was screaming in pain after the bombing of Baghdad, argued that,

> We are not being given the full truth. We see screaming babies in ramshackle hospitals, stripped bare of supplies by a dozen years of medicine sanctions, and we despair at the lie that this war is a humanitarian mission to help a stricken people. We see innocent civilians killed and maimed in their dilapidated homes, and we just don't know why it is happening in our name. (Wells 2007, 65)

Therefore, the strategic performativity of the rhetorical use of images is clear in that photographic accounts of the 2003 US-led invasion of Iraq aim at Othering the Iraqi "enemy." For instance, while *The Guardian* allowed the viewing of victims of the Tsunami disaster in South East Asia (dead children and their grieving parents) in its reports, it did not show even "a single image of a dead child" in its coverage and "parents are absent from every picture of an injured child" (Wells 2007, 58). Media double-standards seem to operate in full synchronization with the national foreign policy (ibid., 59). As Fahmy and Kim (2008) pointed out, "newspapers covered the Iraq War largely according to the level of military involvement and public opinion in their respective country, regardless of the political leaning of their news organizations and the level of importance of the issue being covered" (Fahmy and Kim 2008, 458).

The stereotypical depiction of Iraqis was also extended to TV visual texts about the 2003 Iraq War, which "tend to portray [Iraqi] women as the embodiment of sadness, despair [and] helplessness" (Lipson 2009, 152). Iraqi women were reduced to their sexualized reproductive functions through "de-agentivization" (depoliticized, they became mere "bare live"). When assigned active roles, Iraqi women were reduced to "begging" for water from the coalition forces. In addition, they were cast in roles with which they are stereotypically associated – "the bearers of emotion and feelings" (ibid.). More interestingly, "television participate[d] in the legitimation of the [2003 Iraq War] not by overt propaganda, but through strategies of aestheticisation that represent[ed] the war as a spectacular operation rather than a political fact with humanitarian implications" (Chouliaraki 2005, 3). The BBC World footage of the 2003 aerial attacks on Baghdad suppressed "the emotional, ethical and political issues that lie behind the bombardment of Baghdad" (ibid., 147). This detached "voyeuristic" perspective presented the spectator with a cinematic view of the bombing of the Iraqi capital "not as a scene of suffering," but as "a site of intense military action without agency," "full of spectacularity and striking action" (ibid., 153). Therefore, the Iraqi civilian victims were stripped of their "humanity" by describing them in terms of "non-living targets of coalition fire" (ibid., 152). Such "impersonalization" constructed Iraqis as (Ministry) building(s), Iraqi "positions" and Iraqi "leadership's seats of power." There was "no reference to the Iraqi as a human being, either in language or in image" (ibid., 152).

Instances of "agent concealment" also took the form of "intransitivity" ("[American forces] are pushing on and take ground"), "agentivization" (the inanimate noun can become agentivized in examples like "[buildings] were still ablaze and still under attack"), "passivization" ("[anything that could be an Iraqi position] was targeted") and "nominalization" (e.g., the nominals "heavy fire," "anti-missile flare," and "explosions" become agentive through the process of assigning them the characteristics of processes and actions represented in verbs. This identity "erasure" that failed to "semiotize the persecutor," was meant to cleanse the invaders from any blame attribution. This "radical effacement" of human agency "is a form of power that television exercises in order to constitute the public realm of appearance on the basis of exclusion, be this linguistic exclusion or, even more tellingly, exclusion of the imagery of suffering" (Chouliaraki 2005a, 152).

Similarly, the avoidance of graphic imagery was in line with the official media censorship directives because TV news stories with visual footage of combat could considerably undermine viewers' support for US military presence in Iraq, compared to stories lacking footage (Pfau et al. 2008, 318). Hence, while the Pentagon requires journalists to seek a signed consent from wounded US soldiers before publishing images of them, the release of close-up gruesome death photographs of Saddam's two murdered sons, Qusay and Uday, easily made their way to the media (Entman et al. 2010, 198).[5] It seems that Iraqi victims of atrocity were deemed unworthy of sympathy. These images were widely disseminated across the global media. How Western media make sense of images of distant suffering has a political and ideological dimension in that what made these images publishable is that such killings "offered visually compelling images, symbolized much-desired progress, and above all, offered emotionally gratifying victory against a personalized enemy" (ibid., 199). However, Saddam's videos (e.g., when he was undertaking a medical exam for head lice after his capture and the subsequently leaked hanging video (December 30, 2006)) all served as means to humiliate a pan-Arabist Muslim leader, who had been widely respected in the Arab world. Hence, Saddam's "walk up to the gallows" could only undermine Bush's rhetoric about the US championing of human rights, decency, justice and "rule of law" since these visual strategic narratives could be read as "trophy and humiliation images and as unjust retribution as part of an illegitimate war" (Swimelar 2018, 190).

The justification of the crushing violence of the US oppressor is enacted through the dehumanization of the Iraqi enemy and the representation of

---

[5] Conversely, Western media censured the showing of the gruesome "charred and battered remains of four US contractors hanging from a bridge in Fallujah" (Johnson and Fahmy 2010, 46).

Arabs as "killable," and their death as "ungrievable."[6] For example, a notorious Abu Ghraib photograph showed "Sabrina Harman inanely grinning and giving the thumbs-up over the body of [an Iraqi] man beaten to death" (Carrabine 2011, 17)[7]. Like in Nazi camps, US soldiers rejoiced in documenting their ritualized atrocities against Iraqi civil detainees in Abu Ghraib (Swimelar 2018, 183). The torture photographs are "compositions, containing motifs, which place them in a much larger field of representation – where the victorious pose with the vanquished to gratify the violence of the oppressor" (Carrabine 2011, 6).

It seems that Western visual media gatekeepers disseminated distressing images of Iraqi/Muslim "Others" as a sort of "perverse entertainment" to satisfy their imagined "public's morbid curiosity and unsavoury need for 'atrocity porn'" (Byford 2018, 289), in a way that "mandated engagement with visual material that was often constructed as too repulsive to watch" (ibid., 294). For example, "the promiscuous voyeuristic" trophy snapshots of the "vanquished" Iraqi enemy taken at Abu Ghraib showed

> scenes of US soldiers inflicting atrocities upon helpless captives and inanely grinning as they pose behind piles of twisted, naked bodies. Other notorious images include the hooded man on the box, a female soldier leading a naked prisoner on a leash, dogs poised to attack yet more naked detainees, while others are forced to wear women's underwear and masturbate for the camera or are coerced into simulated sexual positions. (Carrabine 2011, 6)

These sexualized images of violence clearly bear witness to the construction of the racialized Iraqi/Muslim body as a site of "enslaveability," queer erotics and gratuitous violence. This "ritualized" enactment of power or "pornotroping"[8] (turning the Iraqi captive body into a site of enjoyment) echoes other forms of dehumanizing acts of representation of the enemy's body (e.g., the naked African slaves posing on auction blocks or being lynched while

---

[6] BBC Director of News, Richard Sambrook, argued that he would tolerate close-ups of dead bodies of the Iraqis (maybe because Iraqis/Muslims are anaesthetically "desensitized" due to overexposure to political violence in the Muslim World), but not those of the British soldiers (cited in Petley 2003, 75). The US "military had banned photos of flag-draped coffins of America's war dead since the First Gulf War" (Johnson and Fahmy 2010, 46). Consequently, when *Al Jazeera*'s English site posted the videos of the captured and burned bodies of Blackwater contractors in Fallujah during the US-led war on Iraq in 2003, its reporters were banned from the floor of the New York Stock Exchange and *Al Jazeera* (English site) was hacked. The argument was that rendering such graphic images irrevocably public (though they were authentic) violated the norms of journalistic ethics of decency. *Al Jazeera* was also accused of being the "mouthpiece" of Al-Qaeda by allegedly fomenting anti-American sentiment and conveying "coded terrorist recruiting messages" (Jordan 2007, 284–286).

[7] Similarly, the taking of images of the humiliating capture of Saddam Hussein (the unkempt aging man), his mouth examination and the camera footage as he stood at the gallows sought to showcase the US jingoistic dominance over the Iraqi "enemy."

[8] See Spillers (2003, 334).

surrounded by cheering white onlookers). Hence, these images of the tormented Iraqi body resonated with the US "colonial rhetoric of master and slave" (Carrabine 2011, 14). The faces of the victims were erased in these "pornotropic" images as they were "hidden beneath hoods, women's underwear or excrement" (ibid., 15) in order not to provoke any "empathic" or "ethical" response towards the victims. Besides, attention was drawn to the perpetrators, who were amused by ritualizing their strong bonds of "camaraderie" through the aestheticization of their orgies of inflecting sexual abuse on Iraqi prisoners. Hence,

The spectacular inscription of violent subjugation marks the boundaries between "us" and "them", ranks bodies within the larger social order, and helps turn socially recognized categories of difference, such as race, gender, sexuality and religion, into bodily difference. (Richter-Montpetit 2014, 52)

The use of sexualized torture in Abu Ghraib is grounded in "racialized scripts that constitute these bodies and spaces as violable and disposable" (ibid., 56). While the "sneering" Bali bombers were represented in Western mainstream media as "hateful and vengeful madmen with unclear motives for their violence against the west" (Philpott 2005, 237) (which implies that assailants were motivated by a desire not merely to hurt Western tourists, but "unthinking violence is integral to Muslim culture and identity" (ibid.)), no such denunciations have been articulated with respect to the Abu Ghraib images of the "shameless gloating" of the US perpetrators (ibid.). Infamously, the US military tried to rationalize the legitimacy of inhumane and degrading treatment of Iraqi prisoners by invoking the rhetoric of "moral obligation" to save American lives (Carrabine 2011, 19), and thus "enhanced interrogation" was fallaciously framed as an "act of national self-defence" (Richter-Montpetit 2014, 51).[9] More seriously, the US military medical personnel "failed to provide basic health care" and collaborated by "designing and implementing psychologically and physically coercive interrogations" (Miles 2004, 728). They also "falsified medical records and death certificates" (Clark 2006, 570).[10] Hence, the suffering of Iraqi Others was either totally silenced through absence of ethical conscience (as in the Abu Ghraib scandal) or ironically represented as charitable benevolence through individualized "rescue" stories (e.g., the case of the 12-year-old Iraqi boy, Ali Ismaeel Abbas, described below).

---

[9] As many terrorism experts had noted, the use of torture and brutal "enhanced interrogation" techniques to collect intelligence was ineffective and futile because most detainees were "Mickey Mouse" prisoners and "the USA's post-9/11 global torture regime yielded not a single documented case of actionable data" (Richter-Montpetit 2014, 45).

[10] For example, "In November 2003, Iraqi Major General Mowhoush's head was pushed into a sleeping bag while interrogators sat on his chest. He died; medics could not resuscitate him, and a surgeon stated that he died of natural causes" (Clark 2006, 573).

The anti-war cross-national news media challenged the depiction of the 2003 invasion of Iraq as a war of "liberation." For example, the war photos in the Greek press portrayed the US–British soldiers as "faceless" and "emotionless" war machines inflicting "carnage" on "unarmed" "innocent" Iraqi "civilians." However, Iraqis were also constructed as a "potential threat" (angry faces of "turbaned" armed crowds, presence of "mujahideen kamikazes," "Jihad") (Kostantinidou 2008, 149). However, photos of global anti-war protest and scenes of colossal destruction (e.g., a "photo of victims dragged out from demolished buildings by civilians") helped to mobilize against the war.[11] The rhetorical use of visual images of war atrocity performed a strategic moral framing purpose, that of "moral obligation" to feel shamed into doing something to stop the US unjust war against innocent Iraqi civilians. An iconic photo(story) was that of Ali Ismaeel Abbas, the Iraqi 12-year-old child, who had been asleep when a US missile attack hit his home and had both his arms blown off. Ali lost his father, mother (who was five months pregnant), a brother and fourteen siblings. Ali's tragedy was constructed in the Anglo-American mainstream newspaper and political narratives as a "rescue" story (with a happy ending). Ali was flown to Britain to receive "superior" specialized medical care at the hands of British expert surgeons (Kostantinidou 2008, 152).

In today's highly competitive media market, what makes a news image more salient and memorable is its "strategic maneuvering" and "performative" power. While print media frames constructed their readers by evoking shared cognitive schemata about "us" and "them," photographic war discourse defined its public through acts of spectatorship. For example, while the symbolic toppling of Saddam signified a perfect staged "Kodak moment," seemingly justifying the war, the shocking Abu Ghraib images of US soldiers sadistically inflicting torture upon helpless Iraqi detainees and the eroticizing of their bodies in pain contested the "rescue" argument.[12] While the pro-war media might have strived to frame the way the Iraq conflict would be collectively remembered through appealing to textual and visual narratives that propagate the US "humanitarian" narrative, the audience may continue to read these images critically, against their original intentions. Photographic/textual representations enter into a relationship of a "dialectic of exchange and resistance" (Andén-Papadopoulos 2008, 10), as Table 4.1 shows.

---

[11] For example, the gaze of a wounded child in a photograph entitled "The soundless cry of a child" functioned as "a metonym of the Iraqi people looking directly towards the (western) readers" as if telling them "'I dare you' (to care, to respond), backed up with the 'Shame on you' (for refusing), performative speech act" (Kostantinidou 2008, 152).

[12] The photographing of the systematic brutal and humiliating sexual torture scenes at Abu Ghraib was a strategy to blackmail Iraqi prisoners into spying for the US. However, such moral degeneracy and disregard for human integrity went unpunished (Carrabine 2011, 9–10).

Table 4.1 *Iraq War media frames*

Pro-war frame	Anti-war frame
Tone of reporting - Adopted a more pro-war perspective ("liberation"/ "war on terror" arguments). - Reinforcing towards coalition actors and deflating towards Iraqi political actors. - Abundant use of official sources. - Positive definition of the situation (war of "liberation").	**Tone of reporting** - Denounced the war (the "occupation frame"). - Deflating and critical towards coalition actors. - Negative definition of the situation (the "war of aggression" argument). - "Rally round the flag" persisted even amongst the anti-war coalition news media.
Sources - Depended heavily on US government/ military officials as sources of information (perspectivization strategy). - Independent experts, aid workers, environmentalists or human rights activists and international organizations were denied voice.	**Sources** - Abundant use of coalition official sources by most coalition news media. - Use of more Iraqi/Arab sources by Arab/ Muslim news outlets. - Reliance on more Iraqi/international sources for news stories & tendency to use more live reporting and footage from Iraqi and Arab TV channels. - More favorable portrayal of Iraqis in locally produced stories than in foreign wire stories.
Subject agenda - Pro-war editorial content (focus on battlefield operations and war strategy /sophisticated weaponry topics and "coalition heroics"). - Marginalization/vilification of domestic and global anti-war protests. - Disregard for morality and legality issues. - Focus on Iraqi "looting" activities (racialist stereotypes).	**Subject agenda** - Anti-war editorial content: "moral/ legal responsibility attribution." - Stories of global anti-war dissent. - Depiction of military "assault" as failure of diplomacy. - Coverage of a mounting tough Iraqi resistance. - The inadequacy of allied war planning/ the vulnerability of the Allies' long supply lines.
Civilian casualties - Little media coverage of Iraqi civilian casualties. - Depiction of war as mere spectacle and striking action (not as a scene of suffering and human agency). - Attribution of responsibility for civilian casualties to Iraqi "coward" "tactics" (alleged use of Iraqi civilians as "human shields"). - Emphasis on US high-tech "precision" bombing. - Iraqi civilian casualties described in military parlance as "collateral damage."	**Civilian casualties** - The prioritization of the coverage of human suffering and the damage inflicted upon the infrastructure of Iraq (e.g., *Al Jazeera* TV channel). - Portrayal of Iraqi civilians as helpless victims (personal stories), with responsibility attributed to coalition forces. - Scenes of colossal destruction and "collateral damage" of war (shocking graphic images). - Visual messages that (re)humanized the Iraqi victims (portraying their emotions of fear and their suffering).

Table 4.1 (*cont.*)

Pro-war frame	Anti-war frame
Military actors - Positive visual coverage of the Iraq ground war (the portrayal of coalition forces as "brave" and "caring"). - Negative representation of Iraqi soldiers ("disloyal," "cowardly," "unruly," guerilla group. - Domestication of stories: bravery and heroism of deceased soldiers/family prayers in church services.	**Military actors** - Coalition forces depiction as "invaders." - Families questioning the reasons for war ("not in our name" protests). - Mounting Iraqi insurgency/resistance.
Humanitarian issues - Depiction of US/coalition troops as "caring" "humanitarian" aid providers (winning "hearts and minds"). - Some anti-war papers prescribed to this perspective in their visual narratives (e.g., *The Guardian*, see Wells 2007).	**Humanitarian issues** - Representation of US "humanitarian" interventionism as war of aggression. - Failure to deliver aid (interruptions to utility infrastructure, penury of food supplies, physical insecurity for Iraqi civilians).
War rationale - Military: curbing Iraq's weapons of mass destruction (WMD) capability (presupposing Saddam had WMD he could pass to terrorist groups). - Moral: bringing freedom and democracy to Iraqis ("villains" vs. "noble" guys narrative).	**War rationale** Military: challenging the WMD claim and Saddam's ties with Al-Qaeda. Humanitarian: contestation of the humanitarian narrative for the war (US imperialism, "blood for oil").
Media ethics ("graphic imagery") - US full control over images and their usage. - The intentional absence of evidentiary images of Iraqi suffering and Abu Ghraib abuse (denial strategy); canned, unrealistic and decontextualized images of war. - Absence of news media depictions of the impact of war on Iraqi women and children (only Orientalist portrayals in terms of Otherness, essentialism, and stereotypical representation).	**Media ethics ("graphic imagery")** - The right to the image that tells the story in a more "objective" way. - Contextualized visual representation of actual combat activities and human suffering. - Images calling into question the US militarist "humanitarianism." - Different cultural, political, organizational, and audience-related factors determine the visual news framing process.

4.4   Conclusion

US–British viewers have been conditioned to see the world in pre-packaged news frames that flout the central tenets of journalistic ethical codes of "factuality" and "impartiality." The pro-war news media's crucial effect in organizing a picture of the 2003 Iraq War was achieved through media framing in which US/coalition media failed to enable greater spaces for diversity of perspective and sources of information. The type of schematic images that were invoked catered to the ideological positioning of readers/viewers in text. Hence, media (visual) texts were mere "ideological icebergs" in that the stock of topoi, stories and textual/visual frames simply produced a hegemonic Orientalist discourse that does not simply reflect reality but actively seeks to shape it. The "perspectivization" strategy adhered to by pro-war news media involved filtering information by relying heaving on the official "web of facticity" sources and muting the voices of dissent, and thus media frames helped to delimit the bounds of "legitimate" controversy. The US's powerful political and military elite monopolized access to the mainstream media, and indirectly set their ideological agendas and frames by "inundating the media with stories which serve sometimes to foist a particular line and frame on the media" (Herman and Chomsky 1994, 23). This manipulation was "much a result of what was not said as it is of what was said" (Robinson and Livingston 2006, 35). Racialized stereotypical representations of cultural others often occur through the "unsaid," the visual imagery. The US government's control of the journalists' media frames served to cultivate a desired "definition of the situation" and organize focus by deflecting attention from undesirable realities to the effect of shaping the public opinion. Therefore, pro-war media stereotypically reframed the Iraq War by selectively invoking and hiding "history" in a way that reduced the reporters' responsibility to being mere conduits of US perspectives articulated in political officialdom.

Western pro-war new media's coverage of the US-led 2003 Iraq invasion tended to nurture self-glorification and neglect the "collateral damage" of war. Hence, news media framing is a clear "testimony to the West's denial of history and of its own responsibility for the instability in the Middle East" (Machin 2007, 140). Nonetheless, the ability of the Bush administration to enlist the US mainstream media in building a pro-war "consensus" (by marshalling linguistic and visual arguments that intertextually resonated with the "war on terror" rhetoric) was countered by anti-war media, which challenged the US "master frame" by arguing that brute force and daylight "plunder" (dressed up in moral garb and in the language of a "noble ideal") were part of a long Anglo-American colonialist tradition of sexualized and racialized political violence in the Middle East. "Our" violent bodily control of the Iraqi/Muslim "Others" offered the visual "proof" of "their" social subordination and racial difference. Such Orientalist textual/visual rhetoric is a mere "discourse of domination, both a product of subjugation of the Middle East, and an instrument in this process" (Halliday 2003, 200). The stereotypical characterization of the Muslim Others proceeds "not only from dominance and confrontation but also from cultural antipathy" (Said 1997, 163).

References

Aday, Sean, Livingston, Steven, and Hebert, Maeve. 2005. "Embedding the Truth: A Cross-Cultural Analysis of Objectivity and Television Coverage of the Iraq War." *Press/Politics* 10(1): 3–21.
Andén-Papadopoulos, Kari. 2008. "The Abu Ghraib Torture Photographs: News Frames, Visual Culture, and the Power of Images." *Journalism* 9(1): 5–30.
Barker, Gina G. 2012. "Cultural Influences on the News: Portrayals of the Iraq War by Swedish and American Media." *The International Communication Gazette* 74 (1): 3–22.
Brown, Judith. 2006. "Orientalism Revisited: The British Media and the Iraq War." In *Leading to the 2003 Iraq War: The Global Media Debate*, edited by Alexander G. Nikolaev and Earnest A. Hakanen, 97–111. New York: Palgrave Macmillan.
Byford, Jovan. 2018. "The Emotional and Political Power of Images of Suffering: Discursive Psychology and the Study of Visual Rhetoric." In *Discourse, Peace, and Conflict: Discursive Psychology Perspectives*, edited by Stephen Gibson, 285–302. Gewerbestrasse, Switzerland: Springer Nature.
Calabrese, Andrew. 2005. "Casus Belli: US Media and the Justification of the Iraq War." *Television and New Media*, 6(2):153–175.
Carrabine, Eamonn. 2011. "Images of Torture: Culture, Politics and Power." *Crime Media Culture* 7(1): 5–30.
Chouliaraki, Lilie. 2005. "Introduction: The Soft Power of War: Legitimacy and Community in Iraq War Discourses." *Journal of Language and Politics* 4(1): 1–10.
Chouliaraki, Lilie. 2005a. "Spectacular Ethics: On the Television Footage of the Iraq War." *Journal of Language and Politics* 4(1): 143–159.
Clark, Peter, A. 2006. "Medical Ethics at Guantanamo Bay and Abu Ghraib: The Problem of Dual Loyalty." *Journal of Law, Medicine & Ethics* 34(3): 570–580.
Dimitrova, Daniela V. 2006. "The War in Iraq: A View from Australia." In *Leading to the 2003 Iraq War: The Global Media Debate*, edited by Alexander G. Nikolaev and Earnest A. Hakanen, 115–124. New York: Palgrave Macmillan.
Dimitrova, Daniela. V. and Strömbäck, Jesper. 2005. "Mission Accomplished? Framing of the Iraq War in the Elite Newspapers in Sweden and the United States." *Gazette: The International Journal for Communication Studies* 67(5): 399–417.
Dimitrova, Daniela V, Kaid, Lynda L., Williams, Andrew Paul, and Trammell, Kaye D. 2005. "War on the Web: The Immediate News Framing of Gulf War II." *Press/Politics* 10(1): 22–44.
Dimitrova, Daniela V. and Connolly-Ahern, Colleen. 2007. "A Tale of Two Wars: Framing Analysis of Online News Sites in Coalition Countries and the Arab World During the Iraq War." *The Howard Journal of Communications* 18: 153–168.
Entman, Robert M. 1993. "Framing: Towards Clarification of a Fractured Paradigm." *Journal of Communication* 43(4): 51–58.
Entman, Robert M., Livingston, Steven, Aday, Sean, and Kim, Jennie. 2010. "Condemned to Repeat: The Media and the Accountability Gap in Iraq War

Policy." In *Public Policy and Mass Media: The Interplay of Mass Communication and Political Decision Making*, edited by Sigrid Koch-Baumgarten and Katrin Voltmer, 194–214. London: Routledge.

Fahmy, Shahira. 2004. "Picturing Afghan Women: A Content Analysis of *AP* Wire Photographs during the Taliban Regime and after the Fall of the Taliban Regime." *Gazette: The International Journal for Communication Studies* 66 (2): 91–112.

Fahmy, Shahira. 2005. "Emerging Alternatives or Traditional News Gates: Which News Sources Were Used to Picture the 9/11 Attack and the Afghan War?" *Gazette: The International Journal for Communication Studies* 67(5): 381–398.

Fahmy, Shahira. 2010. "Contrasting Visual Frames of Our Times: A Framing Analysis of English-and Arabic-Language Press Coverage of War and Terrorism." *The International Communication Gazette* 72(8): 695–717.

Fahmy, Shahira and Kim, Daekyung. 2008. "Picturing the Iraq War: Constructing the Image of War in the British and US Press." *The International Communication Gazette* 70(6): 443–462.

Goddard, Peter, Robinson, Piers, and Parry, Katy. 2008. "Patriotism Meets Plurality: Reporting the 2003 Iraq War in the British Press." *Media, War and Conflict* 1 (1): 9–30.

Griffin, Michael. 2004. "Picturing America's 'War on Terrorism' in Afghanistan and Iraq: Photographic Motifs as News Frames." *Journalism* 5(4): 381–402.

Haigh, Michel M., Pfau, Michael, and Danesi, Jamie. 2006. "A Comparison of Embedded and Nonembedded Print Coverage of the US Invasion and Occupation of Iraq." *The Harvard International Journal of Press/Politics* 11(2): 139–153.

Halliday, Fred. 2003. *Islam & the Myth of Confrontation*. New edition, London: I.B. Tauris.

Herman, Edward S. and Chomsky, Noam. 1994. *Manufacturing Consent: The Political Economy of the Mass Media*. London: Vintage.

Johnson, Thomas and Fahmy, Shahira. 2010. "'When blood becomes cheaper than a bottle of water': How Viewers of Al Jazeera's English-Language Website Judge Graphic Images of Conflict." *Media, War & Conflict* 3(1): 43–66.

Jordan, John W. 2007. "Disciplining the Virtual Home Front: Mainstream News and the Web during the War in Iraq." *Communication and Critical/Cultural Studies* 4(3): 276–302.

Kellner, Douglas. 2004. "9/11, Spectacles of Terror, and Media Manipulation: A Critique of Jihadist and Bush Media Politics." *Critical Discourse Studies* 1(1): 41–64.

Kellner, Douglas. 2004a. "Media Propaganda and Spectacle in the War on Iraq: A Critique of US Broadcasting Networks." *Cultural Studies ↔ Critical Methodologies* 4(3): 329–338.

Kostantinidou, Christina. 2008. "The Spectacle of Suffering and Death: The Photographic Representation of War in Greek Newspapers." *Visual Communication* 7(2): 143–169.

Kristensen, Nete Nørgaard and Ørsten, Mark. 2007. "Danish Media at War: The Danish Media Coverage of the Invasion of Iraq in 2003." *Journalism* 8(3): 323–343.

Kumar, Deepa. 2006. "Media, War, and Propaganda: Strategies of Information Management During the 2003 Iraq War." *Communication and Critical/Cultural Studies* 3(1): 48–69.

Kuypers, Jim A. and Cooper, Stephen D. 2005. "A Comparative Framing Analysis of Embedded and Behind-the-Lines Reporting on the 2003 Iraq War." *Qualitative Research Reports in Communication* 6(1): 1–10.

Lee, Chang-Ho. 2004. *News Coverage of the U.S. War with Iraq: A Comparison of* The New York Times, The Arab News *and* The Middle East Times. Unpublished Ph.D. dissertation, The University of Texas at Austin. ProQuest Information and Learning Company. UMI Microform Number: 3144550.

Lewis, Justin. 2004. "Television, Public Opinion and the War in Iraq: The Case of Britain." *International Journal of Public Opinion Research* 16(3): 295–310.

Lipson, Maxine. 2009. "'If It Wasn't Rolling, It Never Happened': The Role of Visual Elements in Television News." In *Evaluation and Stance in War News: A Linguistic Analysis of American, British and Italian Television News Reporting of the 2003 Iraqi War*, edited by Louann Haarman and Linda Lombardo, 140–169. London: Continuum.

Machin, David. 2007. "Visual Discourse of War: Multimodal Analysis of Photographs of the Iraq Occupation." In *Discourse, War and Terrorism*, edited by Adam Hodges and Chad Nilep, 123–142. Amsterdam: John Benjamins.

Maslog, Crispin C., Lee, Seow Ting, and Kim, Hun Shik. 2006. "Framing Analysis of a Conflict: How Newspapers in Five Asian Countries Covered the Iraq War." *Asian Journal of Communication* 16(1): 19–39.

Miles, Steven, H. 2004. "Abu Ghraib: Its Legacy for Military Medicine." *Lancet* 364: 725–729.

Nikolaev, Alexander G. and Porpora, Douglas V. 2007. "Talking War: How Elite US Newspaper Editorials and Opinion Pieces Debated the Attack on Iraq." *Sociological Focus* 40(1): 6–25.

Petley, Julian. 2003. "War without Death: Responses to Distant Suffering." *Journal for Crime, Conflict and the Media* 1(1): 72–85.

Pfau, Michael, Haigh, Michel M., Shannon, Theresa, Tones, Toni, Mercurio, Deborah, Williams, Raina, Binstock, Blanca, Diaz, Carlos, Dillard, Constance, Browne, Margaret, Elder, Clarence, Reed, Sherri, Eggers, Adam, and Melendez, Juan. 2008. "The Influence of Television News Depictions of the Images of War on Viewers." *Journal of Broadcasting & Electronic Media* 52(2): 303–322.

Philpott, Simon. 2005. "A Controversy of Faces: Images from Bali and Abu Ghraib." *Journal for Cultural Research* 9(3): 227–244.

Porpora, Douglas V. and Nicolaev, Alexander G. 2008. "Moral Muting in US Newspaper Op-Eds Debating the Attack on Iraq." *Discourse & Communication* 2(2): 165–184.

Ravi, Narasimhan. 2005. "Looking beyond Flawed Journalism: How National Interests, Patriotism, and Cultural Values Shaped the Coverage of the Iraq War." *Press/Politics* 10(1): 45–62.

Richter-Montpetit, Melanie. 2014. "Beyond the Erotics of Orientalism: Lawfare, Torture and the Racial–Sexual Grammars of Legitimate Suffering." *Security Dialogue* 45(1): 43–62.

Robertson, John W. 2004. "People's Watchdogs or Government Poodles? Scotland's National Broadsheets and the Second Iraq War." *European Journal of Communication* 19(4): 457–482.

Robinson, William L. and Livingston, Steven. 2006. "Strange Bedfellows: The Emergence of the Al Qaeda-Baathist News Frame Prior to the 2003 Invasion of Iraq." In *Leading to the 2003 Iraq War: The Global Media Debate*, edited by Alexander G. Nikolaev and Earnest A. Hakanen, 23–37. New York: Palgrave Macmillan.

Sahlane, Ahmed. 2012. "Argumentation and Fallacy in the Justification of the 2003 War on Iraq". *Argumentation* 26(4): 459–88.

Sahlane, Ahmed. 2013. "Metaphor as Rhetoric in Newspaper Op/Ed Debate of the Prelude to the 2003 Iraq War." *Critical Discourse Studies* 10(2): 54–71.

Sahlane, Ahmed. 2015. "Dialectics of Argument and Rhetoric: Protesting Iraq War in US/British Opinion Press." *Discourse & Society* 26(6): 754–74.

Sahlane, Ahmed. 2019. "Discursive (Re)Construction of the Prelude to the 2003 Iraq War in Op/Ed Press: Dialectics of Argument and Rhetoric." In *The Routledge Handbook of Language in Conflict*, edited by Lesley Jeffries, Jim O'Driscoll, and Matthew Evans, 13–43. London: Routledge.

Said, Edward W. 1997. *Covering Islam: How the Media and the Experts Determine How We See the Rest of the World*, revised edition. USA: Vintage Books.

Speer, Isaac. 2017. "Reframing the Iraq War: Official Sources, Dramatic Events, and Changes in Media Framing." *Journal of Communication* 67: 282–302.

Spillers, Hortense. 2003. *Black, White and in Color: Essays on American Literature and Culture*. Chicago, IL: University of Chicago Press.

Swimelar, Safia. 2018. "Deploying Images of Enemy Bodies: US Image Warfare and Strategic Narratives." *Media, War & Conflict* 11(2): 179–203.

Trivundza, Ilija Tomanic. 2004. "Orientalism as News: Pictorial Representation of the US Attack on Iraq in *Delo*." *Journalism* 5(4): 480–499.

Wells, Karen. 2007. "Narratives of Liberation and Narratives of Innocent Suffering: The Rhetorical Uses of Images of Iraqi Children in the British Press." *Visual Communication* 6(1): 55–71.

Wilson, John, Sahlane, Ahmed, and Somerville, Ian. 2012. "Argumentation and Fallacy in Newspaper Op/Ed Coverage of the Prelude to the Invasion of Iraq." *Journal of Language and Politics* 11(1): 1–30.

Part II

Electronic Media and Online Discourses of Conflict

5 Making a Case for War
CNN and the Representations of Humanitarianism, Gadhafi, and NATO in the 2011 Bombing of Libya

Ada Peter and Innocent Chiluwa

5.1 Introduction

The first Libyan demonstration occurred on February 15, 2011. By the same day, there were media reports that civilians were in imminent danger of being killed by the Libyan army. The United Kingdom (UK), France, and Lebanon proposed "Resolution 1973," which was subsequently adopted by the United Nations Security Council (UNSC) on March 17, 2011. They achieved the proceeding by invoking the principle of Responsibility to Protect (R2P) – a doctrine that postulates that sovereignty is not absolute. Thus, the committee of nations led by the North Atlantic Treaty Organization (NATO) validated the war in Libya – allegedly publicizing and citing "humanitarianism" to overlook Libya's sovereignty.

The action and inaction of NATO based on Resolution 1973 was criticized as loosely worded, verbose, and hastily proposed under the guise of taking "all necessary measures" towards protecting Libyan lives. However, suspicions grew over NATO's silence on the part of Resolution 1973 that provided for mediation and calls for a ceasefire. That is the part of the resolution that asserts that before considering the adoption of the R2P doctrine amongst warring factions (rebel groups and constituted Libyan army) within sovereign states like Libya, mediation and ceasefire options must have been exhausted. Hence, Hugh Roberts argues that a sober understanding of the Libyan intervention will only come to light through future work on those (which may include but are not limited to the international media) that manipulated the information (Roberts 2011, 8). In a similar argument, Maximilian Forte indicted Western powers of using media as a propaganda tool for Libya's invasion (Forte 2013, 345). The research in this chapter was sponsored by the Nordic Africa Institute, Uppsala Sweden.

5.2 Gadhafi's Libya before 2011

On gaining power in 1969 in a bloodless military coup, Muammar Gadhafi set about to tackle the unfair economic legacy of foreign domination.[1] He converted Libya into a republic governed by his *Revolutionary Command Council* and transformed the country into a new socialist state called "Jamahiriya" ("state of the masses") in 1977.[2]

Gadhafi was the first leader of an oil-producing state to challenge the oil companies' power to set prices and decide the producer governments' return. "He was the first Arab leader to realize that at a time of rising demand, power lay with the producers. Gadhafi's actions helped to energize OPEC and laid the foundation for the oil price rise of 1973. At that time, Gadhafi emerged the leader who could challenge foreign interests and shift some power from the north to the south."[3] He funded a basic and universal healthcare service and education system for Libyan children from revenue obtained from oil. He also enabled Libya to achieve the highest literacy rates in North Africa. The economic climate in Africa following the structural adjustment programs and IMF economic principles appeared to deepen exploitation, alienation, and dehumanization in Africa. According to Campbell (2013), Libya escaped the worst aspects of this market system by organizing a distributive economy.

Campbell (2013) further drew attention to an examination between Goldman Sachs and the Libyan National Oil Company, the challenge that Libyan independence posed to both oil imperialism and the dominance of NATO over the region of North Africa and the Mediterranean Sea (4). First, Libya was able to reflect alternative financing sources for its resources, and by the end of 2010, China was the top investor in Libya. As a leading producer of petroleum products, with less than 30 percent of its resources untapped, the US oil majors found Gadhafi's flirtation with non-European companies in Libya too threatening. Moreover, in the spirit of international forces opposed to the present scramble for Africa and campaigning against the militarization of Africa, Campbell (2013) argued that Gadhafi's leadership of Libya had become aggressive in its financial operations while committing to the establishment of an African Monetary Union, an African Central Bank, and an African investment bank.

Before the uprisings, Gadhafi had raised the question of nationalizing Western oil companies. The oil companies knew that Libya's nationalization of oil in the 1970s was the precursor to the Iranian nationalization in 1979 and

---

[1] "The Muammar Gadhafi Story," BBC October 21, 2011. www.bbc.com/news/world-africa-12688033.
[2] https://en.wikipedia.org/wiki/Muammar_Gaddafi.
[3] www.theguardian.com/world/2011/oct/23/libya-before-an.

Saudi Arabia's full takeover of Aramco in the mid-1980s (Campbell 2013). According to Campbell, although formal colonialism had ended in Africa, European states such as France, Belgium, and Britain sought to maintain some of their former colonial relationships that Kwame Nkrumah had described as neocolonialism.

In the 1970s and 1980s, Libya's border conflicts with Egypt and Chad, and Gadhafi's alleged support for militants and responsibility for the Lockerbie bombing in Scotland left the country isolated from the global scene. A particularly hostile relationship developed with the United States, UK, and Israel, resulting in the 1986 US bombing of Libya. The UN also imposed some sanctions. From 1999, Gadhafi ignored Arab socialism and encouraged economic privatization, rapprochement with Western nations, and Pan-Africanism (Pereira 2008). The 2011 Arab Spring protests were regarded as civil reactions to widespread corruption and unemployment in eastern Libya.

5.3   Objectives of the Study

Very few studies exist on the detailed textual structures and linguistic strategies applied by Western media (e.g., CNN) in the discursive reproduction of the framework that changed the discourse around the Libyan uprising in the West that potentially shaped the West's involvement in the Libyan uprising and civil war. We apply a discourse pragmatic analytical approach in this study and pay close attention to textual structures and discourse strategies used in CNN news between February 14, 2011 and October 31, 2011. This was the period of intense conflict between Gadhafi's forces and the "rebels" as well as NATO's military intervention in Libya. Muammar Gadhafi was captured and killed on October 20, 2011. Discourse pragmatic analysis in this study takes two forms: first, the analysis of pragmatic acts in CNN headlines and news transcripts on the Libyan civil war, and second, an examination of the language of the narratives in the description of Gadhafi during the conflict.

5.4   News Stories at War: Existing Possibilities of the CNN Effect?

The term "CNN effect" quickly dominated many discussions of media power in the 1990s. Carruthers (2011) highlighted that the phrase emerged after millions of people were so transfixed by CNN's round-the-clock war coverage that they refused to leave their living rooms and loathed missing any breaking developments. As Penley and Ross (1991) put it, the "couch potato of yore had been transformed into scud spud" (2). Susan Carruthers describes the "CNN effect" as "the capacity of images of human sufferings, delivered in real-time, to mobilize outrage worldwide, forcing national governments and international agencies to ameliorate humanitarian crisis or take up arms on behalf of beleaguered underdogs in other people's wars" (2011, 104). It implies that tough national interest calculations were now determined by CNN's "idealistic do-gooding," as lamented by George. F. Kennan – a foreign policy realist. Gilboa (2007) differs after investigating the effects of global television news on the formulation and implementation of foreign policy. While the study found no evidence to support the "CNN effect," it does present evidence and analysis of other significant effects on various phases and dimensions of policymaking. These include, among four others, how to avoid an immediate policy response to an unfolding event without being exposed as a weak leader who is confused and doesn't know how to handle a situation.

Besides studies supporting and debunking the CNN effect, other communication scholars have examined media reports about conflicts. Among many studies in the visual studies context, Ali and Fahmy (2013) reviewed the photographs of Newswire's coverage of the conflict in Gaza (2008–2009). The conclusion was that photo selections in terms of war versus peace journalism ultimately have an impact on shaping public opinion and influencing perceptions of the news event. Using the work of a Norwegian scholar, Johan Galtung, who viewed war and peace journalism as two competing frames in coverage of conflict (Galtung 1986), Lee, Maslog, and Kim (2014) analyzed 1,558 stories on the Iraq War, the Asian conflicts involving Pakistan, and India's tussle over Kashmir. They also studied Tamil Tigers in Sri Lanka, the Muslim Separatist movement in the Southern Philippine province of Mindanao, and the Aceh and Maluku civil wars in Indonesia. The results showed that the Asian newspapers used a war journalism frame in covering local conflicts but deployed a peace journalism frame in covering the Iraq War. Also, Kellner (1992), in a study of ABC, CBS, NBC, and CNN, argued that news media did not report neutrally during the 1991 Persian Gulf War. Amongst other assertions from his findings was the presence of big lies, compliant media, and yellow journalism (emphasizing sensationalism over facts).

In that work, Kellner suggests that though the United States repeatedly accused Iraq and Saddam Hussein of lying and compared the Iraqi leader to Hitler, the Bush administration itself may have systematically disseminated an unfounded accusation of Iraq to promote US war policy. Suspicious claims by the administration began with reports that the Iraqis had positioned an offensive force on the Saudi Arabian border and were poised to invade that country. For instance, on August 3, Forrest Sawyer reported on ABC's Nightline that: "tens of thousands of Iraqi troops are reportedly massed along the Saudi Arabian border, and there was still fear that Saddam Hussein will carry his blitzkrieg across Saudi territory." On Iran, Egypt, and Libya's conflicts, Ali and Fahmy (2013) examined the characteristics of gatekeeping practices by citizen journalists. The study argues that traditional "gatekeepers" continue to maintain the "status quo" regarding news about conflict zones. In a comparative analysis of the editorial column in Danish newspapers, Hjarvard and Norgaard (2014) analyzed how news media acted as a political voice during wartime in Libya, Afghanistan, and Iraq. The study "confirms the influence of elite consensus or dissensus on media coverage" and highlights other factors such as the "semi-autonomous status of newspapers as elite voice competing with other opinion-making elites" (51).

5.5   Methodology and Theory

Our use of "discourse pragmatics" or "discursive pragmatics" refers to "the platform for the pragmatic use of discourse" (Zienkowski 2011, 1) since pragmatics and discourse analysis share the same interest in the study of real-life and authentic discourses described in terms of observable language use (Chiluwa and Ajiboye 2016). We analyze "pragmatic acts" (Mey 2001) rather than "speech acts" (Austin 1962; Searle 1969); however, the former draws on the latter. In their famous speech act theory, John Austin and John Searle have argued that communication through oral language is the same as performing actions or "doing things." These include the acts of ordering, promising, requesting, or inviting – performed in specific contexts and under certain "felicity" conditions (Searle 1969). However, the "pragmatic acts" proposed by Jacob Mey are performed in all contexts (including media contexts) and are not limited to oral "speech acts." Mey (2001) argues that utterances or written communications do not merely provide information for readers and hearers; they perform pragmatics acts, usually not explicitly stated – such as implicit identification with certain people, implicit denial, or denunciation of a group or projection of cultural identity.

Mey proposes a "theory of action (for the study of pragmatic acts) that specifies, for any given situation, the limitations and possibilities of the situation" (2001, 214). Pragmatic acts are then the functions of "the agent" and "the act." In considering the agent, factors such as class, gender, age, or education become essential because they are "the resources that people dispose of as members of the community often referred to as background knowledge" (2001, 214). These resources may be characterized as "constraints and affordances imposed on the individual in the form of necessary limitations on the degree of freedom that he or she is allowed in the society" (2001, 214). In other words, individuals do not just perform speech acts on their own without reference to the context and the level of freedom or affordances that are allowed by society to perform such acts. The "act" is the language used in performing the pragmatic act regarding specific acts in specific contexts (from the individual's perspective) and the language that may be used to create the conditions for achieving a pragmatic act (from the perspective of the context). In sum, "the pragmatic acting can be considered as adapting oneself linguistically and otherwise to one's world" and "all our acts are done in that world, and within the affordances, it puts at our disposal" (215).

The discourse pragmatic study in this chapter pays close attention to persons and organizations, circumstances, events, and actions represented in CNN news headlines and transcripts about the Libyan crisis. News headlines are functional parts of news stories that go beyond the lexicon. According to Chiluwa (2007), they are pragmatically encoded to underscore some unique kinds of social meaning other than mere encapsulation of the body of the news story. Persons in the headlines are designated by expressions that refer to them not so much as particular individuals but as members of influential groups or institutions (Montgomery 2007). Thus, the description of a person proceeds, significantly, not so much by individuation (e.g., through the use of a proper name such as "Muammar Gadhafi"), but by a "membership categorization device" (MCD), (e.g., dictator) (see Housley and Fitzgerald 2002, 59–83). An MCD is always the case except in limited instances where an individual is extraordinarily well known. For events and actions, Montgomery (2007) asserts that MCDs implicate what are described as "category-bound activities" (CBA) (4). The normal application of the device usually activates a set of (stereotypical) assumptions about appropriate behaviors performed by members of a category, while circumstances in headlines routinely refer to the location of an event.

The chapter's narrative investigation explores the news story as the unit of analysis to illustrate the form and regularity of CNN narratives of Muammar Gadhafi and the Libyan conflict. The underlying premise of the narrative analysis is that narratives matter. As Mayer (2002) suggests, not that there aren't "real" interests at work, but politics is also a battle of narratives, counter-narratives, and counter-counter-narratives (4). Narratives have the power to shape beliefs, evoke emotions, and appeal to values. Another supposition is that the news headlines and stories will illustrate acts used to propagate the framework that arguably authenticated NATO's action and allegedly transformed the 2011 uprising in Libya into a civil war.

The pragmatic analyses begin by systematically categorizing the data according to types of pragmatic acts. However, to achieve a comprehensive qualitative analysis of the goal of the discourse of Western media, which are themselves either proponents or opponent of Gadhafi's death or the invasion of Libya, some (written) "speech acts" or indirect speech acts are identified. The entire research further contributes to insights into a theory of how the media construct war and manipulate public opinion.

5.5.1 Data

The data collection tracked the coverage of the conflict in Libya from February 14 to October 31, 2011. Data was collected from *CNN All Sources* on Factiva (CNN Wire, CNN International, CNN Newsroom, CNN 10). Factiva provides access to a reported 35,000 sources, including more than 3,300 US regional and international newspapers; approximately 1,200 newswires; news websites; media transcripts; blogs; and multimedia (Ryan and Simon 2014). The research deployed Factiva over LexisNexis since the former is a more extensive database than the latter.

The following strings *Gadhafi* "AND" *Libya* "AND" *NATO* "AND" *Rebels*[4] were used to run the search on Factiva using the query genius. The search returned 1,625 transcripts with a total duplicate of 542. So, only 1,083 were extracted and used for the analysis. It may be essential to mention that the same search strings on other media outlets like ABC returned 33 results, and Fox News transcript returned 57. It may also be crucial to highlight that when the term "OR" was used in place of "AND" in the search string, ABC returned 1,634. However, since the study's focus is to capture stories that weaved in these four actors (Gadhafi, Libya, NATO, and rebels), only stories from the CNN network were deployed for this phase of the study.

The outcomes of the analysis are presented in stages. The first is the pragmatic analysis of persons, actions, events, and circumstances appearing in the news headlines of stories about the Libyan civil war. The second is a quantitative frequency analysis of six common narratives on Muammar Gadhafi and the conflict. The third examines news stories in two pivotal periods. These were periods (August 20 to August 24 and March 19 to March 29) in which there was the greatest concentration of news stories on the Libyan civil war. These include identifying the pragmatic acts dominantly reported or represented in the media reports about the war. These acts include identifying with or co-opting, denouncing, rejecting, or implicitly denying any of the actors or actions or proposed actions during the civil war.

5.6 Analysis and Findings

5.6.1 Data Analytics

In 259 days, there were 1,083 different stories about Libya, Gadhafi, rebels, and NATO on the CNN network, with more than 500 of these stories repeated at least 3–4 times per day. All 1,083 stories were analyzed using the semantic,

---

[4] "Rebels" as used in this study refers to the anti-Gadhafi forces that opposed and defeated the Gadhafi-led government. These opposition forces included organized and armed militia groups, who switched their support from the Gadhafi government to the protesters.

narrative, and pragmatic frameworks of analysis. Table 5.1 and Figure 5.1 provide a detailed account of the number of each actor's mentions in comparison to other actors. Across all the actors, an unusual and outrageous surge occurs between August 20 and 24, 2011.

The earliest stories from the search string began on February 28, possibly signifying a media chant for NATO's intervention weeks before the multi-state

Table 5.1 *Monitoring the trends and mentions of key actors*

Dates	Gadhafi	Rebels	NATO	Libya
February 22–March 19	2618	449	802	3224
March 19–March 29	2674	559	1095	3036
March 29–April 8	2028	787	905	1962
April 8–April 23	1100	548	1033	1270
April 23–May 13	1090	228	786	1002
May 13–June 8	620	123	444	896
June 8–July 5	758	243	685	994
July 15–August 20	758	373	458	894
August 20–August 24	4404	1813	1011	3579
August 24–September 3	1916	661	345	1495
September 3–October 31	2402	167	740	2183

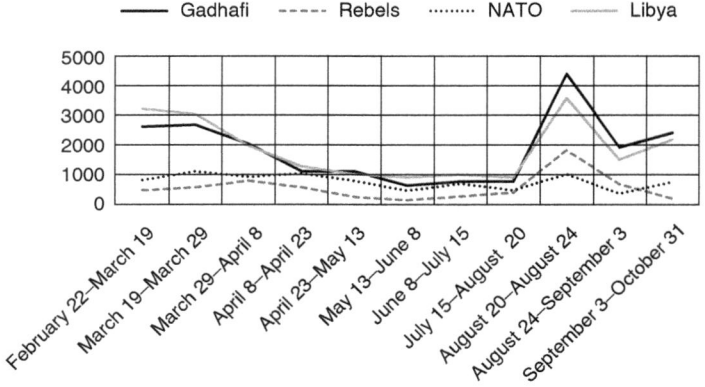

Figure 5.1 Libya 2011: The semantics of CNN headlines on the civil war

NATO-led coalition formally started military intervention in Libya on March 19, 2011. The move possibly represents Herman and Chomsky's (1988) idea of "manufacturing consent" for arguably unacceptable actions. Herman and Chomsky (1988) present the analysis of how individuals and organizations of the media are influenced to shape the social agendas of knowledge and, therefore, belief. The authors argue that the public's world view is shaped by "propaganda'" disseminated by American news media that are heavily influenced by "market forces, internalized assumptions, and self-censorship" (134).

Definitely by March 31, 2011, NATO and its alliance obtained consent from the UNSC to take sole command and control of the international military effort for Libya, ostensibly to implement UNSC Resolution 1973.[5] Subsequently, NATO air and sea assets began to take military action under the umbrella "to protect civilians and civilian populated areas." A few African media reports reiterated the African Union's (AU) Peace and Security Council (PSC) solidarity with Libya and the rejection of "any foreign military intervention, whatever its form." But this narrative was drowned out by the reach and frequency of the news stories making a case for foreign intervention. These drowning views include positions of the Arab League and the Gulf Cooperation Council (GCC), which called for the imposition of a No-Fly Zone over Libya, asking that Gadhafi's government be no longer considered legitimate.

5.6.2 Representations of Persons and Actions, Humanitarianism, and Circumstances

As indicated earlier, persons in the headlines are designated by expressions that refer to them not so much as particular individuals but as members of influential groups or institutions. The semantic rule implicated here by Montgomery (2007) is individuated when the person is already presumed to be famous otherwise categorized by the membership of the most salient or significant group. Within the selected corpus of 1,063 headlines, "Dictator" and "Mad Dog" were the predominant MCDs often used to describe Muammar Gadhafi. Though his last name, "Gadhafi," is used in the question of scale, using an MCD alongside a person's name as famous as Gadhafi indicates a flawed but internalized presumption of his unpopularity.

References to "dictator" and "mad dog" as labels for Gadhafi are shown in the following headlines.

Reference 1: the tipping point and its desperate ***dictator*** is responding by unleashing vicious

---

[5] www.nato.int/cps/en/natohq/topics_71652.htm.

Reference 2: strongest words yet on Libya's **dictator**, but ... "Indescribable" and Deadly Assault
Reference 3: Libyan rebels and an entrenched **dictator**. A sharp contrast to the US
Reference 4: Into US Oil Reserves; Libya's **Dictator** in Denial; Different Kind of
Reference 5: Forces loyal to the Libyan **dictator** mounted vigorous new attacks ... Gadhafi's
Reference 6: Gadhafi, taped earlier today, the **dictator** ... Moammar Gadhafi Speaks on Libyan
Reference 7: The **Mad Dog** is Down

MCDs implicate what are described as "category-bound activities." The device's typical application usually activates a set of stereotypes about the behaviors performed by members of a category (Montgomery 2007). Just as "mothers" as a membership category are assumed (among other things) to nurture children, "dictators" as a membership category are considered to be brutal tyrants who usurp legitimate sovereignty and who are unrestrained by law. From literature such as *The Winter's Tale*, the tyrant is often at last brought down by the people, revolutionaries, tribunes – not heroes, but mere functionaries. Callow suggests that these mere functionaries are akin to the much-maligned professional politicians of democratic congresses and parliaments everywhere.[6] Little wonder the rebels are represented numerous times as fighters subject to defeat without external intervention (see Figure 5.1).

NATO's actions represented in the headlines often cited the protection of Libyans' welfare – suggesting an act of humanitarianism. Humanitarianism as a membership category is a prevalent but stereotypical means of providing security and aid globally. Despite its success, Lauri (2016) highlighted recent scholarly concerns about humanitarianism as an increasing economic enterprise and political tool for controlling territories and governing international relations.[7] In the Libyan case, CNN constructed NATO's action as a humanitarian gesture to rescue Libyan citizens from Gadhafi's brutal onslaught, while Gadhafi was continuously represented as "remaining defiant." Humanitarianism, in this context, also includes arming the rebels. As the sample below exemplifies, Gadhafi was frequently reported as being at war against his own people, and Libyans were in perennial danger of the "current disaster," "a massacre," and being "turned into hell." According to Chouliaraki (2012), mainstream mediation of distant suffering and other forms of humanitarian action have become hypocritical and egoistic Western practices that turn

---

[6] www.nytimes.com/2018/06/20/books/review/tyrant-stephen-greenblatt.html.
[7] www.cmi.no/publications/6037-the-politics-of-humanitarianism-power.

the spotlight instead towards themselves (the Western "ironic spectator") and detach distant suffering from its historical causes and political solutions. Hence, humanitarian communication becomes "a story about how the move from an objective representation of suffering, as something separate from us that invites us to contemplate the condition of distant others, towards a subjective representation of suffering, as something inseparable from our own 'truths' that invites contemplation on our own condition, is also a move from ethics of pity to ethics of irony" (Chouliaraki 2012, 6).

BEN WEDEMAN, CNN SR. INTERNATIONAL CORRESPONDENT: I mean, the picture that's emerging from Tripoli is indeed disturbing. It appears that there is, at this point, zero tolerance for any dissent. People did try to go out after Friday prayers today and demonstrate. But apparently, they came under intense gunfire as soon as they started to gather. We're hearing stories of bodies being taken out of the morgues, bodies of people killed in the protests, and being buried in beaches and in the desert to make it appear that the death toll is, in fact, lower. It appears that the policy of Moammar Gadhafi is similar to that of Attila the Hun or Genghis Khan, simply slaughtering his opponents where he can. Today in Green Square, he made an appearance where he said that he would turn Libya into hell if he has just to maintain his power over this country. (CNN: *Piers Morgan Tonight*, February 25, 2011)

Routinely, circumstances relate to the task of presenting the news as occurring in a spatially dispersed fashion. The headlines achieved this task by regularly referring to the different locations of the conflict in Libya. The predominant locations mentioned in the headlines include Gadhafi's compound and Tripoli. These terms were among the top ten most frequent words in the headlines, as shown in the references below:

Reference 1: grounding flights. Airstrike near **Gadhafi Compound**; Winds Damage St. Louis Airport
Reference 2: Airstrikes Level Buildings inside **Gadhafi Compound**; Feeling the Royal Pressure; Gas
Reference 3: Leveling buildings inside Moammar **Gadhafi's compound** as the dictator continues his
Reference 4: Center of power, bombing his **compound in Tripoli** while cries grow
Reference 5: Allied Air Strike Destroys **Gadhafi Compound**; Anti-Aircraft Fire Over Tripoli
Reference 6: Moammar **Gadhafi's compound** attacked. (INAUDIBLE). The likely weapons
Reference 7: **Gadhafi's Compound** Hit by Missile

By focusing on the "Gadhafi compound," CNN attempted to make the destruction of Gadhafi inevitable, which meant final victory for NATO and its allies.

The report of attacks on Gadhafi's compound is a technique that not only heralded victory for the West but also attempted to expose the vulnerability and weakness and ultimate defeat of Gadhafi. CNN maintained a report that emphasized taking the battle to Gadhafi's home, which gave assurance of victory, much more to the pleasure of Western powers. Thus, the headline news stories were constructed to appeal to Western audiences rather than to African audiences.

5.6.3   Narrative Analysis of CNN News

Narrative techniques provide deeper meaning for readers or listeners and help them to use imagination to visualize situations. A first step in analyzing the narratives about the civil war in Libya was determining what types of stories were being told. Mayer (2002) points out that stories, particularly the shared tales that constitute popular culture, tend to fall into one or another archetype based on their basic plot form and stereotypical characters. Some basic story prototypes seemed to capture the vast majority of the civil war in the CNN Libya narratives. These stories had similar plots and casts of characters and conveyed similar meanings and implications for action. The narratives indicate that viewers or listeners were invited to flashback and visualize the Libyan conflict scenario as an event with a resemblance to the Rwanda Genocide, Bosnia, and Kosovo. These imageries are incidents that most often evoke or incite collective actions to avoid a repeat of what is now perceived as an undesirable past. The frequent representations of "Gadhafi as Dictator," the "Mad Dog of the Middle East," or "Lockerbie culprit" were narratives that invited urgent action to deal with a dictator or the evils of a mad dog. Flashbacks were the predominant narrative plot technique used to recall the sins of past wars (see Figure 5.2).

As pointed out above, the narrative techniques adopted by CNN reporters were primarily those that compared the Libyan crises with previous wars, achieving flashbacks to the incidents of horror, atrocities, and death. In the examples below, the flashback is used to recall the war in Bosnia, Kosovo, and Rwanda. It brings back the memory of "horrific pictures" and "atrocities" and makes the reader relive the war's horrible moments. "NT" stands for "narrative."

NT1. PIERS MORGAN: John, let me ask you – is it sort of a human imperative here for America and the international community to intervene? If you look at what happened in **Bosnia**, in **Serbia**, is what **Gadhafi** is now doing to his people any better, any worse than what **Milosevic** was doing, for example?

KING: It's a great question. And the one part we don't know is the scale. You were having a fascinating conversation just moments ago with Ben and with Ivan. We know the **atrocities** are taking place. We see snippets of the **pictures**. We're beginning to hear

Making a Case for War

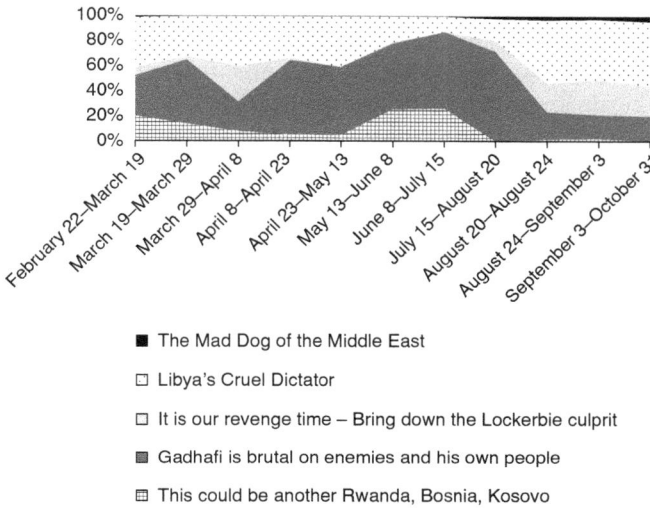

Figure 5.2 CNN news frequency of key narratives

from the people leaving. I spoke to a young Libyan American today who said he remembers seeing more than 100 people shot in just a few moments. (CNN *Piers Morgan Tonight*, February 25, 2011)

NT2. WOOLSEY: Well, I think he should have acted already. We're running out of organizations to get resolutions from. You know, Eliot, in the Clinton administration – Bill Clinton's not normally known as our most war-like President. But in 1995, he went to **war against Serbia** from the air to save Bosnians. And in 1999, he did the same thing against **Serbia to save Kosovar** lives. (CNN: *In the Arena*: Eliot Spitzer, Arwa Damon, Will Cabin, Anderson Cooper, Tom Foreman, Sanjay Gupta, Will Cain, March 18, 2011)

NT3. SLAUGHTER: So I came out in favor of doing something. I mean, we're going to see absolutely **horrific pictures** when things are opened up, where the towns that are right now experiencing real battles, we don't have people there who can send us pictures. Still, we're going to get absolutely **horrific pictures**. And my point was we shouldn't wait the way we waited in **Rwanda**. We should act. (CNN: *In the Arena*. Eliot Spitzer, Will Cain, E.D. Hill, Nic Robertson, Jeffrey Toobin, March 7, 2011).

Further, in the narratives, Muammar Gadhafi is represented as a "brutal" monster, an enemy of his people, "a killer," and "a murderer." Through this demonization technique, the attacks on Gadhafi and Libya were systematically legitimized. Unfortunately, the act that supposedly "set Libya free" actually destroyed Libya. During the attack, not only were physical infrastructures destroyed, oil pipelines and military facilities were bombed. However, in the samples, Gadhafi was consistently referred to as "the Lockerbie culprit," "Libya's cruel dictator," "the man behind the bombing of Pan Am 103," or "mad dog of the Middle East," etc. Again recalling the Lockerbie incident, Gadhafi's attack and eventual killing were construed as "our revenge time" for the West. This echoes the assumption (or the fact) that the West never forgave Gadhafi even after he admitted that Libya carried out the attack but not on his orders. He also agreed to pay compensation for the Lockerbie bombing. In 2013, two senior officials of the Libyan government were acquitted from jail, having decided to pay $2.9 billion compensation to the 1988 Lockerbie bombing victims.[8]

NT4. SESAY: Moammar Gadhafi has directed **attacks against his people in Libya's current crackdown**. He was **the man behind the bombing of Pan Am 103**. So now that a coalition launched attacks on his nation, how far will he go in response? (CNN: *CNN Newsroom*, March 21, 2011)

NT5. BLITZER: Because you make him sound like he's a decent guy when so many people think he is **a killer, a murderer**, especially given the statements that he recently made, that if he goes into Benghazi, if he finds these rebels, he will go and kill them all. You make it sound like he's a decent guy. (*CNN Situation Room*, Wolf Blitzer, Dana Bash, Barbara Starr, Ben Wedeman, April 7, 2011).

NT6. RANDI KAYE, CNN ANCHOR: On our blog, William says, "We shouldn't be helping Libyans. **These are the same Libyans who welcomed home as a hero, the Pan Am bomber**. Pick a side, any side. **One is as bad as another**." (CNN: *CNN Newsroom*, Randi Kaye, Chris Lawrence, Arwa Damon, March 22, 2011)

NT7. FRAN TOWNSEND, CNN NATIONAL SECURITY CONTRIBUTOR: Well, Wolf, I'm a great believer in we ought to take **terrorists** at their word when they threaten us, especially if they've successfully attacked us in the past. Let's **remember Gadhafi was responsible for the La Belle disco bombing** in Germany against our military forces there. He was also responsible for Pan Am 103, the killing of hundreds over Lockerbie (CNN: *The Situation Room*, March 28, 2011)

NT8. COSTELLO: Hala Gorani, many thanks. Syria is quite a conundrum for the Obama administration. Syria's dictator is killing civilians, just as **Libya's dictator is killing civilians**. Yet NATO isn't dropping bombs on military targets in Syria, so what gives? The President's press secretary on the difference between Libya and Syria. (CNN: *CNN Newsroom*, April 26, 2011)

In addition to the demonization strategy, intensification was also used in the news about Gadhafi and Libya. Intensification is a narrative procedure whereby actions attributed to an agent are deliberately exaggerated and ideologically "maximized." According to van Dijk (1995), this is the discursive practice of labeling the "other" and maximizing their bad

---

[8] "Lockerbie compensation: Libyan officials acquitted." BBC News, June 17, 2013. www.bbc.com/news/world-africa-22936678.

aspects and making them appear more evil than they are. Interestingly, under the leadership of Gadhafi, all students in Libya had access to higher education, and Libya had the lowest infant mortality rate in Africa. A lower percentage of people lived below the poverty line in Libya than in the Netherlands. Libya had the highest Human Development Index of any country on the continent of Africa.[9] But at this time of his retribution, everything good he had done for Libya was forgotten. Aided by the media's systematic framing of negative actions attributed to him, his killing by his people (the rebel group) assisted by the West was overwhelmingly legitimized by the international community.

5.6.4 Pragmatic Analysis

The data comprise 10,079 pages of CNN transcripts available on Factiva. The following analysis of the pragmatic acts performed in the CNN news between February 14 and October 31, 2011, by key actors on CNN about the Libyan civil war focuses on acts such as denouncing, identifying with, rejecting, and co-opting (Table 5.2).

The details of the pragmatic acts and the actors that performed them (e.g., Barack Obama, Nicolas Sarkozy, the UN, the AU, etc.) are illustrated in Figure 5.3 and Table 5.3.

In the limited space of this chapter, selected examples that aptly capture the crux of each actor's dominant act towards the war or the key actors in the war are used as samples from the corpus. Table 5.3 shows the type of pragmatic acts dominantly performed by each actor and the actors who performed the most acts. For example, former President Obama's statement rejecting Gadhafi's government as illegitimate is the dominant act he performed throughout the war.

Table 5.2 *Pragmatic acts*

Acts of denouncing	11.30%
Acts of identifying with	18.50%
Acts of rejecting	34.60%
Acts of advancing	22.10%
Acts of co-opting	13.50%

---

[9] Libya, under Gadhafi, was the best place to live: www.africanexponent.com/post/ten-reasons-libya-under-gaddafi-was-a-great-place-to-live-2746.

Table 5.3 *The rate at which each actor performed each act*

Act	Gadhafi	NATO	Rebels	Obama	Sarkozy	UN	AU
Denouncing	9	14	2	6	0	6	0
Identifying with	33	10	6	6	3	2	2
Rejecting	29	7	8	52	10	7	0
Advancing	21	10	16	20	2	3	0
Co-opting	16	13	3	9	0	3	0

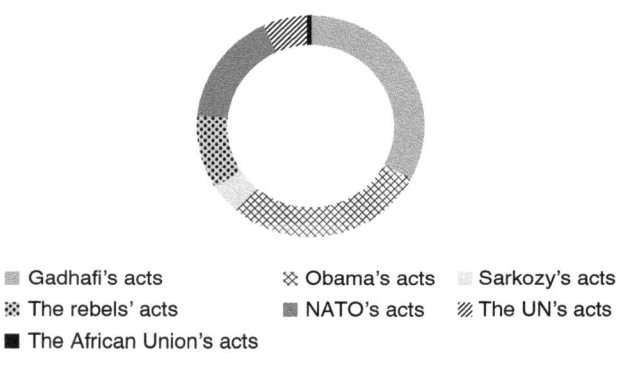

- Gadhafi's acts
- The rebels' acts
- The African Union's acts
- Obama's acts
- NATO's acts
- Sarkozy's acts
- The UN's acts

Figure 5.3 Categorization of key pragmatic actors and analysis

5.6.4.1 Act of Denouncing NATO contributes the most significant number of denouncing acts on US involvement in the war during the study's period. In early March, most of the acts under this category were explicit disapproval of the US getting involved alone, primarily because of the uncertainty and risk. The advanced but failed options included pressure on Gadhafi to leave the country. The successful aspect of the act may have contributed to the US's preferred choice of invading Libya under NATO's umbrella. The NATO alliance took sole command and control of Libya's international military effort on March 31, 2011. The sample below is an opinion showing disapproval of NATO military actions before every available option of peaceful resolution of the conflict was exhausted.

NT9. GEN. GEORGE JOULWAN, FMR. SUPREME ALLIED COMMANDER: I would caution against getting involved. Many of the ships we see passing through the Suez and the Mediterranean are returning and rotating back from Afghanistan and Iraq. The Marines in particular that are there, there are about 800 of them, the Cursards (ph), the Ponce (ph), they are rotating back. And to get involved with the uncertainty we see in Libya is a risk. I'm not sure the US wants to take a unilateral risk in doing that. The European Union, NATO, and particularly the UN need to stand-up. And we need to pull other levers of power, diplomatic, economic, get the Saudis involved in Gadhafi, with Gadhafi, and see if we can get him to leave the country. I think those things need to be tried before we use military power. (NATO, March 5, 2011)

It is essential to highlight that denouncing acts from Obama, NATO, the rebels, and the United Nations *condemn* Gadhafi and Libya's actions. Gadhafi himself denounces NATO's action in Libya, calling it an "unjust war against a small people of a developing country" being embarked by Barack Obama and his government. He described the US and NATO as "traitors."

NT10. FMR. US PRESIDENT BARACK OBAMA: The situation is still very fluid. There remains a degree of uncertainty, and there are still regime elements who pose a threat. But this much is clear ... the Gadhafi regime is coming to an end, and the future of Libya is in the hands of its people. (August 22, 2011)

NT11. *nato*: "Although the surface-to-surface missiles in Gadhafi's arsenal are highly inaccurate, and are not designed to hit a specific target, they are a weapon of terror," NATO said in a statement. "Their use against an urban or industrial area is utterly irresponsible."

NT12. FMR. US PRESIDENT JIMMY CARTER: Gadhafi is an irresponsible animal, who has no scruples; he has no morals.

NT13. FMR. FRENCH PRESIDENT NICOLAS SARKOZY: The embattled Libyan leader's calls to continue fighting were "desperate and irresponsible." (August 22, 2011)

Cumulatively, 76 percent of the times denouncements acts were performed, Gadhafi "the Mad the Dog" was the focus. This implies that the repetition of denouncement and condemnation of Gadhafi by different world leaders may have consolidated the manufactured consent to invade Libya. Remarkably, Nicolas Sarkozy – the French President at the time of the uprising and civil war, was never reported condemning Gadhafi's actions in Libya. The remaining 24 percent of the acts were Gadhafi struggling to call attention to his decrying acts against NATO's invasion of Libya. Specifically, Gadhafi denounced accusations that Libya was on the verge of being destroyed by his military forces.

5.6.4.2 Acts of Identifying with and Co-opting Co-opting acts account for one of the two least performed acts. Gadhafi performed these acts by seeking more supporters to expunge the West from Africa, in this case, Libya. Some other co-opting acts were performed by NATO seeking international support for actions in Libya.

NT14. Gadhafi urges Libyans to fight opposition forces and "cleanse this sweet and honorable land." In a speech broadcast on state television, Gadhafi says: "The strikes will be over, and NATO will be defeated. Move always forward to the challenge; pick up your weapons; go to the fight to liberate Libya inch by inch from the traitors and NATO. Be prepared to fight if they hit the ground." (CNN report, August 16, 2011)

Gadhafi performed the most transmitted acts of identifying with a group, persons, or actions. The continued use of this act referring to who or what he identified with also unwittingly exposed them to targeted attacks. Also, publicizing his strong support for his henchmen to the world supported the dreadful narrative of killing his people. Such representations of Gadhafi may have further stirred the sense of urgency for NATO to attack and oust "the dictator."

It is essential to highlight that in the spirit of the CNN style of broadcasting, the statement (NT14) by Gadhafi was repeated more than once. One hundred percent of Obama's efforts to identify with a group were him standing up for NATO and rarely for the Libyan rebels. Interestingly, on August 22, the French president commended the rebel fighters' courage in fighting for control of the country.

5.6.4.3 Act of Advancing   Obama and Gadhafi predominantly performed these acts by making statements that advanced/put forward specific actions, which included supporting the new Libyan TNC government, enhancing the existing status quo, or seeking improvements on Libya's social and economic status. Obama constituted about 20 percent of these acts. Sarkozy, like the UN, scarcely advanced any ideas. The key actors here were Obama, the rebels, NATO, and Gadhafi. The samples below are Obama's actions and promises that reflect the US enhanced interest in Libya.

NT15. FMR. US PRESIDENT, BARACK OBAMA: The Obama administration has agreed to a NATO request for two additional Predator drones to conduct operations over Libya.

NT16. FMR. US PRESIDENT, BARACK OBAMA: The future of Libya is now in the hands of the Libyan people. Going forward, the United States will continue to stay in close coordination with TNC. We will continue to insist that the basic rights of the Libyan people are respected, and we will continue to work with our allies and partners in the international community to protect the people of Libya and to support Libya, and to support a peaceful transition to democracy.

The rebels and NATO followed Obama closely at the top of the chart of those advancing the idea that ousting Gadhafi's government was the next great idea for Libya.

5.6.4.4 Act of Rejecting   About 34.6 percent of rejections were dominantly unidirectional against Gadhafi and his supporters. Obama performed the highest number of rejections, constituting nearly 50 percent of all rejections against Gadhafi. Statistically, the groups' rejection rates are: the UN 6.9 percent, NATO 6.9 percent, and the rebels 7 percent. Gadhafi, with 25 percent, was less than the rate of propagated rejections from Obama to the rest of the world. President Obama's critical reactions were centered on the illegitimate status of Gadhafi's government and his actions that were viewed as unacceptable. Some of the acts of rejection are exemplified in the following samples:

NT17. FMR. US PRESIDENT BARRACK OBAMA: Gadhafi needs to acknowledge the reality that he no longer controls Libya. He needs to relinquish power once and for all. (March 11, 2011)

NT18. FMR. FRENCH PRESIDENT NICOLAS SARKOZY: We are intervening in Libya under a United Nations Security Council mandate alongside our partners, in particular, our Arab partners. We're doing this to protect the civilian populations from the murderous madness of a regime that, by killing its people, has forfeited all legitimacy. (March 11, 2011)

5.7   Conclusions

The current study focuses on CNN, partly to reflect Western media narratives' cultural dominance in war and conflict in Africa, and somewhat to simplify drawing from endless media outlets. The study's focus on CNN also speaks to questions of subjectivity that all media practitioners face, no matter their professional journalistic orientation. These orientations range broadly from media organizations to narrow personal orientations towards the satisfaction of the audience, towards certain basic principles and values, and towards the interest of the advertising market, or the interest of certain actors in society such as the League of Nations, political parties, companies, associations, and prominent individuals.

And though the analysis is focused narrowly on the American media, ignoring other parts of the world altogether, it expresses the futility of an endless journalistic struggle to engrave a trans-generational notion that media reports are not subjective but objective productions – productions that supposedly wield little or no interest in the slant of outcomes proceeding from propagated narratives. This study has analyzed media representations achieved through linguistic choices or discourse pragmatic strategies that have had some enormous consequences on international diplomacy. Our findings provide initial empirical evidence on the actual textual structures and techniques brought to bear by journalists in the discursive reproduction of the framework which had a great impact in NATO's bombing of Libya and the final ouster of Muammar Gadhafi in a civil war. The findings also suggest that CNN news validated and legitimized the United Nations Security Council decision to attack Libya and provided the impetus for the killing of the former Libyan president through subjective narrative patterns and pragmatic acts. The process of Gadhafi's ouster is likely to remain engraved in the conscience of the world about a procedure that left a lot to be desired.

References

Ali, Sadaf and Fahmy, Shahira. 2013. "Gatekeeping and Citizen Journalism: The Use of Social Media during the Recent Uprisings in Iran, Egypt, and Libya." *Media, War, and Conflict* 6(1): 55–69. doi.org/10.1177/1750635212469906.
Austin, John. 1962. *How to Do Things with Words*. Oxford: Oxford University Press.
Campbell, Horace. 2013. *Global NATO and the Catastrophic Failure in Libya: Lessons for Africa in the Forging of African Unity*. New York: Monthly Review Press.
Carruthers, Susan. 2011. *The Media at War*, 2nd edition. London: Palgrave Macmillan.
Chiluwa, Innocent. 2007. "News Headlines as Pragmatic Strategy in Nigerian Press Discourse." *International Journal of Language, Society and Culture* 27: 63–71. https://core.ac.uk/download/pdf/12356494.pdf.
Chiluwa, Innocent and Ajiboye, Esther. 2016. "Discursive Pragmatics of T-Shirt Inscriptions: Constructing the Self, Context, and Social Aspirations." *Pragmatics and Society* 7(3): 436–462.
Chouliaraki, Lilie. 2012. *The Ironic Spectator. Solidarity in the Age of Post-Humanitarianism*. Cambridge: Polity Press.
Forte, Maximilian. 2013. *Slouching towards Sirte: NATO's War on Libya and Africa*. Montreal: Baraka Books.
Galtung, Johan. 1986. "On the Role of the Media in Worldwide Security and Peace." In *Peace and Communication*, ed. by T. Varis, 12–34. Universidad Para La Paz.
Gilboa, Eytan. 2007. "The CNN Effect: The Search for a Communication Theory of International Relations". *Political Communication* 22(1): 27–44. doi.org/10.1080/10584600590908429.
Herman, Edward S. and Chomsky, Noam. 1988. *Manufacturing Consent: The Political Economy of the Mass Media*. New York: Pantheon Books.
Hjarvard, Stig and Norgarrd, Kristensen. 2014. "When Media of a Small Nation Argue for War." *Media, War, and Conflict* 7(1): 51–69. doi.org/10.1177/1750635213516560.
Housley, William and Fitzgerald, Richard. 2002. "The Reconsidered Model of Membership Categorization Analysis." *Qualitative Research* 2: 59–83.
Kellner, Douglas. 1992. *The Persian Gulf War*. Boulder, CO: Westview Press.
Lauri, Rapeli. 2016. "Public Support for Expert Decision-Making: Evidence from Finland." *Politics* 36(2): 142–152.
Lee, Seow, Maslog, Crispin and Kim, Hun. 2014. "Asian Conflicts and the Iraq War: A Comparative Analysis." *The International Communication Gazette* 68(5–6): 499–518. doi.org/10.1177/1748048506068727.
Mayer, Frederick. 2002. *Stories of Climate Change: Competing Narratives, the Media, and the US. Public Opinion (2001–2010)*, Shorenstein Center for Public Policy. https://shorensteincenter.org/wp-content/uploads/2012/03/d72_mayer.pdf.
Mey, Jacob. 2001. Pragmatics: An Introduction, 2nd edition. London: Blackwell.
Montgomery, Martins. 2007. *The Discourse of Broadcast News: A Linguistic Approach*. New York: Routledge.

Penley, Constance and Ross, Andrew. 1991. "Couch Potatoes Aren't Dupes." *The New York Times*, www.nytimes.com/1991/03/11/opinion/couch-potatoes-arent-dupes.html.

Pereira, Christophe. 2008. "Libya." *Encyclopedia of Arabic Language and Linguistics* 3: 52–58. Leiden: Brill.

Roberts, Hugh. 2011. "Who Said Gadhafi Has to Go?" *London Review of Books* 33(22): 8–18. www.lrb.co.uk/v33/n22/hugh-roberts/who-said-gaddafi-had-to-go.

Ryan, Diane and Simon, James. 2014. "Broadcast News Transcripts in Academic News Databases." *Focus on Global Resources* 34(1). https://www.crl.edu/focus/article/11072.

Searle, John. 1969. *Speech Acts*. Cambridge: Cambridge University Press.

van Dijk, Teun. 1995. "Ideological Discourse Analysis." *New Courant*, 4: 135–161.

Zienkowski, Jan. 2011. "Discursive Pragmatics: Platform for the Pragmatic Study of Discourse." In *Handbook of Pragmatics*, ed. by Jan Zienkowski, Jan-Ola Ostman, and Jef Verschueren, 8, 1–13. Amsterdam: John Benjamins.

6 "The Situation on the Korean Peninsula"

Voice of America and *China Radio International* on China and the USA about the North Korean Conflict

Valerie A. Cooper

6.1 Introduction

On March 10, 2016, news broke across the world that the Democratic People's Republic of Korea (DPRK) had fired two short-range ballistic missiles into the sea off the country's east coast ("North Korea 'fires short-range missiles'," BBC 2016, "DPRK fires short-range ballistic missiles into eastern waters," BBC 2016). This missile launch came after weeks of increasing tension on the Korean peninsula, resulting from increased sanctions against North Korea from the United Nations as well as joint South Korea–United States military exercises.

The tensions and the resulting missile tests gained media attention around the world. Though only South Korea and Japan were directly threatened by these missiles, the small, isolated country led by Kim Jong-Un is globally renowned and reported about, due to its eccentric leadership and dealings with world powers. On one side, South Korea enjoys a cozy military relationship with the United States, putting both countries at odds with North Korea; on the other side is China, seen as one of the DPRK's few allies as well as a provider of much-needed international aid (Bandow 2016). It is therefore unsurprising that those global powers would have very different agendas and approaches in relation to North Korea.

The unusually extreme actions taken by North Korea in March 2016 resulted in highly divisive reactions, with China and the United States on opposing sides of the aisle. This chapter looks at this moment in time, including the lead-up to the missiles' firing and the global reactions to it, through the lens of the state-sponsored media outlets from the United States of America and the People's Republic of China. In doing so, this research interrogates how each country uses discourse to portray the events leading up to the missile launch, and how they seek to justify the stance of their own government on the issue. This is done through a content analysis and critical discourse analysis of each country's state-sponsored news broadcasts in March 2016. This approach is in keeping with Wodak's (2001) assertion that critical discourse studies is less concerned with the existence of ideology itself as with the way that those ideologies are utilized by those in power to promote and maintain a certain perspective over others. According to Wodak (2001), critical discourse studies (CDS) as a whole is defined as a linguistic approach "fundamentally concerned with analysing opaque as well as transparent structural relationships of dominance, discrimination, power, and control as manifested in language," using text as the basic unit of communication and study.

While CDS can be applied to a great number of genres, media outputs are often a focus for language and communications scholars in general, and critical discourse scholars in particular. Bell (1995, 23) explains the reasons behind this: firstly, media outlets provide a rich source of data to be analyzed, and that data is usually readily available; secondly, media usage not only represents people's use of and attitudes about language, but can also influence those attitudes; thirdly, media provide a window into social meanings and stereotypes through language use in a given society; and fourthly, media reflect the formation and expression of culture, politics, and social life. Critical discourse studies have an interest in media outlets especially due to their "manifestly pivotal role as discourse-bearing institutions" (Bell and Garrett 1998, 6), and their role in reproducing or challenging sociopolitical dominance. Such an approach has been used, for example, to analyze Africa Live on CCTV Africa, which found a distinct shift in coverage from a low-profile approach to a more assertive one in terms of the outlet's critique of the current world order over time. In that research, Zhang (2013, 80) states that "discourse analysis is used both as theory and as method ... critical analysis of media discourse, understood as an attempt to show systemic links between texts, discourse practices and sociocultural practices (Fairclough 1995, 16) allows the investigator to examine the intricate relations between media discourse and its political, social and economic contexts."

Existing research on Chinese and American media in general has uncovered a number of approaches and ideologies unique to each nation. One of the major ideologies identified in international media coverage from the United States is the clear preference for and the believed superiority of a capitalist economic system over other systems (especially communist systems). Kobland et al. (1992) identified the predominant frame in the coverage of China as "anti-communism" in their research comparing the reporting of student demonstrations in South Korea in 1980 with similar demonstrations in China in 1989. They found that while government intervention in South Korea was framed as a legitimate response to a "rebellious insurrection," government intervention in China was framed as "cruelly repressive" (1992, 72), arguably because the students were protesting against the communist system that the US disparages. Entman (1991) compared US media coverage of two similar incidents of passenger planes accidentally being shot down by military entities and found drastically different framing approaches. The primary difference between the two incidents were the perpetrators: when it was the Soviet Union downing a Korean passenger plane, the frame focused on the "moral bankruptcy and guilt of the perpetrating nation"; however, when it was the United States downing an Iranian passenger plane, the framing took the focus off the guilt factor and onto the complexity of operating advanced military technology. This perspective has been found for private as well as public media outlets in the United States.

In China, the country's media system in general and China Radio International (CRI) in particular were created to serve as the mouthpiece for the Chinese Communist Party (CCP) in the early 1900s (Zhang 2011). Media liberalization as initiated by Deng Xiaoping allowed marketization and more freedom for the Chinese press, but this had little impact on China's vast state-run media industry overseen by the CCP, which includes CRI, *China Daily* and *China Today* (Shambaugh 2007). Dominant ideology in China is often attributed to the influence of Confucian principles, which emphasize social stability, family values, obedience, and moral discipline above all else (Hu 2007). In the media, this ideology manifests itself through the use of positive, solution-driven narratives in news stories, among other ways. In their analysis of Chinese media coverage of the 4th United Nations Conference on Women, Akhavan-Majid and Ramaprasad (1998, 147) found that the "emphasis on reaching solutions to critical problems was exemplified in part by the general downplaying of conflict, both quantitatively and qualitatively, in the Chinese coverage." The same research found that, despite assumptions of explicit promotion of communist ideology in the media, coverage in *China Daily* contained relatively little praise for China. Similarly, Y. Zhang (2014) argues that the Chinese media approach can be considered "constructive journalism," which focuses on positive solutions to the problems or issues covered in news stories.

6.2 Public Diplomacy through Media

In addition to understanding the grand theories of ideology and discourse, it is also crucial to understand the practical context surrounding the existence of these media outlets. These are not traditional news media sources: they exist in the gray area between journalism and public relations, and are simply one facet within the broader concept of public diplomacy. How these outlets use ideology to tread the line between media outlet and foreign propaganda is one of the core interests of this research.

The most common characteristics of public diplomacy according to definitions are the emphasis on the communication of information (specifically policy), and the building up of relationships through engagement. The former is usually conceived of as a short-term action, while the latter is more long term. This is the recurring theme when attempting to define and describe public diplomacy: one emphasis is on the strategic communications aspect, while the other is on relationship building. Yet these two purposes rarely overlap: the former suggests a unidirectional transfer of information, from a government body to a foreign public, while the other suggests a mutual exchange and relationship that leads to understanding and possibly even respect on both sides. While communication is necessary for such relationship-building purposes, it is certainly not the unidirectional communication that results from mass media that the first dimension emphasizes. It is not surprising that there should be such confusion and debate concerning the definition of public diplomacy when two of its stated dimensions could almost be seen as having contradictory aims.

This question of strategic communication versus relationship building is one of the points of contention among public diplomacy scholars and practitioners. Snow (2009) frames this conflict as the "tender-minded versus tough-minded" approaches to public diplomacy, while Zaharna (2009) describes the division between the "informational framework" and the "relational framework" of public diplomacy.

As Snow (2009) describes it, the tender-minded school favors activities that "foster mutual understanding" between peoples, including through people-to-people and government-sponsored educational and cultural exchanges. Similarly, Zaharna (2009) describes the "relational framework" for public diplomacy as one that focuses on identifying and building relationships.

In contrast, the "tough-minded" school, or the "informational framework" of public diplomacy, is shaped by the first dimension mentioned above: information and influence. According to Zaharna (2009, 88), this approach "is rooted in the view of communication as primarily a linear process of transferring information, often with the goal of persuasion or control." This approach is purposefully unidirectional, as the goal is to send information (often pertaining to government policies) to a target audience in order to sway public opinion. This is particularly true for traditional public diplomacy, which focuses on "governments talking to global publics (G2P), and includes those efforts to inform, influence and engage those publics" and thus "emphasizes citizens in asymmetrical one-way efforts to inform and build a case for a nation's position" (Snow 2009, 6).

Signitzer and Coombs (1992, 137) go so far as to use the words "persuasion and propaganda" to describe the tough-minded school, noting that "objectivity and truth are considered important tools of persuasion but not extolled as virtues in themselves" – a perspective that will be explored more in the following section. While this perspective might seem more applicable to the era of the United States Information Agency, it is actually still heavily utilized in theory and practice.

6.3 CRI and VOA on the World Stage

China Radio International (CRI) and Voice of America (VOA) are ideally situated for this research because, in addition to being global media outlets, they are both voices for their respective governments, existing to "influence public attitudes on the formation and execution of foreign policies" (Cull 2009; Kelley 2009). In the United States, where the First Amendment to the country's Constitution prohibits government interference in the press, the concept of public diplomacy provides an innocuous euphemism to the notorious term "propaganda" (Cull 2009). In this way, Voice of America is unique amongst US media in its ties to the federal government.

In China, CRI's existence is not only less contentious but is, in fact, more of the norm in the media environment. To understand the Chinese approach to public diplomacy, one must understand that (1) propaganda (宣传 – to publicize, advertise, propagate) is not seen as negative, and the term is applied to benign activities such as news and advertisements; and (2) there is no solid distinction between internal propaganda and external propaganda (Wang 2008). Chinese foreign policy scholar Yiwei Wang (2008, 259) declares simply that "public diplomacy is a foreign concept in China."

6.3.1 China Radio International

Research concerning China Radio International often includes it as one component of China's larger public diplomacy and soft power push, which includes Confucius Institutes and the proliferation of other major media outlets like CCTV and Xinhua (d'Hooghe 2005; Kurlantzick 2007). Other research focuses on CRI as a historical component of Chinese media policy overall. The outlet's beginnings predate the Communist Party itself, as overseas broadcasts began during the War of Resistance against Japan in 1941 (China Radio International, "About China Radio International" 2012). It first reached English audiences in 1947, but originally was simply a mouthpiece to broadcast information from Chinese leaders (Chen et al. 2010; Kurlantzick 2007). Since this time, it has grown to the point of broadcasting in more than 60 languages with more than 100 international FM radio partners across Asia, Africa, North America, Europe, and Oceania (Chen et al. 2010; Qing and Shiffman 2015). Its stated mission is to "introduce China to the rest of the world, introduce the world to China, report global affairs to the world, and promote understanding and friendship between the Chinese and peoples from other countries" (China Radio International, "Who We Are" 2017).

Rawnsley (2015, 274) states that a defining feature of China's public diplomacy media outlets is its motivation: "The Chinese have an abiding faith in the ability of international broadcasting to shape the global conversation about China, and an unshakeable belief that the Chinese must explain themselves and their behaviour to an international audience that allegedly misunderstands them. Hence public diplomacy activities are designed around the principle 'To know us is to love us'." Specifically, CRI's primary focus is to deliver political, economic, sport, and cultural information about China (Chen et al. 2010). It also strictly adheres to Beijing's stance and agenda on sensitive issues, such as China's claims to Taiwan and the South China Sea.

CRI's media strategy is often summarized in the Chinese idiom of "borrowing ships to go overseas," (借船跨海) or using existing media structures to broadcast Beijing's message to the world (Chen et al. 2010; Qing and Shiffman 2015). As part of China's public diplomacy approach, some have compared CRI's mission to that of the US's Voice of America or the UK's BBC World Service (Qing and Shiffman 2015). However, Chen et al. (2010) found that CRI often does not enjoy the same perceived credibility and recognition overseas as its Western radio counterparts. Similarly, Zhang (2014) argues that Chinese media outlets in foreign countries continue to be undermined by suspicion on the part of listeners, possibly due to broadcast skepticism from Western media outlets. Despite this, CRI continues to grow and expand its online and broadcast presence, even as competitors such as VOA are cutting back on their expenses and reach (Nye 2008). Rawnsley (2015, 281) attributes this lack of credibility partly to the longstanding disparity between media aimed at domestic audiences within China, and media aimed at foreign audiences outside of China (对内宣传 and 对外宣传, respectively): "What is said in the news on CCTV-1 in Chinese for Chinese audiences must be consistent with the programming in English on CCTV-N and with Twitter feeds for CCTV-America and the People's Daily; and the credibility of the message can be damaged in an instant by film and photographs taken by witnesses or 'citizen journalist' on a mobile telephone, uploaded to the internet and distributed around the world in seconds, even as the recorded event is unfolding."

6.3.2 Voice of America

Similarly to CRI, Voice of America (VOA) emerged in 1942 in order to reach populations in closed and war-torn societies during the Second World War (US Agency for Global Media: "VOA History" 2018). The VOA Charter, signed into law in 1976, established the entity as a "consistently reliable and authoritative source of news," which would be "accurate, objective and comprehensive"

(US Agency for Global Media: "VOA History" 2018). In keeping with its public diplomacy mission, it aimed to "represent America," and "present the policies of the United States clearly and effectively" (US Agency for Global Media: "VOA History" 2018).

VOA is just one branch of public diplomacy overseen by the US Agency for Global Media (USAGM), a government agency which began its existence as the United States Information Agency (US Agency for Global Media: "Who We Are" 2018). Other broadcasters, all with similar public diplomacy goals, include Radio Free Europe/Radio Liberty, Radio Free Asia and Radio Sawa, the Arabic-language station (US Agency for Global Media: "Who We Are" 2018). Altogether, USAGM outlets broadcast in more than 60 languages around the world and claim to have more than 226 million listeners (US Agency for Global Media: "Who We Are" 2018). Interestingly, VOA was kept out of reach of American listeners until 2013, due to the Smith-Mundt Act, which aimed to protect American citizens from taxpayer-funded government propaganda (Hudson 2013). It's noteworthy that in a country that prides itself on the First Amendment and a free, independent press, this radio outlet bears an uncanny resemblance to the state-sponsored propaganda practiced in countries such as Russia and China.

In his book on China's soft power charm, Kurlantzick (2007, 183) claims that US public diplomacy faltered under the Bush administration, when "an increasingly partisan board of governors ... prodded Voice of America, long the flagship of US broadcasting abroad, to become less impartial." In contrast to China's move from strict propaganda to a more nuanced public relations policy, the US seems to have made the opposite shift from a self-professed objective news source to a taxpayer-funded international propaganda machine.

Scholarly research on VOA has often focused on its objectivity and credibility – both understandable concerns given the nature of its existence. In his analysis of the "voices of America," Uttaro (1982) found that VOA itself was less propagandistic than its cousins Radio Free Europe and Radio Liberty, despite the fact that VOA was more directly overseen by the US government. However, Uttaro also notes that while most presidents have promised editorial independence for VOA, "none have been able to refrain from exerting pressure on its news writers to tone down material that might damage or embarrass the administration" (Uttaro 1982, 115). Writing twenty years after Uttaro, Ungar (2005, 7) states that "political interference in programming decisions, thought to be a thing of the past, has returned." Specifically, he highlighted the Congressionally mandated editorials expressing the official views of the US government made in each broadcast that "now blend into or trump objective news reports" (Ungar 2005, 7).

6.4 Methodology

This research is concerned with the ideologies surrounding North Korea that are present in state-sponsored media outlets, and the practices used by those outlets to propagate their ideologies through media. The focus on North Korea is the result of a broader scope of research comparing the ideologies of the two media outlets. The methodological approach involved both quantitative research through content analysis and qualitative research through critical discourse analysis. The dual approach was selected so that the findings from the content analysis and corpus linguistics analysis served to highlight patterns that were critically assessed in more detail through the manual, in-depth discourse analysis (Flowerdew and Richardson 2018).

While a discourse analysis of either outlet could provide a wealth of data on its own, a comparative approach was selected as the best fit for what this research aims to accomplish. Chan and Lee (2017) argue that such comparative approaches to media have many epistemological and methodological advantages. One advantage is that comparative research challenges normative assumptions or approaches by putting the subjects of analysis on a level playing field instead of assuming a singular approach. Furthermore, and what is most crucial to this research, Chan and Lee (2017, 1) state that comparative approaches enable researchers "to more readily identify the influence of social, political, and cultural contexts in shaping media and communication phenomenon."

The data utilized for this research comes from China Radio International (CRI), from the People's Republic of China; and Voice of America (VOA), from the United States of America. Both outlets provide a dedicated daily international news program, which are comparable, and therefore ideal for a comparative content analysis. CRI has *Today*, a "locally produced program with a distinctly international flavour" that airs every weekday with two 54-minute segments (CRI: Today 2018). VOA has *International Edition*, a world news program which airs a 30-minute report and three 25-minute follow-up news segments Monday through Saturday (VOA: International Edition 2018). Data collection took place between March 1 and 31, 2016, the month in which North Korea declared that it possessed nuclear warheads and subsequently test-fired those missiles into the sea off its northeast coast (BBC 2016).

The representative sample comprises Tuesday and Friday broadcasts from each outlet throughout the month, resulting in nine discrete broadcasts from which the data was recorded. These two days were selected because consecutive days were found to have a significant number of overlapping stories and sources for both outlets, albeit especially for VOA. The broadcasts were recorded, then transcribed using online audio transcription software. The unit of analysis was a single news story. For the corpus linguistic analysis, Sketch

Engine text analysis software was utilized to determine frequency for words and multi-word expressions, keywords and collocations. MAXCQD software was used to assist the manual critical discourse analysis.

6.5 Findings

6.5.1 Corpus

The Sketch Engine analysis of China Radio International revealed that the phrase "North Korea" and "DPRK" appeared a combined thirty-eight times in the dataset, while "South Korea" appeared twelve times. It's worth noting North Korea was the most-mentioned country for CRI behind Japan (114 total mentions) and the United States (113 total mentions) (see Table 6.1a).

For Voice of America, "North Korea" was mentioned a total of forty-seven times. This was the second most-mentioned after Syria (seventy total mentions), while China and South Korea were significantly further down the list with thirty-four and seventeen mentions, respectively (see Table 6.1b).

These findings largely reflect the news cycle for both CRI and VOA in terms of country coverage; while the situation on the Korean peninsula and its impact on the world was a frequent news story for both outlets, the Syrian Civil War was much more salient for VOA.

Table 6.1a *Country mentions in CRI*

Word	Frequency	Test
Japan	88	raw frequency
Japanese	26	raw frequency
US	73	raw frequency
United States	40	cluster frequency
North Korea	29	cluster frequency
DPRK	9	cluster frequency
South Korea	12	cluster frequency

Table 6.1b *Country mentions in VOA*

Country	Frequency	Test
Syria	70	raw frequency
North Korea	47	raw frequency
China	34	raw frequency
South Korea	17	raw frequency

6.5.2 Manual Critical Discourse Analysis: CRI

The manual discourse analysis revealed that CRI discussed North Korea in a very distinct and consistent manner. One characteristic of CRI's discourse is the frequent use of the terms "situation" and "issue" to describe North Korea's rocket launches – euphemisms which avoid more militaristic or aggressive depictions. A second characteristic is the regular use of the "Korean peninsula" rather than referring to either North Korean or South Korea, thereby discussing the actions of the DPRK without directly having to place blame on China's ally. These two approaches were frequently used in conjunction with each other, and they are all the more striking because they are in stark contrast to how other countries – namely Japan – are portrayed in CRI discourse.

When discussing China's diplomacy with neighbors, the presenter states: "So Chinese President Xi Jinping is going to attend the meeting and of course the **situation on the Korean peninsula** will be highly expected on the agenda" (CRI_20160301; emphasis added). Later, an international academic says "And there are **issues like North Korea** that have come up quite prominently in recent days, which provide the opportunity for greater cooperation among even the major powers, together with the middle powers, major powers referring to the US, China, Japan and South Korea and Australia" (CRI_20160301; emphasis added). Here, an international academic refers to North Korea as an "issue," but still uses the aforementioned positive language to bring optimism to the situation – namely, phrasing the issue of North Korea as an "opportunity for greater cooperation" among countries. In the same story, the presenter states: "Well there's been lots of dialogue between China and the US recently, we've seen Chinese foreign minister Wang Yi and US Secretary of State John Kerry meeting only last week to discuss the **issue of the Korean peninsula**" (CRI_20160301; emphasis added).

Likewise, in coverage of a press conference with Foreign Minister Wang Yi, a presenter states: "North Korea, nuclear, uh ... **nuclear issue on the Korean peninsula** is not something new." (CRI_20160308; emphasis added). This reference is more interesting because it seems that the presenter originally started to refer to North Korea's nuclear program, then quickly changed tack and instead shifted the focus to the entire Korean peninsula. In that same broadcast, Foreign Minister Wang Yi himself uses this approach when he states: "The resolution 2270 is not only about sanctions, it also reinstated, restated that all the parties shall not take any actions that might deteriorate the **situation on the Korean peninsula**" (CRI_20160308; emphasis added). The term was used again in the "Global Survey of Headlines" segment of a later broadcast. Here, the presenter stated: "And finally, in North America, US President Barack Obama will hold a trilateral meeting with South Korean and Japanese leaders on Thursday on the **issue of North Korea**." (CRI_20160329;

emphasis added). This sentence also serves to highlight the context for the most-mentioned countries: the situation on the Korean peninsula was frequently mentioned in relation to its impact on Japan (the first most-mentioned country) and the United States (the second most-mentioned country).

The result of these characteristics is the careful avoidance of blame on a single country or action, and this becomes more pronounced in the context. The reference to issues on "the Korean peninsula" implies multiple aggressors, rather than placing the blame on North Korea. In one segment, the presenter states: "Well, moving on a little bit north now from Vietnam, moving up to North Korea, we've seen recently that that country's attempts to continue its nuclear programme have somewhat strained relations on the Korean peninsula and in the surrounding area as well" (CRI_20160301). Here, in a story focused on China's diplomacy with its neighbors, the presenter euphemistically refers to North Korea's "attempts to continue its nuclear programme," suggesting that this is a simple continuation of an existing policy without any other provoking factors. Furthermore, it is not North Korea itself that has euphemistically "somewhat strained relations on the Korean peninsula," but instead this "continuation of their nuclear programme," thereby avoiding putting blame on the North Korean government directly.

In another story, in response to Foreign Minister Wang Yi's statement on the Korean peninsula, a presenter stated: "Well Victor, the Minister said that this issue should be solved step by step, and I acknowledge that this Minister when he visited the United States last month, he also stated 'the Korean peninsula must be de-nuclearized, and there can be no more turbulence'" (CRI_20160308; emphasis added). The latter part of this sentence, which quotes the Foreign Minister, not only uses the aforementioned tactic of referring to "the Korean peninsula," but also uses the passive voice. In the English language, the passive voice sentence structure is used to avoid labeling a subject or identifying the entity doing the action. Not only does this quote avoid stating that it is North Korea that must denuclearize by instead including the whole of the Korean peninsula, but the passive voice also allows there to be no actor doing the denuclearization at all, thereby avoiding both assigning action and assigning blame.

A similar sentiment is echoed in this story by a correspondent, who states that "the challenge is really for all the parties concerned to look into this issue squarely and see the true nature and the ever-changing nature of the nuclear weapons programme of the DPRK on the Korean peninsula, and really come up with the very effective way of **achieving the ultimate goal of denuclearization**" (CRI_20160308; emphasis added). Again, denuclearization is seen as a goal, one that all parties must work towards to achieve. Though this statement references both the Democratic People's Republic of Korea and the Korean peninsula as a whole, it again avoids assigning action or blame for the current state of nuclearization on North Korea specifically. This statement also relies on positive language, by phrasing denuclearization as both a "challenge" that can lead to the "achievement of a goal" by all parties, rather than as a problem to be fixed.

The same correspondent, later in that story, also stated: "Simply by talking about the issue will not achieve **the denuclearization goal on the Korean peninsula**. Effective measures **need to be adopted** and the international community **need to be brought** onto the same page in dealing with the DPRK government" (CRI_20160308; emphasis added). Again, we see the Korean situation phrased as a "denuclearization goal" that is shared by all parties on the Korean peninsula; again, we see the use of passive voice sentence construction, in that effective measures "need to be adopted" (by whom?) and the international community "need to be brought onto the same page" (by whom?), in a careful avoidance of delegating action and responsibility. The use of the phrase "international community" is also extremely vague, and seems to simultaneously target all countries and yet no one country specifically.

In the press conference with Foreign Minister Wang Yi, the Foreign Minister himself stated: " . . . we will provide support for North Korea to seek security and development, but at the same time, I want to make clear that we will uphold peace on the Korean peninsula. We will not allow North Korea to proceed with this nuclear programme. Dialogues would be the ultimate way out." (CRI_20160308). This is perhaps the most direct mention of China (through the pronoun "we") condemning North Korea's nuclear program. Here the Foreign Minister balances this direct statement with positive language: "provide support" for North Korea, allowing them to "seek security and development," while at the same time China will "uphold peace," and promote "dialogues" as a way out.

Several weeks later, the situation with North Korea changed when Pyongyang fired projectiles in the direction of Japan. This news warranted a very short segment, however, appearing only in one sentence in the Global Survey of Headlines: "First off, in Asia, North Korea has fired five short-range projectiles into its eastern waters in an apparent show of force toward ongoing US-South Korea joint military exercises" (CRI_20160322). Unlike previous references to the country, this one directly states that North Korea is an aggressor; however, even this short sentence manages to curtail the blame: it is credited as a show of force in apparent retaliation to actions by the US and South Korea. The statement could be interpreted as justification for North Korea's actions, as the initial aggressors were actually the US and South Korea.

This avoidance of blame becomes more pronounced in comparison to how blame is directly ascribed to other international actors in CRI stories. Discourses of blame in other stories typically focused on the territorial disputes in the South China Sea, and Japan was commonly cited as a culprit for such disputes. For example, in the discussion on the situation on the Korean peninsula, a presenter asked: "Do you think what Dr Lin has just said is a good opportunity for Japan to work with China and maybe, mending their relationship, since it's been strained since last year, pretty much, by Japan's new position on its defence law . . . ?" (CRI_20160301). Here, the presenter phrases Japan's potential involvement positively – focusing on an "opportunity" to "mend" their relationship. However, the presenter also makes clear that the reason the relationship needs mending is Japan's fault: " . . . since it's been strained since last year, pretty much, by Japan's new position on its defence law . . . ".

In the same story, the presenter later asked "Do you think that Japan is taking advantage of the territorial disputes in the South China Sea and teaming up with South East Asian countries against China?" (CRI_20160301). This is a leading question, as well as suggesting that the territorial disputes are due to Japan's "taking advantage" and "teaming up" against China – both negative phrases that suggest unethical, devious behavior. Shortly after, the presenter mentions "Japan's so-called 'united front' against China," (CRI20160301), again fashioning Japan as opposed to China without just cause. When discussing Japan's new radar system, the presenter asked if Japan was "trying to cash in on the window in which China has to simultaneously deal with the issues in the South China Sea?" (CRI_20160329), in another example of loaded leading questions.

In the press conference with Foreign Minister Wang Yi, the Minister was less specific about who was to blame for the situation in the South China Sea, but also made clear that the blame lay outside of China. He stated: "On the stage of the South China Sea there is legal occupation. Now **some are stirring up troubles and flexing their muscles**. All these intentions will be in vain. History will prove again that who will be the genuine owner and who will be just passers-by" (CRI_20160308; emphasis added). He very decisively states that China's presence in the South China Sea is legal; any disputes he credits to "some" who "are stirring up troubles and flexing their muscles." Without directly stating a responsible nation, he chalks up any disputes to aggression on the part of outsiders who are interfering with China's rightful claim to the territory.

Similarly, when listing China's peaceful initiatives in the South China Sea, Foreign Minister Wang Yi stated: "I think these all demonstrate fully China's sincere gratitude in the South China Sea, but **due to objections made by other countries**, I think, China's habits in the area's not as smooth as it is expected, but we have full confidence that along with other countries, we can safeguard the peaceful development of the South China Sea" (CRI_20160308; emphasis added). In this statement, Minister Wang says that China's "habits" are "not as smooth as it is expected," which seems to be an acknowledgment that the situation is not exactly as it should be. However, this is prefaced by his assigning blame: the word "due to" establishes direct causation, and the culprits are "objections made by other countries." While this seems a strange way of phrasing this sentence – "objections" themselves are not capable of causing issues – it is again clear that other countries are behind any issues in the South China Sea.

The case against Japan is made more clearly in a story unrelated to North Korea, but focused on territorial disputes between China and Japan. In this story, China repeatedly uses the terms "peace" and "stability," but in such a way that directly implicates Japan. The story starts as "Chinese authorities are calling on Japan to do more to safeguard regional peace and stability" (CRI_20160329). This is followed closely by the presenter elaborating: "A statement from the Chinese foreign ministry said the Chinese side hopes Japan will do much more to benefit regional peace and stability" (CRI_20160329). Several minutes later, the presenter repeats: " ... and Chinese foreign ministry spokesperson said that the Chinese side would hope much more to benefit regional peace and stability instead of doing the opposite" (CRI_20160329). Repetition is a commonly used literary and rhetorical device, used to emphasize a point or make it more memorable. This fourth and final repetition is especially noteworthy, because it explicitly references "doing the opposite" – the implication that has been present since the beginning.

The explicit statement is that Chinese authorities are positively encouraging a desirable outcome ("peace and stability"); however, Japan is considered to be doing the opposite, whether that's causing a dispute or creating instability. With the presenter's mention of "instead of doing the opposite," it's a more direct accusation that the Japanese government is acting aggressively. Examining only these words in isolation, there is a clear dichotomy that can be understood as "the Chinese government works for peace and stability" and "the Japanese government challenges peace and stability." What's most interesting in this story, however, is how CRI is able to maintain its preference for positive language. There is no direct mention of aggression or trouble on the part of Japan; however, through its use of positive language in "peace and stability," and its implications of parties not upholding those desirable values, CRI is able to simultaneously maintain China's image as a peacekeeper and accuse other countries of failing to be likewise.

While CRI discourse carefully avoids blame in relation to the DPRK, it quite directly casts China as instrumental in resolving the conflict, alongside other world powers. In the press conference with Foreign Minister Wang, he states: "China seeks the due track of de-nuclearization and the replacement of the Korean armistice with a peace agreement ... As far as other proposals are concerned, whether three party, four party or five party negotiations, as far as they are conducive to the peace of the Korean peninsula, we remain open to all of these proposals" (CRI_20160308). In another broadcast, a presenter states that "there's been lots of dialogue between China and the US recently, we've seen Chinese Foreign Minister Wang Yi and US Secretary of State John Kerry meeting only last week to discuss the issue of the Korean peninsula" (CRI_20160301_1), while a CRI correspondent similarly opines that "China and the other major countries really need to be on the same page to achieve the ultimate goal of denuclearization" (CRI_20160308_1). Though the situation may be focused on the Korean peninsula, the discourse from CRI impresses on listeners that world powers – including China – must agree together on a solution.

6.5.3 Manual Critical Discourse Analysis: VOA

VOA's coverage of North Korea was characterized both by negative language and by affiliation with countries perceived as non-democratic and with complicated relations with the United States. The concept of "democracy" appeared repeatedly throughout the VOA broadcasts. It was used as both an adjective ("democratic") and a noun ("democracy"), was usually framed using positive language, and was frequently collocated with the terms "human rights" and "freedom." In the VOA broadcasts, the gaining of democracy is presented as a positive step; the loss of democracy is cause for concern.

Therefore, it's little surprise that countries perceived to be non-democratic should have the opposite treatment in the data. "Communism" in particular was presented as the antithesis of "democracy" in many ways. Discourse about communism appeared exclusively as an adjective ("communist") and was used to describe just two countries: North Korea and Cuba. This contrast between democratic and communist countries resulted in very divergent coverage of North and South Korea.

North Korea appeared frequently in VOA's broadcasts primarily due to North Korea's actions on the nuclear front. However, there were also mentions of Otto Warmbier, an American who was sentenced to hard labor in North Korea as punishment for attempting to bring propaganda out of the country (Sang-Hun and Gladstone 2016).

In one story focused on North Korea, a correspondent stated: "So, to elaborate on what you said earlier, **the communist country** fired six projectiles into the East Sea early Thursday, and South Korea's Defence Minister said they were either rockets or guided missiles" (VOA_20160304_1705_1; emphasis added). In a different story, a correspondent said: "The State Department on Twitter shared a video of Deputy Spokesperson Mark Toner commenting on the conviction of Otto Warmbier, and urging Pyongyang to pardon him. Some of the replies asked for a ban on leisure travel to **the communist country**"

(VOA_20160318_2330_1; emphasis added). In both of these instances, "communist" is used to modify the country of North Korea.

Cuba and North Korea were the only countries described by their governmental system in these broadcasts; no country was described as a "democratic country" or a "socialist country" in the way that these countries were described as "communist countries." The inclusion of the government system, without any further description, therefore seems gratuitous and intended to draw attention to communism simply by its association with Cuba and North Korea, two countries that have complicated relationships with the United States government.

North Korea was also lumped together with other such countries in terms of human rights. One VOA editorial ("on behalf of the United States' government") declares "During the 31st regular session of the United Nations Human Rights Council in Geneva, United States delegates raised concerns regarding human rights in Syria, Iran, Burundi, South Sudan, North Korea, and China. They also highlighted abuses in several other countries" (VOA_20160329_2330_6). The editorial goes on to condemn perceived human rights abuses in Cuba and Russia – again, countries deemed non-democracies by the United States. This stance from VOA is in line with the existing literature, which finds a consistent pro-democracy /anti-communist stance in US media, as well as with this research's findings on democracy and communism: according to VOA discourse, democracy is a necessary condition for human rights. Therefore, non-democratic countries, like North Korea and China as mentioned in the editorial, must therefore be lacking in human rights. It's also worth noting that this particular editorial does not state what those alleged human rights abuses are – the countries at the beginning of the editorial are simply listed all together, giving the impression that their transgressions are both equal and obvious.

Similarly, a story focused on North Korea's missile launch included this statement by a representative from a US think tank: "Yes, but there it was pretty clear that everybody was on board to enforcing the sanctions. It's less clear that **Russia**, given the exceptions it introduced today, and **China**, are as much on board. We're just going to have to see by their behaviours" (VOA_20160304_1705_1; emphasis added). In both of the above mentions, China and Russia are portrayed as getting in the way of progress by not "getting on board" as "everybody" else clearly was. The implication is that these countries are obstructing progress on behalf of troublesome countries like North Korea. Regardless of whether Russia and China did stand in the way of sanctions on North Korea, the fact that these countries were specifically mentioned amongst all others seems only to serve the purpose of naming and shaming.

Unlike CRI, there were definite distinctions between North Korea and South Korea in the VOA corpus, and only two mentions of the "Korean peninsula." In addition to the mentions of "North Korea," the VOA corpus also included eleven mentions of "Pyongyang" – in this case, a metonym for the North Korean government. These are important distinctions because VOA often used negative or hostile language when referring to "North Korea" and Pyongyang, and did not shy away from assigning blame.

In one story, a VOA presenter introduces a story as "sanctions tighten around a **defiant** North Korea," and later states that US UN Ambassador Samantha Power "acknowledged that the North Koreans are **masters of evasion**" (VOA_20160304_1705_1; emphasis added). The latter sentence also includes a noteworthy choice of attribution: instead of a neutral "said" or "stated" to repeat the Ambassador's words, the broadcast describes her as "acknowledging," which gives credibility to and supports her accusation of North Koreans as a whole.

Another story referred to "Pyongyang's latest **angry** response to expanded UN sanctions against it" (VOA_20160304_2230; emphasis added). Still another stated definitively that "North Korea **hates** the massive military drills by Seoul and Washington ... " (VOA_20160311_1705). Through negative adjectives, verbs and nouns, VOA discourse paints an unflattering image of Pyongyang in a way that brings to mind a petulant child in defiance of a deserved punishment meted out by the US and UN.

The use of Pyongyang as metonym for the North Korean government is also important because it allows VOA to suggest a distinction between the government and the people. This is seen when VOA refers to then-US President Obama sending "Pyongyang a simple message: abandon these dangerous programmes and choose a better path for the North Korean people" (VOA_20160304_1705_1).

Yet the blame is not exclusively on North Korea – VOA discourse also accuses another non-democratic country, China, of being an accomplice. In one story focused on North Korea's firing of missiles, the presenter states: " ... China's ambassador expressed some concern about the possibility that a US anti-missile system would be deployed to South Korea and he talked about a call for a return to dialogue, the six-party process" (VOA_20160304_1705_1), to which an external source from a US think tank responds: "Well, I think if China had acted like a great power in the first place, North Korea would have never been allowed to develop the Nodong or the Musudan missiles that pose the threat that the THAAD missile system, defence system, is designed to deal with. Now China needs to decide to act like a great power and get those weapons removed from North Korea" (VOA_20160304). Here, the blame for North Korea's actions is placed on China, which is accused of not "acting like a great power." The external source takes the presenter's statement regarding

China's concern of US actions and turns it into China's fault – essentially, the US wouldn't have to be taking those steps if China had behaved properly. It bears repeating that this statement is by an external source and not a VOA presenter; yet the choice of whom to quote and include as a source is always intentional and cannot be considered apolitical.

6.6 Conclusion

In the case of CRI's *Today* and VOA's *International Edition*, the combination of content analysis and manual critical discourse analysis revealed a number of practices and ideologies that largely reflect the cultural or media values associated with these countries from existing literature. As Akhavan-Majid and Ramaprasad (1998, 147) found in their research, CRI used positive language that "generally downplayed conflict." North Korea's firing of missiles was continually referred to as "the situation on the Korean peninsula," (CRI_20160301) or "the issue on the Korean peninsula" (CRI_20160308), euphemisms that mask blame and avoid a direct statement of North Korean aggression. Stories focused not on North Korea's activities, but more on diplomatic efforts surrounding the issues, such as the story where Chinese President Xi Jinping was attending a meeting with this "situation" on the agenda (CRI_20160301), or a trilateral meeting between countries on the "issue" (CRI_20160329).

It's also fascinating to note the extent to which CRI can use positive language to its advantage, even when leveling accusations or assigning blame. This was seen in CRI's discourse around Japan, which provides a sharp contrast to the outlet's portrayal of North Korea. While there is no explicit mention of aggression on the part of Japan (other than vague references to some countries "stirring up troubles and flexing their muscles" [CRI_20160308]), there are repeated uses of the phrase "peace and stability" used to accuse Japan. Through statements such as "Chinese foreign ministry spokesperson said that the Chinese side would hope much more to benefit regional peace and stability instead of doing the opposite" (CRI_20160329), CRI is able to simultaneously portray China as a promoter of peace and stability and reproach Japan for failing to do the same.

The comparison of content with VOA also revealed that CRI did not report on the detention of American Otto Warmbier, though this was a headline story for many international news outlets. This could be attributed to a number of factors: for one, human rights concerns are regularly leveled against China as well as North Korea (as seen in the VOA editorial), and there was possibly a decision made to avoid the topic so as not to bring attention to China's own human rights practices as well as those of its ally. However, as is often the case with media, it could simply be that CRI's editorial board felt it was not a newsworthy enough story: much of CRI's content seen here is focused on large-scale, multinational stories rather than the plight of individuals.

VOA did not show such restraint. In its portrayal of North Korea, VOA discourse used openly negative words such as "defiant," "angry," "hates," and even "masters of evasion." Beyond these, VOA used an accusatory tactic against China similar to what CRI used against Japan. Instead of directly accusing China, a VOA source states that "if China had acted like a great power in the first place, North Korea would have never been allowed to develop the Nodong or the Musudan missiles" (VOA_20160304) – basically accusing China of failing to uphold its responsibility in Asia.

VOA's coverage of North Korea is also similar to what one would expect from an America media outlet, in that it promoted "democracy" and "human rights" while disparaging "communism" (Kobland et al. 1992). In this way, VOA used affiliation to lump together countries seen as problematic to the US government, often without any explanation as to why. This was especially prevalent in the VOA editorial which discussed abuses of "human rights in Syria, Iran, Burundi, South Sudan, North Korea, and China," along with Cuba and Russia (VOA_20160329_2330_6). This method of association suggests that one country's sins are as bad as another's, without having to explain those human rights abuses. In this way, it's almost assumed to be ubiquitously understood and common-sensical that these countries are guilty of human rights abuses – which is precisely the goal of public diplomacy outlets such as VOA.

These findings demonstrate how CRI and VOA are restricted to the informational framework, or tough-minded school, of public diplomacy. As Snow (2009) states, these outlets are limited in their use of one-way informational media that preclude real exchanges and relationship building. Genuine public-to-public exchanges, even through unidirectional media outlets, have the possibility of enjoying more credibility and creating more mutual understanding than government-to-public outlets such as CRI and VOA. There are countless ways that such outlets could contribute to a mutual understanding between peoples and countries around the world, if countries were interested in making this a priority.

Yet as voices for their respective governments, the editorial and linguistic choices made by CRI and VOA are intentional and based on definite agendas. What is obvious in this discourse is the subtle glimpses of ideology, delivered in a way that seems like common sense: of course, human rights abuses should be condemned, and support should be accorded to governments that strive for peace and stability. It is only through recognizing the ideology behind the discourse and identifying the tactics used to deliver that ideology that listeners can fully understand and utilize the "news" delivered to them from CRI and VOA.

References

Akhavan-Majid, Roya, and Ramaprasad, Jyotika. 1998. "Framing and Ideology: A Comparative Analysis of US and Chinese Newspaper Coverage of the Fourth United Nations Conference on Women and the NGO Forum." *Mass Communication Faculty Publications* 1(3&4): 131–152. https://doi.org/10.1080/15205436.1998.9677853.

Bandow, Doug. 2016. *Will China Solve the North Korea Problem? The United States Should Develop a Diplomatic Strategy to Persuade Beijing to Help*. Cato Institute Policy Analysis No. 806, December 2, 2016. www.cato.org/publications/policy-analysis/will-china-solve-north-korea-problem.

BBC News. 2016. "North Korea 'Fires Short-Range Missiles'." March 10, 2016. www.bbc.com/news/world-asia-35770198.

BBC News. 2016. "North Korea 'Has Miniature Nuclear Warhead', Says Kim Jong-Un." March 9, 2016. www.bbc.com/news/world-asia-35760797.

Bell, Allan. 1995. "Language and the Media." *Annual Review of Applied Linguistics* 15: 23–41. https://doi:10.1017/S0267190500002592.

Bell, Allan, and Peter Garrett (eds.). 1998. *Approaches to Media Discourse*. Oxford: Blackwell.

Chan, Joseph M., and Lee, Francis. 2017. *Advancing Comparative Media and Communication Research*. London: Routledge.

Chen, Chwen Chwen, Colapinto, Cinzia, and Luo, Qing. 2010. "China Radio International in the Digital Age: Propagating China on the Global Scenario." *Global Media Journal* 9(16).

China Daily. 2016. "DPRK Fires Short-Range Ballistic Missiles into Eastern Waters." March 10, 2016. www.chinadaily.com.cn/world/2016-03/10/content_23806884.htm.

China Radio International. 2012. "About China Radio International." Accessed August 3, 2018. http://english.cri.cn/11114/2012/09/20/1261s723239.htm.

China Radio International. 2017. "Who We Are." Accessed August 3, 2018. http://chinaplus.cri.cn/aboutus/aboutcri/62/20170216/393.html.

Cull, Nicholas J. 2009. "Public Diplomacy before Gullion: The Evolution of a Phrase." In *Routledge Handbook of Public Diplomacy*, ed. by Nancy Snow and Philip M. Taylor, 19–23. New York: Routledge.

d'Hooghe, Ingrid. 2005. "Public Diplomacy in the People's Republic of China." In *The New Public Diplomacy: Soft Power in International Relations*, ed by Jan Melissen, 88–105. New York: Palgrave Macmillan.

Entman, Robert M. 1991. "Framing U.S. Coverage of International News: Contrasts in Narratives of the KAL and Iran Air Incidents." *Journal of Communication* 41(4): 6–27. https://doi.org/10.1111/j.1460-2466.1991.tb02328.x.

Fairclough, Norman. 1995. *Media Discourse*. London: Bloomsbury Academic.

Flowerdew, John, and Richardson, John (Eds.). (2018). *The Routledge Handbook of Critical Discourse Studies*. London: Routledge.

Hu, Zhengrong. 2007. "The Chinese Model and Paradigm of Media Studies." *Global Media and Communication* 3(3): 335–339. https://doi.org/10.1177/17427665070030030404.

Hudson, John. 2013. "U.S. Repeals Propaganda Ban, Spreads Government-Made News to Americans." *Foreign Policy*, July 14, 2013. https://foreignpolicy.com/2013/07/14/u-s-repeals-propaganda-ban-spreads-government-made-news-to-americans/.

Kelley, John Robert. 2009. "Between 'Take-offs' and 'Crash Landings': Situational Aspects of Public Diplomacy." In *Routledge Handbook of Public Diplomacy*, ed. by Nancy Snow and Philip Taylor. New York: Routledge.

Kobland, C. E., Du, Liping, and Kwon, Joongrok. 1992. "Influence of Ideology in News Reporting Case Study of *New York Times*' Coverage of Student Demonstrations in China and South Korea." *Asian Journal of Communication* 2(2): 64–77. https://doi.org/10.1080/01292989209359549.

Kurlantzick, Joshua. 2007. *Charm Offensive: How China's Soft Power Is Transforming the World*. London: Yale University Press.

Nye, Joseph S. 2008. "Public Diplomacy and Soft Power." *The ANNALS of the American Academy of Political and Social Science* 616(1): 94–109. https://doi.org/10.1177/0002716207311699.

Qing, Koh Gui, and Shiffman, John. 2015. "Beijing's Covert Radio Network Airs China-Friendly News Across Washington, and the World." *Reuters*, November 2, 2015. www.reuters.com/investigates/special-report/china-radio/.

Rawnsley, Gary. D. 2015. "To Know Us Is to Love Us: Public Diplomacy and International Broadcasting in Contemporary Russia and China." *Politics* 35(3–4): 273–286. https://doi.org/10.1111/1467-9256.12104.

Sang-Hun, Choe, and Gladstone, Rick. 2016. "North Korea Sentences Otto Warmbier, U.S. Student, to 15 Years' Labor." *The New York Times*, March 16, 2016. www.nytimes.com/2016/03/17/world/asia/north-korea-otto-warmbier-sentenced.html.

Shambaugh, David. 2007. "China's Propaganda System: Institutions, Processes and Efficacy." *The China Journal* 57: 25–58.

Signitzer, Benno H., and Coombs, Timothy. 1992. "Public Relations and Public Diplomacy: Conceptual Convergence." *Public Relations Review* 18(2): 137–147. https://doi.org/10.1016/0363-8111(92)90005-J.

Snow, Nancy. 2009. "Rethinking Public Diplomacy." In *Routledge Handbook of Public Diplomacy*, ed. by Nancy Snow and Philip Taylor, 3–11. New York: Routledge.

Ungar, Sanford. J. 2005. "Pitch Imperfect: The Trouble at the Voice of America." *Foreign Affairs* 84(3): 7–13.

US Agency for Global Media. 2018. "Who We Are." Accessed August 3, 2018. www.usagm.gov/who-we-are/.

US Agency for Global Media. 2018. "VOA: History." Accessed August 7, 2018. www.insidevoa.com/p/5829.html.

Uttaro, Ralph A. 1982. "The Voices of America in International Radio Propaganda." *Law and Contemporary Problems* 45(4): 103–122. https://scholarship.law.duke.edu/lcp/vol45/iss1/6/.

Wang, Yiwei. 2008. "Public Diplomacy and the Rise of Chinese Soft Power." *Annals of the American Academy of Political and Social Science* 616(1): 257–273. https://doi.org/10.1177/0002716207312757.

Wodak, Ruth. 2001. "The Discourse-Historical Approach." In *Methods of Critical Discourse Analysis*, ed. by Ruth Wodak and Michael Meyer, 63–94. London: Sage.

Zaharna, Rhonda S. 2009. "Mapping out a Spectrum of Public Diplomacy Initiatives." In *Routledge Handbook of Public Diplomacy*, ed. by Nancy Snow and Philip Taylor, 86–100. New York: Routledge.

Zhang, Xiaoling. 2011. *The Transformation of Political Communication in China: From Propaganda to Hegemony.* London: World Scientific.

Zhang, Xiaoling. 2013. "How Ready Is China for a China-Style World Order? China's State Media Discourse under Construction." *Ecquid Novi: African Journalism Studies* 34(3): 79–101. https://doi.org/10.1080/02560054.2013.834834.

Zhang, Yanqiu. 2014. *Understand China's Media in Africa from the Perspective of Constructive Journalism.* Paper presented at the China and Africa Media, Communications and Public Diplomacy conference in Beijing, China on 10-11 Sept 2014. www.cmi.no/file/2922-.pdf.

7 Against a Hard-Earned Peace

(De)legitimation Discourses of Political Violence in Online Press Statements of Dissident Republicans in Post-Conflict Northern Ireland

Stephen Goulding

> We were the Good Friday Agreement generation, destined to never witness the horrors of war but to reap the spoils of peace. The spoils just never seemed to reach us.
> – *Lyra McKee 1990–2019*

> People do not commit political violence without discourse. They need to talk themselves into it.
> – *David Apter*

7.1 Introduction

In the early hours of April 19, 2019, following a confrontation with the Police Service of Northern Ireland (PSNI) – who were attempting to raid houses in the Creggan Estate in Derry City, Northern Ireland – a New Irish Republican Army (New IRA) gunman fired several shots toward police vehicles. Tragically, one of his stray bullets hit and killed a young journalist, Lyra McKee, who was reporting on the growing tensions in the area. Public condemnations of the killing came from political and societal actors in the days that followed. However, one dissident republican political party, Saoradh, gained particular negative media attention in response to a statement it issued from its website in the wake of the killing. Security forces allege that Saoradh is the political wing of the New IRA who would ultimately go on to accept responsibility for the killing. Rather than condemn the killing outright, Saoradh justified it as the consequential, inevitable result of PSNI aggression and intimidation. Moreover, they began to publicly interrogate the impartiality of the media, whose presence on the night of the killing they called into question; accusing the PSNI (and an allegedly collusive news media) of orchestrating a conflict for public relations purposes. Both dissident and state actors took issue with the other's justificatory explanation for the killing. Each side pointed the finger of blame at the other, in what was, essentially, a struggle for that which underlies all acts of political violence: the notion of legitimacy.

Departing from the premise that "embedded within language are dominant ideologies that reinforce group cause and action" (Lau et al. 2011, 7), this chapter aims to demonstrate how discursive toolkits can provide us with insights into how anti-state actors legitimate acts of violence – in spite of a lack of public support. Incorporating Van Leeuwen's (2008) framework of discursive legitimation, the chapter aims to outline the strategies employed by anti-state actors in (de)legitimating actions surrounding the killing. This analytical measure will be complemented by a micro-analysis of key linguistic strategies (proposed by Reisigl and Wodak 2016) used to construct (de)legitimating representations of (opposing) actors. Empirical data is drawn from a series of statements released by Saoradh (and its partner organizations) around the time of the killing.

The following research questions will guide the analysis of this data:

1. How are the actions of dissident republicans legitimated in their press statements?
2. How do these anti-state actors delegitimate the actions of the PSNI and the media?
3. How do (de)legitimating representations polarize actors – (anti-)state actors in the data?
4. What validity claims, value systems and argumentative strategies sustain dissident actors' representations and shift blame to state actors?

This chapter aligns itself with other works aimed at uncovering the role of language in conflict (Nelson 2003). While it is a case study of a specific incident, its approach is applicable to the analysis of the wider (ongoing) conflict. As such, the chapter further aims to demonstrate the expediency of discursive research in understanding political violence in Northern Ireland at a time when ethno-religious tensions and support for dissident republicanism are, arguably, at an all-time high since the cessation of The Troubles. The chapter contributes to local political research by using the semiosis of political actors to provide insight into the value hierarchies, belief systems and truth claims that sustain discourses of anti-state violence. Given dissident republicans' commitment to continued use of armed resistance, the PSNI's unwavering anti-terrorist ethos and the media's questionable impartiality, it is unlikely we have seen an end to social grievances and (mediated) conflict in Northern Ireland. Therefore, this chapter is significant as it raises awareness about the centrality of language in conceptualizing and (de)legitimizing the continuation of violent resistance in a society predicated upon a hard-earned peace.

7.1.1 Historical Grievances of Republicanism

The tensions that prompted the confrontation in the Creggan can trace their roots back hundreds of years through Ireland's past, to the religious divide, (counter)hegemonic ideologies and social movements that developed as a result of the island's colonization.[1] "Irish Republicanism" (simply republicanism hereafter) – taking inspiration from its counterparts in France and America – emerged in response to colonialism in the late eighteenth century, as a political program that strived for sovereignty, secularism, equality and justice for all (Elliot 1978). Most markedly, it advocated the use of armed insurrection to achieve this goal. The course of the late eighteenth and nineteenth centuries were littered with a litany of failed republican insurrections (see Kee 2000). It was not until Easter 1916 that the militaristic endeavors of republicans (rather serendipitously) met with success, when republican combatants launched an insurrection to forcibly bring the capital city of Dublin to a standstill and declare Ireland a sovereign, independent republic (Foy and Barton 2011). Militarily speaking, the Easter Rising was an unambiguous failure: a blood sacrifice aimed at reinvigorating the demand for Irish independence. Ironically, this feat was not achieved by the insurrection itself, but rather by the actions of the British judicial system, who in executing the leaders of the Rising triggered much outrage and shifted public support to the rebels' cause.

Support for Irish independence snowballed thereafter, leading to electoral success for republican candidates in the general election of 1918 (McAllister 2004). These elections – for the first devolved parliament of Ireland or *Dáil* – saw Sinn Féin (the largest Irish republican party at the time) gain a vast majority of seats and declare the parliament sovereign and independent of British rule. An armed conflict – the War of Independence or Tan War – ensued and resulted in both the British and Irish governments calling a truce and entering into peace talks after two years of warfare. The resulting peace arrangements effectively partitioned the island of Ireland into two states: the newly independent Irish Free State, which comprised the twenty-six counties of the modern-day Republic of Ireland, and Northern Ireland, which encompassed six of the nine counties of the northernmost province of Ulster (Phoenix 1994). The partition was designed to appease the substantial Protestant/unionist community who held a majority in four of the six counties.

Politically, Northern Ireland became an ethnocratic state (Yiftachel 2006). With nationalist/Catholics/republicans refusing to recognize the new state or partake in its systems of government, the state ultimately was administered by a unionist-dominated parliament that sought to establish itself as a "Protestant

---

[1] Initially by Normans in the twelfth century, and later by the United Kingdom of Great Britain after the Act of Union 1800.

Parliament for a Protestant People" (a slogan attributed to Lord Craigavon, the first Prime Minister of Northern Ireland). The resulting Protestant dominance led to high levels of civic and political discrimination against the nationalist minority. The ethnic tensions brought about by the partition, and the continued oppression and unjust treatment of the nationalist community in Northern Ireland, led to growing demands for civil rights and equality. These tensions ultimately boiled over in the late 1960s into an era of conflict colloquially known as "The Troubles": an ethno-religious conflict fought between republican and loyalist paramilitaries and the British state security forces that would last for over thirty years and result in the deaths of more than 3,000 people (Kennedy Pipe 2014).

The Provisional Irish Republican Army (Provisional IRA) a newly founded reincarnation of its para-militant predecessor, became the chief combatant on the republican side and engaged in what they perceived as a "long war": a drawn-out conflict which aimed to suck the British state of resources and time (O'Brien 1995). This later developed into a dual strategy of guerrilla warfare and electoral success: a simultaneous commitment to using "the Armalite and a ballot box"[2] (McAllister 2004). The republican struggle of this era gained international notoriety in the early 1980s when a series of hunger-strikes were undertaken by republican prisoners demanding political status. Their leader, Bobby Sands, was elected as an MP shortly before dying of starvation. The provisional republican movement (comprising the Provisional IRA and its political wing Sinn Féin) claimed authority through professing its republican ancestry and constructing itself as the legitimate descendants of previous incarnations of republicanism, against asserting the right of the Irish people to resist Britain's claim to Northern Ireland (Tonge 2012) – claims which would later be recontextualized and appropriated by subsequent (dissident) republican organizations.

As the conflict dragged on, both sides deduced that the war was – from their respective positions – unwinnable and sought out some form of compromise (Schulze and Smith 2000). When a newly elected Labour government came to power in the UK in 1997, the pathway was cleared for Sinn Féin to enter all-party peace negotiations, chaired by US Senator George Mitchell, from which they were previously barred. The signing of the Good Friday Agreement (GFA) in 1998 marked the culmination of this peace process. Measures were taken to ensure that power was shared between both the unionists and the nationalists and both sides committed to demilitarization and peace (Fraser 2005). The Provisional IRA ultimately announced a cessation of its armed campaign in 2005 (Bowman-Grieve and Conway 2012).

---

[2] A phrase attributed to Sinn Féin Director of Publicity, Danny Morrison.

7.1.2 Dissident Republicanism

The signing of the GFA was not lauded or welcomed by all sects of republicanism, however. For many republicans, the adoption of a "new-mode" of republicanism marked a betrayal and desertion of underlying principles of the ideology (Nolan 2014). In their estimation, republicanism was (and always had been) an ideology that advocated the use of physical force to attain its political goal of British withdrawal from Ireland. They contended that as this was a goal which had not yet been achieved, republicans ought to remain committed to its initial modus operandi. Those who adopted this interpretation became known as "dissident" republicans (Horgan and Morrison 2011; Bowman-Grieve and Conway 2012). And although the term cannot be thought of as denoting a cohesive political entity (rather a selection of marginalized splinter organizations), dissident republicans can be broadly characterized by "their condemnation of the Good Friday Agreement and power-sharing arrangements; their rejection of the Police Service of Northern Ireland as a legitimate police force and often (though not exclusively); and their continued commitment to the use of armed resistance to bring about their political goals of British withdrawal and Irish reunification" (Bowman-Grieve and Conway 2012, 72).

In the aftermath of the peace agreement, a first wave of dissident republican splinter groups – such as the Real IRA and Continuity IRA vowed to continue the flame of armed resistance in Ireland (Hearty 2016), carrying out attacks such as the Omagh bombing (Horgan 2013). In spite of a sizeable number of splinter dissident republican organizations (both paramilitary and political wings) abounding in the 2000s–2010s, none achieved significant electoral or military success and have little hope, as Tonge (2012, 2014) argues, of emulating the Provisional IRA's levels of support in the current political climate.

The New IRA formed in 2012 after the remnants of the Real IRA joined forces with smaller republican vigilante and militant groups and immediately began launching attacks on those it perceived as targets: primarily drug dealers, but also members of the PSNI. For the next four years, these attacks continued until interference and internal feuds stifled their operations in late 2016. Earlier that year, an unregistered dissident republican party – Saoradh – was founded in Dublin. Espousing a far-left political program, Saoradh affirmed its commitment to the visions laid out in the 1916 Proclamation and to the "unfinished revolution, the liberation of Ireland and the social emancipation of the Irish People" (Saoradh 2016).

7.1.3 Continued Armed Dissident Campaign

In 2018, the New IRA launched a fresh spate of attacks where its support base arguably remained strongest – the city of Derry. The attacks coincided with rioting in the Bogside area of Derry city in response to an Orange Order parade that was due to take place on July 12 that year, with copycat riots ensuing across the state, predominantly in Belfast. Earlier that year, dissident republicans attempted to commemorate the 1916 Easter Rising in an unauthorized parade organized by "the Derry 1916 Commemoration Committee." PSNI Land Rovers came under missile fire as they accosted the procession and were repeatedly attacked and petrol-bombed in the Creggan housing estate later that evening. In relation to this, eleven men – prominent republicans from the area, some of whom were leading members of Saoradh – were arrested and set to be prosecuted on April 30, 2019.

The arrests heightened tensions in advance of Easter 2019. On April 17, the Derry 1916 Committee released a statement declaring their intention to march again that year and warning the PSNI that if they again attempted to interfere with proceedings, then "the blame for any acts of resistance rests with them alone" (Saoradh 2019). Two days later, on April 19, the PSNI, who were accompanied by members of the Northern Irish media, launched what they claimed were munitions raids on houses in the Creggan area. Rioting by local youths – who some claim were incited by the New IRA – ensued, with burnt-out cars being used as barricades to prevent PSNI vehicles from entering the housing estate. In the course of these riots, a New IRA gunman fired several shots in the direction of the police vehicles. His shots missed and one tragically struck and killed a young journalist, Lyra McKee, who was on the ground to cover the events and positioned to the rear of the police vehicles. The killing caused public uproar and was widely condemned.

In response to the killing, Saoradh released a statement from its website framing the incident as the consequence of the actions of the PSNI, who it accused of engineering a conflict with the presence of the media to "grab headlines." Although the New IRA would ultimately go on to claim responsibility for the killing, Saoradh received high levels of negative media attention in the wake of the attack, owing to its alleged status as the political wing of the New IRA – a link which it fervently denied (Saoradh 2019).

The trial of the eleven men involved in the Easter 2018 parade received high levels of media attention. A week later, the offices of Saoradh at the Junior McDaid House – which also serves as the offices for their youth wing, Éistigí and the Irish Republican Prisoner Welfare Association (IRPWA) – were raided by members of the PSNI investigating the murder of Lyra McKee. Many of Saoradh's social media pages, including its official website, were shut down as they were allegedly being used to promote hatred and incite violence (Saoradh 2019). In response to both of these occurrences, Saoradh released statements via the Junior McDaid House website condemning the PSNI's actions and representing itself as the victim of censorship (Saoradh 2019).

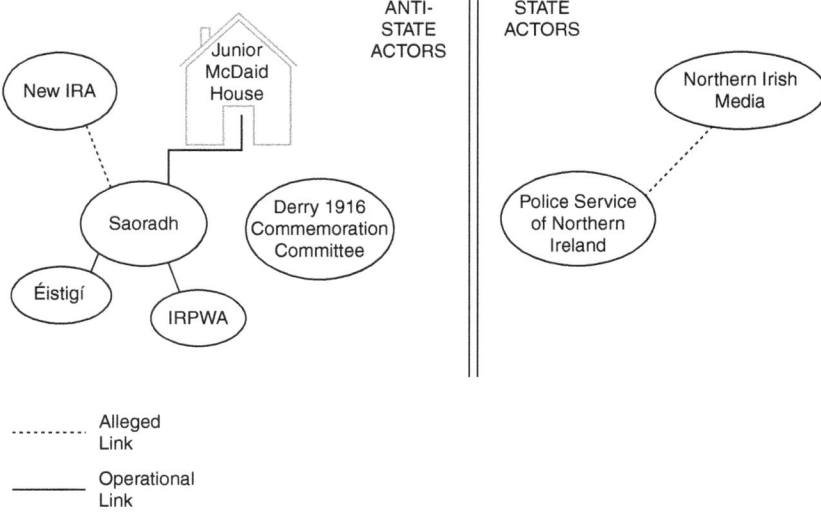

Figure 7.1a (Anti-)state actors and (alleged) operational links)

The temporal focus of the present research finishes with a statement issued in mid-May 2019 directed at the National Union for Journalists (NUJ). Following another raid on Saoradh activists' homes, the party again questioned the impartiality of the media, who it accused of colluding with the PSNI to intensify the hype surrounding the killing. We see, then, that rather than being a simple act of aggression between two combatants, the incident under investigation involves a host of actors who foster (alleged or denied) organizational links. Figure 7.1a illustrates the (alleged) links between actors involved in the incident. In addition, a timeline is provided (Figure 7.1b), illustrating the series of events and release dates of statements during the temporal span under analysis in this chapter. While the start date for the cross-section of the present study was determined by its proximity and contextual relevance to the shooting, the cut-off date of one month was selected as an arbitrary demarcation of time to avoid a selective, cherry-picked upper limit. This ensured a mitigation of researcher bias and a manageable corpus size.

7.2   Legitimation of Political Violence

At a base level, violence of all kinds stands as an affront to established social orders. The transgression, by an actor, of behavioral parameters and norms upon which peaceful societies are premised necessarily leads to social rejection

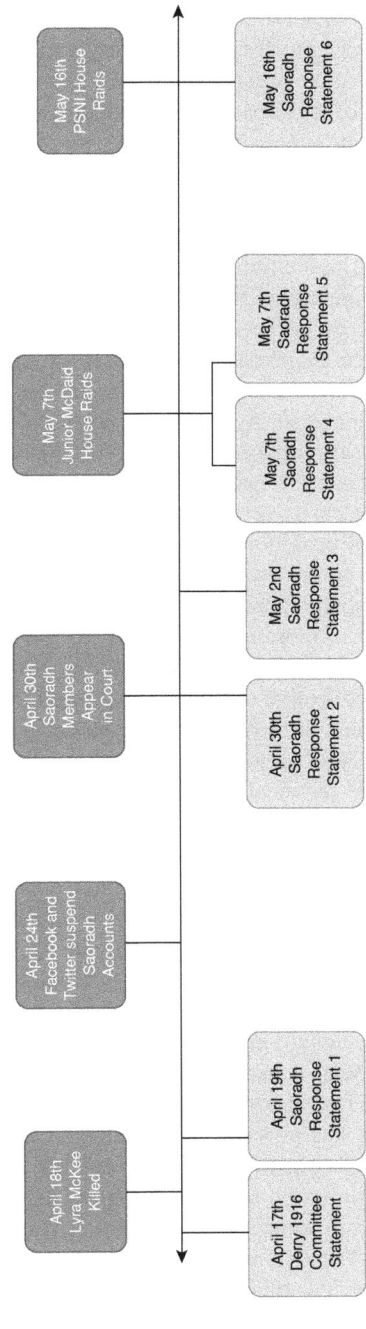

Figure 7.1b Timeline of events and statements

and condemnation from other societal components (Varela-Rey et al. 2013). That is unless the aggressor can proffer a justificatory explanation which is accepted by other components of the social order – thus legitimizing the act. As such, we can view the process of legitimation (i.e., that through which legitimacy is achieved) as a dialogic, communicative action between the aggressor and other components of society. This section is devoted to a conversation on the nexus between political violence, legitimacy and discourse. It begins by outlining how key terms are understood in the context of this chapter, before undertaking an exploration of the literature on discursive legitimation.

A primary distinction that underpins this chapter is that between violence and political violence. Violence can be understood as the intentional (often unbidden) use of physical force against an individual or group; it is typically criminal and often random (insofar as it is reactionary and is not driven by an ulterior motive). Political violence, as Apter (1997) notes, is disordered with a specific, reordering of political purpose: to bring about a change in political structures of dominance and subservience, to dispose or impose a group's religious beliefs or ethnic doctrines, or to achieve territorial sovereignty or quell uprisings. Simply put, political violence is violence with a political slant. It is perpetrated by political actors (state, non-state and anti-state). While interpersonal violence is typically positioned in the ethical parameters of criminality, political violence is morally ambiguous: that is to say, acts of political violence are often more readily defensible and justified by reference to a beneficial outcome for a collective or through appeals to morality, justice and equality. As such, both modalities of violence operate in different moral and justificatory frameworks. Acts of political violence, then, rely heavily on the explanations, reasoning and justifications which beget them.

In order to understand how political violence is legitimated, it is first necessary to have an understanding of what legitimacy entails: a task made difficult by the intangible nature of the concept and a lack of academic consensus on its conceptualization. Taking this convolution and the "considerable surplus meaning(s)" of the term as their impetus, Suddabay et al. (2017) in their interpretive review of the concept, identify three dominant approaches in legitimacy literature: legitimacy-as-property; legitimacy-as-perception and legitimacy-as-process. In this chapter I adhere to the latter of these approaches, and take legitimacy to be a social construct, achieved through interaction of actors – or the process of legitimation. Suchman (1995, 574) presents a definition of legitimacy that has proven to be influential in the canon and accounts for this aforementioned constructedness: in his view, legitimacy is the "generalized perception or assumption that the actions of an entity are desirable, proper or appropriate within some *socially constructed* system of norms, values, beliefs and definitions" (italics mine). We see, then, that legitimacy is not assessed by a universal criterion and is contextually variable. It is conferred by an adherence to (or orientation toward) value hierarchies and belief systems which underpin socio-cultural contexts. For instance, the practice of hand amputation as a punitive measure under Sharia law may seem barbaric to those in the West or Judeo-Christian societies; yet, where it is practiced, it is legitimated by virtue of it being in accord with the culturally endorsed scriptural teachings of the Qu'ran and is enforced by law (Peters 2005).

The above example also touches upon another key characteristic of legitimacy: its close relationship to power and authority. Although often treated as synonymous elsewhere, they are understood here to be distinct. Power is defined here as the capacity of one actor to influence the behavior and attitudes of others (often contrary to their own interests) (Lukes 2004, 37). Power can be conferred through two means: co-option and coercion. Co-option (or soft power) signifies the ability to mold the perceptions, attitudes and, as a result, behaviors of others through non-coercive means, through appeal, attraction or persuasion. Theories such as Lukes' third face of power (Lukes 2004), Gramsci's (cultural) hegemony (see Thomas 2009) and Herman and Chomsky's concept of manufacturing consent (Herman and Chomsky 2010) note that co-option often occurs below the threshold of perception, via control of information flows and exposure of the masses to media texts that are imbued with cultural values and ideologies which, through repeated exposure, become adopted as the norm. They also contend that these normalized ideologies ultimately serve the interests of a ruling elite and not the masses.

Coercion (or hard power) implies the use of force (or threat thereof) to influence the behavior and attitudes of others, generally through military or economic means. For instance, state actors, as noted by Weber (2013), maintain power through a monopoly of violence. Put simply, their statehood relies on their perceived status as the sole entity that can legitimately authorize the use of violence within a demarcated region. The acceptance of this status confers authority. Whereas "power" is the ability to exert control over the behavior of others, "authority" denotes the right to enact power. So while an action might exhibit power, it does not necessarily follow that it exhibits authority. Take, for instance, the practice of taking political hostages by terrorist organizations: while the organization holds a hard, coercive power over the actions of the hostages (and state forces they target), they are not thought of – at least from the perspective of those they are targeting – as having authority, or as having a moral right to do so. Supporters of the terrorists, conversely, may perceive the organization as an authority, and see their actions as justified. Thus, the conferring of authority relies on the acceptance of an actor as legitimate. We see, then, that power is justified through authority which, in turn, is achieved through legitimation.

So when we discuss legitimacy, we speak of a concept that denotes the perceived appositeness of actions in respect to a wider system of beliefs and value hierarchies. Legitimacy is conferred through (persuasively) relating this appositeness and through the exertion of power in its various modalities. But how is the legitimation of political violence achieved?

7.2.1 Discourse and Legitimation

As the quotation from Apter (1997) at the start of this chapter suggests, acts of political violence do not abound randomly. One of the defining characteristics of political violence is that it is spurred by an overarching goal. Rather, those who commit acts of political violence partake and undergo a process of socialization which culminates in violence. An individual's trajectory from passive ideologue to active combatant is fueled by the uptake of group ideology through discourse. Discourse, like legitimacy, is a term which holds much capital in the humanities and social sciences; however, it defies concrete definition, and its meaning is dictated by the context in which it appears. It features in the work of sociologists, linguists, (social) psychologists, anthropologists and both critical and social theorists alike, all of whom (re)define it in line with their respective theoretical positions and disciplines. Scholars who have tended to overviews of discourse have noted that there is a tendency by researchers within these disciplines to assume that the meaning of the term is understood, and to frequently leave it undefined (Mills 2004), often leading to further obfuscation. For the purpose of this chapter, conceptualizations of discourse from two research paradigms are synthesized so as to produce a means of analyzing social phenomena by focusing on linguistic data.

The first of these conceptualizations comes from works in cultural studies and is most associated with the work of Michel Foucault. In his view, discourses are "practices which systematically form the objects of which they speak" (Foucault 1972, 49); in this sense "discourse" seemingly denotes the ideas and institutionalized belief systems or modes of thinking that cause or give rise to utterances and concepts, which are formed in a given context and are discursively realized by statements or utterances. In this view, discourses serve to normalize power dynamics in society. Another understanding of discourse comes from functional text linguistics, which sees it as a type of social action which requires language users to engage in the production and negotiation of meaning (Jaworski and Coupland 1999) and which, when analyzed, should never be considered apart from the functions it undertakes (Halliday 1973, 3). Synthesizing these two approaches, we arrive at a critical interpretation of discourse which is adhered to in this chapter and facilitates the analysis of linguistic features toward a political or normative end so as to address questions and problems of power and ideology from a linguistic approach.

Early work in this critical trend was pioneered by Norman Fairclough, who conceives of discourse as (1) the linguistic manifestation of ideology and (2) as being intrinsically interwoven with social relations and processes (Fairclough 2013). In his view, every social practice involves the use of language (or semiotics) to a certain degree (Chouliaraki and Fairclough 1999). Concurrently, however, he contends that the form of discourse (that is the linguistic form and discursive strategies through which it is constructed) is determined by the social environment (or context) in which it appears (Fairclough 2013). As such, Fairclough argues that discourse and social practice are mutually constitutive: that is to say, they symbiotically influence one another. Summarizing the critical paradigm's interpretation of discourse, Reisigl and Wodak (2016) note that discourse is considered to be:

- a cluster of context-dependent semiotic practices that are situated within specific fields of social action
- socially constituted and constitutive
- related to a macro-topic
- linked to argumentation about validity claims, such as truth and normative validity involving several social actors with different points of view.

(Reisigl and Wodak 2016, 89)

Analyses of political discourses from this perspective aim to elucidate "how some forms of knowledge are privileged over others," how power is "legitimized" and how certain political practices are "normalised" (Jackson 2005, 148). Accordingly, they tend to focus on "the ways discourse structures enact, confirm, legitimate, reproduce, or challenge relations of power and dominance in society" (Van Dijk 2015, 353). If, then, we take legitimation to signify the "the act of justifying and sanctioning a certain action or power, on the basis of normative or other reasons" (Hazaea et al. 2014, 172), we can understand it as discourse that justifies social actions and provides "good reasons, grounds, or acceptable motivations for past or present action" (Van Dijk 1998, 255).

As Van Leeuwen (2008, 93) notes, we can think of legitimation as providing the answers to two pervading "Why" questions: "Why should we do this?" and "Why should we do this in this way?" When analyzing the legitimation of acts of political violence, the aim is to deconstruct the ongoing construction of a "sense of positive, beneficial, ethical, understandable, necessary, or otherwise acceptable action in a specific setting" (Badham 2018, 20). Conversely, when we study the delegitimation of acts of political violence, we focus on the establishment of a negative moral frame which paints the actions as unacceptable and as contravening an overall greater good (Rojo and Van Dijk 1997; Van Leeuwen and Wodak 1999).

Interestingly, an intrinsic link exists between legitimacy and group identity. As Varela-Rey et al. (2013, 86, citing Borja-Orozco et al. 2008) note of conflict legitimation discourses:

First, they have a communicative role, in the sense that it enables to spread the ideology and makes the group more visible. Second, they have a persuasive role, as these types of discourses seek to perform to an audience and to stimulate beliefs within the group itself, with the aim of achieving the legitimacy of its actions.

Rather than solely providing an outward justificatory explanation of actions, legitimation discourses also serve to reiterate commitment to the collective and reinforce in-group ideology. The corollary of this is that out-group actions and interpretations are delegitimized. As such, the polarizing effects of political violence – around affiliations of race, ethnicity, religion, language, class (Apter 1997) – are sustained by the discursive construction of in-groups and out-groups along the line of positive-Self and negative-Other representation (Van Dijk 1993). Moreover, in legitimation discourses, acts of political violence are represented in ways that construct the out-group as the aggressor and ensures the self-victimization of the in-group. A common consequence of this is that the *real* victims of political violence are often, also, delegitimized (Varela-Rey et al. 2013). As such, no consideration of the legitimation of conflict would be complete without an analysis of discursive identification and representation of actors. The analytical framework employed toward this end is outlined in more detail in the subsequent section after a brief discussion on the genre of press statements.

7.3   Methods and Analysis

7.3.1   Press Statements

As the legitimation of political violence relies so heavily on the ability to define and frame an incident in the media, studies of discursive legitimation ought to be drawn to texts which endeavor to do so and are produced in response to and anticipation of acts of violence. Accordingly, this chapter focuses on a series of press statements which were released by anti-state actors in the run-up to or in the wake of the killing of Lyra McKee. As a result of the censorship imposed on Saoradh, statements were sourced from both affiliated organization websites and press articles. Such anticipatory and reactionary press statements, as discursive endeavors, are indicative of actors attempting to define and frame a situation and influence the media discourse (and by extension, public discussion) thereafter (Fishman 1988; Lassen 2006). This has led scholars, such as Lassen (2006: 506), to argue that rather than constituting a distinct genre of text, press statements are more accurately conceived of as a media channel used as a "vehicle to carry a variety of rhetorical objectives." In an age when information subsidy reigns supreme, press statements have become a core feature of news media processes, and their content is often quoted or appropriated "as is" for publication (Gandy 1980). However, who releases a statement remains significant and the treatment it receives by the press largely depends on the political orientation of the media outlet, but also its dependency on and relationship with institutional powers (Lewis et al. 2008).

Reactionary statements released in the wake of instances of violence tend to provide short, succinct summaries of an organization's or actor's representation(s) of events. As such, they are invaluable for analyses of the kind being undertaken here. A final point of insight on statements comes from Filardo-Llamas (2013), who in her study of IRA statements released around the time of the Good Friday Agreement, found that they generally fit into two categories: (1) commemorative statements (which commemorated republican patriot dead) and (2) political statements (which sought to legitimize the conduct of republican actors). A cursory glance at Junior McDaid House's website illustrates that this distinction is still largely applicable. For the purpose of this study, commemorative statements released in the timeframe are omitted, as they represent a formulaic mode of expression for republicanism: they are part of the business of "doing" republicanism and cannot provide insight into the legitimation of acts of violence to the same extent that the anticipatory and reactionary political statements can.

For analysis, an anti-state (AS) corpus of seven press statements released by dissident republican organizations around the time of the killing was compiled (see Figure 7.1b for an illustration of the sample's temporal dispersion). As outlined above, the cross-section timeframe of one month was decided on owing to its capacity to reduce researcher bias (selecting an arbitrary time unit, as opposed to subjectively setting the upper limit of cross-section) and a manageable corpus size. These seven statements represent all statements topically related to the killing within this timeframe. These statements were then labeled AS1 through to AS7. The corpus totaled 1,797 words and featured statements from Saoradh, the Derry 1916 Commemoration Committee and Junior McDaid House (released via its website).

7.4 Analytical Framework

Critical Discourse Studies (CDS) is a research paradigm which endeavors to deconstruct the discursive manifestations of ideologies and power through a systematic analysis of semiotic data (Wodak and Meyer 2016). Two analytical frameworks from within the broad field of CDS are utilized in this study. The first, Van Leeuwen's (2008) framework of discursive legitimation, aims to address the unanswered "why" questions which underlie a given discourse by analyzing discursive strategies employed in legitimation and considering how these reflect power and ideology. The framework presents four general strategies of legitimation (each of which has respective subcomponents). These are:

1. *Authority*, or, legitimation by reference to the authority of tradition, custom, law, and/or persons in whom institutional authority of some kind is vested.
2. *Moral* evaluation, which entails legitimation by (often very oblique) reference to value systems.
3. *Rationalization*, that is, legitimation by reference to the goals and uses of institutionalized social action and to the knowledge that society has constructed to endow them with cognitive validity.
4. *Mythopoesis*, signifying legitimation that is conveyed through narratives whose outcomes reward legitimate actions and punish non-legitimate actions.

(Van Leeuwen 2008, 105–106)

The framework and its subcomponents are outlined in more detail in the matrices in Figure 7.2.

The second framework employed aims to address the polarizing effects of legitimation discourses by investigating the discursive construction of in-groups and out-groups. Toward this end, the analytical categories of the discourse historical approach (DHA) (cf. Reisigl and Wodak 2016) are employed. Only three of the DHA's five proposed strategies are employed in the analysis, owing to spatial limitations, namely: nomination (how actors are linguistically referred to), predication (what characteristics and features are attributed to them), and argumentation (what argumentation schemes and validity claims underlie the discourse). This scaled-down toolkit permits an analysis of the construction of in-groups and negative representations of others as well as the argumentative structures used to convey or justify the legitimacy of actions. An overview of the strategies is provided in Tables 7.1 and 7.2.

A defining characteristic of discourse as it is conceived of in this chapter is its relatedness to a macro-topic (for instance, politics, terrorism). Below this level, discourses can be seen as consisting of key thematic areas or "discourse topics." Discourse topics, as an analytical category, are considered here as the most "important" or "summarizing" idea(s) that underpin a given segment of a discourse (Van Dijk 1984, 56; Krzyżanowski 2008). Discourse topics (DTs) can be signified by "several sentences ... larger segments ... or the discourse as a whole" (Van Dijk 1984: 56) and are indicative of the general gist or aboutness of these sequences. It follows from this that one of the preliminary steps in all approaches to CDS is the identification and categorization of these discursive topics (KhosraviNik 2010; KhosraviNik and Sarkhoh 2017; Reisigl and Wodak 2016). Charting key topics within a discourse enables the analyst to identify how topics stratify its contents and assess the salience of thematic areas. Synthesizing topic identification with the previously outlined analyses of legitimation strategies

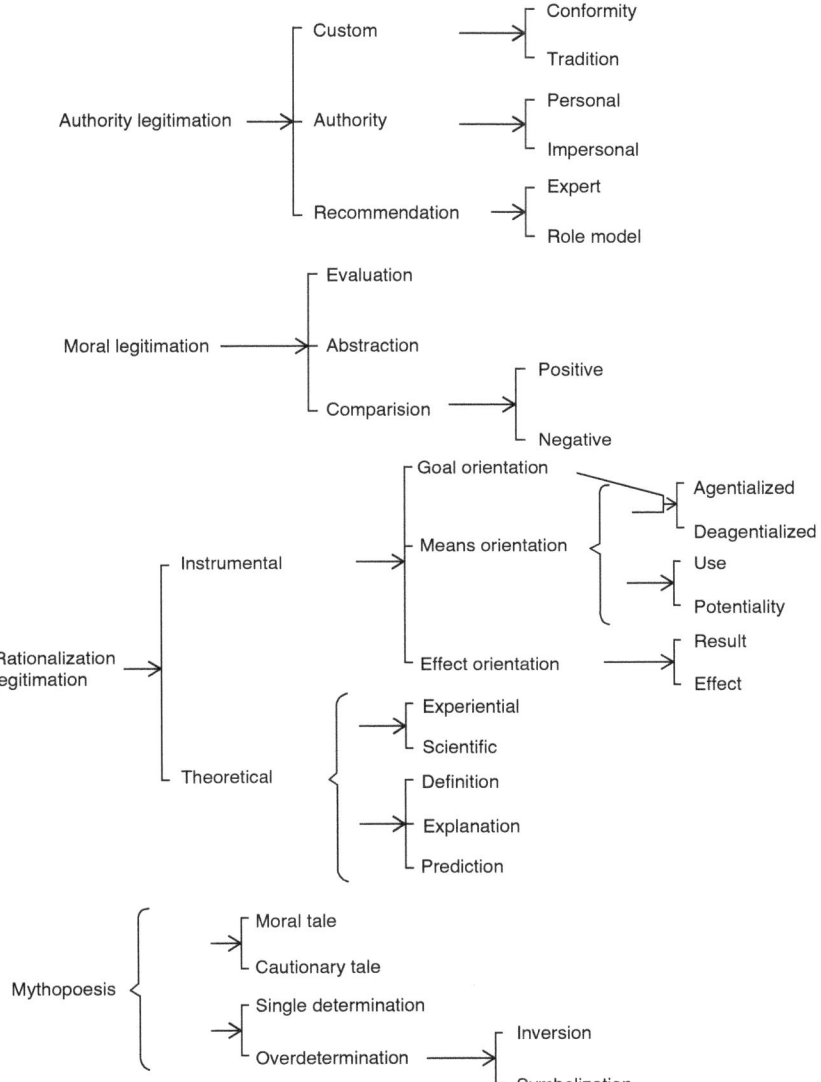

Figure 7.2 Matrices of legitimation
Adapted from Van Leeuwen (2008)

Table 7.1 *Discourse historical approach strategies (adapted from Reisigl and Wodak 2016)*

Discursive strategy and objective	Linguistic forms/realization
Nomination/Referential: Discursive construction of social actors, objects/phenomena/events and processes/actions	• membership categorization devices, deictics, anthroponyms, etc. • tropes such as metaphors, metonymies and synecdoches (*pars pro toto*, *totum pro parte*) • verbs and nouns used to denote processes and actions, etc.
Predication: Discursive qualification of social actors, objects, phenomena, events/processes and actions (more or less positively or negatively)	• stereotypical, evaluative attributions of negative or positive traits (e.g., in the form of adjectives, appositions, prepositional phrases, relative clauses, conjunctional clauses, infinitive clauses and participial clauses or groups) • explicit predicates or predicative nouns/adjectives/pronouns • collocations • explicit comparisons, similes, metaphors and other rhetorical figures (including metonymies, hyperboles, litotes, euphemisms) • allusions, evocations, and presuppositions/implicatures, etc.
Argumentation: Justification and questioning of claims of truth and normative rightness What claims are made/underlie the discourse	• topoi (formal or more content-related) • fallacies

Table 7.2 *Legitimation strategies*

Strategy	Total codes	As a rounded %
Rationalization	24	70
Moralization	8	24
Authorization	2	6
Mythopoesis	0	0

and micro-linguistic techniques facilitates an analysis of what is communicated (in terms of discourse topics) and how it is communicated (in terms of discursive strategies).

As such, the data will undergo three phases of analysis:

1. charting and identifying of discourse topics
2. quantitative coding of legitimation strategies
3. micro-linguistic analysis of discursive strategies.

7.5 Analysis

7.5.1 Discourse Topics

Each statement was coded in terms of discourse topics (at the levels of discourse fragments and topics (Reisigl and Wodak 2016)). Table 7.3 summarizes the percentage of each discourse topic per statement (vertically). The salience of each discourse topic is listed as a (rounded) percentage (horizontally) in the far right-hand column.

The results indicate that dissident republicans dedicated approximately 40 percent of the content of their statements to constructing themselves as the victims of unjust police aggression. The salience of this DT is particularly high in press statements released after raids were conducted on dissident offices or homes (S3, S4, S5). Approximately one-sixth of the anti-state corpus is afforded to positioning dissident republicans as

Table 7.3 *Discourse topic coding results*

Topic	AS1	AS2	AS3	AS4	AS5	AS6	AS7	Total	% (rnd)
Victims of police aggression	8.9	35.65	60.5	6.53	59.22	79.85	16.91	269	38
Media collusion/ bias	0	10.72	0	12.65	2.93	0	82.88	110	16
Compromised republicans	0	5.73	0	1.86	10.73	14.74	0	34	5
Commemoration	41.94	0	8.3	0	0	0	0	50	7
Resilience/ resistance	32.41	29.77	31.17	0	13.93	0	0	107	15
Sympathy	0	18.88	0	44.63	0	0	0	45	6
Non-codable	16	0	0	22.74	13	5	0	23	3

resilient and resistant to this aggression. These insights provide an overall picture of the transitive frame adopted throughout in the anti-state corpus: state forces are the agentive "doers" of aggression and oppression; and dissident republicans are the patients or victims whose acts of resistance are, by virtue of them being reactionary, justified. The corpus also paints the media (16%) and to a lesser extent, non-dissident republicans (5%) as being collusive and abetting these acts of state aggression. Perhaps, given the focus of this chapter, the most notable statistic from the above table is the minuscule portion (a mere 6%) of the corpus that is dedicated to expressions of sympathy for the killing.

7.5.2 Legitimation Strategies

Table 7.4 quantifies the result of the coding of statements in the anti-state corpus for their use of legitimation strategies.

Instrumental rationalization accounts for over two-thirds (approximately 70%) of the (de)legitimation strategies used in the anti-state corpus. Of its twenty-one usages, seven are employed to legitimize the actions of an in-group comprising Saoradh and other dissident actors. For example:

Saoradh is currently pursuing a number of avenues to address these attacks on the freedom of speech.
Saoradh call on the NUJ to investigate the incident and expel any of their members found to have engaged in this mornings attack.
During this attack on the community, a Republican Volunteer attempted to defend people from the PSNI/RUC.

The above goal-oriented instrumental rationalization is employed to frame the actions of anti-state actors as reactions to institutional state aggression. As such, their purpose is constructed as righting wrongs that were committed against the in-group. The quantitative coding employed illustrates the extent to which anti-state actors strive to delegitimize the actions of their opponents: with twice as many instances of goal-oriented delegitimation being found in the corpus:

Heavily armed Crown Forces were sent into Creggan to attack Republicans in advance of upcoming Easter Rising Commemorations.
Today's raid comes after a call by pro establishment parties for British Crown Forces to put in place a tangible plan of action against Republicans.
Saoradh activists homes were targeted by British Crown Forces who colluded with an overzealous media to intensify the hype.

Table 7.4 Statement AS2 legitimation diagram

Actor	Action	Reaction	Purposes	Legitimation
Heavily armed Crown Forces	sent into the Creggan to attack Republicans in advance of upcoming Easter Rising Commemorations		(implicity suggests false purpose of munition raids)	Delegitimation → goal-oriented rationalisation
The Crown Forces	have waged a campaign of oppression in Republican Derry	Saoradh has not shied away from highlighting this		Delegitimation → abstraction to moral discourse of oppression
		gave our analysis that this oppression would inevitably be met with resistance, as has historically been the case		Legitimation → authorisation through appeals to custom
(British Crown Forces)	incursion (to Creggan)	inevitable reaction to such an incursion was resistance from the youth of Creggan	sought to grab headlines and engineered confrontation with the community	Delegitimation → goal-oriented rationalisation
attack on the community		Republican Volunteer attempted to defend people from the PSN/RUC		Legitimation → goal-oriented rationalisation
[Agentless]	a young journalist covering the events, Lyra McKee, was killed accidentally while standing behind armed Crown Force personnel and armoured vehicles			

Actions of state actors are delegitimized by representing their purposes as thwarting the (positively evaluated) actions of republicans, or as being collusive and oppressive. This analysis, again, points toward the transitive position adopted by anti-state actors throughout the corpus: that they are the victims of unwarranted, oppressive state actions. This is compounded by the salience they afford to delegitimating the actions of state actors which are negatively evaluated – with a 2:1 ratio.

Anti-state actors moralize their own actions by distilling them with ethical traits or through abstraction to moral discourses of human and civil rights, as in the below instances:

The Republican community will defend the people and defend the people's right to march in an honourable and dignified manner to commemorate our Republican dead.
Everyone has a fundamental right under international law and European human rights legislation to organise, hold and impart their political opinion and freedom of expression.

Finally, commemorative actions – which state actors argue were (1) illegitimate and (2) the provenance of heightened police attention on dissidents – were justified through authorization, more specifically through appeals to tradition:

Republicans have always honoured the patriots of 1916 along with every patriot who has fallen since.

Considering the above strategies in regard to the earlier analysis of discourse topics provides an overall impression of the anti-state perspective of the incident (and indeed latest phase of the conflict in general): republicans have a right to "do republicanism" and all that that entails; yet they are the victims of aggressive, discriminatory and oppressive measures taken by state actors who are intent on eradicating republicanism. This threat to their very existence serves as an impetus for actions which they frame as part of an ongoing resistance movement, or "struggle" against British imperialism. Presenting the in-group as a victim of the situation is, as Varela-Rey et al. (2013) note, a prototypical means of bolstering in-group support for (re)actions.

One final point of interest is the means through which anti-state actors legitimize (potential) acts of future state-directed violence, using what Van Leeuwen terms theoretical rationalization through "prediction" (3):

If British Crown Forces saturate and hem in this community with armoured jeeps and armed British terrorists then the blame for any acts of resistance rests with them alone.

... we have continually gave our analysis that this oppression would inevitably be met with resistance, as has historically been the case.
it may in future, given the environment endanger members of the press who do go about their profession in an impartial and objective manner.

The less frequent usages of prediction are arguably the most ideologically charged and conflict-oriented of the legitimation strategies in the anti-state corpus; they act as veiled threats, which justify acts of violence in advance of them taking place. In this light, they perform what Kzyrzanowski (2014, 346) terms "pre-legitimation," whereby discourse participants present their "visions rather than accounts" of actions. Below, statement AS2 is deconstructed in order to illustrate how anti-state actors synthesize the above outlined strategies.

7.5.3 Discourse Strategies

7.5.3.1 Positive-Self Representation

Dissident actors construct themselves as a homogeneous republican "community" that is left vaguely delineated and seemingly encompasses all related dissident republican organizations, residents of the Creggan, and dissident support networks around the globe. This mode of self-construction is typical of republican discourse: for instance, Filardo-Llamas (2013) identified a similar mode of self-representation in Provisional IRA statements wherein actors represented themselves through the metaphor REPUBLICANISM IS A FAMILY. Interestingly, dissident actors do not encompass provisional republicans under their definition of the term. Rather, they are denoted through negative, delegitimating and diminutive referentials such as "former republicans" or "crown force cheerleaders." This locates them outside of the republican "community": away from the revolutionary periphery where dissident actors typically position themselves and towards the central state establishment of the out-group. From this perspective, Saoradh and its related organizations, who in common parlance fall under the umbrella of "dissident republicans," are represented as the legitimate successors and puritanical torchbearers of republicanism – explaining their refusal to adopt the "dissident" prefix. "Republican" is used as a prefix to lay claim to collectives and spaces which they position as being distinct from the state and in which the presence of state actors is represented as being invasive or, at the very least, incongruous. For instance, Derry city is referred to as "Republican Derry" as opposed to the city's official title of Londonderry (a title preferred by the unionist/loyalist community). In terms of transitivity, dissident actors are frequently passivized in the data as the patients of state and institutional agency: typically as the victims or "targets" of unwarranted aggression or harassment.

In spite of data only being sourced from organizations that deny any involvement in armed resistance, a high percentage of the statements are dedicated to forwarding a justificatory explanation for the use violence against state forces – which Saoradh refers to as providing "analysis" of the situation. This violence is represented as an "attempt to defend" the republican people against an aggressive, invasive state force. Most significantly, the one line in the entire corpus which represents the shooting and killing of Lyra McKee is de-agentalized:

> Tragically a young journalist covering the events, Lyra McKee, was killed accidentally while standing behind armed Crown Force personnel and armoured vehicles.

The use of passive voice is indicative of attempts to mitigate these organization's association with the negativity surrounding the killing and to distance themselves from the act itself and is, again, reminiscent of wider republican discourse.[3] So while dissident actors devote numerous utterances to justifying the "inevitable" violent reaction elicited by state forces, they frame the young journalist's killing as the consequence of state actions and elide any republican agency.

7.5.3.2 Negative-Other Representation State and institutional actors and their actions are delegitimized through negative evaluation and by framing their purpose as targeting republicanism and repressing its growth. For instance, the PSNI's authority as a national police force is deauthorized in the dataset wherein they are represented as an imperial paramilitary, most frequently through the metonymic referent "British Crown Forces." This represents the PSNI – a cross-community organization – as being the agents of British imperialism and unionism. This strategy simplifies the contemporary conflict into the historic dyad of Irish resistance vs. British imperialism, which – aside from being a far cry from the complex reality of the situation – represents state security measures and dissident political violence as a continuation of this age-old conflict.

In general, state actors are represented as the perpetrators of an ongoing "campaign of oppression" that aims to "thwart" and "diminish Irish republicanism." Whereas the actions of dissident actors are positively evaluated as resistance or pursuits of human rights, representations of out-group actions are negatively evaluated and their purpose is typically depicted as oppressing or thwarting republicanism. This stands in contrast to the moralized institutional discourses of justice or securitization which typically predicate the conduct of criminal investigations and law enforcement (Bogain 2017).

---

[3] Filardo-Llamas (2013) noted a similar usage of passive voice by provisional republican actors in apology statements for the Provisional IRA.

Negatively evaluative constructions of actions and purposes can also be identified in representations of the PSNI's presence in the Creggan on the night of the killing, which is depicted as an intrusive "incursion" into republican territory with the aim of "engineer[ing] confrontation" and manufacturing anti-republican "hype" by eliciting a violent response. Political actors, in particular provisional republicans, are also conceptually linked to imperialism by being encompassed under the term "political aristocracy." The Press's status as an impartial Fourth Estate is also delegitimized by anti-state actors who accuse the media of "unprofessional" conduct, of being "overzealous" in the pursuit of stories and as acting in "collusion" with state forces – a term which holds a particularly strong negative connotation in the socio-historical context of The Troubles.[4]

Overall, dissident actors construct their in-group as an anti-state republican community on the periphery of an imperialist system, a system run by a homogenized out-grouping of illegitimate imperial forces, establishment politicians and a collusive media whose sole purpose is represented as quelling dissident republicanism's growth.

7.5.3.3 Argumentation The legitimation discourse of anti-state actors employs several argumentative strategies which can prove insightful, not only from a discursive perspective but in regard to the general study of the violent dissident republican campaign. For instance, Saoradh justifies and legitimates violent dissident actions by distilling them with ethical qualities or abstraction to moral discourses. This most frequently manifests through invocations of the topos of human rights, as in the below instance:

Those families affected by this mornings [sic] media assisted raids have a right to privacy as a human right.

Such abstraction enables Saoradh to frame itself (and the wider republican community) as the victims of human rights violations but also as the defenders of a value system that is held by the majority of Western society. Similar (im)moral distillation can be identified in their attempts to muster public support for their interpretation of events and resistance to state forces. In the below instance the topos of human rights is used in tandem with a slippery slope fallacy (which is found elsewhere in the corpus) to suggest that any concession to oppressive PSNI measures will ultimately lead to infringements on society's rights as a whole:

Saoradh is currently pursuing a number of avenues to address these attacks on the freedom of speech. What the state does today on Irish Republicans it will not

---

[4] The Troubles saw much collusion between loyalist paramilitaries and British security forces; see Cadwallader (2013) for a comprehensive overview.

hesitate to use tomorrow on the rest of society. You may not share our opinion, you may be diametrically opposed to it, as is your right, but you must understand that the denial of our rights today is the denial of your rights tomorrow.

This statement is a warning addressed to "you" – in this instance the wider public – indicating that dissident actors are seeking support for their perspective outside of the republican community. In addition to the slippery slope fallacy, which denounces concessions to state forces, they aim to muster support by appealing to fear through the relating of hypothetical, negative futures (Reyes 2011). These strategies represent their endeavors as moralized reactions and as *pro bono nobis publico* (for everyone's benefit) and not just the benefit of dissident republicans.

To pre-legitimate actions Saoradh constructs a provocation narrative (Boudana and Segev 2017) which relies on the temporal reordering of events in a narrative structure and produces representations in which "intentions could be falsely attributed, causality hidden or reversed, and blame shifted to the [intended] victim," in this case the PSNI. This narrative manifests as a prediction (Van Leeuwen 2008) or relation of a hypothetical future (Reyes 2011) for potential acts of future violence (as in AS1 for example); and as a version of the *post hoc ergo propter hoc* fallacy (after this, therefore because of this) when it is used to legitimate past violent actions (as in AS2). The re-ordered narrative represents the PSNI's actions as the initial act of aggression which transgressed acceptable behavioral boundaries, rendering it illegitimate and immoral and legitimating any (potential) anti-state reactionary violence as consequent to this initial, antecedent, act of aggression. In this line of argumentation, the reaction has been elicited and is seen as a necessary, predictable and inevitable response. In effect, the narrative shifts the blame for the killing and all subsequent events to the PSNI and is, again, indicative of dissidents' endeavoring to distance themselves from the killing and mitigate their association with the negative public backlash it garnered.

The provocation narrative can first be identified in AS1, which preceded the killing. Here, pre-legitimation through prediction is used to justify a violent response to potential encroachment from the PSNI:

If British Crown Forces saturate and hem in this community with armoured jeeps and armed British terrorists then the blame for any acts of resistance rests with them alone. The Republican community will defend the people's rights.

It is again reiterated and defended in AS2, the statement released in the wake of the killing to legitimate the violent response which resulted in the killing of Lyra McKee:

we ... gave our analysis that this oppression would inevitably be met with resistance

The inevitable reaction to such an incursion was resistance from the youth of Creggan. The blame for last night lies squarely at the feet of the British Crown Forces.

Third parties interrogate the validity of provocation narratives and determine their success (or lack thereof) in presenting the alleged provocateurs as blameworthy (Paris 1989). As such, the dissemination of this narrative can be construed as an attempt by dissident actors to influence the public's interpretation of events and represent the PSNI as blameworthy. This attempt, however, proved a resounding failure with third parties widely condemning Saoradh's interpretation of the events and accusing them of acting as mouthpieces for the New IRA. Moreover, the provocation narrative not only provides dissident in-group members with a lens to view the violence, but it is also designed to provide the wider public with an alternative interpretative framework which appeals to underlying concerns of fear, security and justice. More significant to the study of conflict, however, is that the provocation narrative can also be used to make veiled threats to state or institutional actors.

In instances where the narrative relates a hypothetical future and pre-legitimates potential violent "reactions" (as in AS1), the producers employ *argumentum ad baculum* (argumentation by threat or force). In AS1, for example, dissident actors attempt to dissuade the PSNI from encroaching on their parade with a threat of violence. The privilege of hindsight tells us that, tragically, this subtle threat of violence was actualized the next day. Perhaps more worryingly, however, is the usage of a similar line of argumentation in the statement directed at the NUJ in AS7, which, again, effectively communicates a veiled threat:

This behaviour, if by a media organisation or a Crown Force unit disguised as the media, calls into question the supposed impartiality and objectivity of the media, it may in future, given the environment endanger members of the press who do go about their profession in an impartial and objective manner.

Here again we see rationalization through prediction and *argumentum ad baculum* operating simultaneously within a representation of a hypothetical future to appeal to fear in media professionals. As Mirhosseini (2017) notes, fear appeals and threats are often critical components of legitimation discourses of political violence: "Fear appeals are attempts at triggering a sense of fear leading to possible precautionary positions and reactions (Peters et al. 2013; Ruiter et al. 2004) and threats are various types of discursive hints at overt or imagined vulnerability to potential sources of danger (Dunmire 2007; Gale 2010)."

In this view we see that dissident actors are attempting to deter negative interference or coverage from journalists. They do so by hinting at a future potential source of danger from dissident republican militants for journalists who go about their daily work. In context, this threat becomes more perturbing, however, as it was issued less than a month after the killing of young journalist Lyra McKee.

7.6 Discussion

The multi-level approach to analysis adhered to in this chapter proved an effective means of producing insights into how legitimacy is conferred (or removed) from actions, and how discourses can polarize participants along ideological boundaries. The correlative, quantitative approach to identification of discourse topics and legitimation strategies provided a statistical basis for the analysis of themes and modes of justification in the data. It was shown that dissident actors predominantly (de)legitimated actions by appeals to pragmatism and utilitarianism. Actions of state actors were delegitimated through being represented as being purposively intent on thwarting dissident republican growth and oppressing members of their community. Conversely, dissident actions were justified as defensive or reactionary measures to prevent further oppression of republicans. These actions were further legitimated by abstraction to moralized discourses, such as human rights. Furthermore, the coding of legitimation strategies enabled us to quantify the extent to which dissident actors sought to victimize themselves and paint the PSNI and media as anti-republican.

The analysis also revealed the legitimating effects of referential and qualifying discursive features and how an analysis of these can illustrate the extent to which they are ideologically significant. From a relatively small dataset, CDS was shown to produce an indicative gist of dissident republican ideology and identity. The analysis of discursive identification demonstrated how actors were polarized in the data: dissidents were depicted as a cohesive community and attributed positive characteristics and distanced from negativity surrounding the killing; whereas state forces were imperialized and represented as the doers of oppression. Furthermore, striking parallels were identified between the discursive construction of dissident republicanism and previous insights provided by analyses of provisional republican discourse (Filardo-Llamas 2013). Dissidents position themselves as the true successors and legitimate incarnation of republicanism. Their in-group comprises a wider republican community which is positioned as diametrically opposed to the political establishment out-group, comprising the PSNI, the media and establishment politicians.

Analysis of argumentation strategies revealed the subjective morality which dissidents use to legitimate their existence and actions, as well as the logical fallacies they employ to instill fear or muster support. While the prototypical legitimation of actions targeted at in-group members is found throughout the data (or "analysis" as it is termed by dissident actors), we also find indications of outward legitimation (i.e., legitimation targeting the wider public): for instance, the use of a slippery slope argument directed at "you" (the audience) persuasively appeals to fear and legitimates reactive dissident measures or responses. Further to this, and most ominously, a third intended target was also identified: argumentation analysis revealed the capacity for dissidents to issue subtle threats to opposing institutional actors in public forums and to (pre)legitimate anti-state violence through the relation of hypothetical futures, prediction (of violent reactions) and argumentation *ad baculum*. Finally, the analysis revealed how a temporal reordering of events by anti-state actors in the data produced a frame which positioned them as the legitimate victims of (and justified reactors to) both past and future incidents of state aggression, violence and harassment.

7.7 Conclusion

These findings not only contribute to the study of dissident republicanism, but also to the general study of contentious or sporadic instances of political violence which garner much media attention – both of which will be treated in turn below.

The post-conflict era in Northern Ireland has been characterized by fluctuating levels of support for dissident republicanism and their "prolonged campaign" (Tonge 2012); yet, literature on dissident republicanism positions them as a peripheral threat, content with being political outliers and indifferent to mass support. However, the lingering threat they pose has again returned to the fore of public debate in the wake of a spate of recent attacks (pipe, car and mail bombs etc.). Stagnated power-sharing arrangements and increased political instability prompted by Brexit have created a political climate characterized by uncertainty of national identity and apprehension (Gormley-Heenan and Aughey 2017). It is within this context that the recent surge in dissident republican activity (both political and militant) ought to be seen as more pressing. Analyses such as the above demonstrate the central role played by language in the conduct of dissident actors and in their continuation of violence without a mandate for doing so. The findings indicate an ideological invariance of contemporary dissident republicanism and a continuation of their efforts to accentuate the coloniality of British presence in Northern Ireland through the representation of state institutions as agents of the Crown. The identified threats made in the statements point to dissidents' continued commitment to physical force and violence. However, the chapter's findings also suggest a growing cognizance on behalf of dissident actors of the necessity of public support and mandate for their continued campaign (Tonge 2012, 2014). The striking parallels identified between the discursive patterning of provisional and dissident statements provides some impetus for further comparative (discursive) research between both schisms of republicanism. Finally, the analysis of Saoradh's statements suggests that, while they do not explicitly engage in anti-state violence, they *do* devote much of their communication to threatening it and acting as mouthpieces for its legitimation.

Methodologically, CDS was shown to be an effective analytical approach to deconstructing the contentions and assertions of groups engaged in conflicts. Moreover, it proved expedient in analyzing a violent incident in which the public's opinion was largely shaped by the media's take on the matter. CDS's commitment to addressing the concerns of marginalized voices in society render it an appropriate means of elucidating anti-state grievances. More generally, this chapter reiterates the value of synthesized analysis of two phenomena that are unique to humanity: language and conflict. Studying the inextricable link between these can provide insight into the functionality of language in negotiating and constructing the complexities, agonisms and ideologies which sustain conflicts.

Primary References

Saoradh. *Statement 24/09/16*. (2016)
Derry 1916 Commemoration Committee. *Statement 17/04/19*. (2019) (AS1)
Saoradh. *Statement 19/04/19*. (2019) (AS2)
Saoradh. *Republicans Convicted for Remembering Irish Patriot Dead* 30/04/19. (2019) (AS3)
Saoradh. Saoradh *Facing Unprecedented Internet Censorship* 02/05/19. (2019) (AS4)
Saoradh. *Junior McDaid House Targeted by Crown Forces 07/05/19*. (2019) (AS5)
Saoradh. *Breaking News! 07/05/19*. (2019) (AS6)
Saoradh. Saoradh *statement 16/05/19*. (2019) (AS7)

Secondary References

Apter, David. 1997. *The Legitimization of Violence*. New York: New York University Press.
Badham, Mark. 2018. *Four Media Roles in Organizational Legitimation-News Media Participation in Discursive Legitimation Processes*. Unpublished PhD thesis, Aalto University, Finland.
Bogain, Ariane. 2017. "Security in the Name of Human Rights: The Discursive Legitimation Strategies of the War on Terror in France." *Critical Studies on Terrorism* 10(3): 476–500.
Borja-Orozco, Henry, Idaly Barreto, Jose Manuel Sabucedo, and Wilson Lopez-Lopez. 2008. "Building a Discourse to Delegitimize the Opponent: Government and Paramilitarism in Colombia." *Universitas Psychologica* 7(2): 571–583.
Boudana, Sandrine, and Elad Segev. 2017. "Theorizing Provocation Narratives as Communication Strategies." *Communication Theory* 27(4): 329–346.
Bowman-Grieve, Lorraine, and Maura Conway. 2012. "Exploring the Form and Function of Dissident Irish Republican Online Discourses." *Media, War & Conflict* 5(1): 71–85.

Cadwallader, Anne. 2013. *Lethal Allies: British Collusion in Ireland*. Cork: Mercier Press.
Chouliaraki, Lilie, and Norman Fairclough. 1999. *Discourse in Late Modernity: Rethinking Critical Discourse Analysis*. Edinburgh: Edinburgh University Press.
Dunmire, Patricia L. 2007. "Emerging Threats and Coming Dangers." In *Discourse, War and Terrorism*, ed. by Adam Hodges and Chad Nilep, 19–43. Amsterdam: John Benjamins.
Elliott, Marianne. 1978. "The Origins and Transformation of Early Irish Republicanism." *International Review of Social History* 23(3): 405–428.
Fairclough, Norman. 2013. *Critical Discourse Analysis: The Critical Study of Language*. London: Routledge.
Filardo-Llamas, Laura. 2013. "'Committed to the Ideals of 1916.' The Language of Paramilitary Groups: The Case of the Irish Republican Army." *Critical Discourse Studies* 10(1): 1–17.
Fishman, Mark. 1988. *Manufacturing the News*. Austin, TX: University of Texas Press.
Foucault, Michel. 1972. *The Archaeology of Knowledge*. Translated from the French by AM Sheridan Smith. New York: Pantheon Books.
Foy, Michael T., and Brian Barton. 2011. *Easter Rising*. Cheltenham, UK: The History Press.
Fraser, Thomas G. 2005. *Ireland in Conflict 1922–1998*. London: Routledge.
Gale, Tammy. 2010. *Ideologies of Violence: A Corpus and Discourse Analytic Approach to Stance in Threatening Communications*. Unpublished doctoral dissertation, University of California, Davis, USA.
Gandy Jr, Oscar H. 1980. "Information in Health: Subsidised News." *Media, Culture & Society* 2(2): 103–115.
Gormley-Heenan, Cathy, and Arthur Aughey. 2017. "Northern Ireland and Brexit: Three Effects on 'the Border in the Mind'." *The British Journal of Politics and International Relations* 19(3): 497–511.
Halliday, Michael, and Alexander Kirkwood. 1973. *Explorations in the Functions of Language*. Cambridge: Cambridge University Press.
Hazaea, Abduljalil Nasr, Noraini Ibrahim, and Nor Fariza Mohd Nor. 2014. "Discursive Legitimation of Human Values: Local-Global Power Relations in Global Media Discourse." *GEMA Online® Journal of Language Studies* 14(1): 171–187.
Hearty, Kevin. 2016. "From 'Former Comrades' to 'Near Enemy': The Narrative Template of 'Armed Struggle' and Conflicting Discourses on Violent Dissident Irish Republican Activity (VDR)." *Critical Studies on Terrorism* 9(2): 269–291.
Herman, Edward S., and Noam Chomsky. 2010. *Manufacturing Consent: The Political Economy of the Mass Media*. New York: Random House.
Horgan, John. 2013. *Divided We Stand: The Strategy and Psychology of Ireland's Dissident Terrorists*. Oxford: Oxford University Press.
Horgan, John, and John F. Morrison. 2011. "Here to Stay? The Rising Threat of Violent Dissident Republicanism in Northern Ireland." *Terrorism and Political Violence* 23 (4): 642–669.
Jackson, Richard. 2005. "Security, Democracy, and the Rhetoric of Counter-Terrorism." *Democracy and Security* 1(2): 147–171.
Jaworski, Adam, and Nikolas Coupland. 1999. "Perspectives on Discourse Analysis." In *The Discourse Reader*, ed. by Adam Jaworski and Nikolas Coupland, 1–44. London: Routledge.

Kee, Robert. 2000. *The Green Flag: A History of Irish Nationalism*. London: Penguin UK.
Kennedy-Pipe, Caroline. 2014. *The Origins of the Present Troubles in Northern Ireland*. London: Routledge.
KhosraviNik, Majid. 2010. "The Representation of Refugees, Asylum Seekers and Immigrants in British Newspapers: A Critical Discourse Analysis." *Journal of Language and Politics* 9(1): 1–28.
KhosraviNik, Majid, and Nadia Sarkhoh. 2017. "Arabism and Anti-Persian Sentiments on Participatory Web Platforms: A Social Media Critical Discourse Study." *International Journal of Communication* 11: 20.
Krzyżanowski, Michał. 2008. "Analysing Focus-Group Discussions." In *Qualitative Discourse Analysis in the Social Sciences*, ed. by Ruth Wodak and Michał Krzyżanowski, 162–181. Basingstoke: Palgrave Macmillan.
Krzyżanowski, Michał. 2014. "Values, Imaginaries and Templates of Journalistic Practice: A Critical Discourse Analysis." *Social Semiotics* 24(3): 345–365.
Lassen, Inger. 2006. "Is the Press Release a Genre? A Study of Form and Content." *Discourse Studies* 8(4): 503–530.
Lau, Ursula, Mohamed Seedat, and Victoria McRitchie. 2011. "Discursive Constructions of the Israel-Hezbollah War: The Struggle for Representation." *American Journal of Islamic Social Sciences* 28: 1–33.
Lewis, Justin, Andrew Williams, and Bob Franklin. 2008. "A Compromised Fourth Estate? UK News Journalism, Public Relations and News Sources." *Journalism Studies* 9(1): 1–20.
Lukes, Steven. 2004. *Power: A Radical View*. London: Macmillan International Higher Education.
McAllister, Ian. 2004. "'The Armalite and the Ballot Box': Sinn Fein's Electoral Strategy in Northern Ireland." *Electoral Studies* 23(1): 123–142.
Mills, Sara. 1997. *Discourse: The New Critical Idiom*. London: Routledge.
Mirhosseini, Seyyed-Abdolhamid. 2017. "Discursive Double-Legitimation of (Avoiding) Another War in Obama's 2013 Address on Syria." *Journal of Language and Politics* 16(5): 706–730.
Nelson, Daniel N. 2003. "Conclusion: Word Peace." In *At War with Words*, ed. by Daniel L. Nelson, 449–468. Berlin: De Gruyter Mouton.
Nolan, Paul. 2014. "The Long, Long War of Dissident Republicans." *Shared Space* 16: 41.
O'Brien, Brendan. 1995. *The Long War: The IRA and Sinn Fein*, 2nd ed. (Irish Studies). New York: Syracuse University Press.
Paris, Rainer. 1989. "Der kurze atem der provokation." *Kölner Zeitschrift Für Soziologie Und Sozialpsychologie* 41(1): 33–52.
Peters, Gjalt-Jorn Ygram, Robert A.C. Ruiter, and Gerjo Kok. 2013. "Threatening Communication: A Critical Re-Analysis and a Revised Meta-Analytic Test of Fear Appeal Theory." *Health Psychology Review* 7(sup1): S8–S31.
Peters, Rudolph. 2005. *Crime and Punishment in Islamic Law*. Cambridge: Cambridge University Press.
Phoenix, Eamon. 1994. *Northern Nationalism: Nationalist Politics, Partition and the Catholic Minority in Northern Ireland 1890–1940*. Belfast: Ulster Historical Foundation.

Reisigl, Martin, and Ruth Wodak. 2016. "The Discourse-Historical Approach." In *Methods of Critical Discourse Studies*, ed. by Ruth Wodak and M Meyer, 3rd revised ed., 87–121. New York: Sage.

Reyes, Antonio. 2011. "Strategies of Legitimization in Political Discourse: From Words to Actions." *Discourse & Society* 22(6): 781–807.

Rojo, Luisa Martín, and Teun A. Van Dijk. 1997. "'There Was a Problem, and It Was Solved!': Legitimating the Expulsion of Illegal Migrants in Spanish Parliamentary Discourse." *Discourse & Society* 8(4): 523–566.

Ruiter, Rob. A. C., Bas Verplanken, David De Cremer, and Gerjo Kok. 2004. "Danger and Fear Control in Response to Fear Appeals: The Role of Need for Cognition." *Basic and Applied Social Psychology* 26(1): 13–24.

Schulze, Kirsten E., and M.L.R. Smith. 2000. "Decommissioning and Paramilitary Strategy in Northern Ireland: A Problem Compared." *The Journal of Strategic Studies* 23(4): 77–106.

Suchman, Mark C. 1995. "Managing Legitimacy: Strategic and Institutional Approaches." *Academy of Management Review* 20(3): 571–610.

Suddaby, Roy, Alex Bitektine, and Patrick Haack. 2017. "Legitimacy." *Academy of Management Annals* 11(1): 451–478.

Thomas, Peter. 2009. *The Gramscian Moment: Philosophy, Hegemony and Marxism*. Leiden: Brill.

Tonge, Jonathan. 2012. "'No-One Likes Us; We Don't Care': 'Dissident' Irish Republicans and Mandates." *The Political Quarterly* 83(2): 219–226.

Tonge, Jonathan. 2014. "A Campaign Without End? 'Dissident' Republican Violence in Northern Ireland." *Political Insight* 5(1): 14–17.

Van Dijk, Teun A. 1984. *Prejudice in Discourse: An Analysis of Ethnic Prejudice in Cognition and Conversation*. Amsterdam: John Benjamins.

Van Dijk, Teun A. 1993. *Elite Discourse and Racism*. Vol. 6. New York: Sage.

Van Dijk, Teun A. 1998. *Ideology: A Multidisciplinary Study*. New York: Sage.

Van Dijk, Teun A. 2015. "Critical Discourse Analysis." In *The Handbook of Discourse Analysis*, ed. by Deborah Tannen, Heidi E. Hamilton, and Deborah Schiffrin, 466–485. New York: John Wiley & Sons.

Van Leeuwen, Theo. 2008. *Discourse and Practice: New Tools for Critical Discourse Analysis*. Oxford: Oxford University Press.

Van Leeuwen, Theo, and Ruth Wodak. 1999. "Legitimizing Immigration Control: A Discourse-Historical Analysis." *Discourse Studies* 1(1): 83–118.

Varela-Rey, Ana, Álvaro Rodríguez-Carballeira, and Javier Martín-Peña. 2013. "Psychosocial Analysis of ETA's Violence Legitimation Discourse." *Revista De Psicología Social* 28(1): 85–97.

Weber, Max. 2013. *Politik als beruf*. BoD–Books on Demand.

Wodak, Ruth, and Michael Meyer. 2016. *Methods of Critical Discourse Studies*. New York: Sage.

Yiftachel, Oren. 2006. *Ethnocracy: Land and Identity Politics in Israel/Palestine*. Philadelphia, PA: University of Pennsylvania Press.

8 Ideological Exclusion
Defining the (Dis)believer in Extremist Muslim
Periodicals – *Dabiq* and *Inspire*

Troy E. Spier

> Religion never exists in a vacuum. It is always interwoven with multiple
> strands of culture and history that link it to particular locations. The rhetoric of
> religion must be put into a context, so that we know both the objectives and
> opponents of particular spokespeople.   (Ernst 2003, 30)

8.1   Introduction

Pervez Hoodhbhoy remarked in *Among the Believers* (cf. Levitt and Trivedi 2015) with reference to students of the typical Islamic school that "[a]ll that these students learn is how to read the Qur'ān, and they are not taught about the world around them. They are taught that everybody else is an enemy except that particular sect to which they belong." If such intolerance and insularity are truly propagated among Muslims in these religious institutions, many of whom are self-professed followers of the Wahhabi tradition (cf. Wiktorowicz 2006 and DeLong-Bas 2008), then it is necessary to consider the extent to which these traits will be reflected in and by the existence of publications consulted by Muslims, especially when both are readily employed in establishing ideological borders of "us" and "them" – or, in this case, believers and nonbelievers. In the case of extremists, for instance, the most straightforward means of achieving this interrogation would be through an investigation of the most widely disseminated published propagandistic sources.

The present study investigates the characterization of believers and nonbelievers in the publications of Da'esh and al-Qa'ida, obtained from fourteen issues of *Dabiq* and sixteen issues of *Inspire*, by means of the extraction and analysis of lexical items utilizing the triliteral root $\sqrt{KFR}$ and then consideration of the larger discourse in which they appear. *Dabiq* and *Inspire* have had a widespread impact on geopolitical, militaristic, and religious affairs. While al-Qa'ida is oftentimes viewed as the historic predecessor of similar groups, it has witnessed a gradual increase in the technological and rhetorical skills of its staff, leading to hundreds of films and ultimately the *Inspire* magazine (cf. Martin 2011 for a qualitative analysis of al-Qa'ida's films). Furthermore, the primary goal of *Inspire* is the instruction of its audience to cause as much harm as possible in the name of Islam (e.g., through the creation of explosives with materials found around one's home). Interestingly, many members of Da'esh once belonged to al-Qa'ida and have successfully followed in the footsteps of the propaganda machine of their ancestor through the establishment of their own periodicals (i.e., *Dabiq* and *Rumiyah*), which place far greater emphasis upon issues of historical, spiritual, and philosophical significance. In fact, it is through these publications that one discovers the ideological hallmarks of the Islamism (cf. Mozaffari 2007) that lends support to their actions, namely through unquestionable, literal reliance upon the Qur'ān and the *sunnah* and selective adherence to the *aḥādīth*.

8.1.1 Islamism

Militant implementations of Islam are not novel phenomena, and they serve as proof of the existence of Islamic extremism throughout the world. Although public recognition of al-Qa'ida seemingly reached its peak after the attacks on September 11, 2001, and the subsequent invasion of the Middle East, the official establishment of this group came almost fifteen years earlier – in fact, in the 1980s in Afghanistan as a (then) subsidiary of Maktab al-Khidamat (cf. Farrall 2017). Moreover, despite many nations' awareness of the increasing presence of extremists in Iraq, it was only in the last five years that the political and militaristic strength of Da'esh was recognized through extensive territorial gains, centralization and consolidation of their power in Raqqa, and the gradual expansion of their extremist ideology. However, these two organizations do not only share a historical link and reliance upon violence, but also a shared ideological bedrock that has been defined as Islamism. To this end, this ideology "is brought about by a process of deracinating textual interpretations from contextual factors, and shaping interpretation to fit held extremist beliefs" (Winter and Hasan 2016: 675–676). Although other scholars seemingly utilize a variety of terms interchangeably for this socially shared, evaluative set of (ideological) beliefs, including "extremism," "fundamentalism," "jihadism," and "Islamism," only the final term is used here to refer to the totalizing force described by Shepard (1987):

The tendency to view Islam not merely as a "religion" in the narrow sense of theological belief, private prayer and ritual worship, but also a total way of life with guidance for political, economic, and social behaviour . . . commonly, this takes the form of the claim that Muslims should have an "Islamic State," that is, a state in which all law is based on the Sharia.

Thus, the foundation of this ideology rests upon the desired unification of religion and politics into a single institution, which intends to produce a (more) pious society through religiously sanctioned governance. Although many refer to this governance as reflective of the Sharīʿah, its actual realization can vary greatly and is thus country-dependent (see, e.g., Hefner 2011 and Dupret et al. 2008). However, Cook (2013) argues that the transition from secular to non-secular governance is predicated upon increasingly conservative societal adherence to the beliefs of Islam. Despite being initially apolitical, it may not reach broader acceptance, nor may their objectives be achieved without thorough involvement in the political sphere. Even so, political engagement alone is rarely enough, leading to violent acts becoming the means to solidify power and function as the path to "liberation and freedom" (cf. Chang 2005). As expected, the in-group perception of such violence differs strikingly from the out-group perception. Organizations like Da'esh and al-Qa'ida exist to emancipate the "Muslim world" from the secular bonds of their enemies through acts of terror. Therefore, it is necessary to identify exactly how membership is defined by these groups.

8.1.2 Templatic Morphology and Development of KFR

Arabic is one of the most widely spoken languages in the world and belongs to the Semitic branch of Afroasiatic – a language stock that also includes other notable members in Hebrew, Tigrinya, Amharic, and Aramaic. One of the most distinctive features of these languages is their non-concatenative morphology, sometimes also called templatic or discontinuous morphology. In fact, this type of morphology is manifested most saliently in the Semitic languages through the extensive use and modification of triliteral roots, which are otherwise unpronounceable without the insertion of vowels and/or the doubling of consonants according to the appropriate template and associated semantics (Wightwick and Gaafar 1998, 7). Unsurprisingly, in his examination of √KTB, an often-cited example in Arabic, Tucker (2009, 5) found a "strong meaning similarity among words derived from the same putative consonant root." Furthermore, after considering other lexical items derived from this same root, Tucker (2009) found that thirty of the thirty-two distinct items in Wehr (1976) shared a connection to "writing, letters, or books." As such, both nouns and verbs related to the acts of reading or writing arise as derived lexemes. Similarly, lexical items derived from the particularly relevant (and perhaps most suitable for counterbalance) triliteral root √SLM refer to "submission or acceptance," only a few of which are listed in Table 8.1.

The semantic development of √KFR, not dissimilar from other types of language change, is complicated. Izutsu (1959, 118–119) recognizes √KFR as referring strictly to a sense of covering. In particular, he defines this root with

Table 8.1 *Derived lexemes of* √SLM

Root	Gloss	Template
sala:m	peace	CVCVVC
isla:m	acceptance	VCCVVC
muslim	one who accepts	CVCCVC
tasli:m	to give peace	CVCCVVC
istisla:m	act of submission	VCCVCCVVC
mustaslim	one who submits	CVCCVCCVC

reference to the human subject as the following: "to cover, i.e., to ignore knowingly, the benefits which one has received [from Allah]." Nonetheless, Izutsu (1959, 123) also acknowledges the primacy of this root as relating to ingratitude and disbelief, from which he argues that "it [is] difficult to draw a sharp line of demarcation between them, for ... the two are connected with each other in Quranic thought by a firm conceptual link." As a result, one might understand √KFR as blatant disregard for the will of Allah and a clear refusal to acknowledge the benefits received, a view supported by many contemporary Islamic scholars.

Waldman (1968) recognizes the semantic evolution of √KFR through the compilation of the Qur'ān, instead of viewing the Qur'ān as a single chronological unit like Izutsu (1959). Particular consideration is given the juxtaposition of individual surahs according to their revelation and transcription in Medina or Mecca, the two holy cities that also serve to characterize the content of their respective verses. In doing so, Waldman (1968, 443) recognized three major stages to the (re-)defining of √KFR in the Qur'ān. First, the author describes it as being "merely one of many roots used to describe his [Muhammad's] opponents to being the chief." In a historical sense, this is well supported by the need to consolidate power. Second, it becomes overwhelmingly linked to the practice of idolatry and/or polytheism. In a religious sense, this was necessary to eliminate practices that were inconsistent with the emerging Islamic tradition and which directly contradicted the behavior of the *Jahiliyya*. Although used as an insult in the literature, this refers principally to pre-Islamic societies that deliberately ignored the will of Allah and are thus characterized as ignorant. Finally, it is used to describe any individual or group of individuals who stand in opposition to Muslims as a whole and who, consequently, must be fought by the community of believers. This is quite a different view from that espoused by Izutsu (1959), which strictly addresses the personal connection between the individual and his creator.

Similarly, the exegetical literature seems to support each of these characterizations. Hamza Yusuf (2008, 31) begins with many of the definitions previously offered here, though he remarks that the triliteral root itself need not retain a negative connotation in Arabic, given that the lexical item *kāfir* can additionally refer to a farmer, as "a farmer covers the seed with soil." Nonetheless, he continues by presenting and collapsing the detailed descriptions from Ibn Fūrak and Abū al-Hasan al-Ash'ari into one that foregrounds ignorance as the primary trait, one that "resides in the human heart and is in understanding and not in action" (cf. Fūrak al-Isbahānī 1999). Most importantly, however, this deficiency of the heart is only truly visible through intentionally sinful behaviors, such as "prostrating to an idol or throwing a Qur'an in the garbage" (Abū al-Baqā, quoted in Fūrak al-Isbahānī 1999). Yusuf (2008) then advances his in-depth examination of the types of disbelief and the punishments for them, citing references in the Qur'ān and the *aḥādīth*. Ultimately, however, he concludes that only those who practice idolatry have no recourse to the forgiveness of Allah.

Finally, given the importance of particular sources not only to Muslims generally but more specifically for those who adhere to extremist ideologies, it is necessary to recognize precisely how the subjects of (dis)belief and (dis)believers are approached, especially as it pertains to jurisprudence. According to the *Quranic Arabic Corpus* (Dukes 2009), there are over five hundred instances where √KFR is referenced. Of all the tokens, 83 percent are employed verbally (434/525), while the remaining 17 percent are nominals (91/525). This seems to suggest, at least at the surface, that greater emphasis is placed upon the state of disbelief than on the actions arising from it, and a quick examination of the glosses provided confirms this: These derived lexemes overwhelmingly refer to disbelieving, being ungrateful, denying, rejecting, and removing.

Nevertheless, while all followers of Islam unequivocally agree that the Qur'ān is the undeniable, immutable word of Allah, Brown (2009, 3) notes that "[l]arge portions of the Islamic legal, theological, and popular religious traditions come not from the [Qur'ān], but rather from the legacy of Muhammad, whom they believe God chose to explain and elucidate His message through word and deed." In addition, as Hallaq (2009, 16) explains, there are only around five hundred verses in the Qur'ān that specifically provide contextualized, religiously sanctioned consequences for unacceptable behaviors, i.e., less than 10 percent of the entire text). As a result, consideration must also be given to the *aḥādīth*, i.e., the intergenerationally transmitted, recorded pronouncements of Muhammad that oftentimes encode the customs, traditions, and practices deemed appropriate for a life of piety (*sunnah*). The results provided for "disbelie[f, ves, ver, ving]" on the online database *Sunnah.com* refer overwhelmingly to the stubbornness of disbelievers, the punishment in hell that awaits them, the danger of reverting to impermissible or sinful behaviors (*haram*) after the passing of the Prophet, the omnipotence of Allah, and the danger of a Muslim calling another Muslim a disbeliever.

Thus, while the definitions offered in the *aḥādīth* are less extensive or detailed in their demarcation, the findings of religious and secular scholars are generally in agreement in straightforwardly declaring that those who cannot reside within the fold of Islam are those who have deliberately strayed or shielded themselves from Allah.

8.2   Methodology and Data

The theoretical framework used in this study is Critical Discourse Analysis (Van Dijk 1993, 1995, 1998; Janks 1997; Wodak 1989; Wodak and Meyer 2015; Fairclough 1995, 2003), whose proponents attempt to contemplate and typify the oftentimes tumultuous relationship among language use, power dynamics, societal implications, and – in the case of non-corpus-based analyses – the role of the discourse analyst (see, e.g., Van Dijk 1993, 249). While scholars working within this framework do not adhere to a single, homogeneous approach to the analysis of discourse, there are some shared methodological assumptions. First, discourse is assumed to function above the sentence level but interact with the other levels of linguistic analysis, thus referring to a very particular type of situated language usage. Second, discourse serves to "capture what happens when language forms are played out in different social, political and cultural arenas" (cf. Simpson and Mayr 2010, 5). Third, because discourse reflects larger sociocultural processes, language use can be broadly understood as a complex series of semiotic choices that reflect and constitute one of many (social) realities. Consequently, critical discourse analyses attempt to show how discourse directly or indirectly demonstrates power relations, exposes ideology, portrays individuals belonging to a specific group, and indicates certain perceptions of the world.

Hence, the present study examines the extremist publications of al-Qa'ida and Da'esh to expose how their discursive patterns reinforce, perpetuate, and propagate the ideological underpinnings of the larger sociocultural structures to which these groups adhere and how ideological positioning of the "Self" and the "Other" reflects underlying evaluative beliefs, i.e., the pseudo-religious construction of in-group and out-group membership, based on the conceptualization and definitions of the "(dis)believer" and "acts of (dis)belief." The data are cross-referenced with Van Leeuwen's (2003) representation of social actors, which examines the ideological effects of linguistic choices, and Van Dijk's (1993) ideology schema, which proposes to reduce ideology to a set of questions that correspond roughly to six categories: membership, activities, goals, values/norms, position/group relations, and resources.

The two corpora together contain 694,096 words from *Dabiq* and *Inspire* (see Table 8.2). While the latter was released periodically over a period of six years (sixteen issues), the former was released in much closer increments over

Table 8.2 *Corpora of* Da'esh *and* al-Qa'ida *extremist periodicals*

Periodical	Time range	Total issues	Total words
Dabiq	2014–2016	14	317,613
Inspire	2010–2016	16	376,483
Total:		**30**	**694,096**

a period of three years (fourteen issues). Both publications are written in English and represent a variety of different genres, including letters from the editor, reproductions of accounts in battle, descriptions of historical events, interviews with noted fighters and leaders, and religious dicta.

Following the methodology employed in Spier (2018), each of these thirty periodicals was loaded in two separate stages into AntConc, a freely available concordance and textual analysis program. A regular expression, which is used to search for a certain pattern, was written to identify any possible combinations of the triliteral root √KFR with preceding or subsequent vowels or consonants, which on rare occasions resulted in an ironic false positive, e.g., with the present, preterite, and progressive forms of the verb "backfire." Next, these tokens were abstracted with the one hundred words appearing in equal distribution on the left and right peripheries, in order to discover the larger context in which this derived lexeme appeared and to use this knowledge in the construction of the taxonomy. The Table 9.3 illustrates the nine derived lexemes extracted from these corpora and provides a quantitative analysis presenting the number of tokens and the percentage of total tokens; furthermore, these lexemes are differentiated into the four morphologically least marked classes, the percentages of which are also provided for the reader's consideration.

A few observations are immediately apparent. First, it is quite clear that the authors of *Dabiq* rely much more heavily on religious doctrine to bolster their claims, as evinced by the much greater use of the Arabic term (at a ratio of 8:2). Second, these derived lexemes unsurprisingly occur most frequently in the four least linguistically marked forms (*kafir, kuffar, kufr,* and *takfir*), accounting for 76.29 percent of all tokens. The first (*kafir*) is a singular nominal used to describe a disbeliever, and the second (*kuffar*) is its plural nominal counterpart. The third is a singular nominal that refers to a state of disbelief, and the fourth (*takfir*) is a singular nominal that refers to the act of accusing one of being a disbeliever. Thus, given that both of these periodicals intend to recruit from the English-speaking world, in particular those who are willing to commit to a life of religious struggle, it would be far less effective to reference the more

Table 8.3 *Derived lexemes and statistics*

Derived lexeme	*Dabiq* (Da'esh)		*Inspire* (al-Qa'ida)		
	Number of tokens	Percentage of total tokens	Number of tokens	Percentage of total tokens	Cumulative percentage
Kafir (كافر)	94	11.50%	19	9.95%	**13.09%**
Kafirah (كافرة)	1	0.12%	0	0.00%	
Kafirin (كافرين)	17	2.08%	1	0.52%	
Kuffar (كفّار)	226	27.66%	76	39.79%	**29.96%**
Kufr (كفر)	326	39.90%	83	43.45%	**42.76%**
Kufri (كوفري)	22	2.69%	0	0.00%	
Takfir (تكفير)	123	15.05%	11	5.76%	**14.38%**
Takfiri (تكفيري)	8	0.97%	1	0.52%	
Takfiriyyin (التكفيريين)	2	0.24%	0	0.00%	
Total:	**817**	**100%**	**191**	**100%**	**100%**

marked forms, such as the singular feminine *kafirah*, with which readers are less likely to be familiar without additional framing or greater linguistic competence (cf. the Arabic-language periodicals *Al-Shamika* and *Al-Khansaa*, which were developed for a female audience).

8.3 Discussion

Each of these tokens and the larger discursive environments in which they occur illustrate how positive-self presentation and negative-other presentation arise. In order to determine precisely how this occurs, one needs first to recognize who the "Self" and the "Other" truly are. In the case of extremist groups, the "Other" is defined ostensibly as, at a minimum, the total sum of those who fall prey to the violence of those who perpetrate it. However, such a definition doesn't address the motivation for the victimhood of the "Other" in the first place. As such, after close examination of the approximately one thousand tokens extracted for this study, it becomes clear that the motivation for becoming the "Other" can be reduced taxonomically for a fuller characterization of the disbeliever and acts of disbelief that would lead one to a state of disbelief, through in-group and out-group membership constructed on the basis of behaviors, affiliation, and characteristics. Although there are general behaviors that are described as forbidden, there are others that specifically refer to violations of the Five Pillars or the basic religious teachings. Affiliations correspond to one's national, ethnic, and/or religious identity. Finally, the characteristics arise at the level of the individual or the community.

The primary discursive strategies employed include inclusion and exclusion, foregrounding and backgrounding, personalization and impersonalization, individualization and collectivization, generalizations, and high-stakes religious ultimatums. While inclusion and exclusion can be demonstrated directly, it is perhaps even more interesting when done indirectly, such as through a lack of acknowledgment to imply the corollary. For instance, if only those who are included are mentioned, then those who are excluded are implied by default. Foregrounding and backgrounding function similarly in that the presence of one often implies the other, whether both are present or not; however, foregrounding and backgrounding serve more generally as focal markers to direct or obscure the reader's attention deliberately. Personalization is frequently accomplished through the provision of proper nouns (typically in leaders' or countries' names) or through personal pronouns (typically *you* and *we*). In contrast, impersonalization often arrives through vague third-person (pro) nominal descriptions, e.g., *a person*, *one*, or *any party*. Likewise, individualization and collectivization are distinguished according to the subject under investigation. It should be noted that these are not mutually exclusive strategies. For example, an ultimatum can be issued to an impersonalized person, or an individual can belong to a collective group that is excluded.

Furthermore, there are recurring themes that arise through the use of these discursive strategies, including the notion of a perpetual existential threat, the necessity of a state governed by Islamic principles, the ever-looming final judgment at the end of time, the historical precedents that inform synchronic events, the punishment(s) assigned for impermissible behavior, and the constant tension between legislation divinely inspired and that which was created by humankind. Each of these discursive strategies and themes receives a fuller exemplification below through a representative sample of tokens from both periodicals.

8.3.1 Behaviors

Specific behaviors that are recognized in the corpora of *Da'esh* and *al-Qa'ida* as placing one outside the fold of Islam range from general statements to direct condemnations of those who do not adhere to the basic teachings, especially those revealed through the Qur'ān and the *aḥādīth*. Specific references are also made to the *Five Pillars*, i.e., the profession of faith (*shahadah*), the five daily prayers (*salat*), charitable giving to the poor (*zakat*), fasting from sunrise to sunset during the month of Ramadan (*sawm*), and undertaking the holy pilgrimage to Mecca (*hajj*).

General statements often establish the existence of such a state of disbelief (*kufr*) and identify the consequences for those who have entered it. For instance, from the samples numbered below, the text in (1) uses an impersonal reference to self-professed Muslims and offers a warning: Those who continue to live in predominantly non-Muslim countries but who abstain from engaging in the common, mutual religious struggle are more likely to enter a state of disbelief, regardless of their otherwise pious activities. On the other hand, the exemplar in (2) issues to the collective community a multi-generational warning cloaked in a reminder: It presupposes the common liturgical knowledge that voluntarily leaving the Muslim world situates one dangerously close to a life of sin, and it also reinforces the reader's internalization of this fact through a reminder that their actions will affect the totality of their lineage. Finally, the passage in (3) is addressed to an impersonalized individual reader. It assumes not only that the reader is a pious defender of the faith, but also that there is shared recognition that the United States, especially through its continued support of Israel, is a haven for disbelievers; as such, the reader is inclined to take up arms even if alone in this endeavor.

(1) Even if one were to spend all his hours at a masjid in prayer, dhikr, and study of the religion, while living amongst Muslims who reside amid **kuffar** and abandon jihad, then such a person would only be establishing the strongest proof against himself and his sin. (*Dabiq* 3)

(2) Therefore, it should be known that voluntarily leaving Darul-Islam for darul-**kufr** is a dangerous major sin, as it is a passage towards kufr and a gate towards one's children and grandchildren abandoning Islam for Christianity, atheism, or liberalism. If one's children and grandchildren don't fall into **kufr**, they are under the constant threat of fornication, sodomy, drugs, and alcohol. (*Dabiq* 11)

(3) Yes, O zealous mujahid Muslim, be the first inside America to revive this uproar inside the head of worldwide **kufr**. Let it be pressure to the government to stop their support to Jews and sacrifice for the reward of Allah. Look around at the reward if you decide to revive the tradition of this uprising in the land of **kufr**, America. You will be blessed with the honor of reviving up the lone wolf operations. The **kuffar** will live in constant fear in America and would not be able to taste the security. Our lofty Sheikh Usama Bin Laden (May the mercy of Allah be upon him) once said, "America and Americans will not dream of security nor gain it except when we experience it in Palestine." (*Inspire* 15)

Additionally, there are behaviors that are contrary to the basic teachings of the religion through which one becomes a disbeliever. The passage in (4) begins by establishing authenticity by calling upon (unknown) Islamic scholars and the ten acts that cause a person to go astray. However, the three clearly prohibited actions (consuming alcohol, committing adultery, and stealing) mentioned are then absolved of their sinful nature if and only if the leader of that area has deemed them permissible. It should be noted that this is the same rationale that has been used historically and contemporaneously by both groups to justify behavior that is otherwise unequivocally considered *haram* (forbidden). Both of the following exemplars present to the impersonalized reader an expanded list of prohibited behaviors, albeit in quite different ways. While both offer the very real threat of violence as a consequence, (5) provides a straightforward intertextual reference to the earlier description of willful rejection of the faith and distinguishes a simple disbeliever and a disbeliever who practices polytheism (*shirk*).

(4) Islamic scholars have given a little over ten major acts that would lead one to apostasy. One has to be careful to not take some one outside the fold of Islam (i.e. **takfir**) on major sins such as drinking alcohol, committing adultery, stealing and such unless if it's a ruler who clearly permits these sins under his rule (i.e. istihlal). (*Inspire* 4)

(5) So if a person who adheres to all the laws of the religion but resists the prohibition of gambling, usury, or fornication is a **kafir** whom it is obligatory to fight, how much more so is the case of he who practices shirk with Allah and is called to offer the religion sincerely to Allah and declare bara'ah and **kufr** towards everything worshipped besides Allah, but instead he arrogantly refuses and is from the **kafirin**. (*Dabiq* 8)

On the other hand, the passage in (6) offers such syntactic, semantic, and extralinguistic (i.e., historical and religious) complexity that it is unclear which message the reader actually receives. One is straightforwardly encouraged to adhere to the Five Pillars, though only three are listed explicitly. Hereafter appears a litany of behaviors that must be either strenuously avoided (e.g., the consumption of alcohol, which, as the reader may recall, was permissible in (4)) or deliberately followed (e.g., requiring non-Muslims to pay their annual tax, the *jizyah*), after which the reader is reminded that ignorance does not excuse one from the consequences of one's actions or behavior.

(6) So any resistant party that resists some of the obligatory prayers, fasting, hajj, or resists abiding by the prohibition of spilling blood, looting wealth, alcohol, gambling, incest, or resists adherence to jihad against the **kuffar** or the enforcement of jizyah upon Ahlul-Kitab, or abiding by anything else of the obligations and irja' – the most dangerous bid'ah prohibitions of the religion, those rulings which no one has an excuse for being ignorant of or abandoning and which the individual commits **kufr** by denying, then the resistant party is fought over these rulings even if it acknowledges them. (*Dabiq* 8)

To this end, given the significance of the five daily prayers, a reference to their obligatory nature appears both at the start and end of this passage in (6), though

Ideological Exclusion 205

the emphasis arguably shifts in tone from one of a reminder to one of a warning: Those who deliberately abandon their prayer have committed an act of disbelief. This theme continues in (7), which begins with a personalized, inclusive referent ("we") before establishing credibility through the invocation of the name of Muhammad and the legislation of appropriate punishment for the abandonment of prayer, i.e., the non-trivial loss of life. Similarly, (8) provides the consensus of the Companions of the Prophet (the *Sahabah*), once again establishing credibility, and notes that the fulfillment of the daily prayers is the most significant of them all.

(7) We then mentioned the reports narrated from the Prophet (sallallahu 'alayhi wa sallam) declaring the **kufr** of he who abandons prayer, expelling him from the religion, and legalizing the killing of one who resists performing it. (*Dabiq* 8)

(8) The Sahabah explicitly agreed that abandoning prayer was major **kufr**. As for the other three pillars, then there is difference of opinion amongst the later scholars regarding the ruling on a person who abandons one of these three. (*Dabiq* 8)

8.3.2 Affiliation

Despite the fact that many countries have waged war against al-Qa'ida or are currently engaged in warfare against Da'esh, not all opposing belligerents are readily recognized as non-believers. Although one's national affiliation is certainly a contributing factor, how one identifies ethnically and religiously also serves to discriminate among these opposing forces. Many countries from the "West" are foregrounded as categorically excluded from the realm of believers. In fact, although Americans are frequently the first to be singled out, as in (9), other countries are also personally referred to when the issue of retribution is raised in (10). Additionally, the benefits of serving valiantly are reinforced in (9) when an equivalence is made between the loss of a believer's life in exchange for the death of many disbelievers, who the reader is told were condemned to hell (*Jahannam*).

(9) It was a call to which Abu 'Umar responded, living great days in the city that stood defiantly in the face of the American transgression on the lands of the Muslims. Time passed, many **kuffar** were sent to Jahannam, and the brother was hit by a crusader airstrike in which all those who were with him were killed. (*Dabiq* 10)

(10) I hate the leaders of **kufr**. I want to assassinate the US president, the French president, the British PM or their ministers. (*Inspire* 10).

Furthermore, Muslims' frustrations are concurrently foregrounded while they are called to action for living in such nations; in fact, the believer has the moral obligation as in (11) to assist in the violent struggle to regain Muslim territory and the integrity of the religion. The agent ("you") is personalized, and the patients are collectivized. If this religious responsibility is not undertaken, however, the editor offers a historical precedent to the reader in (12). The Quraysh, a specified historical opponent of the faith, are equated with the present-day leaders of the collective West.

(11) The first thing I say to Muslims in America and the European countries is that you are in the heart of nations of the **kuffar**. You are in a place that too many Mujahedeen wish they were in, so that they can beat the **kuffar** in their own countries, destroy their peace as they destroy ours; force them to stop the war against Muslims. And force them to leave the Arabian Peninsula as well as all other Muslim countries, move the war from our lands to theirs and keep fighting them until we let Islam rule the whole planet. (*Inspire* 13)

(12) And here we are again, history repeating itself, the heads of **kufr** once again using the same ways in the war against Islam but in new forms. As the Quraysh, the head of **kufr** at that time, fought the Muslims laying sieges and economic blockades – doing their best to dry the resources of the Muslims. The same applies to the head of **Kufr** in our times, America and the West, fighting the Muslims by all means and methods. Exploiting the resources of the Muslims by imposing and tightening their grip, control and authority in the Muslim lands. And the Muslims are left with crumbs of their wealth. Seeing in front of their eyes how their wealth and treasures are used in building and strengthening the civilizations of the enemy – who later on use their strength in fighting the Muslims. (*Inspire* 15)

Nevertheless, ethnic affiliation plays a pivotal role in the daily military offenses. For example, in their quest to conquer the Middle East, Da'esh has deliberately attacked predominantly Kurdish or Yezidi villages. Strangely, the exemplar in (13) initiates a defense of such attacks by proposing that these are motivated by a disbelieving subset of the larger ethnic group. Moreover, their disdain for the Kurds cannot be nationalistic, since they do not recognize the existence of a Kurdish nation. This gives the impression, whether borne out by the data or not, that the military leaders carefully distinguish future victims of their violence. In contrast, there is no attempt made in (14) to defend themselves against criticism for the enslavement of Yezidi women; instead, an effort is made to discredit the credibility of the media's portrayal. This is accomplished through the invocation of lexical items that connote a powerless or defensive position, such as *astonishment, awake, asleep, alarmed*, etc.

(13) Our war with the Kurds is a religious war. It is not a nationalistic war – we seek the refuge of Allah. We do not fight Kurds because they are Kurds. Rather we fight the **kuffar** amongst them, the allies of the crusaders and Jews in their war against the Muslims. As for the Muslim Kurds, then they are our people and brothers wherever they may be. We spill our blood to save their blood. The Muslim Kurds in the ranks of the Islamic State are many. They are the toughest of fighters against the **kuffar** amongst their people. (*Dabiq* 10)

(14) So I say in astonishment: Are our people awake or asleep? But what really alarmed me was that some of the Islamic State supporters (may Allah forgive them) rushed to defend the Islamic State – may its honor persist and may Allah expand its

territory – after the **kafir** media touched upon the State's capture of the Yazidi women. So the supporters started denying the matter as if the soldiers of the Khilafah had committed a mistake or evil. Thus, after the matter transcended its limits and the barking of the charlatans – the wicked scholars – rose upon the pulpits of deviance, it became necessary to face their declarations with a declaration, but one of truth, to suppress their falsehood and restrain their tongues. (*Dabiq* 9)

Finally, it is unsurprising that one's religious affiliation is also a defining factor in the attribution of in-group or out-group membership, especially given repeated mentioning of both groups' shared interest in establishing Muslim states by invoking particularly polemic nomenclature (e.g., *Khilafah* and *Sharī'ah*). Nonetheless, these publications repeatedly foreground the other members of the Abrahamic religions, as in (15) and (16). To this end, those who follow the Judeo-Christian tradition are excluded from the believers, and the collectivized Muslim community is cautioned against coexistence with them, as they [Christians and Jews] will continue to victimize the Muslims until the final judgment.

(15) How many Jews are there in America, Europe and other **kufr** countries! So take matters in hand and follow the advice of your Prophet, if any of you gets hold of a Jew anywhere, let him finish him off. (*Inspire* 15)

(16) O Muslims! Whoever thinks that it is within his capacity to conciliate with the Jews, Christians, and other **kuffar**, and for them to conciliate with him, such that he coexists with them and they coexist with him while he is upon his religion and upon tawhid, then he has belied the explicit statement of his Lord ('azza wa jall), who says, And they will continue to fight you until they turn you back from your religion if they are able. So this is the condition of the **kuffar** in dealing with the Muslims until the establishment of the Hour. (*Dabiq* 9)

On the other hand, accusations are made even against other Muslims. For instance, the Sunni majority within the Muslim community oftentimes perceives the Shi'a as practicing an improper form of Islam and of following improper practices; consequently, the Alawis and the Sahwa Movement, another extremist group, are both positioned alongside those who directly oppose their agenda, e.g., those who rule not by that which has been revealed by Allah (*tawaghit*) and those who reject the revelation (*rafida*). The passage in (17) demonstrates this perpetual existence threat and analogizes the future to the historical precedents set in Rome.

(17) And nothing changes for the Islamic State, as it will continue to pronounce **takfir** upon the Jews, the Christians, the pagans, and the apostates from the Rafidah, the Nusayriyyah, the Sahwah, and the tawaghit. It will continue to wage war against the apostates until they repent from apostasy. It will continue to wage war against the pagans until they accept Islam. It will continue to wage war against the Jewish state until the Jews hide behind their gharqad trees. And it will continue to wage

war against the Christians until the truce decreed sometime before the Malhamah [Great War]. Thereafter, the slave markets will commence in Rome by Allah's power and might. (*Dabiq* 12)

8.3.3 Characteristics

Communities of believers and disbelievers are also distinguished from one another based on their self-presentation as perceived by the Other. In the case of (18), Muslims are urged to recognize the disbelieving community based on their own most salient characteristics. Although these generalized behaviors are foregrounded, the reader understands that backgrounded is the implication that believers do not exhibit any of these traits. Furthermore, the credibility of this statement is established through the personalized attribution of the statement to the historical theologian Ibnul-Qayyim, which is subsequently reinforced by comparison to the actions of Iblis, i.e., if a believer were to retain these characteristics, then he would be acting in tandem with Iblis.

(18) Ibnul-Qayyim (rahimahullah) said, "The pillars of **kufr** are four: arrogance, envy, anger, and desire" [Al-Fawa'id]. These four pillars push the person and party to commit **kufr**. How so? Arrogance and envy are what pushed Iblis to resist prostrating to Adam after he was ordered to by Allah. He then angrily promised to wage war against Adam and his offspring despite knowing that he would be burnt in Hellfire. Arrogance and envy also prevented the Israelites from accepting Islam, believing that the final messenger should only be from them. (*Dabiq* 2)

Moreover, such communities of disbelief are described as places where the laws of men are prioritized over their Islamic counterparts (i.e., the *Sharī'ah*), which itself is perceived as a major sin. Those who freely associate with disbelievers and their laws, especially those who do so in an attempt to oppose or defeat believers, are committing apostasy. These are represented by the personalized reminder in (19) and the impersonalized warning in (20), respectively. Finally, certain groups self-identify as more effective protectors of the Sharī'ah by disassociating themselves from those who practice man-made law. Hereafter, they urge the reader to consider the cognitive dissonance of simultaneously disavowing the privileging of man-made laws while accepting individuals who live in societies where they are practiced, as the exemplar in (21) indicates.

(19) Remember that if you were able to capture one hand span, one village, or one city from it, the law of Allah in that area would be replaced with the laws of men. Then ask yourself, "What is the ruling on someone who replaces or is a cause for the replacement of the law of Allah with the law of man?" Yes, you commit **kufr** by such. (*Dabiq* 12)

(20) And if the power in the coalition is for other than Allah's Shari'ah – and this is the reality – is their action considered to be merely requesting the help of the **kuffar** against the Muslims, which is absolutely prohibited and blatant deviance, or is it considered to be aiding the **kuffar** against the Muslims, which is extreme apostasy! And those who permitted seeking the help of the **kuffar** against other **kuffar** (not against Muslims) listed many conditions, which are not fulfilled by the Shari'ah claimants in the action they take with their allies from amongst the apostate factions against the Islamic State. (*Dabiq* 10)

(21) Al Qaeda is amongst the strongest Islamic groups in relation with declaring its barâ'ah (disassociation) from the **kuffâr**, whether it is an original **kâfir** or an apostate kâfir. And how astonishing it is when someone proclaims that man-made laws are **kufr** as well as quoting the ijmâ` (consensus) of ahl as-sunnah which states that these laws are **kufr**, and in spite of this he does not make barâ'ah from its people regardless of the fact that these man-made laws are clearly found in the constitutions of these regimes to the extent of their availability by its page number? Hence, how do you reject **kufr** but do not reject its people? (*Inspire* 6)

8.4 Conclusion

This study has demonstrated qualitatively and quantitatively through the use of particular instantiations of the triliteral root √KFR how the propaganda of two different extremist groups can be utilized in the (re)defining of disbelievers – and believers by extension – through the delineation of individuals into classes, namely, those who believe in the religion of Allah and those who retain any other religious beliefs. Interestingly, this strict bifurcation completely alienates the remaining members of the Ahl al-Kitab (Christians and Jews) by limiting the class of believers to those who identify strictly as Muslims (and sometimes even only as Sunni). On the other hand, the category of disbelievers is defined in terms of one's behaviors, affiliation, and characteristics. More specifically, the first includes those who engage in general behaviors believed to be forbidden, specific behaviors against the basic teachings of Islam, or acts that repudiate the Five Pillars. The second emphasizes national, ethnic, and religious identity as contributing to one's immediate rejection from the fold of Islam. Lastly, the third refers to particular characteristics of the disbelieving community and the disbelieving individual, by extension.

Nevertheless, after careful consideration and close textual analysis of the specific tokens in which √KFR appears, it becomes clear that members of al-Qa'ida and Da'esh are not strictly consulting the religious denotations of the triliteral root (e.g., Izutsu 1959 and Waldman 1968). Instead, they have presented a litany of acts and traits that, at best, establish the "Self" and the "Other" on the basis of pseudo-religious grounds. At worst, they perpetuate antiquated stereotypes and contemporary prejudices that misrepresent all those who adhere to the Islamic faith. A variety of strategies are found in the discursive construction of these two groups, including exclusion and inclusion, personalization and impersonalization, individualization and collectivization, generalization, and religious ultimatums.

Finally, although this paper demonstrates one meaningful method for extracting and analyzing derived lexemes from a single triliteral root in corpora of extremist periodicals, there remains much to be done. For instance, although the present study analyzes strictly the usage of √KFR, a subsequent study could examine the use of other terms of significance in English and/or Arabic, such as *munafiqûn* ("hypocrites"), *murtaddin* ("apostates"), *rafidah* ("those who reject the faith"), *crusaders*, *infidels*, *invaders*, etc. to expand our collective understanding of the overarching narratives being perpetuated, especially as some of these are not only utilized in distinguishing believers from non-believers, but are also employed by some as sectarian insults. Additionally, each of the thirty issues considered here could realistically be examined individually to see how their component parts serve the larger objectives of the periodical, especially given how different the overall objectives appear to be for al-Qa'ida and Da'esh. Moreover, each periodical has numerous sections that fit within different genres, such as interviews, calls to arms and *fatawa*, summaries of recent engagements, historical accounts of military events, etc. This could demonstrate the importance of genre writing and provide a preliminary characterization of each genre individually. Furthermore, as the present study focuses solely on textual analysis, an additional area for future research would be in the more multimodal aspects of the larger propaganda campaign of both groups, such as through the images in these periodicals and their online audiovisual content. Nonetheless, although an anonymous reviewer suggested investigating the social media accounts of associated individuals, this avenue has been unsuccessfully pursued in the past, in large part due to the ever-changing digital landscape and the inability of scholars to verify the authenticity of particular accounts as reliably belonging to a genuine member of the group.

References

Brown, Jonathan A.C. 2009. *Hadith: Muhammad's Legacy in the Medieval and Modern World*. London, UK: Oneworld Publications.

Chang, Byung-Ock. 2005. "Islamic Fundamentalism, Jihad, and Terrorism." *Journal of International Development and Cooperation*, 11(1): 57–67.

Cook, Michael. 2013. "The Appeal of Islamic Fundamentalism." *Journal of the British Academy* 2: 27–41.

DeLong-Bas, Natana. 2008. *Wahhabi Islam: From Revival and Reform to Global Jihad*. Oxford: Oxford University Press.

Dukes, Kais. 2009. *The Quranic Arabic Corpus*. Available at: https://corpus.quran.com/.

Dupret, Baudouin, Barbara Drieskens, and Annelies Moors (Eds). 2008. *Narratives of Truth in Islamic Law*. New York: Palgrave Macmillan.

Ernst, Carl W. 2003. *Following Muhammad: Rethinking Islam in the Contemporary World*. Chapel Hill, NC: The University of North Carolina Press.
Fairclough, Norman A. 1995. *Critical Discourse Analysis: The Critical Study of Language*. New York: Pearson Longman.
    2003. *Analysing Discourse: Textual Analysis for Social Research*. New York: Routledge.
Farrall, Leah. 2017. "Revisiting al-Qaida's Foundation and Early History." *Perspectives on Terrorism* 11(6): 17–37.
Hallaq, Wael B. 2009. *An Introduction to Islamic Law*. Cambridge: Cambridge University Press.
Hefner, Robert W. (ed). 2011. *Shari'a Politics: Islamic Law and Society in the Modern World*. Bloomington, IN: Indiana University Press.
Ibn Fūrak al-Isbahānī, Abū Bakr. 1999. *Kitāb al-Ḥudūd fī al-uṣūl. Beirut: Dār al-Gharb al-Islāmī*.
Izutsu, Toshihiko. 1959. *The Structure of the Ethical Terms in the Koran: A Study in Semantics*. Tokyo: Keio Institute of Philological Studies.
    1966 [2002]. *Ethico-Religious Concepts in the Qur'ān*. Montreal, McGill-Queen's University Press.
Janks, Hilary. 1997. "Critical Discourse Analysis as a Research Tool." *Discourse: Studies in the Cultural Politics of Education* 18(3): 329–342.
Levitt, Jonathan Goodman and Hemal Trivedi (Producers). 2015. *Among the Believers*. Film, Hemal Trivedi and Mohammed Ali Naqvi (Directors). Pakistan: Changeworx Films LLC and Manjusha Films LLC.
Martin, Jessica M. 2011. "The Information Battlefield: Al-Qaeda's Use of Advanced Media Technologies for Framed Messaging." *UNLV Theses, Dissertations, Professional Papers and Capstones*. Paper 1257.
Mozaffari, Mehdi. 2007. "What Is Islamism? History and Definition of a Concept." *Totalitarian Movements and Political Religions* 8(1): 17–33.
Shepard, William E. 1987. "Islam and Ideology: Towards a Typology." *International Journal of Middle East Studies*, 19(3): 307–335.
Simpson, Paul and Andrea Mayr. 2010. *Language and Power: A Resource Book for Students*. London: Routledge.
Spier, Troy E. 2018 "Extremist Propaganda and Qur'anic Scripture: A 'Radical' Corpus-Based Study of the Dabiq." *Discourse & Society* 29(5): 553–567.
Tucker, Matthew A. 2009. "The Root-and-Prosody Approach to Arabic Verbs." Unpublished draft. https://citeseerx.ist.psu.edu/viewdoc/download?doi=10.1.1.387.7497&rep=rep1&type=pdf.
van Dijk, Teun A. 1993. "Principles of Critical Discourse Analysis." *Discourse & Society* 4(2): 249–283.
    1995. "Discourse Analysis as Ideology Analysis." In C. Schäffner and A. Wenden (Eds.), *Language and Peace*, 17–33. Amsterdam: Harwood.
    1998. *Ideology: A Multidisciplinary Approach*. London: Sage.
Van Leeuwen, Theo. 2003. "The Representation of Social Actors." In Carmen Rosa Caldas-Coulthard and Malcolm Coulthard (Eds.), *Texts and Practices: Readings in Critical Discourse Analysis*, 32–70. London: Routledge.
Waldman, Marilyn R. 1968. "The Development of the Concept of Kufr in the Qur'ān." *Journal of the American Oriental Society* 88(3): 442–455.

Wehr, Hans. 1976. *A Dictionary of Modern Written Arabic*. Ithaca, NY: Spoken Language Services, Inc.

Wightwick, Jane and Mahmoud Gaafar. 1998. *Arabic Verbs and Essentials of Grammar: A Practical Guide to the Mastery of Arabic*. New York: McGraw Hill Books.

Wiktorowicz, Quintan. 2006. "Anatomy of the Salafi Movement." *Studies in Conflict & Terrorism* 29: 207–239.

Winter, Charlie and Usama Hasan. 2016. "The Balanced Nation: Islam and the Challenges of Extremism, Fundamentalism, Islamism and Jihadism." *Philosophia*, 44: 667–688.

Wodak, Ruth. 1989. *Language, Power, and Ideology*. Amsterdam: John Benjamins.

Wodak, Ruth and Michael Meyer. 2015. "Critical Discourse Analysis: History, Agenda, Theory, and Methodology." In Ruth Wodak and Michael Meyer (Eds.), *Methods of Critical Discourse Analysis*, 1–22. London: Sage.

Yusuf, Hamza. 2008. "Who Are the Disbelievers?" *Seasons* Spring: 30–50.

9 Violence for Social Change
An Analysis of the *#FeesMustFall* Movement in South Africa

Fiona Chawana and Ufuoma Akpojivi

9.1 Introduction

Much research has been conducted around the *#FeesMustFall* movement that began in South Africa on October 12, 2015. As Hodes (2016, 141) puts it, *#FeesMustFall* "is the subject of acute academic interest and a rapidly growing literature." Researchers have been interested in the movement because it can be regarded as the first social movement in post-apartheid South Africa since the attainment of independence in 1994 that challenged inherent values (i.e., inequality, transformation, and calls for decolonization) of the higher education sector.[1]

Studies such as Gillespie and Naidoo (2019a), Naicker (2016), and Hodes (2016) among others, have focused on the examination of the rationale behind the protest, and the contestation of ideas between the different stakeholders during the protest. There are few, if any, studies that examine how violent discourse was used as resistance and for advocating social change. Habib (2019) mentioned violence within the movement in his book, *Rebels and Rage: Reflecting on #FeesMustFall*. His discussion was, however, a critique of the movement and not necessarily a critical discourse analysis of violence. Likewise, Malabela's (2017) account of the violence within the University of the Witwatersrand was not a critical discourse of how violence was used for social change but an analysis of events that happened during the protest and students' reaction to the university's management.

This chapter critically examines the discourse of "violence" within the *#FeesMustFall* movement, and how violence was used as a strategy and call

---

[1] Although some scholars might see the *#RhodesMustFall* movement as the first movement for challenging racial and transformation issues at the University of Cape Town (UCT), this movement was limited to just UCT. *#FeesMustFall* was a nationwide protest from students across South Africa.

for social change within higher educational institutions in South Africa. The *#FeesMustFall* movement was birthed at the University of the Witwatersrand, also known as "Wits University," before it moved to other universities in South Africa. Also, the University of the Witwatersrand, as a historically "white university," presents a good vantage point to analyze how violence was used by students to disrupt the university space and push an ideological position of social change within this space (see Malabela 2017).

To interrogate the discourse of violence and its usage within the *#FeesMustFall* movement, thematic analysis was carried out on interviews conducted with eleven stakeholders and a collection of tweets at the peak of the protests in 2015 and 2016. Consequently, this chapter addresses the following questions: Why did the *#FeesMustFall* movement adopt violence as an ideological weapon during the 2015 and 2016 student protests? How was this violence played out within the protests of 2015 and 2016? To what extent did the violence aid and advocate social change?

The chapter posits that in order to understand violence within social movements, there is need for a nuanced reading of violence and its adaptation in addressing social issues in society.

9.1.1 Background of #FeesMustFall

#FeesMustFall started on October 12, 2015 at the University of the Witwatersrand, South Africa. Gillespie and Naidoo (2019a) explain that the formation of *#FeesMustFall* was influenced by two unique factors that reflect the relationship between the university and society. According to them, these factors are the emergence of the *#RhodesMustFall* movement in March 2015, which demanded the removal of the statue of Cecil John Rhodes from the University of Cape Town, and a call for the university to move from Eurocentric knowledge to African knowledge (Gillespie and Naidoo, 2019a). These two factors influenced the establishment of the *#FeesMustFall* movement at Wits University. Dasai (2019), while buttressing the above points, stated that "Wits was and remains an elite university" shrouded in whiteness. This position is maintained by Xaba, who stated that "historically white universities [like Wits University] **maintain colonial and racist institutional cultures** due to their histories" (2017, 97, emphasis added).

This protest started as a reaction to the increase of tuition fees by over 10 percent, and this meant that Black students from poor or disadvantaged backgrounds would be excluded as they would be unable to afford the fees. According to the university management, this increase was a result of the "decline in government subsidies which left the universities with no option but to increase fees" (Malabela 2017, 132). Similarly, Steyn and De Villiers (2006) state that:

> The effect of this (decrease in government funding) has been to create conditions of austerity in universities, as well as to force universities to grow their revenue by increasing tuition fees and "third stream" income from corporate and other non-governmental funders. High student fees caused student exclusions from university programs, and students have been stressed by mounting debt, which has risen sharply since the mid-1990s. (Cited in Gillespie and Naidoo 2019a, 192)

The shortfall in government funding from "49 percent in 2000 to 40 percent," despite an increase student enrollment since the end of apartheid (Hodes 2016), meant that students have to bear the burden of such shortfall in the form of increased fees. According to the Department of Higher Education, the "average cost of higher education in most historically white institutions such as the University of Cape Town, Rhodes University, University of Stellenbosch and the University of the Witwatersrand is more than R90000 (US$6200) annually which is unaffordable for the middle-class" (2015, 22). For instance, Statistics South Africa (2019) reported the average monthly earnings for an employee in the formal non-agricultural sector to be R20,833 (US$1,400). The Black working class rarely earns this much due to the history of apartheid, where Blacks were denied formal education and excluded from the formal sector. Most often, Blacks are limited to informal or menial jobs, where the minimum wage is R3,500 (US$239) (Omarjee 2019). Gillespie and Naidoo (2019a), while elaborating on the above, posit that since the end of apartheid and the embrace of democracy in 1994, the government under the African National Congress (ANC) failed to address the social inequality in society that has continued to keep Black people at the bottom of the economic structure. Furthermore, university is pivotal to moving Black people into "the upper strata of capitalist economy and society" (Gillespie and Naidoo 2019b).

Consequently, students had to protest and resist such fee increments and their possible exclusion from seeking a university education that could increase their chances of leaving their present economic condition and reaching a higher level in the social and economic structure. Using social media and its affordances, the students shutdown Wits University and blocked the entrances to the university, forcing management to engage with them, because the students felt that they were not being listened to. This protest action subsequently moved to other universities – hence drawing nationwide attention to the issue. Habib (2016) argues that the protest from the students nationwide was not just anger toward universities' management but also toward the state for "failing to serve the needs of its polity and to drive an agenda of democratic redress" (cited in Hodes 2016, 141).

Although the movement was established to call for free education, it was also at the forefront of calling for a free decolonized education (see Ahmed 2019).

The call for a decolonized education was meant to advocate and promote African indigenous knowledge systems that are in line with inherent African societal beliefs over Eurocentric knowledge. To Gillespie and Naidoo, the students' use of the "decolonization language is to mark their objection not only to the racism caused by fifty years of apartheid rule but also to the much longer colonial period that informed it" (2019a, 192).

In order to achieve their objectives of "free" and "decolonized" education, the movement embraced radical strategies of the anti-apartheid struggle and these strategies include singing a decolonized national anthem, dancing, nude protest, use of violence, and the call to the government and the police to their struggle. The use of these strategies was to pronounce their "renewal of the struggle to overcome the long history of subjugation in South Africa: a commitment to ongoing struggle" (Gillespie and Naidoo, 2019a). Of these strategies, the use of violence by the movement generated much interest, both in mainstream media and in social media. This violence was attributed to the militarization of campuses, where the police and private security personnel were highly visible and clashed with students. Nicolson (2016) extended this thought by arguing that the presence of the police and private security agents created some form of tension; hence, violence was to be expected as the students distrusted the state and university management. This manifested itself in different ways (e.g., clashing with the police, throwing of stones, and burning and destroying of infrastructure). At Wits University, there was an attempt to burn down the Wartenweiler Library in which a hundred books were damaged (Wits University statement 2016). A bus was also destroyed. According to the former Minister of Higher Education, Naledi Pandor, the destruction of public property in South African universities during the 2015 and 2016 #FeesMustFall protests was estimated at R800 million (about US$55 million) (Dentlinger 2018).

Such large-scale damage to the university attracted numerous criticisms against the movement as the use of violence was condemned. Xaba (2017) notes that following the violence that erupted at South African universities and the level of destruction that took place, all public sympathy for the movement disappeared. The mainstream South African media were also critical of the students, referring to them as "violent and unruly." According to Mtengwane (2019), there was no need for violence during the protests as social change comes as a result of ideological exchange and not through violence. The protesters instead argued that the institution and society had been violent towards them, and the only solution to address that is the use of counter-violence (Mkatshwa and Ntshingila 2018). The students' position was influenced by their understanding of Frantz Fanon's readings of violence as a way of attaining true decolonization. This is fully discussed in the theoretical framework section.

However, President Jacob Zuma's announcement of free education for the poor and working class whose annual income does not exceed R350,000 (US$23,943) in December 2017 brought relative peace to higher education campuses. Zuma's announcement goes contrary to the Heher Commission – a commission set up to establish the feasibility of free higher education. The findings of the Commission state that there is "no capacity for the state to provide free tertiary education to all students" (Areff and Spies 2017). Therefore, it can be argued that the decision of former President Zuma to go against the findings of the Commission was to stabilize the higher education sector and stop the violence that had become a common phenomenon within the South African higher education institutions.

9.2   Social Movements, Activism, and Protest

Social movements are generally considered to be groups of people who rise to stand against ills in society, usually against the state and the elite. Over the years, social movements have morphed to include issues that revolve around quality of life and issues that generally concern the allocation of material wealth in society to address poverty and socioeconomic inequality. To Tarrow (2011), a social movement is a group of people united by common challenges and purpose, leading to social solidarity toward achieving set goals, mostly through sustained interaction amongst themselves or actors such as the government. Tarrow's definition of social movement falls within Tilly's (1987) four critical elements of a social movement, namely collective challenge, shared purpose, social solidarity, and sustained interaction (Tarrow 2011, 9). On the other hand, Leslie (2006, 21) defines a social movement as "a sustained interaction between a specific set of authorities and various spokespersons holding a set of opinions and beliefs and preferences for changing some aspects of the social structure and reward distribution of a society."

The above definition embodies the characteristics of social movements and identifies actors as well as the element of change that social movements seek to achieve, whether socioeconomic or ideological. This definition is best suited for the view expressed in this chapter, as it emphasizes the sustained interaction between the different actors, which is what distinguishes social movements from protests. Also, this chapter will borrow the notion of contentious politics by movement actors from Tarrow (1998, 2011) as it includes collective acts by movement actors to coerce the state into giving in to their demands. To Tarrow, "contentious politics occurs when ordinary people, often in league with more influential citizens, join forces in confrontation with elites, authorities, and opponents" (1998, 2). The notion of contentious politics brings to the fore the issues of confrontation between movement actors and the state, particularly authorities such as the police and army during the processes of the sustained interaction.

The development of social movements has been characterized in a multiplicity of ways, but one key component that arises consistently in debates is collective behavior. Tarrow (2011) points out that the collective is critical in social movements as it guarantees the impact that a movement can make. Leslie (2006) situates the notion of the collective within the classical model of social movements by arguing that social-movement actors rely on each other and maintain their existing social networks for increased opportunities for success. According to Dobash and Dobash (1992), social movements can be traced along the lines of the resource mobilization theory, with particular focus on how social movements mobilize financial, human, and social resources. They further state that for social movements to make more significant impacts, the resource mobilization stance allows them to lie dormant for periods and resume when issues they focus on re-emerge in communities, or when there are new possibilities for change. This is indicative of the ever-transforming nature of social movements and how the element of the collective has remained key in their operations. While the collective is inherently good for social movements, Dobash and Dobash (1992) argue that a critical component within a collective is the existence of radical factions, because they ultimately push for the most extreme of changes through the most radical means, making the demands of moderate factions seem more moderate from within and outside the movement.

The kind of social change that a movement seeks to achieve sets the tone for the actions the movement organizes and implements to achieve maximum impact. According to Leslie (2006, 42), "in order for social movements to realize their potential to effect social change, they need to exert control over the state apparatus." This can only be achieved through exerting pressure on the state, as the state is the key actor that most movements seek to transform, therefore making the state key to the operations of social-movement action. While identifying the state as a key actor within social-movement politics, Leslie adds that "social movements make demands on the state yet, paradoxically for social change to prevail it has to have the support of the state ... the state is the architect of the political environment within which social movements emerge and operate, thus creating the opportunities for action and, alternatively, imposing restrictions on movement activities" (Leslie 2006, 35). Thus, social-movement actors are in a precarious position because social movements are born out of the failures of the state, but the social change can only be realized with the support of the state. Whether it relates to policy changes or the provision of essential services, social movements rely heavily on responses from the state.

Owing to their dependence on the state to realize social change, the process of bringing about that change has often led to a confrontation between the state and social movements, and such confrontations are often violent. According to Tarrow (2011), violence could emanate from police brutality or be used by movement actors as tactics to gain attention and retain it. However, within the African continent, social movements formed by university students have long been embedded in student politics and grounded in the culture of violence (Fomunyan 2017). This culture of violence "is an inherited ideological trait that is gradually manifesting itself among students" in contemporary society (Fomunyan 2017, 38). Such violence from student movements was evident in the early 1940s at the dawn of nationalist movements against colonialism, and this has continued. Nyamnjoh (2005) buttressed this further in his statement that continuity of colonial legacies has ensured continued subjugation of Africans and the colonized, which is being resisted violently.

In recent years, student movements such as *#YoSoy132* in Mexico (Garcia and Trere 2014) and the Penguins Revolution in Chile are examples of violent student protests emanating from deep issues involving government failure to cater for the needs and demands of society, all resulting in the deployment of security forces to quash the resistance. Fomunyan (2017, 38) states that "because the culture of violence is an inherited one, the process will continue unless urgent steps are taken to ensure transformation and decolonization ... universities need to create environments where students are comfortable to learn, thereby eradicating the need for protest."

Within the South African context, violence can be traced to the apartheid era, which was inherently violent towards marginalized Blacks. Violence was perpetrated against Blacks through harsh apartheid laws such as pass laws that segregated Black South Africans into camps and Bantu reserves, where their movement was restricted. Furthermore, the Bantu Education Act of 1953 (Thompson 2001) segregated students along racial lines, leading to the current challenges in higher education that the *#FeesMustFall* students sought to address. Segregation allowed for the creation of separate universities for white and Black students, therefore leading to the existing challenges in historically white universities and historically Black universities. According to Morrow (2008), apartheid created disparities in the allocation of resources among racially segregated universities that were never resolved after apartheid, leading to protests in tertiary institutions that were historically Black as they remained underequipped. This juxtaposes Fomunyan's (2017, 54) argument that "violence is a legacy of racial discrimination and colonialism, high levels of unemployment, and pronounced increasing income inequality" – legacies that have continued years after independence in 1994.

On the violence during the *#FeesMustFall* protests, Oxlund (2016, 1) notes that "violent struggle protests that were formerly associated with the institutional life of historically Black institutions are becoming common in historically white institutions as well." Hence, it appears that the violent protests in historically white universities are aimed at condemning the hostile and untransformed teaching and learning space. More so, violent protest has always been a part of student protests in other universities before the start of the *#FeesMustFall* protests. For example, there were violent protests as early as 2006, at the Mahikeng Campus of North West University and the Mamelodi Campus of the University of Pretoria, which were previously Black campuses of historically white universities (Morrow 2008). Hence, we argue that violence is an inherent tactic of social movements in Africa.

9.2.1 Theoretical Framework: "On Violence"

The acts of violence used by student protesters as a tool for social change was rooted in their understanding of Fanon's philosophical work entitled *The Wretched of the Earth*. This is not farfetched, as Achille Mbembe (2011) labelled the *#FeesMustFall* movement the "Fanonian moment" (Gibson 2017). Such a label from Mbembe points to the adaptation of Fanon's ideology and its influence on the students during the 2015 and 2016 protests. According to Mbembe, the current generation of students are "impatient, brash, and angry ... and they reject the logic of normalcy. In a sense, the typical youth want to change society" (Gibson 2017, 580). The anger of the students is based on the systematic and epistemic violence of the university spaces against Black students, thus their rejection of peaceful dialogue, and the use of violence as a tool for achieving social change. Jonathan Jansen, the former Vice-Chancellor of the University of Free State, while buttressing the above argument, stated that, "mainly middle-class black students who attend white schools and white universities ... their complaint is very simple: they are still not free. They see a generational break between the old-timers' accounts of struggle and victory and a new generation caught in the daily grunt of a white-dominated economy and untransformed universities" (cited in Gibson 2017, 585).

The above quote emphasizes that the students' struggle during *#FeesMustFall* was not only about free education, but to address systematic and epistemic issues inherent during colonialism that have continued in post-apartheid South Africa, hindering and making Black students uncomfortable within the university's space. Gillespie and Naidoo (2019a and 2019b) argue that universities in South Africa are still rooted and structured along colonialization (apartheid) in which Black bodies feel unwelcome and the curriculum is built around Eurocentric knowledge. These colonial structures have been normalized, and education is an instrument that is used to entrench this colonialism in South Africa (Xaba 2017). Therefore, the students' struggle and resistance were grounded on Fanon's ideas of violence. According to Fanon, "colonialism is both created and sustained by violence; it can be destroyed only by violence" (Riley 2017, 10). This idea immediately resonates with the students in their drive for a real transformation and decolonization of the universities (Gibson 2017). The word decolonization presents a new lens through which the legacies of colonialism and apartheid can be easily understood and dismantled (Xaba 2017). Fanon posited that true decolonization in postcolonial societies will be advanced by the "lumpen-proletariat of shanty towns-all fall into line with the stand made by the rural masses" and not by the privileged people, i.e., "puppet bourgeoisie of businessmen and shopkeepers, the urban proletariat" (1961, 10). This is because the "lumpen-proletariat" want to bring about social change and not maintain the status quo, which has privileged the bourgeoise or middle class that emerged in post-independent African states. This process of decolonization is non-negotiable, and it is a violent process because the colonizer and settler dehumanize the natives or subjects. This process of decolonization should see the replacement of one group by another, and this is only possible via their rebellion and resistance to dehumanization, which in itself is a violent process.

This description by Fanon fits the postcolonial South African state, as the *#FeesMustFall* movement was established by Black students who were worse off with limited or little economic resources, refused to continue with the status quo and wished for the decolonization of the university space and curriculum. According to Xaba (2017, 96), South Africa as a postcolonial state inflicts violence on poor Black South Africans daily, and such violence has been normalized. Hence, the only option to resist such normalized violence is by violence, as the state responds to violence (2017, 96).

However, a literal understanding/interpretation of Fanon's work "on violence" as was done during the protest is problematic. Fanon's call for violence as a way of achieving true decolonization was not a call for direct violence, as Fanon argues that "decolonization is the meeting of two forces opposed to each other by their very nature" (Xaba 2017, 100). This refers to the contestation of ideas and ideology. This could mean that Fanon's notion of violence was ideological violence between the colonizer and the colonized people. It is this ideological violence that will help disrupt colonial structures and legacy. Riley (2017) argues that Fanon's argument in *The Wretched of the Earth* was challenging the dominant ideology that the colonizer is "powerful" and "expert" over the colonized people. This notion of ideological violence is similar to Cabral's (1966) idea of ideological weapons. According to him, one salient way for postcolonial states to achieve freedom and bring about social change is through ideological contestations between the African states and their colonizers, as such ideological weapons will facilitate and promote African ideas and uproot inherent Western or colonial structures that are dominant in the society (Akpojivi 2018). This falls within

Fanon's argument that "decolonization is quite simply the replacing of a certain 'species' of men by another 'species' of men ... decolonization never takes place unnoticed, for it influences individuals and modifies them fundamentally ... it brings a natural rhythm into existence, introduced by new men, and with it a new language" (Fanon 1961, 27–28).

9.3 Methodology

In order to understand the discourse of violence for social change within the University of the Witwatersrand, South Africa, during the *#FeesMustFall* protests in 2015 and 2016, semi-structured interviews were conducted with eleven university stakeholders, including two senior management staff, two members of the academic staff union, six students that participated in both protests and Student Representative Council (SRC) members, and one member of staff from the Department of Higher Education South Africa. These interviewees were purposely selected based on their positions and their involvement in the said protests. Their experiences and exposures to the *#FeesMustFall* protests will help to ascertain the ideological contestations and the discourse emanating from the use of violence. Each interview was recorded and lasted between 45 and 60 minutes. Each participant signed a consent form, and participants who requested to be anonymized in data reporting due to the sensitivity of the issue had their names replaced with pseudonyms. Also, an online ethnography, i.e., collecting tweets from the official hashtags of *#FeesMustFall*, was carried out. Tweets were collected between October 8 and November 20, 2015 and September 19 and October 11, 2016, because these periods marked the peak of protests. A total of 2,678 tweets were collected, and these tweets were purposively selected for the analysis.

A thematic discourse analysis was carried out. Using thematic analysis will enable attention to be paid to the text and language used based on emerging themes. Jupp (2006, 186), while substantiating this methodology, stated that "the emphasis is on the content of a text, 'what' is said and how it's said."

9.4 Violence and Social Change: A Critical Analysis

9.4.1 Shutdown: Speaking to Power

This study found that the students utilized the shutdown of the university via mass sit-ins as a violent ideological weapon to elicit a response from the university, the state, and the corporate world regarding the issues raised during the *#FeesMustFall* protests. This strategy entails occupying strategic university buildings and entrances and ensuring that activities at the university came to a standstill. As the system had been inherently violent towards Black students, and so there was need for epistemic violence to ensure the disruption of university business in a bid to gain the attention of the government and university management. The students revealed that by conducting mass sit-ins at university entrances and critical points, such as Solomon Mahlangu House,[2] they were speaking back to power and holding hostage the very institutions that perpetrated coloniality and exclusion of young Black students from gaining economic emancipation. According to Interviewee 4, a student activist at the university, "the system is violent; it is violent towards us the children of apartheid, they do not want to see us progress. So, it was our duty as 'fallists' to stand our ground and demand to be heard ... we were not going to move, and we wanted them to understand our pain" (Personal interview, Johannesburg, December 14, 2019).

Also, Sphiwe Ndlovu, a student activist, opined that "the university and government have for long disregarded our demands for opening up education, to allow more economically disadvantaged Black students to get into tertiary education. Over the years, we see that the government only responds to threats and blockades, so that is what we implemented" (Personal interview, Johannesburg, January 18, 2019). From the above assertions, it is evident that the students were determined to get the relevant response via shutting down the institution. Based on previous experiences of protests at other tertiary institutions and the history of the country, the students were aware that governments respond to violent disruption. This is supported by Heffernan's (2019) argument that universities and government have always been known to respond when the situation/protest is violent, forcing them to negotiate, since non-violent protests were often ignored without any decisive reaction. This position on violence and shutdown of the university to attract the needed attention was evident in social media discourses, as the tweets revealed that the students intended to continue with the shutdown until the university and government responded to their demands. For instance, @WitsFMF posted, "we will #Shutdown till management listens to us" (October 19, 2016). The students in 2015 had echoed similar sentiments as @WitsFMF tweeted "Student: way forward, we must continue to occupy Solomon house. Next year we must say no free quality education no local elections" (November 1, 2015). The tweets also indicated students' intentions to extend the fight for free quality education by holding the electioneering process hostage.

Nevertheless, to the students, occupying Solomon Mahlangu House was a strategic decision to violently disrupt the day-to-day business of the university, which will in turn result in the university losing revenue via working

---

[2] Formerly Senate House – the name was changed to Solomon Mahlangu House as part of the decolonizing the university space program of the University due to the *#FeesMustFall* protests. This is the main administrative building for the University, which holds administrative and management offices.

hours. Such a strategy led to the protests attracting media attention as they managed to force a shutdown of university business for periods of days at various stages of the protests. According to Chinguno et al. (2017), the shutdowns implemented by the students forced the university to engage with the students, indicating the effectiveness of the tactics utilized by the students. Consequently, due to its success, this approach of disruption spread to other universities.

Furthermore, this shutdown strategy was a tactic to elicit a response from the private sector, which the students accused of not investing in higher education. By shutting down the university, the semester would inevitably be delayed and graduate programs would be affected. Sphiwe Ndlovu, while buttressing the above, held that, "as a movement we wanted to send a clear message to the corporate sector that our needs have to be met, and the best way to achieve that was through a shutdown of the university" (Student activist, personal interview, Johannesburg, January 18, 2019). Similarly, Motimele (2019) posits that the university operates in neo-liberal time, pushing for deadlines and the timely completion of degrees so they can continue churning out students for the corporate sector. This represents students' awareness that if the movement was to be effective, they needed to violently challenge the university structures that perpetuate the commodification of South African education, therefore, forcing the private sector to contribute to university infrastructure and the needs of students.

In line with this, Ballard et al. (2005) articulate that capitalism and neo-liberal policies have drawn the focus of the South African government towards pleasing market forces at the expense of the people that elected them into power. More so, Satgar (2019) argues that the current economic situation in South Africa is influenced by the reluctance of the private sector to assist student development through a more extensive base of scholarships tailored explicitly for poor Black students. Ballard et al. (2005) previously stated that student revolts were inevitable because the government had seemingly relinquished all power to the private sector, thereby neglecting the economic transformation they had promised before independence. Therefore, there was need to question the private sector's commitment to students' development. For example, @WitsFMF tweeted "RT @starstart: Private sector exploitation of students for bursaries is being called into question – Free quality education @WitsFMF #feesmustfall ..." (November 27, 2015). The above tweets highlight the need for all stakeholders, i.e., public and private sectors, to be actively involved in addressing the challenges confronting South African students, especially Black students, due to economic inequalities. This is in line with Tarrow's (2011) and Dobash and Dobash's (1992) arguments that the effectiveness of social movements in achieving social change can be judged through their ability to stimulate a response from stakeholders, and a clear way of doing this is through upsetting the balance of power by threatening corporate structures.

In this light, the *#FeesMustFall* protests succeeded in getting the attention of the country, as by shutting down an institution of the magnitude of the University of the Witwatersrand, and subsequently other institutions, the movement made history by holding government, university management, and the private sector accountable. However, such an approach was criticized by other stakeholders. For instance, a senior member of the university management posited that such a strategy was holding the institution hostage. According to him, "Fasiha put it well on TV when she said, we cannot attack the government, but we can only hold the university hostage, but that was a dangerous kind of thought" (Interviewee 1, December 14, 2018). Nevertheless, it should be noted that disruptive tactics and violence have long been used as tools for expression, and students were only using them to express and confront institutional powers.

9.4.2 Decolonizing the University Space through Violent Protests

Another salient theme that emerged was the conversations about disrupting university spaces and the colonial knowledge reproduction within the university. The students articulated that the South African knowledge project is violent towards Black bodies, thereby perpetuating colonial practices and knowledge within the university space. As indicated earlier, *#FeesMustFall* protests erupted in the background of the calls for decolonizing knowledge practices through curriculum change and inclusion of more Black experiences in academia. Some of the students interviewed articulated that the university space was exclusionary due to language practices and the exclusion of decolonial and African thoughts. According to Sphiwe Ndlovu, "this university and other white Universities out there are tough on Black bodies, we are bruised and battered just by trying to compete with other students from white Universities. How do you expect a student from Tembisa who has to be here for 8 am classes to be equally competitive with a person from student accommodation or a white student who drives to school?" (Personal interview, Johannesburg, January 18, 2019).

Similarly, Ashley Mabasa opined that the struggle for inclusion reared its ugly head through limited availability of resources and the high cost of education at the institution. He stated that, as members of the SRC, they had to negotiate with a private off-campus accommodation provider, "South Point," to acquire a reprieve for students who were homeless. "For instance, if you were in residences last year, you would get free meals, residence, and tuition. At some point, the SRC had to approach Financial Aid to get them to talk to South Point and bail out about 200 students. So, some students were bailed out"

(Personal interview, Johannesburg, January 22, 2019). While the efforts of the student union brought respite to some students, many students were still left homeless, and the SRC was not well equipped to assist them all. Swartz et al. (2018, 76), while expressing the challenges Black students encounter within the university, argue that only one in four Black students complete their degrees on time because "financial factors were the most debilitating obstacles that inhibited access and continued participation in universities." In addition to this, several academic factors hindering the completion of degrees on time by Black students have been identified, including "being inadequately prepared to choose a course to study, poor quality lecturing, ineffective channels for complaints about staff, lack of academic support, lecturer inaccessibility, fears of intellectual inferiority, coping with high workloads and technological unpreparedness" (Swartz et al. 2018, 76). These were some of the aggregate demands raised by students during the *#FeesMustFall* protests in 2015 and 2016. The above is an indication of the violent nature of the academic space at the university and other universities that students from poor Black families have to endure.

Accordingly, in order to address the economic inequalities that have impacted their development right from apartheid to the post-apartheid era, the protesting students believed that violence was the only option available to them. For example, @WitsFMF, while buttressing the above, tweeted that "Phetani on violence – us destroying buildings or burning tyres is NOT violence. Our poverty and dispossession IS violence. #Asinamali" (February 13, 2016). Another tweet by @WitsFMF read "Lushaba: At the heart of our struggle, we want to be HUMAN in our own country!" (October 7, 2016). Both tweets speak of state violence towards Black bodies despite the embrace of democracy, and this violence is rooted in the inherited apartheid structures that have continued to promote economic inequalities (Thompson 2001). Such structural inequality has resulted in dehumanizing standards of living across South Africa. For one to demand to be human in the country of one's ancestors speaks of expression of the coloniality and violence entrenched within South Africa.

9.4.3   *Violence as a Strategic Tool*

From the interview data, the use of violence was considered a strategic tool for achieving the overall objectives of the *#FeesMustFall* protests of 2015 and 2016. The use of violence resulted in people adopting different positions concerning its place in bringing about social change. For example, John Smith,[3] a former member of the Academic Staff Association of Wits University, posited that

---
[3] A pseudonym.

"while most staff members supported the need to address accessibility and inclusivity embodied in FMF, the tactics and violence used were not palatable to many across the institution" (Personal interview, December 12, 2018). A similar sentiment was shared by the Vice-Chancellor, Professor Adam Habib, who not only denounced the violence but blamed it on the factionalism within the movement along political lines. In his words:

I argue that there was a difference between the 2015 and 2016 movement. 2016 was more violent, it was far more factional, and parts of it were far more racist. The lazy answer is a belief among some of the students that violence is a product of police action. However, research has shown differently ... Factionalism starts at the end of October 2015 because after Zuma made the concession and students came back, the African National Congress (ANC) tried to control the movement. Then the Economic Freedom Fighters (EFF) tried to control the movement, and as each tried to control the movement, the violence starts. (Personal interview, Johannesburg, December 12, 2018)

This position was criticized by the students, who attributed the violence to the militarization of the campus and the belief that the only way to address an institutional culture of violence is through violence. The militarization of the campus by police and private security forces led to inhumane treatment or police brutality against Black students during the #FeesMustFall protests. The humanity of Black bodies was questioned, as the students argued that they were met with physical violence because Black lives in the country were currently treated as worthless and subjected to violence. This assertion is evident in the following tweets by @WitsFMF: "They believe that black people must be dealt with violence because they are objects" (October 7, 2016). @WitsFMF retweeted "RT @mphomakitla: 12Jan16 Solomon House Forced Removal Part 1 https://t.co/zorXLQVDk1 via @YouTube" (January 12, 2016). The tweet had a video link showing fewer than ten students who had occupied the concourse at Solomon Mahlangu House being dragged by at least twenty members of campus and private security agents. The altercation eventually turned violent, with the police and private security staff shoving students and eventually firing rubber bullets and tear gas at them. Similarly, @WitsFMF tweeted "RT @UJFMF: @AmandlaMobi help is currently needed at Wits by @WitsFMF as students have been brutalized by armed police and private security # ..." (January 12, 2016) and "RT @patriciahlengz: We asked for poor students to be included in the system, not for armed police and guards @WitsFMF @UJFMF #ViolenceAtWits" (January 12, 2016). The above tweets position Black lives as objects of torture and disrespect, and the students attributed this to the challenges and dynamics of race discourses in South Africa. Some social critics argue that the Blackness of the students was the reason for police brutality, as such brutality has never been extended to white movements such as #ZumaMustFall that calls for the resignation of President

Jacob Zuma (Haupt 2015). For instance, a student account on Twitter explained how a student was shot with rubber bullets: @WitsFMF posted "Stdnt [student] narrates how he was brutally attacked by police last night! He was shot in the back three times as he lay on the floor! #WitsPeaceAccord" (October 19, 2016). The tweet further highlights the difference between how Black bodies are treated as against white bodies, drawing a comparison from the thirty-six Black miners that were killed by the police at Marikana following a protest. Such could be seen in the tweet below: @WitsFMF tweeted "Lushaba: We know what we would see if those 36 miners were white. Similarly, had the students been white, we would see no police brutality" (October 7, 2016).

This difference was further highlighted in the profiling that occurred during the militarization. According to @WitsFMF, "militarisation of campuses is automatically racial profiling. White kids and staff attend without intimidation. Blcks [Blacks] are ALWAYS suspects!" (October 19, 2016). These conversations further bolstered student attempts to address decolonial issues of inequality and coloniality through the same violence that has been meted out to Black bodies over the years. According to Riley (2017), colonialism thrives within violence and the students challenging that violence with violence was a means to end the cycle of violence against Black bodies within and outside of academic spaces. This thought was further reflected in @panashechi's tweets: "Violence begets violence twitter aka middle-class SA neglects discussion of structural violence black people endure daily ... " (October 15, 2016). The tweet above also alludes to the ignorance of the middle class towards the students' challenges that resulted in violent clashes across the university.

9.5 Conclusion

The study determined that the *#FeesMustFall* movement protests of 2015 and 2016 were established to challenge deeply inherent colonial structures of inequality as well as lack of transformation that has systematically excluded and impacted on poor Black and middle-class South African students. The movement saw and used violence as a strategic tool to advocate for social change. Such a strategy was influenced mainly by their interpretation of Fanon's "violence" as a means of achieving true decolonization. The use of violence resulted in getting the needed attention of the government – a key stakeholder – to address the issues of free education and bring decolonized education to the fore. Hence, the Vice-Chancellor of Wits University, Adam Habib, while summing up the impact of the movement, held that through their advocacy, the movement was able to achieve in ten days what Vice-Chancellors had been unable to achieve in ten years.

Such a feat from the movement to bring about social change is commendable as the students fall within Fanon's category of "lumpen-proletariat," whom he envisaged will bring about the needed change and true decolonization in postcolonial African states. However, the students' use and understanding of Fanon's notion of violence is problematic as Fanon's call for violence as a way of addressing colonialism or coloniality that is perpetuated using violence was not through physical violence but by ideological violence. Such ideological violence will bring about contestation of ideas, which will eventually lead to true decolonization, as the ideological contestation between the colonizer and the colonized will facilitate social change. Nonetheless, we argue that within a postcolonial state like South Africa, where government and other stakeholders only respond to the language of violence to facilitate and bring about change, the students' usage of violence was understandable. Therefore, we suggest that any reading of violence and its usage within social-movement protests should be nuanced within the context in which such movements exist.

References

Ahmed, Abdul. K. 2019. *The Rise of Fallism: #RhodesMustFall and the Movement to Decolonize the University*. Ph.D. thesis, Columbia University. https://academic commons.columbia.edu/doi/10.7916/d8-63y6-2245/download.

Akpojivi, Ufuoma. 2018. *Media Reforms and Democratization in Emerging Democracies of Sub-Saharan Africa*. New York: Palgrave.

Areff, Ahmed and Spies, Derrick. 2017. "Breaking: Zuma Announces Free Higher Education for Poor and Working Class Students." *News24*, December 16. www.news24.com/SouthAfrica/News/zuma-announces-free-higher-education-for-poor-and-working-class-students-20171216.

Ballard, Richard, Habib, Adam, Valodia, Imraan, and Zuern, Elke. 2005. "Globalization, Marginalization and Contemporary Social Movements in South Africa." *African Affairs* 104(417): 615–634.

Cabral, Amilcar. 1966. *The Weapon of Theory*. Address to the First Tricontinental Conference of the Peoples of Asia, Africa and Latin America held in Havana. www.marxists.org/subject/africa/cabral/1966/weapon-theory.htm.

Dasai, Rehad. 2019. "#FeesMustFall: How Student Movements Shaped a New South Africa." *AlJazeera*, May 10. www.aljazeera.com/features/2019/5/10/feesmustfall-how-student-movements-shaped-a-new-south-africa.

Chinguno, C., Kgoroba, M., Mashibini, S., Masilela, B.N., Maubane, B., Moyo, N., Mthombeni, A. and Ndlovu, H. (Eds.). 2017. *Rioting and Writing: Diaries of the Wits Fallists*. Johannesburg: SWOP and the University of the Witwatersrand.

Dentlinger, Lindsay. 2018. "#FeesMustFall Damage Cost Soar to Nearly R800M." *EWN*. https://ewn.co.za/2018/08/08/feesmustfall-damage-costs-soar-to-nearly-r800m.

Department of Higher Education. 2015. *Report of the Presidential Task Team on Short-Term Student Funding Challenges at Universities*. www.justice.gov.za/commissions/FeesHET/hearings/set2/set2-day03-DHET-Presentation.pdf; last accessed February 10, 2019.

Dobash, Emerson and Dobash, Russell. 1992. *Women, Violence and Social Change*. London: Routledge.
Fanon, Frantz. 1961. *The Wretched of the Earth*. New York: Grove Press.
Fomunyan, Kehdinga. 2017. "Student Protest and the Culture of Violence at African Universities: An Inherited Ideological Trait." *Yesterday and Today* 17: 38–63.
Garcia, Rodrigo and Trere, Emiliano. 2014. "The #YoSoy132 Movement and the Struggle for Media Democratization in Mexico." *Convergence: The International Journal of Research into New Media Technologies* 20(4): 496–510.
Gibson, Nigel. 2017. "The Specter of Fanon: The Student Movements and the Rationality of Revolt in South Africa." *Social Identities Journal for the Study of Race, Nation and Culture* 23(5): 579–599.
Gillespie, Kelly and Naidoo, Leigh-Ann. 2019a. "#MustFall: The South African Student Movement and the Politics of Time." *The South Atlantic Quarterly* 118 (1): 190–194.
Gillespie, Kelly and Naidoo, Leigh-Ann. 2019b. "Between the Cold War and the Fire: The Student Movement, Antiassimilation, and the Question of the Future in South Africa." *The South Atlantic Quarterly* 118(1): 226–239.
Habib, Adam 2016. "Reimagining the South African University and Critically Analyzing the Struggle for Its Realisation," *University of the Witwatersrand: In Their Own Words*, January 25, 2016. www.wits.ac.za/news/latest-news/in-their-own-words/2016/2016-01/reimagining-the-south-african-university-and-critically-analysing-the-struggle-for-its-realisation.html.
Habib, Adam. 2019. *Rebels and Rage: Reflecting on #FeesMustFall*. Johannesburg: Wits University Press.
Heffernan, Anne. 2019. *Limpopo's Legacy: Student Politics and Democracy in South Africa*. Johannesburg: Wits University Press.
Haupt, Adam. 2015. "#ZumaMustFall: Whose Hashtag Is It Anyway?" *Mail&Guardian*, December 17. https://thoughtleader.co.za/adamhaupt/2015/12/17/zumamustfall-whose-is-it-anyway.
Hodes, Rebecca. 2016. "Questioning 'Fees Must Fall'." *African Affairs* 116 (462): 140–150.
Jupp, Victor. 2006. *The SAGE Dictionary for Social Research Methods*. New York: Sage.
Leslie, Ngoma. 2006. *Social Movements and Democracy in Africa: The Impact of Women's Struggle for Equal Rights in Botswana*. New York: Routledge.
Malabela, Musawenkosi. 2017. "We Are Not Violent but Just Demanding Free Decolonized Education: University of the Witwatersrand." In M. Langa (Ed.), *#Hashtag: An Analysis of the #FeesMustFall Movement at South African Universities*. Johannesburg: Centre for the Study of Violence and Reconciliation, 132–147.
Mbembe, Achille. 2011. "Fanon's Nightmare, Our Reality." *Mail&Guardian*, Available at: https://mg.co.za/article/2011-12-23-fanons-nightmare-our-reality, accessed 10/07/2019.
Mkatshwa, Nompendulo and Ntshingila, Omhle. 2018. "South Africa-A Violent Reality (Policy Brutality, A FeesMustFall Account with Omhle Ntshingila)." *Polity*, November 1. www.polity.org.za/article/south-africa-a-violent-reality-police-brutality-a-fees-must-fall-account-with-ms-omhle-ntshingila-2018-11-01/.

Morrow, Sean. 2008. "Race, Redress and Historically Black Universities." In K. Bentley and A. Habib (Eds.), *Racial Redress and Citizenship in South Africa*. Cape Town: HSRC Press, 263–288.
Motimele, Moshibudi. 2019. "The Rupture of Neoliberal Time as the Foundation for Emancipatory Epistemologies." *The South Atlantic Quarterly* 118(1): 205–214.
Mtengwane, Gcina. 2019. "Students Who Violently Protest Need to Catch a Wake Up." *City Press*, April 18. www.news24.com/citypress/Voices/students-who-violently-protest-need-to-catch-a-wake-up-20190418.
Naicker, Camalita. 2016. "From Marikana to #FeesMustFall: The Praxis of Popular Politics in South Africa." *Urbanisation* 1(1): 53–61.
Nicolson, Greg. 2016. "#FeesMustFall: Another Day of Violence as the State Kicks Issues Forward." *Daily Maverick*, October 12. www.dailymaverick.co.za/article/2016-10-12-feesmustfall-another-day-of-violence-as-the-state-kicks-issues-forward/.
Nyamnjoh, Francis. 2005. "Media and the State in Africa: Continuities and Discontinuities." In P. Kareithi and N. Kariithi (Eds.), *Untold Stories: Economics and Business Journalism in African Media*. Johannesburg: Wits University Press.
Omarjee, Lameez. 2019. "Everything You Need to Know about the National Minimum Wage." *Fin24*. www.fin24.com/Economy/everything-you-need-to-know-about-the-national-minimum-wage-20190101.
Oxlund, Bjarke. 2016 "#EverythingMustFall: the use of social media and violent protests in the current wave of student riots in South Africa." *Anthropology Now*, 8(2): 1–13.
Riley, Quinn. 2017. *An Analysis of Frantz Fanon The Wretched of the Earth*. London: Macat International.
Satgar, Vishwas. 2019. *Racism After Apartheid: Challenges from Anti-Racism and Marxism*. Johannesburg: Wits University Press.
Swartz, Sharlene, Mahali, Alude, Moletsane, Relebohile, Arogundade, Emma, Khalema, Nene, Cooper, Adam, and Groenewald, Candice. 2018. *Studying While Black: Race, Education and Emancipation in South African Universities*. Cape Town: HSRC Press.
Statistics South Africa. 2019. *Quarterly Employment Statistics March 2019*. Pretoria.
Steyn, G. and de Villiers, P. 2006. *The Impact of Changing Funding Sources on Higher Education Institutions in South Africa*. Research Report for the Council of Higher Education. Higher Education Monitor no 4.
Tarrow, Sidney. 1998. *Power in Movement: Social Movements and Contentious Politics*, 2nd Ed. Cambridge: Cambridge University Press.
Tarrow, Sidney. 2011. *Power in Movement: Social Movements and Contentious Politics*, 3rd Ed. Cambridge: Cambridge University Press.
Thompson, Leonard. 2001. *A History of South Africa (Yale Nota Bene)*. New Haven, CT: Yale University Press.
Tilly, Charles. 1987. "The Contentious French: Four Centuries of Popular Struggle." *Journal of Peace Research* 24(1): 101–102. doi:10.1177/002234338702400118.
Wits University. 2016. "Fire in the Wartenweiler Library." www.wits.ac.za/news/latest-news/general-news/2016/feesmustfall2016/statements/fire-in-the-wartenweiler-library.html.
Xaba, Wanelisa. 2017. "Challenging Fanon: A Black Radical Feminist Perspective on Violence and the Fees Must Fall Movement." *Agenda* 31(3–4): 96–104.

Part III

Media Discourse and Conflict Resolution

10 The Language of Peace in Conflict Transformation

A Critical Analysis of the *New York Times'* Coverage of the Israeli–Palestinian Peace Agreement and Its Role in the Discursive Context of the Oslo Negotiations

Giuliana Tiripelli

10.1 Introduction

This chapter provides a qualitative analysis of news coverage of peace, in a context of changing relations between historical enemies in an internationally relevant conflict. It focuses on the coverage of the first six months of the Israeli–Palestinian Oslo peace process by the *New York Times*. By means of a media content analysis, the chapter shows how this important newspaper covered developments during the first months of the political negotiations on its front page, and how it framed the meaning of peace. These results are then discussed through a critical analysis of the discourses of peace available at the time. By unpacking the process of meaning-building in the new era of "dialogue" between Israelis and Palestinians, the chapter first reveals what discourses the newspaper linked the idea of peace to; secondly, it maps the transfer of dominant discourses of peace from the political and social levels to the diplomatic and media ones. In doing so, it also shows how the formation of such media and diplomatic discourses of peace was the result of the intense, multiple, and opposite power pressures unfolding behind the attempt to bring peace to the area. Finally, the chapter discusses how these media and diplomatic discourses may have strengthened conflict-nourishing ideologies at the political and social level in the years leading to the *Second Intifada*, and beyond.

10.2 News Media and Israeli–Palestinian Peace

While media studies have rarely focused on peaceful events, some scholars have specifically investigated the relation between media coverage and the Israeli–Palestinian peace process. Wolfsfeld (2004) analyzed the role played by the Israeli media during the Oslo peace process and stressed the primacy of politics as a trigger of change in media coverage of news. Shinar analyzed the common strategies applied in media discourses of the peace processes (2000) and recognized that the news media served as a channel for the dialogue between Yitzhak Rabin and Yasser Arafat (Shinar 2003). In general, scholars have maintained that public support for the peace process was affected by the news media in the long term. We may discern two tendencies: the news media either nourished very high expectations of change, reducing the process to an accomplished, generic peace (Mandelzis 2007) without relying on a new discourse of change (Shinar 2000), or they placed emphasis on the remaining political polarization that followed the inauguration of the peace process, without paying attention to important achievements that could have lessened internal tensions (Wolfsfeld 2004). The Declaration of Principles (DoP, also called the Oslo Accord or Agreement) that Arafat and Rabin signed in September 1993, which officially inaugurated the Oslo peace process, was not a comprehensive agreement detailing the new and peaceful status quo, but it was a promise of change to achieve peace.

A critical and qualitative analysis of the specific meaning of "peace" that was legitimized through news coverage makes it possible to evaluate the role of mediated information in bringing about, or preventing, change in societies in conflict. Such evaluation of the meaning of "peace" allows us to clarify whether the latter may correspond to the idea of a new situation where existing expectations are met or to a change of expectations, or even the abandonment of demands for change. Any of these situations – or a variety of their combinations – can lead to an end of visible violence and, in some cases, provide a basis for structural conflict transformation. In the context of the Israeli–Palestinian political dialogue of the early 1990s the question of whose expectations had to change and how was never clarified in consistent ways for all those involved. Consequently, "peace" assumed different meanings for different groups. It is therefore very important to analyze the role of the news media in representing the beginning of this peace process, as it is there that scholars can identify which conceptualizations of peace were legitimized in the public debate, during an extraordinary time of predisposition to change.

This chapter examines how the *New York Times* navigated this time, and how it approached the tension between different meanings of peace. The hypothesis underlying this chapter is that, by setting the frames to interpret these developments for many other news media at the time, this globally important coverage embodied far more than generic expectations of peace. Its coverage was the outcome of a "complex dance" (Schudson 2011, p. 147) between developments, media agents, and politicians, which had important consequences for the way peace could be understood and supported by regional and international publics in the long term.

10.3 The *New York Times* and the Israeli–Palestinian Conflict

In representing and interacting with the context of the Israeli–Palestinian negotiations, the news media contributed to the formation of narratives about peace. In order to explore how this was done and what the outcomes were, this chapter presents an analysis of the coverage of these negotiations on the front page of the *New York Times* between 1993 and 1994. In those years, TV had only just started providing 24-hour real-time coverage of foreign events, starting with the 1991 Gulf War, and the *New York Times* was still a very important definer of events. Noakes and Gwinn Wilkins (2002, p. 655) talked of this newspaper as one of the major sources of international news for US citizens, and for foreign news media. Slater (2007) affirmed that the *New York Times* "determines what will be considered important news and how that news is likely to be understood" (p. 88). Luyendijk (2009, p. 46) further stated that much of what was published by the *New York Times*, and by a few other media outlets, tended to be published everywhere. The paper's former editor Max Frankel described it as "'the house organ' of the smartest, most talented, and most influential Americans at the height of American power," which "reaches the most influential, interesting, and powerful people on earth" (Frankel 1999, pp. 414–415).

The opportunity for a dialogue between the Israelis and Palestinians in the early 1990s particularly attracted the attention of US newspapers. Such opportunity allowed the US administration to show the world its capabilities as the only remaining superpower after the end of the Cold War. For this reason, the US had been the official host and facilitator of the negotiations for peace in the Middle East since 1991, when it inaugurated the Madrid Conference (Bentsur 2001, pp. 150–152), which proposed multilateral negotiations to stabilize the region. However, these negotiations, which were carried out without the Palestinian Liberation Organization (PLO), soon reached a standstill (Ashrawi 1995; Beilin 1999, pp. 67–68; Morris 2001, p. 614), and in the summer of 1993 the Israeli government and the PLO secretly agreed on the draft of a peace agreement through an alternative diplomatic channel, which was developed in Norway (the so-called Oslo secret channel, see Waage 2000; Corbin 1994; Beilin 1999; Heikal 1996). Despite this, the Israeli government wanted the official support of the US administration, and the Palestinian leader Yasser Arafat wanted to present himself as the legitimate representative of the Palestinians in an international context. An agreement between Israelis and Palestinians was also crucial for the development of normalized international relations and stability in the region, under the supervision of the USA. For all these reasons, the USA remained the official host of the signature of the peace agreement. Due to this centrality of the US administration, the *New York Times* became a primary force in shaping discourses about peace in the Middle East.

In his study of the records of the *New York Times*, Daniel Chomsky (1999) presented it as a newspaper whose internal decisions remained carefully hidden, and whose editors and reporters always aligned themselves with the publisher's position on the important issues of the day. Zelizer et al. (2002) studied thirty days of coverage of the *Second Intifada* in mainstream US newspapers, and concluded that "the *Times*, while upholding conventional US journalistic practices, appeared to be the most slanted in a pro-Israeli direction" (p. 303). Jerome Slater compared coverage of this issue in *Haaretz* and the *New York Times* between 2000 and 2006, and discovered that the latter was "rarely as critical of Israeli policies as are the Israeli media" (Slater 2007, p. 119). Handley (2009) analyzed how the news of an Israeli settler's killing of twenty-nine Palestinians in Hebron at the end of February 1994 disrupted the paper's peace narrative, and how it repaired this narrative by "blaming the massacre on 'extremism'" (p. 260). Finally, Noakes and Gwinn Wilkins (2002) discovered that the PLO started to be depicted under "a more positive frame" in particular "from 1994 on, after the first round of agreements reached in Oslo" (p. 663). They also found that, at the same time, official Israeli sources were being quoted around twice as much as their counterparts (Noakes and Gwinn Wilkins 2002, pp. 660–661).

10.4 Methodology

The data for the analysis consists of all sixty-three articles published on the front page of the *New York Times* and dedicated to the peace process, between two key dates: August 28, 1993 and February 26, 1994. The front-page articles were chosen on account of the relevance that the editors accord to these, as well as their enhanced visibility to the readers. On August 28, 1993, the news broke that a secret agreement had been reached in Oslo. February 26, 1994 was the day after the Hebron massacre, perpetrated by the settler Baruch Goldstein at the Cave of the Patriarchs in Hebron; this was the first event that clearly showed the unresolved tensions behind the peace process to audiences abroad.[1]

The analysis of these articles was conducted in two stages. The method chosen for the first stage of analysis is adapted from Allan Bell (1998, pp. 64–104), who suggests investigating four of the journalist's "five Ws": who (sources and actors); what (events); where (places); when (time). Bell excludes what is commonly referred to in media studies as the fifth "W," namely the "why." He also advises the examination of the structure of the story (i.e., how the four questions are structured in, or absent from, the media text). Therefore, how the journalists organized the elements of the story to create a compelling

---

[1] Four articles in this selection are about the Hebron killing, and they are not included in this analysis. For an analysis of the *New York Times* coverage of the Hebron massacre, see Handley (2009).

narrative (the internal cohesion) in each article was also part of the analysis. Finally, in addition to Bell's approach is the coding of terminology and strings of text which highlighted a specific explanation of story elements by the journalists and by the sources used.

In a second stage, these results were evaluated in relation to the developments in negotiations, as these were knowable to journalists at the time (see Tiripelli 2016). In this respect, the articles analyzed can be divided in three specific negotiating periods, namely: articles published before the mutual recognition between Israel and the PLO (August 29 to September 8, 1993); articles covering the signing ceremony in Washington (September 9–14, 1993); and articles covering the period following the ceremony (September 15, 1993 to February 26, 1994).

10.5 The *New York Times* Coverage

The confirmation of a deal between the Israelis and the PLO, secretly achieved in Norway, reached the media at the end of August 1993. The news was unexpected, because the official negotiations between the Israelis and Palestinians had been taking place in Washington since 1991. This was especially true for the Palestinian negotiators in Washington, who were not members of the PLO and did not know about the draft agreed in Oslo (Ashrawi 1995, p. 260). As a result, over just eleven days (August 29 to September 8), the *New York Times* published sixteen front-page articles about the peace process, which focused on this secret channel.

The articles from this period were dominated by a feeling of extreme surprise, and they expressed strong criticism of the deal. They also reflected the political anxiety that dominated during these eleven crucial days. The news of the accomplishment was spread, but the final confirmation was still pending. To make the Oslo Agreement effective, it was necessary to achieve formal and mutual recognition between Israel and the Palestinians. This did not occur until September 9 – only a few days before the prescheduled signing of the agreement in Washington and the bilateral negotiations between the two sides.

The opposition that the journalists drew in these articles, namely between the quickness and unexpectedness of the deal, and the conflict's duration, emphasizes the relevance of the change, as shown in these examples:

irreconcilable foes, who demonized one another for decades, suddenly breaking down a barrier for peace (Friedman 31/8 par. 1)
the coming days will witness a positive and an historic development, which has been awaited, expected by both people for a long time (Yasir Abed Rabbo, senior PLO, speaking, Haberman 30/8 par. 8)
the draft declaration will be made public within days [...] two sides that have endured 45 years of war, suspicion and hostility (Engelberg 30/8 par. 17)

The focus on the temporal dimension, together with the way the articles were structured, constituted the main device through which the journalists expressed their early criticism of the Oslo deal. The best examples of this are Thomas Friedman's article of September 1, entitled "Israel and PLO Ready to Declare Joint Recognition." In the first part of the article, Friedman hooks the reader by stressing the speed of the change, and he lets highly optimistic official sources speak of the imminent success of the alternative diplomacy. Expressions used are:

already drawn up [...] quickly followed (Friedman 1/9 par. 3); early today (par. 4)
within two years. (par. 7); no more than five years (par. 8); within nine months (par. 9); At the same time (par. 10)

However, in the central part of the article, Friedman introduces new arguments, opinions and doubts, and time expressions stress the prospect of a long and exhausting process lying ahead, as demonstrated in these examples:

This could take months. (par. 11); Israeli officials said it was not certain that they would succeed (par. 12); Israeli and Palestinian negotiators are hoping (par. 16); that cannot be done on short notice. (par. 18)

By opposing fastness to slowness, the journalist frames the official statements as mere auspices and contrasts them with the unsolved outcome of that process.

The representation of the Palestinians' attitudes and insecure locations further stresses such uncertainty:

disillusioned young Palestinians who live in the Israeli-occupied Gaza strip and West Bank (Cohen 3/9 par. 12); a civil war among Palestinians in the occupied territories. (4/9 par. 4); in the Gaza Strip, Fatah activists battled (5/9 par. 27)
delegates from the territories lacked the authority (Haberman 30/8 par. 29); the troubled Gaza Strip and West Bank town of Jericho. (1/9 par. 6); losing ground fast in the occupied territories (5/9 par. 15)
whether the Palestinians living in the Israeli-occupied territories will be as eager to reach agreement as [the PLO] (Engelberg 30/8 par. 14)

By highlighting the idea of a fragmented and tense society, these articles provide an image of the Palestinian community as one that was not ready to give the level of support needed for a successful peace process.

The way in which journalists used spatial elements in these early articles also reveals the nature of the *New York Times*' early criticism of the alternative Oslo Agreement. In this coverage, the US – and Washington in particular – constitute the most recurrent spatial references and the lens through which the developments were usually evaluated. Washington was not only the national political center, it was also the place where US politicians had facilitated negotiations between Israel and its neighbors since 1991.

The articles stress the differences between the US and Norway, and between official and alternative channels of negotiations. Thus, they mention a "Washington channel" and an "outside Washington channel." The latter corresponded to the vaguely defined and faraway settings of the long and secret negotiations that had already been conducted, where "they" had allegedly reached an agreement. By contrast, Washington was where events were happening in the present, and where journalists and the US administration, the "us," were located:

[the Oslo agreement is] a closely guarded secret (Engelberg 30/8 par. 5);
American officials expect (par. 17); American officials remain cautious (par. 14)
[the Oslo agreement is] delicate [...] reached secretly in the serenity of Norway (Friedman 31/8 par. 3)
Israeli and Palestinians negotiators resumed their formal Middle East peace negotiations here today, but officials said the real diplomatic action was going on secretly in Europe (1/9 par. 1)
their now-secret peace negotiations (par. 13)
their secret blueprint [...] in Norway and [...] in another country (par. 15);
in Washington [...] today [...] Arab and Israeli officials said [...] the Washington channel is simply a facade (par. 24)

Through this spatial opposition, journalists propose a precise political expectation about the US's role in a time when, following the surprising news of the alternative agreement being achieved, American officials tended not to speak directly or make demands through the news media; Washington was the place "peace" should have emerged from.

The criticism of this exclusion of the US is fully revealed by the analysis of the representations of, and communicative approaches to, the actors involved in the new dialogue. A coherent appeal is specifically addressed to the Israelis, with warnings about the risks of autonomously dealing with the PLO. Friedman evokes the leitmotifs of the mainstream Israeli discourse about the dangers of the Palestinian organization, and he frames the delays that Israelis were experiencing in negotiating with the PLO over the eleven tense days as the evidence of such dangers:

They toss grenades, not leaflets; they write death warrants, not Op-Ed pieces. (Friedman 31/8 par. 15)

Israeli officials are only getting their first dose of something that American officials have known for some time [...] is not like negotiating with another state. (2/9 par. 15)

[the PLO] has a loose organizational structure, unclear lines of authority, varied factions, no fixed address, nocturnal meeting habits and a preference for ambiguity [...] [the PLO] is the embodiment of the idea that there is a single Palestinian nation, spread inside and outside the historical boundaries of Palestine (par. 18)

The way in which the Israelis were represented contributes to stress the potential dangers brought by these autonomous negotiations with the PLO. Haberman gives extensive space to the feelings of the Israeli people, and describes their perceptions of the PLO and the Palestinian leader (August 29, 30, and 31). The journalist often speaks for them, declaring that Israelis did not trust Arafat, and that his presence in the territories could increase social tension, as shown in these examples:

the core of the issue for many Israelis is the West Bank and, even more so, Jerusalem, where not only security questions but also deep emotional and religious imperatives come into play. (Haberman 29/8 par. 19)

the P.L.O. has been such a hated group (30/8 par. 19)

Arafat, such a reviled figure in Israel [...] formal recognition would undoubtedly be a profound shock for many Israelis [...] And the thought of Mr. Arafat in Jericho, not 20 miles from downtown Jerusalem, could only intensify the jolt. [...] a big pill for many Israelis to swallow, and some officials acknowledged that "making Arafat kosher," as one of them put it, could take time. (31/8 par. 27)

In these articles, Haberman highlights the Israelis' extant difficulty of accepting the change, and he represents this as a problem for the unfolding process. In general, no article appears to clearly address the Palestinians in a similar way, by warning them of the dangers of these negotiations in relation to their own perspectives. Palestinians remain an object of journalistic analysis and representation, for what appears to be a preferred and imagined Western and Israeli audience.

In particular, the Palestinian negotiator Yasser Arafat progressively emerges as a weak politician, lacking the determination to fulfill his first promise of peace. This promise entailed recognizing Israel, which would ensure mutual recognition and therefore confirm the beginning of the peace process. For Arafat, the problem was that this specific recognition – formulated within the Oslo channel – initiated a process that he wanted, but which also left the duty to define the boundaries of the state he had recognized to subsequent and bilateral negotiations (Corbin 1994, p. 185; Savir 1998, pp. 68–76).

In most cases, the *New York Times*' front page represented Arafat's moves from the point of view of the other negotiating side. Descriptions of Arafat often come from Israeli officials, who question his authority, stress his political weakness, and hint at the possibility of following alternative paths towards pacification of the region, which would have ousted Arafat once again from the political negotiations. In particular, the hypothesis of negotiations between Israel and Syria, as an alternative to those with the Palestinians (Haberman 6/9),[2] increased pressure on Yasser Arafat; for him, any development of the Israeli–Syrian channel would have meant a dangerous shift of attention away from the Palestinians, and his own loss of leadership in their cause.

However, on the eve of the PLO's acceptance of the mutual recognition, the coverage provided by Roger Cohen gradually reverses this representation of Arafat. Cohen reports from Tunis on September 3, 4, and 5, while Arafat is trying to gain political support within the PLO for a mutual recognition on the terms set out in Oslo. The success of Arafat's efforts contributes to the first change in the framing of the Palestinian leader:

September 3:
Palestinian Officials Say Pact With Israel Is Near (headline)
"There are no reserves of patience if the current momentum disappears" (Western diplomat speaking par. 11)
It appears certain that [...] Mr. Arafat will have to demonstrate quickly (par. 13)

September 4:
ARAFAT BATTLING FOR ISRAEL ACCORD IN HIS FATAH GROUP (headline)
Yasir Arafat, the leader of the Palestine Liberation Organization, struggled today to rally his mainstream Fatah movement behind proposal for peace (par. 1)

September 5:
Arafat Wins Approval of Fatah for Peace Agreement with Israel (headline)
"he's desperately trying to force" (Western diplomat speaking "on the condition of anonymity" par. 14)
Mr. Arafat [...] appeared nonetheless confident (par. 18)
"The greatest contribution the United States and Western Europe could make right now would be to convince the Israelis to take a flexible line" (Western diplomat speaking par. 24)

---

[2] This hypothesis kept reappearing during the deadlocks that followed the signature of the DoP, usually a few days before a new deal was finally reached.

While this media attention stressed the urgency of coming to a deal within the official Washington channel, Israeli and Palestinian demands were still very different. The perspective of the Israeli negotiators articulated peace as a means towards security for Israel and the end of Palestinian violence. The Palestinians' demands (about settlements, borders, Jerusalem, refugees, and statehood) were not equally justified, and sometimes they indirectly emerged as problems preventing the eventual achievement of peace. The articles failed to highlight the fact that Israel's non-acceptance of Palestinian demands was, for the PLO, the fundamental cause of its delay in supporting the recognition of Israel.

The ways in which two of the more important UN Resolutions on the conflict, namely Resolutions 338 (United Nations 1973) and 242 (United Nations 1967), were represented contributed to the lack of clarity about the meaning of "peace." These resolutions were fundamental references in the negotiations, the interpretation of which was and still is subject to endless debate, but the two journalists who discussed these resolutions defined them in the same way, without mentioning two of their main elements, namely withdrawal and boundaries:

"Resolution 242 and 338 [...] implicitly recognize Israel's right to exist and call for negotiations towards/on a durable peace" (Friedman 2/9 par. 9, Cohen 3/9 par. 17)

Through this formulation, the newspaper weakened the connection between peace achievement and its territorial aspects, a connection that has legal and international value, and which was particularly relevant in the Palestinians' demands. Presented during a period dominated by high expectations of a mutual recognition, this partial definition of the resolution rendered more plausible the explanation that the PLO was reluctant to negotiate with Israel altogether. The coverage thus lacked evidence to appreciate an alternative explanation for the delay in obtaining mutual recognition, for example that the PLO was resisting Israeli refusal of the Palestinians' demands.

The achievement of mutual recognition was announced on September 9, and at this point the signing of the Oslo Accord in Washington, on September 13, became a certainty. From September 9 to 14, the *New York Times* hosted twelve articles on its front page, all focused on the official signing ceremony.

The confirmation of mutual recognition triggered a change in the general tone of the articles. Under these special circumstances, journalists abandoned their previous criticisms and, instead, provided enthusiastic reports. The certainty of the forthcoming peace ceremony of September 13 allowed for wider, relaxed reflections and for focused representations. The new rhythm of the articles reflected the suspense and expectancy on the eve of the big event, until the entire news story reached its climax in the moment Arafat and Rabin shook hands.

Politicians, especially American and Israeli, were quoted widely and directly, with the coverage focusing on their preparation for the ceremony. Enthusiasm often led to irony, or to intense and intimate portraits (Shinar 2000). Clinton, together with the Israeli prime minister, became a main actor in the story, and Rabin's feelings received special attention:

Israel's Old Soldier Is Edgy, Yet at Peace, About Accord (Haberman 13/9 headline)
Inside, the old soldier was in a jumble (entire par. 1)
In not too many hours, he [Rabin] would be standing on the White House lawn, face to face with Yasir Arafat, perhaps even shaking his hand, although that remains one of the greatest unanswered questions of this epochal moment in Middle Eastern history. (par. 4)

The representation of Arafat changed as well. The PLO leader stopped being a dangerous partner, and for a short time, his reliability was no longer under scrutiny. However, his "rehabilitation" – in the media – as an international leader was never fully achieved. Journalists mostly used old clichés and Western frames of interpretation to describe him, and they did not generally focus on his point of view or sentiments. In this new context, he emerged as a surreal and anachronistic character:

In the meantime, get ready for the pictures: Yasir Arafat in his permanent stubble-beard discussing peace on a couch in Tunis with the dapper Warren Christopher; Mr. Arafat in his checkered headcovering chatting with Yitzhak Rabin about the modalities of self-rule over thick Arabic coffee in Jericho; Mr. Arafat in his P.L.O. fatigues admiring Bill Clinton's newly redecorated Oval Office on his first official visit to Washington. (Friedman 10/9 par 27)

Arafat had become a normalized character in the story, but one whose presence still did not fully match the settings and behaviors of public foreign relations. In this coverage, the Palestinian leader had left behind the intransigent and threatening attitude of the Palestinian fighter, but he had also lost his aura of a powerful symbol of the Palestinian cause.

The DoP emerged as a product of Arafat's change, and Arafat had changed because he had made promises: "We haven't changed – it changed," Peres said, referring to the PLO (Haberman 10/9 par. 16). As a consequence, the mutual recognition marked the beginning of a period during which the PLO needed to fulfill its promises by guaranteeing smooth and successful negotiations.

The outcomes of the agreement were explained from the Israeli point of view, and Israeli security became the major and tangible element in the story. Friedman let Clinton speak about this issue:

Israel is the country that will have to trade tangible security assets for promises (Friedman 12/9 par. 12)
the people of Israel had to be made to feel secure
"by hosting the event on Monday is to reassure the people of Israel that the United States is committed to their security" (par. 13)
"that they are more secure not less secure because this is done" (par. 15)
"the issue in Israel is security, and the opposition to the agreement are people who believe that it will weaken rather than enhance their security" (par. 19)
"Monday has to be a signal to the people of Israel that this is about security" (par. 20)

This focus was an invitation to support the peace agreement for the Israelis, whom Haberman had described as being very anxious about the upcoming change. At the same time, however, this focus contributed to framing the DoP as a means by which to maintain and increase Israeli security tout court; it implied that the Israelis could not be asked for more and should only expect to receive the benefits of this agreement.

During the third period considered, which lasted more than five months, the front page hosted only thirty-five articles about the Oslo peace process, four of which were dedicated to the Hebron massacre of February 25. Excluding the general evaluations that followed the ceremony, the first key theme that emerged from this coverage was the new central role of the US and its politics for the Middle East. A special concentration of articles about the new process (five articles between November 6 and 13) appeared on the front page, on the eve of Rabin's visit to the US, scheduled for November 12. These articles discussed the American role in the Middle East in connection to its aid to Israel. On November 12, Friedman delved into this aspect, widely illustrating the kind of aid the US was ready to give to Israel:

Clinton is planning to present [...] Rabin [...] with a package (Friedman 12/11 par. 1)
the White House also seeks to address Israel's desire to import more American computer and electronic technology (par. 3)

The journalist explained that this offer was made in order to convince Israel to consider a wider, regional normalization under American terms:

American strategic interests lie even more importantly with getting a Syrian-Israeli peace accord, since this would eliminate the greatest threat to a major war in the region and help to further isolate Iran (par. 11)

The Language of Peace in Conflict Transformation 247

However, on the day of Rabin's visit to the US, this sub-story was unexpectedly interrupted by an official press release of the Israeli Defense Force (IDF), concerning the imprisonment of pro-PLO Fatah members for the killing of a Jewish settler:

Prime Minister Yitzhak Rabin suffered a potentially serious political blow today when his army announced that five captured Palestinians suspected of killing a Jewish settler two weeks ago had identified themselves as members of Yasir Arafat's faction (Haberman 13/11 par. 1)

Following the publication of this release, the discussion of the political coordination between US and Israeli politics in the Middle East vanished from the front page, and no articles written in Washington would appear there until the Hebron massacre. The signing of the DoP in Washington had opened the official peace process, which was composed of a series of bilateral negotiating stages that should have led to a definitive peace agreement after an interim period of five years. However, the *New York Times*' front page did not give much space to these new bilateral negotiations.

Arafat's image kept changing following the developments in the negotiating process that the DoP had inaugurated. The first critique of Arafat's management of the process was raised while Rabin was visiting Clinton, with both leaders asking Arafat to condemn the killing of the Jewish settler by the pro-PLO Fatah members, the incident reported by the IDF press release (Haberman 13/11 par. 2). From that day on, doubts of Arafat's authoritativeness and willingness to engage in the peace process progressively resurfaced and became the focus of Israeli officials' sources, parallel to the new crisis in the bilateral negotiations.

On December 13, the first postponement of the accord's implementation was officially announced; from that moment onwards, postponements became the main theme in the front-page coverage of the process. After this postponement, the discussion concerning Arafat's role changed to overwhelming criticism, and his political weakness once again became a central theme. Instead of also clarifying how the rejection of Palestinian demands contributed to both the postponements and the tension on the Palestinian side, journalists gave voice to Israeli officials:

[Arafat is] despondent (Hedges 13/12 par. 1)
[Arafat] stood slumped over the podium with his arms folded (par. 2)
growing concern [...] that a wave of defections [...] may be undermining the ability of Yasir Arafat (Ibrahim 29/12 par. 20)
mounting criticism of Mr. Arafat's leadership and a wave of defections from the P.L.O. Command [...] Mr. Rabin may be wondering whether there is any

point in giving concessions to an organization that appears to be tottering (30/12 par. 28)

In contrast to the first period, these delays were no longer being framed as a violation of peace. According to the Israeli representatives, flexibility was now a natural fact, and a new principle for the implementation of the peace process. After December 13, the idea of the peace process deadlines as "no sacred dates" became the leitmotiv of the front page, and the lens to explain the new delays:

Rabin suggested today that there could be still further delays (Haberman 14/12 par. 1)
his remark that there are no holy dates included not only today, the missed target for starting the troop withdrawals in Gaza and Jericho, but also April 13, the scheduled completion day (par. 4)
[Rabin] received public backing even from the most dovish members of his Cabinet (par. 7)
"We are not in a hurry. We are under no pressure whatsoever. We will give it as
much time as needed." (Rabin's spokesman speaking, Ibrahim 30/12 par. 25)
"In my assessment, another month will be needed to finish the details of the agreement to a full accord" Mr. Rabin said. "I hope a month will be enough. It could take a little more. Remember, in our eyes there are no sacred dates." (Haberman 11/2 entire par. 32)

The articles provided the necessary elements to understand how postponements both guaranteed the Israelis' security and reduced their anxiety about it:

> "we must not make concessions on things that are security related." (Rabin speaking, Haberman 14/12 par. 5)
> with many Israelis [...] increasingly anxious about the security implications (par. 7)

Through this representation, delays shifted from being a tool for Arafat to try to resist Israeli intransigence towards Palestinian demands to being a tool in the hands of the Israeli representatives, to exert pressure on Arafat and his constituency. What the front page usually omitted was a full explanation of what each side demanded at each stage, and who eventually agreed to compromise his own requests.

The image of the Palestinians also changed during this third period. Articles increasingly stressed their lack of control, and their unruly and violent attitude. However, they left not much space for discussing their anxieties and expectations in the new context. On October 9, before the first postponement, the *New York Times* hosted a front-page article dedicated to a Palestinian football match, which highlighted these problems:

Palestinians Rule Jericho, at Least in Soccer (Haberman 9/10 headline)
it took a long time to clear spectators off the field so that play could begin, raising an inevitable question for a while about how the organizers hoped to liberate Palestine if they had so much trouble liberating a soccer stadium (par. 10)
far from the stadium, movement continued toward translating that control from theory into reality (par. 13)

In the middle of the negotiating crisis, on December 24, Hedges supported this perspective by presenting Palestinian police as violent, unreliable, and a menace to Israeli security:

dozens of young men with pistols tucked into their belts [...] One tossed a hand grenade up and down in his hand (Hedges 24/12 par. 2)
"We make the laws and punish the offenders" (Mr. Tafish, 24, the local leader of the Fatah Hawks, the military wing of Yasir Arafat's faction in the Palestine Liberation Organization' speaking, par. 3)
Israeli troops have quietly ceded whole sections [...] to Palestinian guerrillas (par. 4)
Israeli military officials [...] permit them to operate unmolested in some areas (par. 6);
But even those not covered by the amnesty nonchalantly roam the Gaza Strip, often heavily armed (par. 10)
the fighters say they will not protect Israeli settlers (par. 23)
"If the Israelis think we will turn on our brother Palestinians, they are wrong" (Fatah Hawks member speaking, described at par. 21 with "an AK-47 rifle cradled in his arms," par. 24)

Once again, the Palestinians and their leader represented the only element in this story that ought to change, to clear the way for peace. When the negotiations started to show signs of success (Enderlin 2004, p. 695), Arafat was again presented as a reliable partner:

Mr. Arafat's "very constructive" attitude in these meetings [...] the Palestinian leader was "very much in command, is in charge, and is aware of all the details of the talks" (Yossi Sarid, Israeli negotiator, speaking, Ibrahim 31/1 par. 32)

10.6 From Content to Discourse

This section reviews the social, political, and diplomatic discourses of peace "against the codes of the content analysis" (Petrina 1998, p. 31), in order to explain the function of the *New York Times*' coverage within the wider communicative dynamics of the Oslo peace process.

During the official ceremony which took place in Washington in September 1993, both sides had signed the peace agreement so that each could decode and present it as the symbol of the beginning of its own peace. Israelis decoded "peace" as the guarantee that their lives would not be marked by violence (Mac Ginty 2010, p. 153), and that the Israeli government could maintain full control of its own security as it defined it (including Palestinian territories conquered in 1967), while at the same time separating Israelis from the Palestinians (LeVine 2009, pp. 102–112). This ran opposite to what the Palestinians demanded: a viable Palestinian state in the West Bank and Gaza, with Jerusalem as its capital, and the possibility for refugees to return to Palestine.

The reasons why the PLO and Israel decided to sign the very ambiguous DoP are worth exploring, to help to unveil the complex dynamics in which the news discourse of peace intervened in 1993. When the Madrid Conference on the Middle East started, on October 30, 1991, just eight months after the end of the Gulf War, the then exiled PLO was not invited to the negotiating table. The Palestinian representatives were selected from among the residents in territories occupied in 1967 (Ashrawi 1995, pp. 121–129). However, these official negotiations between Israeli and Palestinian representatives continued throughout 1993, though without any success. Paradoxically, it was the Palestinians' concreteness in these official negotiations that led Israel to support the opening of an alternative channel, where a peace deal was agreed. The main reason for this support was that the internal tension unleashed by the *First Intifada* of 1987 was not decreasing, and that it was necessary for Israel to find a partner willing to negotiate soon (Guyatt 1998, p. 29). This explains why, in the middle of the Madrid Conference impasse, the PLO started to appear more attractive than in the past. Unlike the Palestinians in Washington, the PLO also had its own priority, which made it more willing to compromise: the maintenance of the PLO leadership. The secret dialogue initiated in Norway gave the PLO an opportunity to achieve this (Gresh 1998).

This specific factor tellingly played a crucial role in the Oslo secret channel. At the end of July 1993, after six months of secret negotiations in Norway (Abbas 1995; Beilin 1999; Perry 1994; Corbin 1994; Enderlin 2004, pp. 637–660), the secret agreement was still far from being reached. The Israeli negotiators came to the eleventh secret meeting with new requests, which would have greatly limited the new Palestinian authority. The PLO had already accepted a variety of demands (Enderlin 2004, p. 661), and during that meeting they agreed to more. However, they also had more requirements, among which the need to include a clear connection between the final negotiations and the full application of Resolutions 242 and 338, something that the Israelis were not ready to concede. In the middle of this stalemate, Israeli negotiators announced that Israel would recognize the PLO in exchange for a certain guarantee. Recognizing the PLO meant that Arafat could enter Gaza as the representative of the Palestinians. This was a very tantalizing option for the chairman (Makovsky 1996, p. 62; Corbin 1994, p. 136).

The outcome of this approach was that it framed what Robert L. Rothstein has defined "an unequal process" (2002, pp. 30–31), stipulated on the basis of the PLO's political weakness, and according to which the only guarantee that the Palestinians could reach their outcomes resided in the Israeli government's willingness to concede these. The DoP included a separation between the interim period and the final settlement, as the Israelis wished (Shlaim 2000, p. 519). It did not define the extent of the territories to be assigned to the future "Palestinian self-government authority," which should be agreed upon by the parties ('Abd Al-Shafi 1993, p. 15).[3] Since it did not mention a Palestinian state, the right to return was totally excluded from the negotiations of the interim period.[4] The Palestinian refugee problem, as well as the Israeli settlements, the status of Jerusalem, the determination of borders, security, and cooperation with other countries, were all excluded from the interim negotiations (Art. V.3). The only principle to which the parties were, in general, obliged to respond was the reference to Resolutions 242 and 338 for the final negotiations.[5] While the DoP left Arafat with very little power, the *New York Times* represented the Palestinian leader as the actor who had to change in order to guarantee mutual recognition and peace, shifting the power further towards the Israeli side.

In addition, through its discussion of what the agreement ought to be about for the Israelis, the newspaper reinforced one of the interpretations of peace that existed at a social level, instead of giving equal space to the variety of views circulating in Israel/Palestine. The Palestinians generally saw the agreement as "herald[ing] the prospect of a State and ... an end to the occupation" (Maher 2003, p. 92). However, while two-thirds of Palestinians supported the agreement (Morris 2001, p. 622), the majority considered it "the only available choice," and they believed that they could quickly turn away from the

---

[3] Israel was the recognized jurisdiction in the sectors not transferred to the Palestinian Council (specific understanding of Article VII). In other words, the powers of the Palestinian Authority in the Palestinian territories did not represent an alternative, territorial jurisdiction.

[4] This is the thesis that prevailed in the DoP, although the UN General Assembly Resolution 194 had already called, in December of 1948, for the return of refugees "at the earliest practicable date" (United Nations 1948).

[5] These resolutions had been accepted by the PLO in 1988. Palestinian demands for the right to return were based on the land occupied by Israel in 1967 and Resolution 242. This meant that they had accepted the right to return for the 1967 refugees, but not for those of 1948.

agreement if the political and economic situation did not improve (Rabbani 1993, p. 16). According to Morris, two-thirds of Israelis supported the agreement (Morris 2001: 622), while Yediot Aharonot reported that 53 percent supported it (Bar-Siman-Tov 2001, p. 47). About half of the members of the Knesset opposed the agreement. This opposition was led by the new leader of the Likud party, Benjamin Netanyahu, and supported by the radical settlers (Sprinzak 1999, pp. 228–233).

Among the Israeli supporters of the negotiations, however, the majority held views that had little to do with Palestinian ideas of peace. The wider, dominant Israeli political discourse saw Israel as having the right to be in control of its own security, and the right to guarantee the Jewish nature of the state. Security meant being in control of the borders with neighboring countries in the West Bank and along the Gaza Strip, and controlling strategic parts within these areas. As Mansfield has argued, the idea of partition had been accepted by the majority of the Palestinians, but Zionist Jews now rejected it (Mansfield 1992, p. 319).

Other changes had forced the Israelis to start a dialogue with their enemy. The *First Intifada*, which started in 1987, had jeopardized the possibility of managing the territories conquered in 1967, and it had made direct control of this land too costly for Israel, in both economic and political terms. What Israeli citizens most wanted was "peace" as a stop to the *Intifada* protests and the consequent international blaming of Israeli policies. In this context, the main sentiment driving Israeli representatives towards the negotiations in the early 1990s was a desire to end Palestinian reliance on, and relations with, Israel. All measures had to be considered to achieve this desired separation, once Israel had regained control over its own security.

This interpretation of "peace" was embodied in the diplomatic proposal to transfer several *functional* powers to the Palestinians for the management of the territory, which was included in the DoP and developed during the Oslo peace process between 1993 and 2000. In parallel, separation measures were implemented from 1993 onwards. The device through which these undemocratic solutions were often justified was the idea that Palestinian violence against Israelis was an ideological phenomenon, with no social or contextual roots, and that Palestinian deprivation and constraints were an unavoidable (albeit unwanted) outcome of the indispensable Israeli actions to prevent Palestinian violence.

By focusing on Israeli security and Palestinians' unruly attitude, and by framing Arafat as a guarantor of advancements in the context of an increasingly unproductive negotiating process, the *New York Times* provided fundamental elements to justify this Israeli dominant discourse of "peace" at critical stages in the negotiations. This discourse – along with the separation politics that progressively limited encounters between Israelis and Palestinians – nourished an ideological cohesion among Israelis against concessions to the Palestinians, rather than promoting substantial change that could have transformed the conflict.

At the same time, however, the idea – included in the DoP – of withdrawing and redeploying to transfer functional powers to the Palestinians represented a historic change for Israel; it created a new precedent, that of a Palestinian territory, that would have been difficult to rediscuss (Makovsky 1996, pp. 152–153). Even the very proposition of discussing issues such as Jerusalem, refugees, and settlements, albeit in the final negotiations, was a major concession for many Israelis, because it implied that they were ready to consider an undesirable compromise in the long term (Makovsky 1996, p. 141). The *New York Times* accurately reflected the magnitude of this change for Israeli citizens. Regrettably, no equally supportive reflection of Palestinians' fears and hopes was present in the front-page articles, to explore why Palestinians were resisting certain demands.

There is a crucial, final element, which entered the social-political-diplomatic-media discursive nexus during these early negotiations between Israelis and Palestinians. This is Resolution 242, a pillar of the transformation of the Israeli/Palestinian conflict since its adoption by the UN Security Council (1967), together with Resolution 338 (1973).

The Palestinians had asked to insert a call for the full implementation in the DoP, to make the resolutions binding in the negotiations for the final agreement with Israel. The Israelis did not oppose the inclusion of a reference to the two resolutions, but they followed a different logic. As exemplified by this brief excerpt by Yoel Singer, the Israeli lawyer in Oslo, the Israelis tended to see the negotiated accords themselves as the application of the two resolutions:

They [the Palestinians] want the accord to establish that the negotiations on the permanent status will lead to the application of these resolutions, but we can only agree to a formula establishing that the final accord represents the application of these resolutions. (Enderlin 2004: 661–662, author's translation)

The DoP then established that "negotiations on the permanent status will lead to the implementation of Security Council Resolutions 242 and 338."[6] This ambiguous language embodied both the Israeli and the Palestinian perspectives. The *New York Times* was less ambiguous: by partially representing Resolutions 242 and 338 as the international tools that "implicitly recognize Israel's right to exist and call for negotiations towards/on a durable peace," the newspaper's front page emphasized the Israeli understanding of Resolution 242.

The few but fundamental elements of conflict transformation that the DoP recognized were formulated as an ambiguous compromise, which each party could have read as it wished. In this sense, the DoP represented a conservative and exemplary diplomatic example of what Dougherty et al. have dubbed "language convergence/meaning divergence" (Dougherty et al. 2010); it reframed old

---

[6] See also Abbas (1995, p. 176) and Beilin (1999, p. 124).

social and political tensions and set it free to evolve according to political power dynamics, which the *New York Times*' front page did not fully acknowledge.[7]

10.7 Conclusion

The *New York Times* coverage of the Oslo Agreement was the outcome of very complex and dynamic interactions which involved the newspaper, the development of the negotiations, and the evolving powers of the negotiators. The newspaper's coverage reflected the existent power imbalance between Israelis and the US, on the one side, and the Palestinians, on the other. Journalists defined security in Israeli terms without examining the role of the DoP in guaranteeing security for the Palestinians. A comprehensive analysis of the changes that the Israelis needed to guarantee peace maintenance was omitted, while Arafat's expected transformation became fundamental to creating peace. Although journalists generically spoke of "occupied territories," they did not highlight the ambiguity of the DoP in relation to the principle of land for peace as established in 1967 by the UN Resolution 242. The Palestinians, like the Israelis, had specific reasons for the delays in the negotiation timetable, but the legitimacy of their points was not interrogated with the same depth.

While this kind of coverage highlighted some of the pressures and difficulties behind the attempt to bring peace to the area, it did not widely challenge the imbalance of power embedded in the diplomatic discourse and negotiations, and it did not comprehensively investigate the less visible forms of violence that Palestinians experienced. In this way, the *New York Times* gave more visibility to political and social discourses of peace that framed it as the end to visible violence and the achievement of Israeli security tout court. Thus, the *New York Times* coverage only partially clarified how peace could be achieved in the area. Equally partial, and conflict-nourishing, ideologies, which blamed the Palestinians as the responsible agents for the absence of peace, and which fostered mistrust between Israelis and Palestinians, gradually re-emerged and gained strength at the political and social level in the late 1990s, in parallel with the growing difficulties in the Israeli–Palestinian interim negotiations.

References

'Abd Al-Shafi, Haydar. 1993. "The Oslo Agreement. An Interview with Haydar 'Abd Al-Shafi." *Journal of Palestine Studies* 23(1): 14–19.

Abbas, Mahmoud [Abu Mazen]. 1995. *Through Secret Channels: The Road to Oslo: Senior PLO Leader Abu Mazen's Revealing Story of the Negotiations with Israel.* Reading: Garnet Publishing.

---

[7] The journalistic factors that may have led to this outcome are explored in Tiripelli (2016).

Ashrawi, Hanan. 1995. *This Side of Peace: A Personal Account*. New York: Simon & Schuster.
Bar-Siman-Tov, Yaacov. 2001. "Peace Policy as Domestic and Foreign Policy: The Israeli Case." In S. Sofer (Ed.), *Peacemaking in a Divided Society: Israel after Rabin*. London: Frank Cass, 27–54.
Beilin, Yossi. 1999. *Touching Peace. From the Oslo Accord to a Final Agreement*. London: Weidenfeld & Nicholson.
Bell, Allan. 1998. "The Discourse Structure of News Stories." In A. Bell and P. Garrett (Eds.), *Approaches to Media Discourse*. Oxford: Blackwell, 64–104.
Bentsur, Eytan. 2001. *Making Peace: A First-Hand Account of the Arab–Israeli Peace Process*. Westport, CT: Praeger.
Chomsky, Daniel. 1999. "The Mechanisms of Management Control at the *New York Times*." *Media Culture & Society* 21(5): 579–599.
Corbin, Jane. 1994. *The Norway Channel: The Secret Talks That Led to the Middle East Peace Accord*. New York: Atlantic Monthly Press.
Declaration of Principles on Interim Self-Government Arrangements – Oslo Agreement [DoP]. 1993. September, 13. www.unhcr.org/refworld/docid/3de5e96e4.html.
Dougherty, Debbie S., Mobley, Sacheen K. and Smith, Siobhan E. 2010. "Language Convergence and Meaning Divergence: A Theory of Intercultural Communication." *Journal of International and Intercultural Communication* 3 (2): 164–186.
Enderlin, Charles. 2004. *Paix ou Guerres: Les Secrets des Négociations Israélo–Arabes 1917–1995*. Paris: Fayard.
Frankel, Max. 1999. *The Times of My Life and My Life with the Times*. New York: Random House.
Gresh, Alain. 1998. "From PLO to State: The Palestinians Dream On." *Le Monde Diplomatique*, September. http://mondediplo.com/1998/09/12gresh.
Guyatt, Nicholas. 1998. *The Absence of Peace: Understanding the Israeli–Palestinian Conflict*. New York: Zed Books.
Handley, Robert L. 2009. "The Conflicting Israeli-Terrorist Image: Managing the Israeli–Palestinian Narrative in the *New York Times* and *Washington Post*." *Journalism Practice* 3(3): 251–267.
Heikal, Mohamed. 1996. *Secret Channels: The Inside Story of Arab–Israeli Peace Negotiations*. London: HarperCollins.
LeVine, Mark. 2009. *Impossible Peace. Israel/Palestine since 1989*. Halifax: Fernwood Publishing.
Luyendijk Joris. 2009. *People Like Us: Misrepresenting the Middle East*. New York: Soft Skull Press.
Mac Ginty, Roger. 2010. "No War, No Peace: Why So Many Peace Processes Fail to Deliver Peace." *International Politics* 47(2): 145–162.
Maher, Joanne (Ed.). 2003. *The Middle East and North Africa 2003*. Regional Surveys of the World 49th edition, London: Europa Publications.
Makovsky, David. 1996. M*aking Peace with the PLO: The Rabin Government's Road to the Oslo Accord*. Boulder, CO: Westview Press.
Mandelzis, Lea. 2007. "Representations of Peace in News Discourse: Viewpoint and Opportunity for Peace Journalism." *Conflict & Communication Online* 6(1). http://www.cco.regener-online.de/2007_1/pdf/mandelzis.pdf.

Mansfield, Peter. 1992. *A History of the Middle East*. London: Penguin Books.
Morris, Benny. 2001. *Righteous Victims: A History of the Zionist–Arab Conflict 1881–2001*. New York: Vintage Books.
Noakes, John A. and Gwinn Wilkins, Karin. 2002. "Shifting Frames of the Palestinian Movement in US News." *Media Culture & Society* 24(5): 649–671.
Perry, Mark. 1994. *A Fire in Zion: The Israeli–Palestinian Search for Peace*. New York: Morrow.
Petrina, Stephen. 1998. "The Politics of Research in Technology Education: A Critical Content and Discourse Analysis of the *Journal of Technology Education*, Volumes 1–8." *Journal of Technology Education* 10(1).
Rabbani, Mouin. 1993. "'Gaza-Jericho first': The Palestinian Debate." *Middle East International* 24 September: 16–17.
Rothstein, Robert L. 2002. "Oslo and the Ambiguities of Peace." In J. Ginat, E. J. Perkins and E.G. Corr (Eds.), *The Middle East Peace Process: Vision Versus Reality*. Portland: Sussex Academic Press.
Savir, Uri. 1998. *The Process: 1100 Days That Changed the Middle East*. New York: Random House.
Schudson, Michael. 2011. *The Sociology of News*. New York: W. W. Norton & Company.
Shinar, Dov. 2000. "Media Diplomacy and 'Peace Talk': The Middle East and Northern Ireland." *International Communication Gazette* 62(2): 83–97.
Shinar, Dov. 2003. "The Peace Process in Cultural Conflict: The Role of the Media." *Conflict & Communication Online* 2(1) http://cco.regener-online.de/2003_1/pdf_2003_1/shinar.pdf.
Shlaim, Avi. 2000. *The Iron Wall: Israel and the Arab World*. London: The Penguin Press.
Slater, Jerome. 2007. "Muting the Alarm over the Israeli–Palestinian Conflict: The *New York Times* versus *Haaretz*, 2000–2006." *International Security* 32(2): 84–120.
Sprinzak, Ehud. 1999. *Brother against Brother*. New York: The Free Press.
Tiripelli, Giuliana. 2016. *Media and Peace in the Middle East: The Role of Journalism in Israel/Palestine*. London: Palgrave Macmillan.
United Nations. 1948. *General Assembly Resolution 194: Palestine – Progress Report of the United Nations Mediator*, December 11. https://pij.org/app.php/articles/610.
United Nations. 1967. *Security Council Resolution 242: The Situation in the Middle East*, November 22. www.securitycouncilreport.org/atf/cf/%7B65BFCF9B-6D27-4E9C-8CD3-CF6E4FF96FF9%7D/IP%20S%20RES%20242.pdf.
United Nations. 1973. *Security Council Resolution 338: Cease-Fire in the Middle East*. October 22. http://unscr.com/en/resolutions/doc/338.
Waage, Hilde Henriksen. 2000. *Norwegians? Who Needs Norwegians? Explaining the Oslo Back Channel: Norway's Political Past in the Middle East*. Evaluation Report, September 2000. International Peace Research Institute Oslo. https://norad.no/en/toolspublications/publications/2010/norwegians-who-needs-norwegians-explaining-the-oslo-back-channel-norways-political-past-in-the-middle-east/.
Wolfsfeld, Gadi. 2004. *Media and the Path to Peace*. Cambridge: Cambridge University Press.
Zelizer, Barbie, Park, David and Gudelunas, David. 2002. "How Bias Shapes the News: Challenging the *New York Times*' Status as a Newspaper of Record on the Middle East." *Journalism: Theory, Practice, and Criticism* 3(3): 283–307.

11 The Historical Context in Media Narratives in Search of Peaceful Resolution to the Israel–Palestine Conflict

A Comparative Study of BBC and Al Jazeera

Jelena Timotijevic

11.1 Introduction

This study is a comparative analysis of the BBC's and Al Jazeera's online reporting of the Israeli elections, examining a period from August 2019 (the pre-election period) through to October 2019 (the immediate post-election period). Its aim is to analyze the role of the historical context (the long-standing and highly contested conflict between Israel and Palestine) in the reporting of such a significant political event. The comparative textual analysis is twofold: a comparison of the Israeli and Palestinian representations in the media, and a comparison of the two media outlets in order to explain some of the findings related to the first aim.

Central to the examination of the news reports in question is the framework of Critical Discourse Analysis (CDA) which, amongst many particulars, addresses a dialectical relationship between discourse and society – a dynamic that is of particular importance to the topic of the chapter (cf. Meyer 2001; Fairclough 2001a, 2001b). A further aim is to supply additional theoretical rigor by engaging with discourse analysis as a form of "history writing" in which history and context are taken seriously and responsibly within the developing actions of the topic in question (e.g., Fowler 1996). The following section thus examines the key facets of CDA and discusses some theoretical and methodological complexities that CDA presents. It then looks at ways in which *history and context* should be considered central elements in any theory of communication by drawing on the work of Vygotsky, whose principal concern was with the importance of questions of language use in social life. The application of CDA to the analysis of data is thus supported by additional insights from the Cultural-Historical and Activity Theory. Section 11.3 is dedicated to the complex and long-standing Israeli–Palestine conflict. It briefly shows that the historical narratives surrounding the conflict are highly contested by the different parties involved, all of whom tell the story from their own perspectives, often in order to legitimize their own actions. Here, the reader is also directed to existing literature for much richer and well-evidenced historical summaries. Section 11.4 discusses the sources of data and the "histories" of the BBC and Al Jazeera. An examination of the reporting of the Israeli elections, and the role historical context has played in the production of such reporting, is represented in Section 11.5. In the final section, some concluding remarks focus on two elements for further discussion: ways in which language is linked to wider social processes, and the role media narratives might play in how meaning and communication contribute to divisions in society. In methodological terms, following Philo (2007), we ask whether frameworks such as CDA, which remain focused on text, should always incorporate an analysis of the ways in which media accounts are produced and then received by their audience. In ideological terms, following Jones (2000) and Jones and Collins (2006), we ask whether CDA's ideological leanings ought to provide a clearer set of political principles to be used in the analyses of the socio-historical elements of events under scrutiny.

11.2 Critical Discourse Analysis Meets Cultural-Historical and Activity Theory

The general premise of CDA is to critically analyze real-life situations through an ideological lens, and engage with discourse analysis and language use as a method to expose inequalities, including how these affect social change in and through language. Accordingly, the study of communication processes and practices is an essential element in attempting to understand and critically respond to what is going on in the world, and so supports various attempts by CDA researchers to critically investigate "social inequality as it is expressed, signalled, constituted [and] legitimised ... by language use" (Wodak 2001: 2). Communicative practices therefore can play a decisive role in contributing to the unmasking of social inequalities. However, there are issues with an examination of the living processes of social action, conflict and change that are solely conducted on the grounds of linguistic analysis combined with the ideological role of communicative practices. Methodologically, therefore, the CDA project is faced with a contention that it does not represent "the whole" of discourse analysis (cf. Jones and Collins 2006; Philo 2007). The problem appears to be in the attempt of the CDA method to grasp the discourse itself at an integral moment in the generative process of social life through particular interactions, in particular times and in particular places. To attempt to address this problem of *history and context*, support is sought from a perspective that, together with CDA, can help concretize this kind of thinking, namely in the tradition of the Cultural-Historical and Activity Theory. Section 11.2.2 introduces its key tenets.

11.2.1 The Dialectical Elements of CDA

Discourse analysis has become a diverse area of study which subsumes a variety of approaches in a number of disciplines. Various surveys make a binary distinction between "critical" and "non-critical" approaches, where the former not only describe discursive practices (typically a characteristics of the latter) but also examine how "discourse is shaped by relations of power and ideologies, and the constructive effects [it] has upon social identities, social relations and systems of knowledge and belief" (Fairclough 1992: 12). This distinction is not absolute by any means. CDA is a sociolinguistic approach that incorporates a number of practices which investigate discourse from a perspective of the social but which differ in theory, method and the type of issues critical language researchers focus on (Fairclough 2001b).

Discourse has been commonly used to include "meaning-making as an element of the social process" (Fairclough 2012: 11). It can also be associated with a particular social field of practice (e.g., political discourse), or it can represent a particular social perspective constructed around an aspect of the world we might be grappling with, such as the topic of this chapter. Fairclough (2012: 11) further points out that the first, most abstract sense could be equated to *semiosis*, and as such discourse is understood as being concerned with various "semiotic modalities, of which language is only one ... [O]thers are visual images and 'body language'." These elements of the social process are *dialectically* related to each other; in other words, they are different but not *discrete* (i.e., fully separate): "each one 'internalises' the other without being reducible to them" (Harvey 1996, cited in Fairclough 2012: 11; see also Fairclough 2001a: 123).

This model of *dialectical theory of discourse* figures in social practices in three ways. Firstly, it is a "part of the social activity within a practice" (Fairclough 2001b: 232): this entails that we use language in a particular way as part of what we do, for example, as part of doing a job as a flight attendant, a teacher, as well as a leader of a country. The second way in which discourse figures in social practices is in "representations" (2001b: 232). Social actors *see* and represent social life in different ways. In this chapter we will examine how conflict between Israel and Palestine is *seen* through the ideas of different media outlets. Thirdly, Fairclough argues that "discourse, as part of ways of being, constitutes styles" (2001b: 232). For our purposes, we will examine *styles* of reporting of the conflict in question, as well as some of the interactive aspects of the modes of discourse exemplified above.

Fairclough (2001b: 232) pays particular attention to social order and the way social practices constitute it. This order can be examined by assessing a particular social ordering of relationships (through different discourse, genre and style) or it can be viewed through "dominance," where "some ways of making meaning are dominant or mainstream, some are marginal, oppositional or 'alternative'" (2001b: 232). The political concept of *hegemony* appears to play a significant role in Fairclough's *dialectical theory of discourse*, a role that is not as explicitly applied in other forms of critical practices within CDA. That there are concerns with the philosophical positioning of this aspect of CDA, as understood by Marxist thinkers, is another element of contention amongst those who take issue with the overall approach of CDA (cf. Jones 2007). Nonetheless, Fairclough insists that the ideological and discourse analytical elements of CDA are in line with Gramsci's view of hegemony and hegemonic struggle. He characterizes hegemony both as leadership and domination within political, social, cultural and ideological realms of society (1992: 92). This conception of hegemony, he argues, is in line with the dialectical view of the relationship between "discursive structures" and "events" (Fairclough 1992: 93). So, on the one hand *order of discourse* in itself is hegemonic in nature as it can contribute to the changes in meaning in relation to *dominance*. On the other hand, how social actors articulate or rearticulate orders of discourse and consequently change those in relation to *dominance* is an essential aspect of hegemonic struggle. Then, relatedly, the "production, distribution and consumption (including interpretation) of texts" which constitute discursive practice, are all aspects of hegemonic struggle because they contribute to the changes of the existing order of discourse as well as impacting on existing social and power relations (Fairclough 1992: 93). Arguably, based on the findings of this chapter and the research of many studies illustrated throughout, a *rearticulation* of the Israel–Palestine conflict is necessary, yet it is still a missing element in the attempts to seek peaceful resolutions to the conflict.

In summary, the concept of hegemony can help us to do three things: analyze the social practice within which the discourse belongs; enable us to use it as a model or a way in which we analyze discourse that itself is an instance of hegemonic struggle; and thirdly, it can help us facilitate a way to pursue various struggles through language (Timotijevic 2016).

11.2.2 Language, Context, and History

In the previous section some of the central elements were sketched out within the tradition of critical language research and specifically Critical Discourse Analysis, in order to illustrate ways in which the method of CDA has developed towards linking the tools of linguistics and discourse analysis to a critical theory of power and ideology. However, concern remains with CDA's engagement, or lack thereof, with the question of *history and context*, as reflected in the concerns by arguably one of the key figures in the creation of the critical language school – Roger Fowler. An issue Fowler (1996) was grappling with early on centered around a contradiction that was developing in critical language research, where, on the one hand, practitioners were, rightly, placing great emphasis on the role of *context*, and on the other, there was an assumption by practitioners that (ideological) context was somehow assumed, and shared, by audiences. Consequently, notwithstanding the importance of the role of linguistics in this respect, linguistic analysis of discourse was likely to "provide some privilege of access to the interpretation of text" (Fowler 1996: 9–10). Instead, what is needed to "understand the text" is to first "bring to it relevant experience of discourse and context." The "[l]inguistic description" would then take place "at a later stage, as a means of getting some purchase on the significances that one has heuristically assigned to the text" (Fowler 1996: 9). Collins and Jones (2006: 52) express similar concerns with the method in CDA: the significance of linguistic analysis in processes of social and political change cannot be claimed "outside of a concrete understanding of the interconnected circumstances in and through which [discourse] arises." The CDA analyst does of course take these circumstances into consideration; however, these are considered by means of a *textual analysis*. The procedure of CDA in this respect appears problematic as it attempts to make claims about the interrelationship between aspects of sentence structure and the alleged ideological orientation of a relevant section of discourse. It follows that we can somehow draw reliable conclusions about the events in question, and about the consequences of those events, from linguistic descriptions of the sentences. In critical language research, some of the solutions to this issue are offered using other theoretical frameworks simultaneously with CDA's methods, as is suggested here with the use of some aspects of Cultural-Historical and Activity Theory. In media studies, other methodological approaches have been proposed. For example, Philo (2007: 175) argues that text-based studies are limited in terms of the conclusions they can offer because they do not engage in the examination of the "production factors in journalism" nor in the analysis of how audiences understand news messages. In the case of production processes, Philo (2007: 181) suggests that studying the "professional ideology of journalists and the institutions which they represent" is important in understanding and explaining the credibility and legitimacy of news, particularly on issues where there are sensitivities surrounding the relationship between the broadcasting institutions and the state. One such sensitive topic is the Israel–Palestine conflict. There are many other factors that play a role in the production of news, such as political links among countries, sources of data and use of such sources, market pressures, and so on. Secondly, Philo (2007) argues, it is important to study how audiences perceive news messages before it is possible to draw conclusions on the meaning of concrete social contexts and potential impact of texts on the public's consciousness and understanding of events and their history. In order therefore to fully understand how the media exert power, we need to study both the ways in which power and dominance are embedded in texts, and the ways in which audiences might interpret media narratives.

At this point, it should be noted that CDA's sense of responsibility and commitment to social justice are not contested. Its overriding aim has been to illustrate how language can be used to exercise power over the oppressed, who are often subject to exploitation and discrimination, and whose human rights have been suppressed (Widdowson 1998). Unmasking such injustices in and through language is as urgent now as in past decades, and centuries before, marked by systematic discrimination of certain groups in society. Questions, however, remain as to the theoretical routes for Fairclough's (and other CDA researchers') political and economic arguments. Fairclough in particular seems to have an affinity with a Marxist perspective associated with Althusser and with the journal *Marxism Today* in Britain (as well as Gramsci, as illustrated above), which critics argue, presents a view of capitalism as "a social form whose driving forces are less and less material and economic, and increasingly 'cultural' and 'ideological'," thus in keeping with Western-Marxist origins that ideology is the most important element in "maintaining class rule" (Jones 2004: 103). Further theoretical influences stem from the poststructuralist and postmodernist traditions of Foucault, and other discourse-oriented social theorists such as Habermas. Jones (2004) points to Fairclough's affinities with the work of Voloshinov and the Bakhtin circle, works which, together with Vygotsky's, present important contributions to analyzing the role of language in the social process, in the tradition of historical-materialism.[1] While what is being advocated in this chapter is coherent with many facets of CDA, CDA's political (and economic) arguments sit away from the historical-materialist tradition and toward a view of capitalism as a social form whose driving forces are cultural and ideological, and less material and economic.[2] The application of CDA in this chapter is thus supported by additional insights from the Cultural-Historical and Activity Theory tradition. By way of an analysis of historical events through this historical-materialist theoretical prism the aim is to show that such an approach helps us to grasp significant moments of social change, which can then be examined using text-based studies, and those that look into the production and perception of news messages (see above).

---

[1] Collins (2000) and Jones (2000) engage in detail with the historical-materialist tradition.
[2] Jones (2004) suggests that a detailed critique on this question was presented by Barker and Dale (1997), who say that in "postmodernity" questions of "identity" and "symbolism" are central in analyzing social conflict, whereas previously "material" questions took center stage in such analyses.

The Cultural-Historical and Activity Theory tradition is rooted in Soviet psychology, mainly reflected in the writings of Vygotsky, and other historical figures of his time. Vygotsky is indeed mostly regarded as a psychologist, although his work has recently been largely reinvigorated in educational and pedagogic research, as well as within studies on language and communication. One of the key contributions of Vygotsky's work (mainly obscured, and banned throughout the Stalinist era) is his account of the development of human consciousness (Vygotsky 1934 [1986], 1934 [1987]; Collins 2000). The particular tradition is rooted in historical-materialism, which sees language as humans' *concrete* "practical consciousness" Marx and Engels (1845: 51), only able to exist if socially organized individuals engage and communicate through the use of *sign* (Voloshinov 1929). Thus, utterances, and discourse, are concrete manifestations of language use. They are spoken by living subjects, located within a specific social and historical perspective, and are interactive in the sense that they are responses to others' utterances. Communication understood in this way reveals the various processes of change, shifts and developments "without which language would have no history to speak of" (Collins 2000: 44). Utterances are accordingly spoken by "living subjects" in concrete social contexts (Collins 1996: 74), and at the same time represent verbal interaction between interlocutors in continually shifting real socio-historical conditions (Timotijevic 2018: 195).

Similarly, for Vygotsky, grasping *sociocultural and historical* elements means grasping social phenomena *concretely*, "in their 'internal relations' to other phenomena in a developing system" (Collins and Jones 2006: 53). This idea applies to consciousness as a whole and also to the *internal* dynamics of consciousness itself. Thus, understanding consciousness is understanding not only how human mental functions operate but also what the interrelations are between those functions, such as speech, memory, perception and so on (Collins 2000). In order to grasp the constitution of consciousness, we need to understand that is it intrinsically linked to the *social* and the *historical* means, language being the key instrument in that process which connects individuals to the world, to other people, and to themselves. Collins and Jones (2006: 53) argue that discourse is produced "*in* and *through* the 'logic of evolving activity'," which then gives relevance to the study of social change (our emphasis). This perspective thus suggests that an engagement with discourse starts from a form of *history writing* in order to firstly examine how it evolves as a product of the real historical development that considers significant moments of social change, be that within communities or other social structures. This position is arguably controversial because it invites a language researcher to consider seriously an adoption of historical-materialist principles in the analysis of events, and consequently texts, and also the production and interaction of audiences with those texts, if we were to adopt these additional constructs in discourse analyses. How we explain political events theoretically inevitably has consequences for how we analyze changing ideas and the ways in which these affect change through discourse. While a truism, it is an important consideration in the application of CDA as well, since its advocates, too, claim that the framework is ideologically "biased and proud of it" (van Dijk 2001: 96). They argue that conducting research free from ideological judgment is difficult to do; thus CDA, like other frameworks, has to start from a predetermined ideological position (cf. van Dijk 2001; Meyer 2001). In terms of historical analyses of events, Philo and Berry (2011), and Philo (2007) (among others)[3] have shown that, in the case of the Israeli–Palestine conflict, where there is agreement on some information, much is still disputed, for example on the account of the development of political Zionism, the military and administrative occupation of Palestine, settlement building, the rise of opposition movements, and violence, to name but a few. Analyses of such contested events are themselves contested. Philo and Berry (2011) and Philo (2007: 182) describe the media in their work as a "contested space," where the news "is not a neutral product" (The Glasgow Media Group 1976: 339). Thus, the engagement with discourse from the point of history writing, following a well-defined set of theoretical premises, enables then an analysis of discourse in this new light by examining how particular uses of language were generated from "within, and out of" particular historical developments (Collins and Jones 2006: 53). Therefore, following Vygotsky, a more "historically focused" CDA is applied to the analysis of news texts in an attempt to produce a more substantive account of socio-historical developments, which in turn can help account for discursive processes in language use.

11.3 Histories of the Israeli–Palestinian Conflict

It has already been indicated that the *histories* and the origins of the Israeli–Palestinian conflict are complex and contested by different parties. Any attempt to examine such histories in this chapter would undermine the complexities surrounding them, and would not provide a full account of the struggle faced by the Palestinian people in the region. The reader is directed towards well-researched historical summaries[4] that to a large extent adopt a historical-materialist approach to the examination of the origins of the conflict. The question of Palestinians as refugees is one such contested history. The Palestinian view is that they were forced out from their homes in 1948, and then had to live as refugees in countries such as Syria, Jordan, Lebanon, and in the Gaza Strip and on the West Bank (Philo and Berry 2011; Saïd 1992). Thus

---

[3] See, for example, Pappe (2006, 2015); Saïd (1992); Saïd and Mohr (1998).
[4] See footnote 3; also see: Badarin (2016), Philo and Berry (2004), and Philo and Berry (2011).

accounts of how Palestinian people were displaced when the Israeli state was formed in 1948 vary. Israel's claims about the displacement of Palestinians focus on the fighting between Arab neighbors and Israel, which resulted in Palestinian leaders telling their people to leave. Philo and Berry (2011) show through evidence of Israeli historians, including a statement by Moshe Dayan – one of the most prominent Israeli politicians – who confirmed this to be a contested claim and that Palestinian people were indeed forced to leave their homeland. Amongst many serious and devastating conflicts, one might single out one of the most significant events known as the 1967 Six-Day War, during which Israel occupied the West Bank and East Jerusalem, the Gaza Strip and the Golan Heights. This occupation has been widely seen as a violation of international law since the Israeli government occupied and exploited the land and its resources, by building settlements and placing the Palestinian people under its military control (Philo and Berry 2011; Karmi and Cotran 1999). Some mainstream news broadcasters have referred to such settlements as "illegal" (for example, *The Guardian* in the UK). There are two uprisings (or intifadas) that stand out as conflicts in the occupied territories; one in 1987 and the second in 2000. These were followed by a series of peace efforts, led mainly by the American government, notably the Oslo agreements of 1993 and 1995, and then the Wye Accords of 1998. In practice, these achieved little: an example of a small achievement is self-rule of the Palestinians in the West Bank and Gaza. Philo and Berry (2011) report on a number of *Guardian* stories between 1998 and 2000 about the demolition of Palestinian homes and control of their water supplies, suggesting Israel's complete control and sovereignty (cf. also Pappe 2006). The peace process negotiations have continued into the 2000s without success, frustrating the process itself and possibilities for a peaceful resolution.

Anyone who has any appreciation of Palestine and Israel, whether through the academy or otherwise, will recognize an exposure to particular vocabulary that has become a marker, a signal, a judgment on the question. One of those words is *conflict*. The phrase *Israel–Palestine conflict* arguably represents an equal dispute between two equal parties, thus implying equity in responsibility for the conflict, and consequently equity in responsibility for its resolution. The use of such discourse is not only present among politicians, but also in newspapers, television and other media outlets, as well as filmmakers, artists and ordinary people who engage with social media and other available means of information gathering.

As argued earlier, complex histories impact on the media reporting of events. One such example is the conceptualization of *resistance* into acts of *terrorism* by the Palestinians. Pappe (2015: 34) argues that most historical analyses of the *conflict* on the side of Zionist histography see Palestinian resistance to the colonization of their land as synonymous with terrorism (Pappe 2015: 34). He further claims that it is difficult to find amongst published views (whether academic, political or ideological writings) contributions that propose any action on the side of Israel as a possible explanation for Palestinian violence. Under the rubric of *terrorism*, Israeli published documentation that combines the sporadic activities of dissent by the expelled Palestinians (often acts of rock throwing) with the guerrilla warfare of Fatah. This representation of *terrorist acts* has continued over decades of *conflict* and has turned Palestinians into terrorists in their attempts to claim back their homeland and resist the ongoing colonial settler project (Pappe 2015).

11.4 Data and the "Histories" of the BBC and Al Jazeera

The chosen data focus on the media reporting of the most recent presidential elections in Israel. The period examined is from August 2019 (pre-election) through to early October 2019 (post-election), focusing on two prominent media outlets: a British public service broadcaster, the BBC (British Broadcasting Corporation) and Al Jazeera (specifically Al Jazeera English), a Qatari state-funded broadcaster of the Al Jazeera Media Network. The chosen samples of data include a number of articles on related topics written in the same period. The aim has been to understand the ways in which the two media outlets represented the contested history of the region, and by doing so to illustrate the ever-present process of "evolving activity" and its impact on a possible (re)shaping of some of that history (Collins and Jones 2006). The related topics included in the data sample are, for example, the timing of a release of the US peace plan (after the election) and reports related to Israel's most recent prime minister's court hearing linked to corruption cases. The aim has been to consider possible effects these might have on the overall reporting of the specific event in question.

The election period is captured by fourteen and fifteen online news reports from the BBC and Al Jazeera, respectively, of which six and nine reports, respectively, were written by either Middle East editors or guest editors/writers of the two media outlets.

Since the establishment of the state of Israel in 1948, much has been written on the issue of media bias in reporting the Israel–Palestine conflict. The contested historical context has thus played a key role in the journalistic coverage of the conflict, linked to the reputation and influence of different media outlets and corporations that provide such coverage, often in the process creating a broader impression on the views of a state's press and the state itself on the Israel–Palestine conflict (e.g., Zelizer et al. 2002). Extensive research in discourse and media studies has been undertaken comparing the narratives of the various British news corporations in order to show media bias one way or another (e.g., Philo and Berry 2004; Gaber et al. 2009; Richardson and Barkho

2009), North American corporations (e.g., Zelizer et al. 2002), comparisons of the British and North American press (e.g., Barkho 2010), including analyses of global media coverage (e.g., Kalb and Saivetz 2007; Deprez and Raeymaeckers 2010). In Zelizer et al.'s study we find evidence of clear bias towards Israel by the North American press. Philo and Berry's (2004) extensive content study of BBC and ITV (a UK commercial television network) news showed significant differences in the language used to discuss the two sides in the conflict. It found that Israeli voices were heard twice as many times as the voices of the Palestinian people. Their conclusions were that substantial bias towards Israel was present.

The BBC, in particular, has been the subject of intense debate and scrutiny related to biased reporting. Some of the research alluded to above, as well as broader research field on the topic, well documented in Philo and Berry (2004), examines an abundance of evidence of mainstream media reporting that clearly points to a more substantiated pro-Israel bias than that of anti-Israel bias. Gaber et al.'s (2009) work indicates, however, that the complaints received by the corporation come from both sides of the debate. For example, they report findings by the pro-Israeli campaign group BBC Watch, which claimed that the BBC discriminates against Israel in its reporting. The report findings by pro-Arab media campaigners who, in their analysis of the BBC reporting of the conflict suggest a similar picture to that presented in Philo and Berry (2004), and the research conducted by Loughborough University (Downey et al. 2006)[5] argues that the BBC is "innately biased towards Israel" (Gaber et al. 2009: 240).

In comparing the BBC and Al Jazeera, some studies have adopted a research strategy that focused on the differences in terms of worldwide ratings and influence of a news corporation, thus categorizing the BBC as the "first world broadcaster" and Al Jazeera as the "third world broadcaster." This approach has made it possible to investigate how a global "third world broadcaster" might shift its discourse in comparison to that of the BBC (Barkho 2008: 127). The findings show that Al Jazeera's reporting is based on regional, historical, cultural and religious systems. The discursive strategies used in the reporting of the Israel–Palestine conflict were related to the sociocultural composition of Al Jazeera's audiences. The findings from the qualitative data also show that Al Jazeera's mission is to "give voice to the voiceless" and so the pattern of vocabulary used in the representation of Palestinians and Israelis is that of "victim" and "victimiser," respectively (Barkho 2008: 128). Such "oppositional" practices in the choice of vocabulary in Al Jazeera's coverage of the

---

[5] "Researchers at Loughborough University conducted a content analysis on BBC news and current affairs programmes over a six-month period. They concluded that the majority of news reports failed to provide sufficient historical context, or to mention the ongoing land annexations taking place in East Jerusalem and the West Bank" (Gaber et al. 2009: 241).

conflict appear manifestly to represent *oppositional discourses*, using these as a vehicle to carry out its own ideological strategies (Fairclough 1989: 113; Barkho 2008: 127). We see this in the data sample discussed below.

In the light of the findings of the previous research studies mentioned above, the analysis in this chapter additionally seeks to consider whether the coverage of the Israeli presidential elections by the BBC and Al Jazeera contributes to this widely reported view of bias in the coverage of the conflict, namely towards Israel by the BBC and towards the Palestinians by Al Jazeera. Further, as has consistently been reported in other research studies (some illustrated here), amongst a range of contributing factors to reporting is putting the event reported on into context. A lack of contextual material, or the choice of what contextual/historical material is provided (see Philo and Berry (2011) for an extensive discussion on this topic), is one of the most contested points made by many independent commissions tasked to investigate bias in media reporting. We see illustrations of this issue, too, in the data analysis below.

11.5 The Role of the Historical Context in the Reporting of Israeli Elections

11.5.1 Al Jazeera

The emergent picture suggests a distinctly different construct in the reporting of the elections between the two media outlets. Starting with Al Jazeera, a notable focus in all news reports engages with some form of analysis of the impact the election results would have on the Palestinian population. At the forefront of the reports is the parties' position on 'Israel's occupation of the Palestinian territories.'[6] Al Jazeera engages in detailed summaries of the historical events we illustrated previously, using those summaries to expose a number of key issues: the outcomes of the Oslo Accords which partitioned the occupied West Bank into three areas and 'left Israel in complete control of the Palestinian economy, its civil and security matters,' 'limited voting rights of the Palestinian people,' further expansion of 'illegal' settlements, 'de-facto annexation' of the Jordan Valley and the 'future of the peace process.' The language used in the analysis of the issues is explicit in pointing out the living conditions and rights of the Palestinians under the 'occupation': 'decades of systematic crimes,' 'violation of international law and a very dangerous escalation against the Palestinians,' the peace process being 'clinically dead and [with the annexation of the Jordan Valley] it will literally end it.' Further reported is the 'endless' support by the United States giving Netanyahu 'the courage to publicly talk

---

[6] The elements of discourse within single quotation marks come from the media sources used in the analysis.

Resolution to the Israel–Palestine Conflict   269

about annexation,' the pledge (to annex the Jordan Valley) is denounced as 'dangerous and racist' [by the Palestinian leaders]. [In areas A and B of the West Bank] Al Jazeera reports that 'the Israeli military retains the right to enter these areas at any time, typically to raid homes or detain individuals under the pretext of security.' Al Jazeera says that 'there are more than 200 illegal Jewish settlements in the West Bank, where more than 400,000 settlers live'; 'Palestinians are unable to access basic resources such as water,' and similar.

Another poignant issue Al Jazeera engages with are the views of a number of Palestinian people interviewed during the reporting of the elections. The content of the reports rests on the issue of annexation and the prospects of a recognition of the future Palestinian state. On both accounts, the messages are consistent: these speak of a 'de facto occupation' [of the Jordan Valley] where 'Israel [already] denies access to land, water and electricity, making living conditions difficult.' The reports further emphasize that the said conditions 'also apply across the whole of Area C, which constitutes about 60 percent of the West Bank.' Al Jazeera reports on Israel's reiterated intentions 'to maintain military control over the area [in Netanyahu's election pledges]', supporting such reports with the views of the Palestinian people interviewed, one of whom reportedly says that 'they want us to leave as life becomes harder and settlements around us increase.' Since Palestinians in the occupied West Bank do not have voting rights, Al Jazeera further reports 'little hope of change' and 'business as usual' [whatever the election outcome]. One Palestinian says: 'whether it's the right or the left that comes to power, we're doomed anyway.' Other Palestinians are reported to consider and 'shrug off the elections as irrelevant.'

Additionally, Al Jazeera engages in meticulous detail of the consequences of various parties' election pledges on current Palestinian leadership and factions, their proposed actions (including 'suing Israel in international courts'), management of a potential publication of the United States' 'peace plan,' which Al Jazeera reports 'is likely to depart from even theoretical support for an independent Palestinian state in the territories occupied in 1967.' Al Jazeera's detailed reporting also focuses on the turnout both by Israeli and Palestinian populations to vote and offers, arguably, an objective summary of Netanyahu's inability to form a majority government, thus offering analyses on the impact of various forms of coalition and eventual formation of government. In that light, we note that Al Jazeera publishes an interview with a Hamas official, an organization regarded by several countries and international organizations (most notably Israel, the United States, Britain, and the European Union) as fundamentalist militant and terrorist. In the interview, the following language is used to portray the views of the organization: 'nationalist and extreme right-wing Jews, in general, believe in greater Israel that expands beyond the borders of historic Palestine,' 'we are supporting the establishment of a Palestinian state in the 1967-occupied West Bank, Gaza and Jerusalem as its capital.' The quoted paragraphs below are responses to questions of choice between the two leading election candidates, and the concept of peaceful vs. violent protests, respectively:

Well, the 2014 war against Gaza that killed over 2,000 Palestinians was led by none other than Benny Gantz [opposition candidate in the elections], so that tells us who the man is. Moreover, we are a resistance movement, which means the only form of contact between me and my enemy is resistance in nature. We don't differentiate between Gantz and Netanyahu.

These are peaceful demonstrations in part to let the world know of our plights in Gaza. Even though many of our young men and women have been killed by Israeli soldiers at the demarcations, we are forced to this kind of action as a direct response to the brutal siege by Israel ... Do you expect the protesters to fly out flowers to their oppressors? People used whatever they have around them to express their rejection of Israeli policies against them. Gazans are prevented from travelling and prevented from having normal lives because of this blockade. Gazans feel as if they live inside a pressure cooker. Our goal is to channel this explosive energy out towards the enemy, otherwise the situation will explode beyond control.

[Al Jazeera, 24 Sept 2019 www.aljazeera.com/news/2019/09/hamas-official-difference-gantz-netanyahu-190923142051143.html]

The content analysis presented above shows how Al Jazeera depicted the news and explained the conflict, including the representation of the Palestinian struggle (Philo and Berry 2011). Its reporting attempts to concretely and critically apply particular discursive practices to the ongoing processes of colonialization of the said territories. The contested elements in the reporting, in particular perhaps the engagement in the dialogue with a Hamas representative, pose questions around the role of the ideological perspectives reflected in the Al Jazeera narratives, and how these elements might impact on prospects for a peaceful resolution to the conflict. Further, Al Jazeera gives more space to the Palestinian actors to tell their stories about life under occupation (see below for comparison with the BBC). Lastly, Al Jazeera reporting offers a great deal more of the historical context in its reporting, stretching its news stories to include views of the Palestinian people on the prospects of a peaceful resolution and the future of Palestine more generally.

11.5.2 The BBC

The BBC's reporting of the same period predominantly focuses on the reportage of the competing political parties, namely that of the long-standing prime minister Netanyahu and his right-wing Likud party, and that of his chief rival in the elections, Benny Gantz and his centrist Blue and White party. The news reports are overwhelmingly written in the Passive Voice and focus on the *nature* of the fight between the two candidates, thus mainly describing the developments using the following vocabulary: 'tough fight,' nature of the 'pitch to voters,' 'promises' by both key contenders, candidates 'weakened,' candidates 'headed for deadlock,' both candidates 'facing difficult tasks,' and similar. The news reports further focus on the analysis of various election outcomes, possible coalitions of parties and government formation. This textual material seemingly suggests a *neutral* reporting style used by the BBC to *naturalize* its Middle East discourse (Chilton 2004). There is no attempt to link any of the electoral happenings with the historical and political situation of the region, nor to use any vocabulary associated with the decades-long conflict, which is explicit in the Al Jazeera discourse: '(military) occupation,' 'illegal settlements,' 'violation of human rights,' and so on. The BBC avoids using the word 'occupation' as part of its own lexical range. That, and similar lexical items, are only used as part of a direct statement quoting Palestinian officials. The lexical items used are thus neutral in their representation of the conflict (if there is any representation at all), yet the actors at the heart of the production of those discourse strategies give little discursive leeway in reporting on the construct of social and discursive realities for those they are reporting on. Only one BBC news discourse engages in the reporting of the response of the 'Arab nations' to Netanyahu's annexation plan of the Jordan Valley, using the collective phrase throughout the report to predominantly refer to the responses offered by officials in Jordan and Saudi Arabia. The report quotes the chief Palestinian negotiator, whose views on the annexation issue mirror those of the Palestinian people in the discourse of Al Jazeera, namely that the move is 'illegal' and would 'bury any chance of peace.' Netanyahu's previously reported statement of Israel's commitment to retaining a presence in the Jordan Valley 'for security purposes' is offered by the BBC, presumably in an attempt to present a balanced view of the situation. In the BBC coverage we also see the narrative of *security* used by the Israeli prime minister to mask the contentious discourse of illegal settlements and the total annexation of the Jordan Valley; the security of the Israelis is given as the reason for the annexation. The same narrative is then adopted by the BBC in its reporting of the news item.

It is notable that during the recounting of the election period, the BBC reports on the killing of an Israeli 'teenage girl [who was] killed in the bomb attack in the West Bank,' which the prime minister described as a 'harsh terrorist attack' and repeated his commitment on 'strengthening settlements' and 'deepening [their] roots and strik[ing] at [their] enemies.' In its second news coverage indirectly related to the topical news item, the BBC describes events associated with the 'hunt' for 'the killer' of an Israeli off-duty soldier. 'The killer' is described as a 'despicable terrorist' by the prime minister on the assumption by the Israeli security forces that 'there is a terrorist cell in the area that carried out the attack.' The BBC also reports on the tweet from the US ambassador to Israel who was 'heartbroken and outraged by the brutal terrorist attack.' These narratives indicate that Palestinians appear to be at a disadvantage, both discursively and socially. They and their groupings are labeled as 'terrorists' and 'bombers,' who 'kill,' suggesting that our earlier analyses in which we discussed the conceptualization of 'resistance' into acts of 'terrorism' point to accuracies in a common perception of Palestinian people in most historical analyses: the Palestinian resistance to the colonization of their land is synonymous with terrorism (Pappe 2015). In contrast, reports of Israeli actors responsible for killing and injuring Palestinians are not included in the BBC texts examined.

These illustrations are further evidence of the asymmetry present in the reporting of the conflict, indicating how the socially more powerful side (Israel) is given preferential discursive treatment compared to the dominated side (Palestinians). Palestinians are not given any due space in the reporting of the elections. The historical background of the region and the conflict are represented in two out of the fourteen news reports within the chosen sample. In the two reports the BBC offers four paragraphs (repeated in the two sets of news) in which the occupation of the West Bank is labeled an 'issue' that 'goes to the heart of the Israel–Palestine conflict.' The BBC further reports that the building of the 140 settlements is 'considered' illegal under international law (rather than stating that these *are* illegal), and swiftly adds in the same sentence that 'Israel disputes this.' The choice of vocabulary testifies to the instability in the social relations of power; the decision by the BBC to employ certain lexical items and discard others plays a vital role in conserving the dominant narrative of the more powerful side.

11.5.3 Reflections

Based on the examination of the BBC reports, and previous findings of significant pro-Israel bias of the corporation, we see the relations between Al Jazeera and the BBC as indicative of *oppositional discourses* in the deconstruction of news associated with the Israel–Palestine conflict. The second contention of the narrative found in the BBC reporting rests on the question of *neutrality* of the reports or, to put it another way, raises an issue of *bias* (Barkho and Richardson 2010; Barkho 2011). Barkho (2011: 300) comments on the use of lexicon and the role it plays in BBC's and Al Jazeera's internal guidelines, suggesting that these are "indicative of social relations of power." He argues that in managing their vocabulary, media institutions show how they work "as agents and sustainers of one particular ideology rather than the other" (2011: 300), supporting our comments, following Vygotsky, on the importance of the analysis of the socio-historical developments that can help account for discursive processes in language use, and our historical-materialist position on the role of media as advocates and agents of the state and contemporary narratives. Thus, BBC departs from Al Jazeera in this respect. The latter is far more explicit in describing the struggle between Israel and Palestine and has no apparent problems in describing the Israelis lexically, as we saw above. The former, in the words of Barkho (2011: 300), "re-word and over-word [the Palestinians]" to match their own "distinctive lexicalisation agenda that fits [their] own interpretation of the social and discursive world of the Israeli–Palestine struggle." Through the representation of a number of language examples above, we hope to have showcased some of these issues.

11.6   Conclusion

The results highlight that the issue at stake is historical contextualization *in the media text*, from two perspectives: one centers on the question of the theoretical choice a discourse analyst makes in explaining how, and from which viewpoint, discourse might be socially constructed; the second is the adoption of varied historical contexts by the news corporations, and the ways in which those penetrate into the construction of news stories. As illustrated by the work of Philo (2007: 195), the latter needs to be methodologically supported by the analysis of other elements, such as processes of content, production, reception, and also "circulation of social meanings" in the media.

From the view of the first perspective, the chapter has argued that a historical-materialist approach advocated by Vygotsky in the application of the Cultural-Historical and Activity Theory helps in deciphering more clearly the contested narratives of the Israel–Palestine conflict, and at least challenges the academic readership to take note of such political tradition in the efforts to seek a peaceful resolution. The connections among language, context and history are striking, particularly when the socio-historical analyses are placed at the center of our understanding of how, in the case of Israel and Palestine, institutional and discursive levels enter into the relations of dominance as represented here through news stories.

The second perspective shows that the historical contextualization in the media text is complex and can lead to the employment of deliberate discursive practices by institutional actors engaged in the reinforcement of certain narratives and claims of the more powerful side in the conflict. It is our duty to continue to challenge them.

Appendix A Links to the BBC Data Sources

www.bbc.co.uk/news/world-middle-east-49275899
www.bbc.co.uk/news/world-middle-east-49447035
www.bbc.co.uk/news/world-middle-east-49657915
www.bbc.co.uk/news/world-middle-east-49714067
www.bbc.co.uk/news/world-middle-east-49714279
www.bbc.co.uk/news/world-middle-east-49740981
www.bbc.co.uk/news/world-middle-east-49753221
www.bbc.co.uk/news/world-middle-east-49768172
www.bbc.co.uk/news/world-middle-east-49790505
www.bbc.co.uk/news/world-middle-east-49833050
www.bbc.co.uk/news/world-middle-east-49904296
www.bbc.co.uk/news/world-middle-east-49973217
www.bbc.co.uk/news/world-middle-east-50132760
www.bbc.co.uk/news/world-middle-east-50167387

Appendix B Links to the Al Jazeera Data Sources

www.aljazeera.com/news/2019/9/24/hamas-official-no-difference-between-gantz-and-netanyahu
www.aljazeera.com/news/2019/9/18/israel-election-exit-polls-show-race-too-close-to-call
www.aljazeera.com/news/2019/9/16/israeli-pm-again-vows-to-annex-all-west-bank-settlements
www.aljazeera.com/news/2019/9/15/what-does-israels-election-mean-for-palestinian-factions
www.aljazeera.com/news/2019/9/15/were-doomed-anyway-palestinians-on-israeli-election
www.aljazeera.com/news/2019/9/13/palestinians-in-israel-netanyahus-racism-makes-us-want-to-vote
www.aljazeera.com/news/2019/9/12/palestinians-in-jordan-valley-our-lands-are-already-annexed
www.aljazeera.com/news/2019/9/12/israel-election-where-do-the-parties-stand-on-the-occupation

www.aljazeera.com/news/2019/9/11/what-are-areas-a-b-and-c-of-the-occupied-west-bank
www.aljazeera.com/news/2019/9/11/netanyahu-annexation-pledge-denounced-as-dangerous-and-racist
www.aljazeera.com/news/2019/9/11/netanyahu-announces-post-election-plan-to-annex-jordan-valley
www.aljazeera.com/news/2019/9/11/israel-election-five-key-things-to-know
www.aljazeera.com/news/2019/9/1/palestinians-slam-netanyahu-pledge-to-annex-west-bank-settlements
www.aljazeera.com/news/2019/8/27/how-will-the-joint-list-fare-in-israels-snap-election
www.aljazeera.com/news/2019/8/19/trump-us-peace-plan-likely-to-be-released-after-israel-election

References

Badarin, Emile. 2016. *Palestinian Political Discourse between Exile and Occupation.* London: Routledge.
Barker, Colin, and Gareth Dale. 1997. "Class Will Out? Some Remarks on Social Movements in Europe." Paper for the *European Sociological Association Conference*, University of Essex, August 1997.
Barkho, Leon. 2008. "The Discursive and Social Power of News Discourse: The Case of Aljazeera in Comparison and Parallel with the BBC and CNN." *Studies in Language and Capitalism* 3, 111–159.
Barkho, Leon. 2010. *News from the BBC, CNN and Al-Jazeera: How the Three Broadcasters Cover the Middle East.* New York: Hampton Press.
Barkho, Leon. 2011. "The Role of Internal Guidelines in Shaping News Narratives: Ethnographic Insights into the Discursive Rhetoric of Middle East Reporting by the BBC and Al-Jazeera English." *Critical Discourse Studies* 8(4), 297–309.
Barkho, Leon, and John E. Richardson. 2010. "A Critique of BBC's Middle East News Production Strategy." *American Communication Journal* 12(1), 1–16.
Chilton, Paul. 2004. *Analysing Political Discourse: Theory and Practice.* London: Routledge.
Collins, Chik. 1996. "To Concede or to Contest? Language and Class Struggle." In *To Make Another World: Studies in Protest and Collective Action*, ed. by Collin Barker and Paul Kennedy, 69–90. Aldershot: Averbury.
Collins, Chik. 2000. "Vygotsky on Language and Social Consciousness: Underpinning the Use of Voloshinov in the Study of Popular Protest." *Historical Materialism* 7 (1), 41–69.
Collins, Chik, and Peter E. Jones. 2006. "Analysis of Discourse as 'a Form of History Writing': A Critique of Critical Discourse Analysis and an Illustration of a Cultural-Historical Alternative." *Atlantic Journal of Communication* 14(1&2), 51–69.

Deprez, Annelore, and Karin Raeymaeckers. 2010. "Bias in the News? The Representation of Palestinians and Israelis in the Coverage of the First and Second Intifada." *The International Communication Gazette* 72(1), 91–109.

Downey, John, David Deacon, Peter Golding, Ben Oldfield, and Dominic Wring. 2006. *The BBC's Reporting of the Israeli–Palestinian Conflict*. A report for the BBC Board of Governors, March. Loughborough, UK: Communications Research Centre, Loughborough University.

Fairclough, Norman. 1989. *Language and Power*. London: Longman.

Fairclough, Norman. 1992. *Discourse and Social Change*. Cambridge: Polity Press.

Fairclough, Norman. 2001a. "Critical Discourse Analysis as a Method in Social Scientific Research." In *Methods of Critical Discourse Analysis*, ed. by Ruth Wodak and Michael Meyer, 121–137. London: Sage.

Fairclough, Norman. 2001b. "The Dialectics of Discourse." *Textus* 12(2), 231–242.

Fairclough, Norman. 2012. "Critical Discourse Analysis." In *The Routledge Handbook of Discourse Analysis*, ed. by James P. Gee and Michael Handford, 9–20. Oxford: Routledge.

Fowler, Roger. 1996. "On Critical Linguistics." In *Texts and Practices: Readings in Critical Discourse Analysis*, ed. by Carmen R. Caldas-Coulthard and Malcolm Coulthard, 3–14. London: Routledge.

Gaber, Ivor, Emily Seymour, and Lisa Thomas. 2009. "Is the BBC Biased? The Corporation and the Coverage of the 2006 Israeli–Hezbollah War." *Journalism* 10(2), 239–259.

Harvey, David. 1996. *Justice, Nature and the Geography of Difference*. Oxford: Blackwell.

Jones, Peter E. 2000. "The Dialectics of the Ideal and Symbolic Mediation." In *Evald Ilyenkov's Philosophy Revisited*, ed. by V. Oittinen. Helsinki: Kikimora Publications.

Jones, Peter E. 2004. "Discourse and Materialist Conception of History: Critical Comments on Critical Discourse Analysis." *Historical Materialism* 12(1), 97–125.

Jones, Peter. E. 2007. "Why There Is No Such Thing as 'Critical Discourse Analysis'." *Language & Communication* 27, 337–368.

Jones, Peter. E. , and Chik Collins. 2006. "Political Analysis Versus Critical Discourse Analysis in the Treatment of Ideology: Some Implications for the Study of Communication." *Atlantic Journal of Communication* 14 (1&2), 28–50.

Kalb, Marvin, and Carol Saivetz. 2007. "The Israeli–Hezbollah War of 2006: The Media as a Weapon in Asymmetrical Conflict." *The International Journal of Press/Politics* 12(3), 43–66.

Karmi, Ghada, and Eugene Cotran (Eds.). 1999. *The Palestinian Exodus 1948–1998*. London: Garnet Publishing.

Marx, Karl, and Friedrich Engels 1845 [1974]. *The German Ideology*, ed. by Christopher J. Arthur. New York: New York International Publishers.

Meyer, Michael. 2001. "Between Theory, Method, and Politics: Positioning of the Approaches to CDA." In *Methods of Critical Discourse Analysis*, ed. by Ruth Wodak and Michael Meyer, 14–31. London: Sage.

Pappe, Ilan. 2006. *The Ethnic Cleansing of Palestine*. London: Oneworld Publications.

Pappe, Ilan. 2015. *The Idea of Israel: A History of Power and Knowledge*. London: Verso.

Philo, Greg. 2007. "Can Discourse Analysis Successfully Explain the Content of Media and Journalistic Practice?" *Journalism Studies* 8(2), 175–196.
Philo, Greg, and Mike Berry. 2004. *Bad News from Israel*. London: Pluto Press.
Philo, Greg, and Mike Berry. 2011. *More Bad News from Israel*. London: Pluto Press.
Richardson, John E. and Leon Barkho. 2009. "Reporting Israel/Palestine: Ethnographic Insights into the Verbal and Visual Rhetoric of BBC Journalism." *Journalism Studies* 10(5), 594–622.
Saïd, W. Edward. 1992. *The Question of Palestine*. New York: Vintage Books.
Saïd, W. Edward, and Jean Mohr. 1998. *After the Last Sky*. New York: Columbia University Press.
Timotijevic, Jelena. 2016. "The Sociolinguistic Transition of the Discourse of Nationalism in Serbia from Tito to Neoliberal Crash in the 2000s." In *Sociolinguistic Transition in Former Eastern Bloc Countries: Two Decades after the Regime Chang,*. Volume 4, ed. by Marian Sloboda, Petteri Laihonen, and Anastassia Zabrodskaja, 207–231. Frankfurt am Main: Peter Lang.
Timotijevic, Jelena. 2018. "The Relevance of Marx to Contemporary Perspectives on Utterance Meaning in Context: A Re-examination of Voloshinov's Philosophy of Language." *Language Sciences* 70, 193–204.
The Glasgow Media Group. 1976. "Bad News." *Theory and Society* 3(3), 339–363.
van Dijk, A. Teun 2001. "Multidisciplinarity in CDA: A Plea for Diversity." In *Methods of Critical Discourse Analysis*, ed. by Ruth Wodak and Michael Meyer, 95–120. London: Sage.
Voloshinov, N. Valentin. 1929 [1986]. *Marxism and the Philosophy of Language*. Cambridge, MA: Harvard University Press.
Vygotsky, S. Lev. 1934 [1986]. *Thought and Language*. Cambridge, MA: MIT Press.
Vygotsky, S. Lev. 1934 [1987]. "Thinking and Speech." In *The Collected Works of L.S. Vygotsky, Volume 1*, ed. by Robert W. Rieber and Aaron S. Carton. London: Plenum.
Widdowson, G. Henry. 1998. "The Theory and Practice of Critical Discourse Analysis." *Applied Linguistics* 19(1), 136–151.
Wodak, Ruth. 2001. "What CDA Is about – A Summary of Its History, Important Concepts and Its Developments." In *Methods of Critical Discourse Analysis*, ed. by Ruth Wodak and Michael Meyer, 1–13. London: Sage.
Zelizer, Barbie, David Park, and David Gudelunas. 2002. "How Bias Shapes the News: Challenging the New York Times' Status as a Newspaper of Record on the Middle East." *Journalism* 3(3), 283–307.

12 From Peace Talks to Military Operation
Pakistani Newspapers' Representation of the TTP Conflict

Lubna Shaheen and Muhammad Tarique

12.1 Introduction

News discourses are constructed around ideologies and disseminated through language. These ideologies comprise the shared beliefs of a group or institution (van Dijk 2006). According to Fairclough (1992), language is neither a tool of communication nor is it impartial; "it is a manipulative instrument that reflects ideologies through lexical, syntactic, and discursive choices" (see Munday 2009, 196–197). Those with power in society "have access to and control over the media" and are in a position to "subtly imprint their views on discursive practices" (Youssefi 2013, 1343). They also present their views through reports written by journalists working in the media – the media then generate the desired meanings through discourses that support and legitimize these views to the readers. Such partisan information can mislead and cause unrest, disparity, biases, and differences in narratives. This chapter explores how peace talks and the subsequent Zarb e Azab operation were constructed in two English-language newspapers in Pakistan, namely *Dawn* and the *Nation*. It does so by analyzing the ways in which language is used as a tool for constructing the ideologies of pressure groups within the selected newspapers.

This chapter argues that, although the Taliban were declared a terrorist organization by the Pakistani government, they deserved a fair chance to be heard, by bringing them to a peace negotiating table. There are examples from other countries where governments have engaged in negotiation as the only route to avoid violence and war. For example, in 2012, the Colombian government initiated peace talks with the "Revolutionary Armed Forces of Colombia" (FARC) to resolve an armed conflict that had lasted fifty years (Beittel 2014), although there was little serious effort from either side and the media simply made an already bad situation worse.

12.2 Language and Ideology in the Media

Discourses have ideological effects (van Dijk 1998; Parker 1990) and assist in "establishing, maintaining and changing social power relations" (Omondi 2019, 13). Johnstone (2017) suggested that language shapes the world in which people live and its use is influenced by ideological positions, value systems, biases, and different perspectives (see Thetela 1999). In the news media, the construction of information and its dissemination reflect the cultural mindsets and the accompanying worldview of those controlling the media. Hence, the presentation of news may be constructive as well as destructive, depending on the objectives of the writers of the news.

Omondi (2019) further observes that different cultural conventions shape discourse and these conventions influence the aspirations and motives of those that construct discourse. Similarly, newspapers have their own ideologies and belief systems around which news discourses revolve. This is why the same incident is reported differently by different newspapers.

As highlighted above, ideologies are generated and shared within a specific social group; however, members of a social group are not always aware of these ideologies (van Dijk 2006). "Members are able to speak or act on the basis of their acquired knowledge of that ideology, but they are not always able to express their beliefs explicitly" (van Dijk 2006, 119).

The function of ideology in the media induces the notion of "embedded journalism," where journalists simply become a part of the system, and where powerful groups disseminate their ideological positions through "embedded journalists." This was most evident in the case of the Iraq war, where, before it began in 2003, a sense of paranoia was already created around "weapons of mass destruction" (WMD) that was brought to the center stage of media representations. Likewise, throughout the various phases of the Cold War, the follies of the communist system were strongly highlighted and presented as a failed system of government by Western media. The media portrayal of the Taliban is another example.

The Taliban are a Sunni Islamic fundamentalist political and military group nurtured in Afghanistan to combat the Soviet invasion and fight the Afghan–Soviet war in 1979. However, when the war ended, they were described in the media as "terrorists." The general strategy that controls the structure of media representations of people and situations is the "in-group" and "out-group" polarization of ideological "Us" and "Them" (van Dijk 2006). This strategy largely controlled Western media portrayals of the Iraqi war and the events following 9/11. For a "socially constituted ideology, language becomes the primary instrument through which it is transmitted, enacted, and reproduced" (Teo 2000, 11).

The word "critical" is a key theoretical concept in Critical Discourse Analysis (CDA) (van Dijk 2006). It signifies the need for analysts to undertake an extremely thorough investigation into the ideological underpinnings of discourse – aspects that are typically taken for granted and deemed common, acceptable, and natural features of discourse. Adopting a "critical" bent of mind enables the researcher to "elucidate such naturalisations, and bring clarity to the objectives of a discourse, which are otherwise obscure to the reader" (Fairclough 1985, 739).

Although ideologies play a role in legitimizing the domination of certain groups, they also help articulate resistance to such groups. For instance, feminist movements emerged to resist prevailing notions or ideology that women should adopt certain stereotypical roles in society and are incapable of performing others. Similarly, pacifist ideologies emerged as a resistance movement against war (van Dijk 2006, 117).

12.3 Discourse, Media, and Conflict

While the media are required to play their role in times of conflict, they are all the more important as mediators when a conflict is feared likely to result in destruction of lives and property at a national or international level. Hence, news coverage inevitably plays a crucial role in conflicts (Hackett 2007), and this role largely depends on the ideology of a newspaper whether it speaks in favor of or against the conflict. The use of language or discourse by a newspaper may change the dimensions of an entire problem. While a substantial body of literature highlights media roles in the escalation of conflict (e.g., Galtung 2003; Lee and Maslog 2005; Lee 2010), there is a paucity of research on the media as peace-builders (Bratić 2015). Literature on the Colombian peace talks, the separatist movement in Spain, the Irish peace process, the Philippines' Mindanao conflict, and the Palestinian–Israeli conflict, among others, provides evidence to indicate that the media prioritize the coverage of discrimination, biases, oppression, violence, and war; by contrast, peace-related news are rarely portrayed (Lee 2009; Şahin and Ross 2012; Ozohu-Suleiman 2014; Tarique and Shaheen 2016). Moreover, in relation to chronic conflicts such as the Palestinian–Israeli and Balochistan conflicts, the media prefer and sensationalize war, rather than peace, and promote language that escalates unrest (Wolfsfeld 2004; Tarique 2017). If the media have the power to escalate conflicts, they also have the power to de-escalate them (Bratić 2006).

In the production of news, the media sometimes appear to represent the views and opinions of groups that have either power or money. Media reports are thus based on the ideology of interest groups. Nevertheless, the media have a responsibility to help maintain a peaceful society, especially in relation to resolving conflicts (Thetela 1999). Hence, it can be argued that if the media's portrayal of a certain issue is positive, the prospects of a successful resolution are multiplied; conversely, if they are not, the chances of an immediate solution become bleak and the possibility of any sustainable peace efforts in the future is undermined. Following the Afghan war in 1979, Pakistan provided help and shelter to millions of Afghan refugees. Following 9/11, when the US decided to wage a war against the Taliban, Pakistan supported the decision. Consequently, Pakistan lost the trust of the Taliban, who then engaged in terrorist activities in their own land. To avoid a direct clash, the Pakistani government decided to initiate a peace process through mutual dialogue. Regrettably, the peace talks failed miserably, and the government had to resort to its last option (i.e., a military operation known as Zarb e Azab). Interestingly, the Taliban were once supported by the media, and discourses favored them in their struggle against the Soviet Army. However, after 9/11, their positive image declined abysmally, which consequently led to an accompanying shift in media ideology. The Taliban were then termed a criminal organization; and as Soherwordi (2011) observed, the image change of the Taliban transformed them from a militant organization into a criminal one (42), as the media subsequently labeled them "terrorists" (Nadeem 2017). Ever since, the prevailing perception of the Taliban in Pakistani society has mostly been negative, although a few positive impressions still exist (Malik and Iqbal 2010).

12.4 The Making of the Taliban

In 1979, the Soviet Union invaded Afghanistan; the US did not want the Soviet Union to have control over South Asia and therefore developed an alliance with Pakistan and heavily funded the Mujahidin (i.e., the Taliban) in Afghanistan (Bew et al. 2013; Fazli et al. 2015; Khan and Wei 2016). In the aftermath of Pakistan's decision to support the US government in its war against terror after 9/11, Pakistan became a breeding ground for Taliban insurgency, and the heroes of US and Arab nations were suddenly declared villains, enemies, and terrorists (Khan 2013). This was the point at which the Taliban became a violent and terrorist organization. They were now ready to fight, and Pakistan became the only country to face the wrath of the Taliban. The possible reason for this may be the discontinuation of the help and support provided to the Mujahidin by the US and Pakistan. Furthermore, Pakistan provided the US with operational air bases to launch operations against the Mujahidin (Malik and Iqbal 2010), which created resentment and triggered terrorist activities against Pakistan.

A large number of the Taliban, both domestic and foreign, took refuge in North Waziristan (Pakistan). This infiltration destroyed the peace in Pakistan. Consequently, "Talibanization encouraged a culture of terrorism in Pakistan that includes frequent ambushes on armed forces by Tehreek-e-Taliban Pakistan (TTP), target killings and suicidal attacks" (Afzal et al. 2012, 197).

As a result of major violent incidents, including the assassination of the ex-prime minister of Pakistan, Benazir Bhutto, approximately 50,000 people, including 5,000 armed personnel, have been killed, and a massive economic loss has been incurred (Hussain and Munawar 2017).

12.5 From dialogue to operation Zarb e Azab

When the elected government of Prime Minister Nawaz Sharif took office in Pakistan in 2013, it decided to tackle the Taliban issue through dialogue. The Pakistan government finally brought the TTP to the negotiating table in January 2014. The Taliban committee arrived with a fifteen-point agenda, some of which were highly unlikely to be accepted by the government of Pakistan (*Dawn* 2014).[1] A major breach of trust occurred while talks were still ongoing when the Taliban killed twenty-three army officers, which resulted in the suspension of the talks. On June 8, 2014, the peace talks were dealt another blow by a Taliban attack at Karachi Airport. Consequently, the government decided to launch a military operation in North Waziristan on June 15, 2014. In contrast to the popular belief that Zarb e Azab would control the violent activities of the TTP, the country witnessed the worst ever episode of terrorist attacks. Some of the most heinous acts of violence in the history of mankind occurred during and after Zarb e Azab, including the bombing and shooting at the Army Public School that killed 144 innocent children and teachers in 2014 (*Dawn* 2015).[2] Furthermore, Zarb e Azab resulted in the displacement of more than a million tribal people in the Federally Administered Tribal Area (FATA) and the loss of 190 billion rupees. Despite this, the terrorist threat to Pakistan was far from being eradicated (Basit 2016, 6).[3] A summary timeline of the important events in this period is given in the Appendix.

12.6 Methodology

The socio-cognitive approach of CDA is applied to the two phases of news reports under study. The analysis examines how ideologies are reflected in the news relating to the representation of the Taliban and the peace talks leading to Zarb e Azab. van Dijk's socio-cognitive approach connects the "microstructure of language to the macrostructure" of society (Kintsch and van Dijk 1978). Instead of discursive practice, "focuses on social cognition as the mediating component between text and society" (cited in Jahedi et al. 2014,

---

[1] www.dawn.com/news/1085920/ttp-finalises-15-point-draft-for-talks-sources.
[2] www.dawn.com/news/1226622/aps-one-year-after.
[3] https://thediplomat.com/2016/06/pakistans-counterterrorism-operation-myth-vs-reality/.

32). The data for this study comprises five complete news stories, including their headlines, sub-headlines, and the body of news stories published on the front pages of *Dawn* and the *Nation*.[4] Both newspapers are English-language national newspapers in Pakistan. *Dawn* is the oldest newspaper and is read by policy and decision makers within the country. It follows a socialist leftist agenda and is considered an elite class newspaper. The *Nation* is a supporter of Pakistan ideology and is extremely conservative in its views. The news stories were collected online from the newspapers' websites[5] from January 2014 to June 2014.

12.7 Analysis

The analysis examines how ideology plays a significant role in the construction of news stories in the newspapers under study pertaining to the peace talks between the Taliban and the Pakistani government – how the peace talks were politicized and how operation Zarb e Azab was constructed in news stories.

12.7.1 Ideological Construction of Taliban as Terrorists and Unworthy of Peace Talks

In most of the news stories during the selected period, the Taliban were constructed negatively – as terrorists and as members of a banned outfit and unworthy of peace talks. The excerpt below from the data reflects the common tone of the regular description of the Taliban in *Dawn* newspaper.

No **room** in law for talks with **terrorists**: The government faces **a moral dilemma**, as it gets ready for talks with the Tehreek-i-Taliban Pakistan. **One of the 60 outfits officially banned** and declared as **terrorist organizations**. (*Dawn*, February 2, 2014, 1)

The textual macrostructure of the paragraph presents a categorical denial of any possibility of peace talks. It presents a mental model that imposes the writer's evaluation of the situation, suggesting that the government is taking the wrong decision by seeking peace through dialogue. This news report indicates that the journalist presupposes certain knowledge in his discourse and attempts to extol the issue beyond its actual magnitude owing to his political or ideological beliefs. As such, this obscures the real issues in contention, placing the reader in a situation where they are unlikely to separate facts from opinions. The writer implies that "terrorist organizations and banned outfits" do not deserve dialogue, hence should not be invited to the negotiating table. And rather than

---

[4] https://nation.com.pk/09-Feb-2014/mulish-taliban-insist-on-sharia-precondition.
[5] www.dawn.com/newspaper and www.thenation.com/archive/.

discuss the political issues leading to the conflict and possibility of peace talks, the newspaper rather dwells on an intangible "moral dilemma," that tends to obscure the constitutional rights of the TTP members and the peace process. Furthermore, the newspaper's stance indicates the unwillingness of the writer to support peace talks, which they label as a "dilemma" in an effort to persuade the incumbent government (Pakistan Muslim League-Nawaz) to reconsider its decision to conduct peace talks with the group. The use of "moral dilemma" by the news writer speaks more of imposing an obligation on the government to avoid peace talks. And by highlighting the sensitive aspects of the topic, that "Tehreek-i-Taliban Pakistan is one of the 60 outfits officially banned and declared as terrorist organisations in Pakistan," the journalist further attempts to persuade the reader about the supposed unconstitutionality of initiating a peace process with the TTP. As the excerpt below from *Dawn* shows, the demonization of the Taliban as a terrorist organization also suggests that the writer is trying to convince the reader that whatever the government is doing is wrong and that the only way to handle the Taliban is through the use of force.

The government keeps on saying that negotiations with the TTP would be held within the **framework of the Constitution**, but **experts** believe that there is **no room** in the Constitution to enter into a dialogue with **terrorist groups**. (*Dawn*, February 2, 2014, 1)

The tone in this paragraph is clearly challenging and explains the mood of the discourse in the mind of the reader. To make his assertions more authentic, the writer refers to the "framework of the constitution" and the "experts" as his source of legitimacy against the peace talks without referring to any specific clauses of the constitution that deal with the subject of dialogue in a conflict situation. Likewise, using a general term like "experts" without any names further indicates the disposition of the writer and suggests that the news may be fictional. The news also indicates the attitude of the journalist as only wanting to influence and persuade the reader by sounding somewhat authentic. Unfortunately, this argument reflects the leftist social ideology that this particular newspaper (*Dawn*) espouses. *Dawn* is one of the largest English-language newspapers in Pakistan and has always supported social causes opposed to government policies, which are sometimes unfavorable to the general public. The author accuses the government of initiating the peace process without considering its legal provisions in the constitution. Such an argument can create a polarity of ideology among readers and supporters of peace talks and influence the peace process negatively by turning promoters into critics. It can also create a permanent impression in the minds of the public that the only route to resolve any conflict, especially with terrorists, is the use of force. In the sample below, expressions such as "maintaining the status quo" and "not lifting the ban" are terms that represent a *positive appraisal* of government policy and also strongly imply that the TTP has no legitimate right.

Asked if the government was considering **lifting a ban on TTP** before the start of talks, Information Minister Pervez Rasheed told *Dawn* there was no such possibility and the **status quo** would be maintained. **The TTP, with Baitullah Mehsud as its head, came into being in Dec 2007 – five months after the Lal Masjid operation. The organisation was banned on Aug 25, 2008.** (*Dawn*, February 2, 2014, 1)

However, the mental model being created in this report is such that would remind the reader of the previous problems and troubles caused by the TTP. This report has the tendency to instigate negative emotions, so that the reader would read the news with a preconceived negative evaluation of the TTP. This study argues that the role of the media in a conflict situation such as that of Pakistan, should be to pacify both the public and the groups involved in the conflict in order to facilitate the peace processes and not to tilt the news in favor of one party against the other. The use of *memory discourses*, especially those highlighting the painful past, can arouse negative feelings even when the news appears positive; this can seriously hinder conflict resolution. In the next sample the writer is trying to establish the fact that the government's efforts for peace dialogues have proven futile.

The TTP **has claimed responsibility** for a number of **terrorist attacks**, including **suicide bombings on military convoys**, and it **is accused of killing** a number of civilians. Before the last general elections, the TTP had agreed to hold peace talks with the government, **but the killing** of one of its **key leaders changed** the scenario. **A fresh initiative** taken by the government for talks after adoption of a **unanimous resolution** by an all-party conference **did not work either** because **another drone attack killed TTP** chief Hakeemullah Mehsud. (*Dawn*, February 2, 2014, 1)

This paragraph clearly presupposes the failure of peace talks owing to certain extreme incidents of violence by the Taliban at different stages. In the process of building the argument, the journalist applies *transitive verbs* to construct the Taliban as the main actors. Thus, the TTP are presented as the most dominant group in this discourse. The positive ideology of the government's peace talks initiative with the TTP is highlighted. The use of *semantic moves* such as the "TTP had agreed to hold peace talks with the government, *but the* killing of one of its key leaders changed the scenario" serves to legitimize the decision to wage a war against them. In the next extract from the same news story the writer claims that the time for peace talks is long gone and action is necessary at this crucial time. By doing so, he criticizes the government for the option of peace talks, which is viewed as a lackluster approach.

But the government **kept on saying** that the dialogue **was its top priority**. When the **TTP killed a number** of Frontier **Corps personnel in Bannu** it **was thought** that the **government was ready for a final showdown** and that **a military operation was**

imminent. But Prime Minister Muhammad Nawaz Sharif **announced the formation** of a four-member committee for talks with the TTP. (*Dawn*, February 2, 2014, 1)

The assertive part of the discourse (i.e., "a military action was imminent") denotes a negative ideology representing the Taliban as "terrorists" while also giving the impression that war is the only solution befitting such lawbreakers. Furthermore, the use of temporal words such as "imminent" affords the situation a sense of urgency that demands an immediate reaction. This paragraph expresses the negative stance of the journalist towards the Taliban, who describes them using strong adjectives such as "outlawed organisation." This negative evaluation gives the reader no room to form their own opinion on the conflict. The criticism of the government for taking a lenient approach and offering talks instead of launching a war suggests that the newspaper prefers war, rather than peace. *Repetition* is a discursive strategy used by the news writer to assert that the opinion of the newspaper is more authentic and absolute than the actions of the government.

12.7.2 Highlighting the Taliban's Orthodox Extremes

As noted above, in Pakistani newspapers, the Taliban are usually represented as extremists, and their religious extremism is often highlighted in news stories. In the sample below from the data, the news portrays the Taliban as orthodox extremists.

Mulish Taliban Insist on **Sharia Precondition.** The TTP named 3-member team of negotiators Saturday met with Taliban leadership who put forward **three conditions** to proceed with dialogue process with the government. The conditions include are: holding negotiations **within limits of sharia**, withdrawal of troops from conflict areas and release of captured members of Tehrik-i-Taliban Pakistan (TTP) from Pakistani prisons. Professor Ibrahim, Yousaf Shah and Samiul Haq's were airlifted from Peshawar to Miranshah on a **government helicopter**. They met with TTP leaders at **an undisclosed location** in North Waziristan and conveyed them government's message. (*The Nation*, February 9, 2014, 1)

The headline in the news report from which the above excerpt was culled appears to be extremely harsh, again reflecting the ideological bias of the journalist. In the first sentence of the sample above, the news report refers to the Taliban as "Mulish Taliban"; however, the author does not attempt to prove his claim anywhere in the report. Rather, the reporter tries to make the lead more sensational by blaming one party. The overall macrostructure of the news represents the biased mental model of the journalist about the Taliban. His overall ideological strategy also reflects the negative presentation of "Them" and the positive presentation of "Us," which follows the usual ideological discourse structure generally found in Western media. Another example of bias in the news report lies in its explicit language about the Taliban. The report is precise when it captures the names, actions, and activities of the government in positive terms but extremely vague when referring to the Taliban. Hence, the image conveyed by the news story expresses the negative opinion that resides in the mental model of the journalist, and it also reflects the presupposed ideology of the newspaper about the Taliban. The following news extract also presents the same ideology of emphasizing the negative actions of the "other" while de-emphasizing their positive actions.

According to sources, negotiations between committee members and Taliban could last two to three phases and JUI-S chief Samiul Haq, who is a member of the original TTP-named team, is also expected to join the negotiations. Sources said that Taliban's Shura **was providing complete security** to the visiting peace delegates. (*The Nation*, February 9, 2014, 1)

The use of *a rhetorical device* such as "sources" denotes an attempt by the author to validate his point of view. The positive point regarding the Taliban providing complete security to the visiting peace delegate was not given importance as the newspaper quoted it in the middle of the news rather than making it a lead or subheading. Within the news, a box is presented in which it is stated that, "Sharia can't be enforced by killing innocent." The newspaper is thus employing the *innocence/threat* rhetoric by placing the two parties in opposing positions as "innocents and killers."

12.7.3 Politicizing Peace Talks

In almost all the selected stories both *Dawn* and the *Nation* newspapers see peace dialogues as a political issue rather than a national issue. The following extract depicts the same ideology:

PPP (Pakistan People's Party) Chairman Bilawal Bhutto Zardari has said that Taliban are **deceiving the government** and the people of Pakistan in the name of negotiations, vowing that his party won't bow before "**savages**". Criticising PML-N government, he said those who termed Quaid-e-Azam as 'Kaafir-e-Azam' are being negotiated with today. Bilawal said peace cannot prevail in smaller provinces unless terrorists are denied sanctuaries in Punjab, accusing the PML-N government of **protecting and patronising militants**. (*The Nation*, April 5, 2014, 1)

This report comprises a speech by Bilawal Bhutto Zardari.[6] The communicative event is described in a compound paragraph. The analysis of the semantic macrostructure demonstrates that the discourse focuses on different themes of hate towards the Taliban and criticizes the new political government of

---
[6] The son of assassinated former prime minister Benazir Bhutto and chairman of the Pakistan People's Party (PPP) a center-left, social-democratic political party of Pakistan. It became the second most popular party in the 2013 general election.

Muhammad Nawaz Shareef. The selection for the lead and headline expresses the same negative mental model of the news writer, as it portrays the Taliban as deceivers of the nation. In this paragraph, ideological content is presented through the presupposition that the Taliban are not trustworthy and that any peace negotiations with them would be dangerous. Adjectives such as "*protecting* and *patronising*" express negative opinions that are enshrined in the description of the negative acts undertaken by the present government, such as the government attempt to broker peace with the Taliban. Only the first paragraph is relevant to the topic; other paragraphs revolve around round Bilawal discussing the present government's failure in other projects.

12.7.4 Vilifying the Government's Intentions for Peace

The newspapers under study frequently referred to other militant organizations related to the Taliban. In the news stories, writers were fond of associating them with different violent organizations without naming them in order to pressurize governments against their intentions for peace.

The militant groups, including the Tehreek-i-Taliban Pakistan (TTP) and some **other banned outfits**, are operating with "**virtual impunity**" in Pakistan as the country's civilian and military institutions are either "**unable**" or "unwilling" to prevent terrorist attacks, says report of an international human rights organisation. The militant groups such as the ostensibly banned Lashkar-e-Jhangvi (LeJ), a Taliban affiliate, operate with virtual impunity across Pakistan as law enforcement officials either turn a blind eye or appear helpless to prevent attacks," says Human Rights Watch (HRW) in its World Report 2014 released on Tuesday. (*Dawn*, January 22, 2014, 1)

The tone of the author in this paragraph is extremely assertive in demonstrating either his or the newspaper's ideological perspective. The macrostructure presents only one theme, which is that the "Taliban are terrorists and governments are unable to tackle them." The overall strategy of the writer involves the negative presentation of "them," through which he emphasizes the cruel and immoral behavior of the Taliban. The newspaper discusses the Taliban and the political government's weaknesses and negative aspects extremely precisely and explicitly. To increase the *evidential value* of the presentation, a reference of other banned organizations alongside the TTP is given, but such a weak and incomplete reference "and some other banned outfits" shows that the journalist only wants to validate his point of view. The tone of the news is also sarcastic in referring to the banned organizations and blaming the government for providing them with virtual impunity with a license to kill people. Elsewhere, the use of the word *ostensibly* gives the impression that the government is not capable of undertaking any action or that this is part of the scheme. This mental model also expresses the critical stance of the journalist regarding government

From Peace Talks to Military Operation 289

institutions. The ideologically biased context suggests that, by accusing and blaming the political administration, law enforcement agencies, civil and military institutions, and the Taliban, the author has tried to present them as members of the same group. In the following excerpt, the same tone of criticism of the government's policy of peace talks is also obvious.

> Taliban attacks, amounting **to war crimes**, have increased in **scope and magnitude** even as Prime Minister Nawaz Sharif's government has renewed offer for peace talks in the aftermath of atrocities," said Mr Hasan. The HRW report has come at a time when the militants have stepped up their attacks across the country and the media has reported that the militants have already carried out 25 major terrorist attacks in the first 20 days of 2014. TTP and its affiliates, who had declared elections "**un-Islamic**" and warned voters to stay away from the rallies of the formerly ruling coalition parties. (*Dawn*, January 22, 2014, 1)

The overall strategy involves presenting "them" as bad, and the author is playing a *numbers game* by referring to the number of terrorist attacks during the first twenty days of January 2014. In the first few lines of the excerpt, Human Rights Watch (HRW) is quoted, whereas the last few lines represent the ideological perspective of the newspaper. Repetition of the same impressions is designed to convince readers that what is given is true. To validate this point of view, memory/past events are employed as a discursive tool (Neiger et al. 2011). For instance, in this text, reference to previous elections is made to refresh bad memories of the past in the minds of the reader so as to connect these to the present events. The use of stereotypical arguments, namely "un-Islamic," is another type of strategy employed to shape readers' minds. It provides the reader with the context of a social group sharing the same religion. The last lines convey the message that voters (readers) were once threatened by the TTP and its affiliates, so there is a need to be careful now as the Taliban are more dangerous than they (the voters) think. In the next sample from the data, the writer attempts to rekindle past memories related to the Taliban.

> **Numerous** government installations and law enforcement personnel have been targeted by the Taliban. At least 22 polio vaccination workers were killed, and 14 wounded in 2012 and 2013 in attacks for which the Taliban **claimed responsibility**, says the HRW. The human rights organisation says "a climate of fear impedes media coverage of militant groups and the Taliban and other armed groups **regularly** threaten media outlets over their coverage". The report alleges that "**security forces routinely violate basic rights**" in the course of counter-terrorism. (*Dawn*, January 22, 2014, 1)

The theme of this excerpt focuses on the overall macrostructure of the news article. The same impression is given to explicitly present "them" as violent and evil. Applying the strategy of *evidentiality*, the writer, though without giving any specific reference, uses the word *numerous* to indicate the amount of damage done by the Taliban. The first line sounds like the writer is not confident about the numbers of the incidents being reported. This type of weak impression expresses the biased mental model. The use of lexical choices such as *numerous* and *regularly* tends again to remind the present government of the negative "them." At the end of the news text, a critical view is offered regarding the violations committed by security forces; this was an important aspect of the HRW report but is given the least importance. But there is continuous emphasis on the negative "others" (i.e., the political government and government institutions) in terms of not taking any steps against the terrorist groups while criticizing "them" (the TTP and other armed groups) for their terrorist activities, reflecting the polarization of ideology.

12.7.5 Admiring the Government's Decision of War

In all the stories, the newspapers criticize the government's decision to engage in peace talks with the banned outfits, and in the following extract, the writer supports the government's decision to initiate war against the TTP.

Zarb-e-Azab is **war of survival**, says **ISPR Chief**: The ongoing military operation in North Waziristan is a **"war of survival"** and **will pave** the way for the **dawn of permanent peace** in the country, **the military's spokesperson**. (*Dawn*, June 27, 2014, 1)

The central theme of the above extract is elimination. There appears to be an ideological content communicated through an unfair presupposition that the military operation in North Waziristan will finally pave the way to permanent peace within the country. The use of *semantic moves* (e.g., "war of survival") in the news text gives the reader the impression that only the proposed war "solution" is what society needs; otherwise, the situation will become critical. The mental model created by the writer of this headline shares a sociocultural ideology of *innocence and threat* – presuming that "we" are innocent and that the Taliban are the threat to the country. This mental model also expresses *attribution* – the view that the Taliban are wholly and solely responsible for all the troubles and only their elimination will ensure the restoration of ultimate peace in the country.

In the next sample the writer expresses the strength of Pakistan armed forces.

In **a formal briefing** to the media on Operation Zarb-i-Azb, Inter-Services Public Relations (ISPR) **Director General Major General** Asim Bajwa told reporters that the operation was being carried out without **any discrimination** between "**good or bad Taliban**". This is the **biggest** and **most well-coordinated** operation **ever conducted against terrorists**. It is **the beginning** of **the end** for terrorism in the country. (*Dawn*, June 27, 2014, 1)

From the beginning, the sample uses the authoritative polarized view of "us," emphasizing that the newspaper is not discriminating between "good Taliban" or "bad Taliban." It is also possible to observe a linguistic presupposition of the writer at work, which is that the reader already knows the definition of good and bad Taliban. They are also made aware that the Taliban have already been given a fair chance to seek redress for their atrocities and, because they have not shown any remorse for their terrorist activities, there is going to be a decisive operation. Notably, the fact that this decisive operation would be heavily funded by the US government is not included in the report. Only superficial information has been emphasized, primarily to communicate the writer's point of view to the reader. The use of metaphoric adjectives such as the *biggest, most well-coordinated* gives an impression of the magnitude of the problem and the urgent need for action against the Taliban. Similarly, in the excerpt below, the same rhetoric of constructing the army as saviors is emphasized.

Maj Gen Bajwa said **army troops, Frontier Corps personnel, Khasadars, Levies, intelligence operatives and the Pakistan Air Force were jointly conducting** the operation in North Waziristan. "**We have surrounded** the entire agency and sealed the 180 km border with Afghanistan, as well as the boundary with South Waziristan, **making it impossible** for **terrorists to escape**." (*Dawn*, June 27, 2014, 1)

Although this news discourse reiterates prior knowledge of the army and its operation, it also gives the reader the details of the operation. Like all discourses, this text presents an *argument* in favor of the government action/operation, quoting credible sources to make the point more authentic and reliable. The use of military rhetoric such as army troops, the Frontier Corps personnel, Khasadars, levies, intelligence operatives, and the Pakistan Air Force reflects the mental model employed by the journalist to explain the complexity of and technicalities associated with the conflict. This is designed to highlight the efforts of the government in managing the conflict in terms of cost, intelligence, and manpower and to create a false sense of assurance that the war with the terrorists will be won easily.

The terrorists could not anticipate the launch of the operation. Terrorists of all kinds, involved in different activities **from Fata to Karachi**, are based in North Waziristan. They **include local and foreign militants, including Uzbeks and Chechens**. Now, it is up to them whether they **surrender or fight**. (*Dawn*, June 27, 2014, 1)

As shown in this extract, the writer uses an *inclusion* strategy to construct a comprehensive discourse around local and foreign militants, Uzbeks, and Chechens. The rhetorical emphasis of "all kinds" – a hyperbole employed to express the mental model of the journalist regarding the government's actions – serves to represent the government's actions against the Taliban as legitimate and acceptable. *Local coherence*, which refers to the relatedness of each sentence to previous sentences, can also be seen, as there is repetition of the same ideological perceptions explained in previous excerpts. The excessive use of modal verbs including *must, shall, should, will, would, can, could, may*, and *might* affect the level of possibility and also construct the ability of the government to demonstrate their obligations towards the Taliban, such as giving permission to the armed forces to continue a one-sided action. This clearly indicates the ideology and affiliation of the journalist towards the army and the government.

In the next paragraph, the writer is involving the whole nation in the discussion.

The entire nation and the **political leadership** of the country were on the **same page** as the military on the issue of terrorism **and fully supported the army** in the operation. He said that since the launch of the operation on June 15, a total of 327 terrorists had been killed and 45 of their hideouts had been destroyed. He said 19 terrorists had surrendered to security personnel **but did not reveal any details about their nationality or allegiances**. (*Dawn*, June 27, 2014, 1)

In this text, the mental model of the writer regarding Pakistan reflects the tendency toward *homogenization* (i.e., presenting all important parts of the society as one uniform whole) of the Taliban; for example, as depicted in the phrase "the entire nation and the political leadership were on the same page." Furthermore, *lexical choices* such as "the entire nation ... fully supported" also emphasize the rhetoric of polarization as one of "us" against "them" and serve to construct a positive in-group and negative out-group divide. The news describes the intensity of the military operation and its achievements since its launch, also highlighting that the killings of the terrorists is a welcome development. *Historical comparison* is employed to provide a picture of the previous pact and to seek positive appraisal from the reader.

12.8 Conclusion

Newspapers play an important role in the reproduction of ideologies, and the presupposed biased ideology against the Taliban contributes substantially to the production of news discourses in Pakistan. News reports not only reflect reality, they also represent the ideological perspective of those working on the news and of the newspapers. The selection of headlines underpinned by a polarized ideology depicting "them" as bad and highlighting their negative actions reflects the stereotypical biases of the newspapers. The overall presentation, including the selection of images with the news report, also presents the leftist ideology of *Dawn* and the conservative ideology of the *Nation*. The lexical analysis of news discourses demonstrates that the newspapers have a certain tone that shapes the structure of news stories. The pessimistic and negative tone of the writers against the perceived terrorists is evident from the rhetorical selection of language, which ultimately plays a crucial role in the presentation of the polarized in-group ideology reflected in the discourses. The

From Peace Talks to Military Operation   293

overall tone of the discourse with respect to the TTP is condescending, contemptuous, demonizing, and demoralizing rather than conciliatory. Thus, it can be argued that both newspapers contribute to generating an unfavorable public opinion towards the peace talks.

Throughout the entire process of the talks, *Dawn* and the *Nation* disseminated information that was based on ideological presuppositions regarding the Taliban and tended to argue that, because they were terrorists, peace talks were neither an option nor a solution. To further validate their ideology, the newspapers often used different rhetorical devices to persuade their readers. Generally, the role of the newspapers is reflective of war journalism in that they negated the principles and practice of peace journalism in their discourses. van Dijk's ideological square, characterized by a positive in-group and negative out-group divide, provides an understanding of how the peace talks were presented negatively in the reports through the use of rhetorical and discursive devices. For instance, the government and security forces were portrayed as strong and having control over resources. Moreover, the newspapers characterized the military operation (Zarb e Azab) as the only way to bring peace to the country. To make this point more valid and authentic, the newspapers cited the opinions of "experts" without mentioning their names. An impression of national support for the military operation was also created by suggesting that the army was the only savior of the country, and war was a vital and imminent choice. It can be argued that these newspapers therefore played a part in the failure of the peace talks. Both newspapers criticized the government for its policies and the way in which it tackled the Taliban as well their peace initiative.

The Taliban were constructed as a problem, and the use of strong negative adjectives such as *barbaric*, *extremists*, *unlawful*, and *terrorists* constructed their activities as evil and antisocial overall. Throughout the news reports, the government, the army, and the US were constructed as part of the in-group with the writer and were addressed as "us." They were always represented as powerful and ready to take action. The newspapers created the impression that the number of "militants" killed did not matter, unlike the number of "us" killed (e.g., "Two troops, 25 militants die in North Waziristan" – *Dawn*, June 24, 2014). Soldiers killed in operations or suicide bombings were called "martyrs" whereas the Taliban killed in operations or in drone attacks were referred to as "terrorists" and "militants." The use of suggestive and insinuating language such as *our army, national heroes, war of survival, biggest war in Pakistan history, nation is supporting war, war is the solution, support for operation is every citizen's religious duty*, and others made the messages more involving and personal for the readers. By contrast, the Taliban were constructed as "them," their side of the story was excluded from the news, and only the official version was given importance. Overall, the discourses demonstrate how the ideologies in newspapers are shaped, reproduced, and rendered dominant through the presentation and selection of language.

Appendix: Chronology of Events (from Peace Talks to Military Operation Zarb e Azab)

Date	Month	Year	Event
27	Dec	2012	Talks were offered by the Tehrek e Taliban e Pakistan (TTP)
14	Feb	2013	First All Parties Conference (APC) was held by ANP (Awami National Party) to discuss option of peace talks with the TTP. Many of the party's political activists were bombed down by the TTP
28			Second APC was held. Note that in peace talks with the TTP were supported
12	March	2013	US drone killed 14 TTP militiamen including 2 TTP commanders, in Waziristan – stronghold of TTP activists.
14	April	2013	ANP leader was killed in blast. The ANP is considered among three secular-leaning political parties which the Taliban had threatened to attack during May 11, 2013 election campaigns. The other two parties were the Pakistan People's Party (PPP) and Muttahida Oaumi Movement (MQM). The assassination of ex-Prime Minister Benazir Bhutto was also considered to be in the anti-Taliban party mindset.
14			bomb blast killed 9 people in Peshawar
15			attack on ANP 2013 election rally killed 15 political party workers
25			bomb blast on ANP election meeting killed 11
06	May	2013	Twin blasts killed 14 people in Karachi office of the MQM (in connection with secular-leaning political parties who opposed peace talks with TTP)
07		2013	Suicide bomber attack on JUI-F election rally killed 19 (though the religious cum political party favors TTP, a section of its leaders opposed talks)
17		2013	An attack on a mosque killed 13 in Malakand. The incidents were a challenge to the new provincial government Pakistan Tehreeki, Insaf (PTI), which stands for talks with Taliban for peace in the province (Khyber Pakhtunkhwa-KPK which is still considered a stronghold of the Taliban due to its adjacent borders with Afghanistan) and the country

19			May 2013 "Dialogue with TTP is best option" – the newly elected Prime Minister of Pakistan Nawaz Sharif once again reiterated the need of talks with TTP
26			Pakistan Muslim League - Nawaz (PMLn) and JamiatUlma e Fazal ur Rahman (JUI-F) sat together to devise a mechanism for talks with Taliban. The JUI(F) is a far-right wing religious cum political party who strongly favors dialogue with TTP
28			2013; Waliur Rehman, TTP's second-in-command, was killed in US drone attack. It is pertinent to mention here that Pakistan had been verbally opposing US drone attacks but on the other hands at least two of its bases were facilitated to the US for such operations
02	June		The Taliban withdrew their offer for peace talks and vowed to avenge the killing of Waliur Rehman
17		2013	29 people killed in suicide bomb attack in funeral of a local person
20		2013	bomb blast at mosque in Peshawar killed 15
26			TTP conducted two coordinated suicide attacks against a Shia community at a market in the Kurram. Agency - then the Federally Administered Tribal Area (FATA) left 60 people dead and 180 wounded, which the TTP claimed responsibility. It is important to be noted here that the TTP had its religious ideology in opposition to Shia religious faith
09	Sep	2013	APC backed by PM Nawaz Sharif also attended by army chief. The country's political leadership and army were trying to build consensus for holding talks with TTP
22			The TTP conducted a dual suicide bombing during a service at a Christian Church in Peshawar, which left 81 people dead and 145 wounded
01	Nov		HAKIMULLAH Mehsud (the TTP chief) was killed in a US drone attack, where both government and one of the opposition parties, Pakistan Tehreek e Insaaf (PTI) (now in power after 2018 general elections), termed the killing of TTP leader as an attack on the peace process
1–18	Jan		In seventeen days, 41 revenge attacks after the death of TTP chief were conducted throughout Khyber Pakhtunkhwa (KPK), claiming 24 lives
19		2014	Immediately after the Bannu garrison blast, TTP claimed responsibility for the attack and said the outfit wanted "meaningful" dialogue with the government
30			the PM Nawaz Sharif offered peace talks to TTP after a series of endless attacks and formed a 4-member committee to represent the government of Pakistan
31			Invited TTP to nominate its members for talks
01	Feb	2014	TTP announced 5-member committee
02			According to *Dawn* report published next day, TTP offered full security to members of government in fear of the outfit's

			indiscriminate attacks on the committee for talks. Imran Khan (the current Prime Minister of Pakistan) and Mufti Kifayatullah of the JUI-F refused to become members of the TTP committee
03			Suicide blast in Peshawar. Four volunteers of an anti-Taliban peace body were killed in a clash with militants
09			First round of peace talks with TTP was held where the TTP came forward with two demands i.e., withdrawal of troops from tribal areas and release of their prisoners
13			TTP claimed responsibility for the bomb attack on a police van in Karachi in which thirteen commandos were killed. In this connection, the TTP spokesperson Shahid Ullah Shahid said that About twenty Taliban fighters had been killed over the past month in fake encounters and their bodies were thrown in different places. "We are justified in continuing a defensive war until a formal agreement on ceasefire is reached with the government"
17			Talks were suspended due to killing of 23 army men
21			TTP demanded government to declare ceasefire
25			TTP rejected government offer of unconditional ceasefire
01	March	2014	target strikes in tribal areas by Pakistan Military
02			TTP announced unliteral ceasefire. A TTP spokesman said in a statement released to the media that the ceasefire was being declared with all seriousness and good intentions. The spokesman expressed the hope that the government would reciprocate the offer (according to *Dawn* March 03, 2014 report)
04			Government decided to resume talks with TTP
26			Government held first round of direct peace talks with TTP

References

Afzal, Saima, Hamid Iqbal, and Mavara Inayay. 2012. "Terrorism and Extremism as a Non- Traditional Security Threat Post 9/11: Implications for Pakistan's Security." *International Journal of Business and Social Science* 3, no. 24: 194–203. https://ijbssnet.com/journals/Vol_3_No_24_Special_Issue_December_2012/21.pdf.

Basit, Abdul. 2016. "Pakistan's Counterterrorism Operation: Myth vs Reality." *The Diplomat*, June 27. https://thediplomat.com/2016/06/pakistans-counterterrorism-operation-myth-vs-reality/.

Beittel, June S. 2014. "Peace Talks in Colombia. 2014." Library of Congress, Congressional Research Service. www.everycrsreport.com/files/20140403_R42982_966a8af4e1b86effee73950f1c40ef2819a7b12d.pdf.

Bew, John, Ryan Evans, Martyn Frampton, Peter Neumann, and Marisa Porges. 2013. "Talking to the Taliban: Hope over History?" ICSR, http://indianstrategicknowledgeonline.com/web/ICSR-TT-Report.pdf.

Bratić, Vladimir. 2006 "Media Effects During Violent Conflict: Evaluating Media Contributions to Peace Building." *Conflict & Communication* 5, no. 1. https://regener-online.de/journalcco/2006_1/pdf_2006–1/bratic.pdf.

Bratić, Vladimir. 2015. "Beyond Journalism: Expanding the Use of Media in Peacebuilding." In Julia Hoffmann and Virgil Hawkins (Eds.), *Communication and Peace: Mapping an Emerging Field*. New York: Routledge.

Fairclough, Norman L. 1985."Critical and Descriptive Goals in Discourse Analysis." *Journal of Pragmatics* 9, no. 6: 739–763.

Fairclough, Norman. 1992. "Discourse and Text: Linguistic and Intertextual Analysis within Discourse Analysis." *Discourse & Society* 3, no. 2: 193–217. https://doi.org/10.1016/0378–2166(85)90002–5.

Fazli, Reza, Casey Johnson, and Peyton Cooke. 2015. *Understanding and Countering Violent Extremism in Afghanistan*. Special report, United States Institute of Peace. www.usip.org/sites/default/files/SR379-Understanding-and-Countering-Violent-Extremism-in-Afghanistan.pdf.

Galtung, Johan. 2003. "Peace Journalism." *Media Asia* 30, no. 3: 177–180. https://doi.org/10.1080/01296612.2003.11726720.

Hackett, Robert A. 2007. "Journalism Versus Peace? Notes on a Problematic Relationship." *Global Media Journal: Mediterranean Edition* 2, no. 1: 47–53. www.sfu.ca/~hackett/JournalismVSPeace.doc.

Hussain, Shabbir, and Adnan Munawar. 2017."Analysis of Pakistan Print Media Narrative on the War on Terror." *International Journal of Crisis Communication* 1, no. 1: 38–47.

Jahedi, Maryam, Faiz Sathi Abdullah, and Jayakaran Mukundan. 2014. "An Overview of Focal Approaches of Critical Discourse Analysis." *International Journal of Education and Literacy Studies* 2, no. 4: 28–35. doi:10.7575/aiac.ijels. v.2 n.4p.28.

Johnstone, Barbara. 2017. *Discourse Analysis*. John Wiley & Sons.

Khan, Hidayat. 2013. "Pakistan's Contribution to Global War on Terror After 9/11." *IPRI Journal* 13, no. 1: 37–56. www.ipripak.org/wp-content/uploads/2014/02/art3hidw13.pdf.

Khan, Muhammad Khalil, and Lu Wei. 2016. "When Friends Turned into Enemies: The Role of the National State Vs. Tehrik-I-Taliban Pakistan (TTP) in the War Against Terrorism in Pakistan." *Korean Journal of Defense Analysis* 28, no. 4: 597–626.

Kintsch, Walter, and Teun A. van Dijk. 1978. "Toward a Model of Text Comprehension and Production." *Psychological Review* 85, no. 5: 363–394. https://psycnet.apa.org/doi/10.1037/0033-295X.85.5.363.

Lee, Andrew Wei-Min. 2009. "Tibet and the Media: Perspectives from Beijing." *Marquette Law Review* 93, no. 209. https://heinonline.org/HOL/LandingPage?handle=hein.journals/marqlr93&div=12&id=&page.

Lee, Seow Ting. 2010. "Peace Journalism: Principles and Structural Limitations in the News Coverage of Three Conflicts." *Mass Communication and Society* 13, no. 4: 361–384. https://doi.org/10.1080/15205430903348829.

Lee, Seow Ting, and Crispin C. Maslog. 2005. "War or Peace Journalism? Asian Newspaper Coverage of Conflicts." *Journal of Communication* 55, no. 2: 311–329. https://doi.org/10.1111/j.1460-2466.2005.tb02674.x.

Malik, Shaista, and Zafar Iqbal. 2010. "Construction of Taliban Image in Pakistan: Discourse Analysis of Editorials of *Dawn* and *The News*." *China Media Research Journal* 7, no. 2: 46–56.

Munday, Jeremy. 2009. *The Routledge Companion to Translation Studies*. Routledge.

Nadeem, Muhammad Umar. 2017. "Pakistani Print Media and Taliban: A Test of Media Conformity Theory." *VFAST Transactions on Education and Social Sciences* 5, no. 1: 55–60. http://dx.doi.org/10.21015/vtess.v13i2.454.

Neiger, Motti, Oren Meyers, and Eyal Zandberg. 2011. *On Media Memory: Collective Memory in a New Media Age*. Springer.

Omondi, Clarice Atieno. 2016. *Media Discourse and Ethnic Conflicts: A Critical Discourse Analysis of Online Newspaper Editorials in Kenya*. Unpublished Master's thesis, University of Helsinki, Finland. http://urn.fi/URN:NBN:fi:hulib-201611072962.

Ozohu-Suleiman, Yakubu. 2014. "War Journalism on Israel/Palestine: Does Contra-Flow Really Make a Difference?" *Media, War & Conflict* 7, no. 1: 85–103. https://doi.org/10.1177%2F1750635213516697.

Parker, Ian. 1990. "Discourse: Definitions and Contradictions." *Philosophical Psychology* 3, no. 2–3: 187–204. https://doi.org/10.1080/09515089008572998.

Şahin, Sanem, and Susan Dente Ross. 2012. "The Uncertain Application of Peace Journalism: The Case of the Turkish Cypriot Press." *Conflict & Communication* 11, no. 1. www.cco.regener-online.de/2012_1/pdf/sahin-ross.pdf.

Soherwordi, Hussain Shaheed. 2011. "A Theoretical Discourse on the Pakistani Taliban." *Pakistan Horizon* 64, no. 1: 39–51. www.jstor.org/stable/24711141.

Tarique, Muhammad. 2017. *Balochistan Unrest through the Lens of Pakistani National Print Media (1999–2008)*. Unpublished PhD thesis, University of the Punjab, Pakistan.

Tarique, Muhammad, and Lubna Shaheen. 2016. *Not What Does Bollywood Mean, but What Does Bollywood Do? A Critical Peace Journalism Appraisal*. 26th International Peace Research Association (IPRA).

Teo, Peter. 2000. "Racism in the News: A Critical Discourse Analysis of News Reporting in Two Australian Newspapers." *Discourse & Society* 11, no. 1: 7–49. https://doi.org/10.1177%2F0957926500011001002.

Thetela, Puleng. 1999. "The Linguistics of Blame in Media Discourse: Language, Ideology and Point of View in Media Reports on the 1998 Lesotho Conflict." *Lesotho Social Science Review* 5, no 1: 111–132. https://opendocs.ids.ac.uk/opendocs/bitstream/handle/20.500.12413/6187/Puleng%20Thetela.pdf?sequence=1.

Van Dijk, Teun A. 1993. *Elite Discourse and Racism*. Vol. 6. Sage.
Van Dijk, Teun A. 1998. *Ideology: A Multidisciplinary Approach*. Sage.
Van Dijk, Teun A. 2006. "Ideology and Discourse Analysis." *Journal of Political Ideologies* 11, no. 2: 115–140. https://doi.org/10.1080/13569310600687908.
Wolfsfeld, Gadi. 2004. *Media and the Path to Peace*. Cambridge University Press.
Youssefi, Kazem, Alireza Baghban Kanani, and Amir Shojaei. 2013. "Ideological or International Move? A Critical Discourse Analysis Toward the Representation of Iran Sanctions in Western Printed Media." *Journal of Language Teaching and Research* 4, no. 6: 1343–1350. http://citeseerx.ist.psu.edu/viewdoc/download?doi=10.1.1.656.8635&rep=rep1&type=pdf.

13 From Collision to Diplomatic Compromise
"We are very sorry" – One Official Utterance, Different Interpretations in the Chinese and US Mainstream News Coverage of the 2001 Mid-Air Collision

Lutgard Lams

13.1 Introduction

Peter Hessler, former news reporter for the *Boston Globe*, tendered his resignation upon noticing how two news workers published two ideationally different articles in the *Boston Globe* on the Chinese reactions to the spy plane incident in April 2001. For Hessler, the journalistic enterprise became quite problematic when he realized how both authors witnessed the same event, interpreted it completely differently, but adopted the same impersonal and authoritative tone (Hessler 2006: 301). The present chapter aims to illustrate how news discourse indeed produces variations of reality and how it can influence perceptions of this constructed reality. Drawing on theoretical and methodological insights from the disciplines of pragmatics and critical linguistics, it examines how these variations of reality are mediated through the powerful instrument of language. The concrete issue under investigation concerns the way language was employed in the diplomatic tension between the United States of America (hereafter US) and The People's Republic of China (hereafter PRC or China) after the April 1, 2001 mid-air collision of the respective countries' military aircrafts. The study particularly deals with how the insistence by the Chinese authorities that the US government should apologize was mediated in both the Chinese and US media. Chinese and American press accounts of this incident/accident diverged considerably in terms of problem definition, blame attribution, and responsibility for the solution. As the collision and its ensuing diplomatic standoff between China and the US bore the potential of triggering a larger conflict between the then world's superpower and an emerging "competitor," the EP-3 (or Hainan) incident, as it was also called, received wide media coverage on an international scale. More importantly, the intense media discussion of the Chinese official demand for a formal US apology and the US refusal to apologize raised the question of whether the meta-discussion in the press had contributed to the final production of the US "letter of two very sorries" (Ensor 2001; Keefe 2002)[1] and whether they had influenced the popular interpretations that followed the announcement of the letter.

Since the event essentially revolved around blame attribution/avoidance and the Chinese government's demand for an official apology from the US, as well as the latter's refusal thereof, this chapter focuses on the significance of the speech acts of apologizing and expressing regret and the role of the media in constructing, interpreting, and translating these utterances. That the speech act of apology constitutes a major issue in international diplomacy is also evidenced by a number of other international conflicts between China and Japan or Taiwan and Japan.[2] Much literature has been produced within the theoretical language-pragmatic discipline on the speech act of apologizing. This study adds an extra dimension by discussing the media's constitutive role in political apologies in international conflictual contexts like the one discussed here.

As Table 13.1 shows, the corpus of media texts examined consists of all relevant articles about the event published in April 2001 by *The International Herald Tribune* and *CNN Online* for the US press, and by the dailies the *Renmin Ribao* (*RMRB* – the Chinese Communist Party paper), and the English-language *China Daily* (*CD* – equally the mouthpiece of the Chinese Communist Party) for China. The corpus also included the feature articles, published in April and May, by the *Beijing Review* (the PRC government's official monthly magazine), and 170 headlines of the *People's Daily* (*PD* – the English-language online version of the *Renmin Ribao*).[3]

---

[1] The letter entered the history of important historical documents under this name (Source: https://en.wikisource.org/wiki/Letter_of_the_two_sorries#:~:text=The%20letter%20of%20the%20two,plane%20crisis%22%20in%20April%202001). It was also reported as such by David Ensor, CNN correspondent, in the article "CNN Breaking News: China Promises Releases of U.S. Crewmembers," April 11, 2001 ("As far as the letter, it's being called the letter of the two very sorries here" (Ensor 2001).

[2] Just to take one more example from the Asia-Pacific region, we refer to the ROC–Japan dispute about the collision of a Japanese patrol guard boat with a Taiwanese fishing boat near the Diaoyutai [Spratley] islands on June 10, 2008. The collision of this Japanese patrol guard boat with the Taiwanese fishing boat resulted in the sinking of the Taiwanese vessel. The location of the Diaoyutai islands is especially sensitive, as China and Taiwan as well as Japan claim sovereignty over the island group. In a parallel with the present case, the Taiwanese government insisted on an apology, and when the Japanese authorities did not immediately meet this demand, the Taiwanese withdrew its representative to Japan. Eventually, the Japanese government did offer some type of apology, as presented in the editorial of the Taiwanese English-language paper, *The China Post*, June 25, 2008.

[3] Most of the Chinese-language research units consisted of the newspapers' hard copies, which were retrieved from the KU Leuven University library archives and coded manually, as no electronic versions were available (except for accounts on *CNN Online*, *China Daily*, and the *People's Daily* articles that served for the headline analysis). Search criteria included an approach to the accident/incident as a continued narrative. Hence, short descriptive factual accounts or "faits divers" were not selected, since the focus lay on longer, in-depth reports, commentaries, and editorials.

Table 13.1 *Units of analysis*

News outlet	Number of articles	Periods in which relevant articles were found
RMRB (Renminribao) (daily)	123	April 2–25, 2001
CD (China Daily) (daily)	23	April 5–12, 2001
Beijing Review (weekly)	20	April 12–May 17, 2001
PD (People's Daily: for headline analysis)	170	April 2–23, 2001
IHT (International Herald Tribune)	85	April 2–22, 2001
CNN Online	9	April 09–12, 2001

As the main speech act, leading up to the final resolution, was uttered on April 11, many articles of interest appeared between April 11 and 13, which explains the cut-off date on April 14 for most of the newspapers, except for the Chinese *Renmin Ribao* and the *International Herald Tribune* (*IHT*), the articles of which were followed up until the news value had diminished to a negligible number of articles per day.

Since media organizations in the PRC are conceived of as tools to serve politics, they are supposed to faithfully reflect the government's point of view. This type of institutional practice differs from the media concept held by private, profit-driven media organizations in countries like the US. Therefore, it is to be expected that the disparity in the nature of the Chinese and US press systems will have considerable effect on the output. The PRC's foreign press corps echoes the official pronouncements while keeping true investigative reporting, especially pertaining to sensitive issues, such as tensions in foreign relations, to a minimum. According to Scollon (2000: 777), beyond the regular news categories, there were five distinct genres of hard news in Mainland Chinese newspapers of those days: "officials meet," "official statements," "press conferences," "China develops," and "sport achievements," although in the English-language paper, these genres were often blurred.

13.2 The Sino–US Diplomatic Impasse Following the Plane Collision

The lack of hard evidence for the particular circumstances of the collision on April 1, 2001 complicated the determination of responsibility, which was nonetheless an essential part of the framing practice engaged in by the authorities and the media alike. As Entman (1993: 52) notes, framing refers to:

the selection of some aspects of a perceived reality to make them more salient in a communicating text, in such a way as to promote a particular problem definition, causal interpretation, moral evaluation, and/or treatment recommendation for the item described.

The collision and ensuing diplomatic standoff between the US and China gave rise to multiple interpretations articulated by both government officials and media professionals. The following account, however, can be made with relative certainty as it selects only empirically verifiable facts. The accident between the two military planes – an American Navy EP-3 surveillance aircraft with twenty-four crew members and a Chinese F-8 jet fighter with one pilot – happened above the South China Sea. Initially, the precise location of the collision was also a point of contention, the Chinese arguing it had happened in Chinese airspace, in particular in the Exclusive Economic Zone (EEZ) of its coastline, and the Americans insisting it was above international waters. There were also diverging views on what operations foreign aircraft are allowed to execute in the airspace of the EEZ of coastal states. One of the legal documents which both sides referred to was the United Nations Convention on the Law of the Sea (UNCLOS, UN 1982). It provides aircraft with freedom of overflight over EEZs, but does not specify overflight rules, thereby leaving room for interpretation. An in-depth survey into the international legal aspects of both the Chinese and American claims is provided by M.K. Lewis (2002).

After the collision, the American plane made an emergency landing at the nearest Chinese military airport on Hainan Island. The Chinese jet fighter crashed and the pilot, Wang Wei, went missing and was not found despite extensive search operations. There was, however, a witness to the event – the pilot of the second Chinese interceptor, who landed at the same airport a few minutes before the American plane. A few days after the collision, US State Secretary Colin Powell sent a letter to the Chinese Vice Premier, Qian Qicheng, expressing regret for the pain this accident had caused. This was followed by President Bush's reiteration of the regret for the missing pilot and one of the Chinese airplanes. Yet, for the Chinese, this expression was considered too mild, as it did not suggest remorse or an assumption of responsibility. The Chinese authorities had instantly blamed the American plane for "ramming and destroying" their fighter and illegally intruding into Chinese airspace by landing at the airport without verbal clearance. Hence, China demanded that the US government accept full responsibility, articulate a formal apology, and halt all routine surveillance flights along China's coastal line. The US refused to apologize, standing firm in their conviction that the American pilot was not to blame, and asked the Chinese to release the crew and return the stranded airplane.

Within the US military, there was speculation that the Chinese jet had caused the accident by undertaking a dangerous flight maneuver. Arguments such as previous near-misses between a Chinese F-8 jet, flown by the same pilot, and American spy planes, of which the military already had video-taped evidence, fueled this conjecture. Other reasons were the size of both planes, suggesting that the "lumbering" US plane did not have the maneuverability of the Chinese jet, and the assumption that the American pilot would not imperil twenty-four crew members by "veering" into the Chinese fighter. The official American position in guilt attribution was that no comments could be made until the crew had been heard and a joint investigation into the collision had been set up. The Chinese government, on the other hand, claimed they had proof of US responsibility, based on the second pilot's account of the event and the particular damage to the surveillance plane.

The twenty-four crew members were detained in the military compound on Hainan Island until the American Ambassador, Joseph Prueher, delivered a "letter of regret/apology" to the Chinese Foreign Minister ten days after the event. That the letter had to go through a number of versions until it reached its final shape bears witness to the intense diplomatic negotiation that preceded its issue. The precise content of the letter will be discussed in the next section with the empirical analysis. Suffice it to mention here that State Secretary Powell and President Bush added essential adjectives and adverbs as sentiment intensifiers. They expressed "*sincere* regret" over the missing pilot and airplane and to the Chinese people and the pilot's family, they said they were "*very* sorry" for their loss. In addition, they were also "*very* sorry the entering of China's airspace and the landing did not have verbal clearance."[4] The climate leading up to this famous letter and the interpretation of its content is the very subject of the present article.

As for the literature about this plane collision, Avruch and Wang (2005) and Lams (2010) offer extensive reviews of studies conducted by academics from various disciplines, ranging from political science and intercultural communication to legal studies. The present article supports the position taken by Chang (2001) that the standoff should be viewed not only as a cultural matter involving face issues, but also, from a geopolitical perspective, as an exercise "testing the compatibility of co-existence between the hegemonic status-quo and an emerging great nation power in the Asia-Pacific region" (2001: 106). In the same vein, it seconds the propositions by Gries and Peng (2002), and by Zhang (2001), who point at the danger of essentialist readings of the standoff as originating in cultural differences, since an exclusively cultural reading would diminish the political analysis of the ideological struggle at hand. But one also needs to beware of any potential nationalist bias when engaging in

---

[4] Ambassador Joseph W. Prueher's Letter to Foreign Minister Tang Jiaxuan, Beijing, China, April 11, 2001. Available at https://china.usc.edu/amb-prueher-foreign-minister-tang-ep-3-incident-2001.

political analyses of complex issues, such as geopolitical relations. For example, Zhang's conclusion concerning China's concession to the US in accepting "a letter of regret" instead of a "letter of apology" due to unequal power relations is based on a preconceived determination of guilt in this case. Yee (2004) adopts a more balanced approach in leaving the guilt question open and probing into the issue of joint deflections, commenting that "both leaders made mutual concessions that enabled them to placate enough of their respective domestic critics to render their concessions politically sustainable" (2004: 82). While exclusively culturalist readings distract from additional interpretations, it is, however, important not to neglect the complicating role of culture for a better understanding of apologies in international negotiation. Differences in cultural meanings of apologies and what they entail underpin the work of Avruch and Wang (2005), who link the Chinese insistence on an apology in this spy plane crisis to the Asian "high context" cultures, where apologies are connected to face, social status, hierarchy, and relative power (see also Cohen 1997; Solomon 1999; Gries and Peng 2002). Securing an apology from the perceived offender often takes a central role in Chinese conflict management, whereby China presents itself as the injured party (Solomon 1999), thus constructing a victimization narrative of suffering at the hand of Western actors during the "Century of Humiliation" (Gries and Peng 2002; Lams 2005, 2010). According to Avruch and Wang (2005), the role of culture in studies on apologies has too often been neglected. Former works in the broad field of conflict resolution that have analyzed the concept of apology in interpersonal or intergroup communication have indeed primarily focused on the usefulness of apologies for unblocking stalemates and on the risks involved in assuming legal liability. Pruitt and Kim (2004) present an extensive review of studies on tactical apologies in the domain of courtroom litigation. While Avruch and Wang (2005) zoom in on the cultural aspects involved in the official game of words between the Chinese and the American authorities, the current article embeds this ingenious practice of linguistic engineering in a broader theoretical context of speech act theory, discusses the cultural aspect of apologies in conflict situations against the background of cross-cultural pragmatics, and interrogates the intertextual uptake of this language game by the Chinese and US media.

13.3 Theoretical Perspectives on the Speech Act of Apologizing and Application to the Case Study

Apologies have generated ample research in the academic field of speech act analysis, given their importance in conflict resolution on interpersonal, institutional and international levels. Speech act research has been conducted in the disciplines of sociolinguistics, philosophy, foreign language teaching, and pragmatics. Within the field of pragmatics, the analysis of speech acts is particularly relevant for politeness theories. In early speech act theory, John Austin (1962, 1975) argued that language could be used to perform actions beyond merely producing sentences with a sense and reference. Utterances are intended to contribute some interactional move to communication. To illustrate this point, Austin made a distinction between constative and performative utterances, the former describing or reporting events, structures, or processes, and the latter "doing" something more than "just" saying or reporting something (Austin 1962: 5). These speech acts are, in English, commonly given labels, such as complaint, invitation, compliment, request, promise, apology (Yule 1996: 47). As an example of the speech act of promising, one can distinguish between the constative and reporting utterance of "He promised to be back home early today" and the performative utterance of "I promise to be back early today," where the utterance itself constitutes the act of promising (Cummings 2005: 6).

Reconsidering the theory in that, in effect, *all* utterances can be seen as performing some sort of action, Austin later replaced the dual constative–performative distinction by a classification of acts into three aspects of performativity: a locutionary, illocutionary, and perlocutionary act. The first entails producing a meaningful linguistic expression that the hearer/reader can understand and interpret. The second and the most often discussed dimension in speech act theory relates to the intended function or communicative purpose, generally referred to as the illocutionary force of an utterance. The last aspect involves the intended effect of the utterance. For an apology, for example, one would not articulate an apology without intending it to have the effect of being recognized as such by the interlocutor or the targeted audience. Illocutionary force indicating devices (IFIDs), such as performative verbs preceding the speech act, as well as word order, stress, and intonation, facilitate audience recognition of the illocutionary force as intended by the speaker. In addition, certain conditions, technically called "felicity conditions," need to be fulfilled for the audience to recognize the intended speech act. For example, the speech act needs to be uttered by a specific person in specific circumstances (such as a judge sentencing a convict to a life sentence in a courtroom), or the language chosen has to be comprehensible to the audience. As for content conditions, speech acts such as a warning or promise presuppose the propositional content of the speech act to relate to a future event. Other conditions pertain, for example, to the sincerity of the utterer, an aspect of specific relevance to the present case study of how the speech act of apology is accepted by the intended audience as genuine. All these conditions are called constitutive rules for the successful performance of a speech act (Searle 1969: 51–52).

Early studies on apologies were primarily influenced by the dominant paradigm of "face," as developed in Brown and Levinson's politeness theory

(1987). Since then, research has moved on from the latter's universalistic approach to a greater consideration for contextual relevance (Suszczyńska 1999; Blum-Kulka et al. 1989). Jeffries (2007), Harris, Grainger, and Mullany (2006), and Yamazaki (2004) have provided useful insights for the present analysis.

Harris et al. find the emphasis on "politeness not as a normative set of prescripts but as, in particular, a contested concept emerging dynamically from discursive struggle" (2006: 718) especially relevant to identifying the pragmatics of political apologies in the context of public debate and controversy. The authors explore the pragmatics of the political apology as a generic type of discourse by identifying certain characteristics, derived by analyzing examples of public apologies in the UK. Secondly, they argue for an approach to political apologies which is culturally as well as situationally grounded. Although they agree with Mills (2003) that it is hardly possible to define the apology precisely as a formal speech act comprising a fixed semantic set of components, they argue that

(T)he judgments by the hearers, at least in the case of the political apology, contain a degree of consistency which is not purely individual but culturally and socially defined and then produced and reproduced by the media, in particular. (Harris et al. 2006: 720)

As will be clear from the empirical analysis, the findings of the present corpus support the argument about culturally based consistency in political apologies and that this is co-produced by the media.

The following characteristics of political apologies, as listed in Harris et al., are all relevant for our case study. Firstly, they are in the public domain and highly mediated. Secondly, they are often generated by and spark further conflict and controversy: they are not usually a spontaneous offering but rather come in response to a demand from the group offended. Conflicts also arise over the nature of the offence, the actors who should apologize, and the question of whether or not an apology is warranted. (2006: 721). Most importantly, what constitutes a valid apology in terms of the language used is mostly considered quite contentious by both parties involved. Even though a wide range of linguistic forms is conceivable, a lack of explicitness in political apologies tends to undermine both the perceived validity of the expression as a formal apology as well as the sincerity of the speaker. Again, this is also borne out in the present case study.

Thirdly, both an explicit IFID token (e.g., "sorry," "apologize") and an expression indicating responsibility for the "offence" appear to be crucial parts of political apologies in the eyes of the receiver (i.e., offended party, media and its viewers). Explicit apologies can be defined as those which include sorry-based units and/or some form of apology as a performative verb (Robinson 2004: 293). In an attempt to draw conclusions about the likely formal structures of the apology, Suszczyńska (1999) compares textual components of the apology in English, Polish, and Hungarian. Her version of the more general model of components of an apology provided by Olshtain and Cohen (1983)[5] includes the very elements that, in the present study, are part of the journalists' meta-discussion about the expected US apology and were essentials of the Chinese authorities' demands for a US apology. The current analysis also demonstrates that these components, constituting the culturally and socially defined "prototypical" Anglo-Saxon apology, were indeed part of the US attitude and verbal expressions (or lack thereof) in the diplomatic standoff.

Crucial in this discussion, however, is the constructive ambiguity of the IFID "sorry," which does not necessarily refer to speaker responsibility but can be a mere expression of regret. It can be a polite speech act of expressing condolences or commiserating, based on the "sympathy maxim" (Leech 1983) and a positive politeness strategy of attending to the hearer's wants and needs (Brown and Levinson 1987). In the case study examined, it is precisely this aspect of ambiguity in the IFID "sorry" that generated the main difference in interpretation between the Chinese and US sides. While the Chinese government read the IFID "sorry" as a straightforward apology, the American administration meant it to be a mere expression of sympathy, at least in the initial expressions of regret during the first days in the standoff and also in the first expression of regret over the missing pilot and aircraft in the US Ambassador's letter to the Chinese Foreign Minister. The second phrase "we're very sorry the entering of China's airspace and the landing did not have verbal clearance, but very pleased the crew landed safely" is an interesting example of linguistic gymnastics, illustrated by the disparate ways of indirect reporting and media interpretations of this phrase. In this case it is no longer an expression of condolence. Yet, can it be viewed as an apology? It may harbor the illocutionary force of an apology, but it could equally have the ideational function of subtle criticism against the Chinese military airport control officers for not giving verbal clearance for the emergency landing. According to the US claims by the EP-3 pilot, emergency calls were made, but the Chinese version refutes this argument. The ambiguity revolves around the meaning of the verb "have" in the utterance "We are very sorry the entering of China's airspace and the landing did not *have* verbal clearance," which leaves implicit whether the request for clearance was made. A non-agentive gerund is used for the carrier element ("the entering" and "landing"), combined with the verb "have," which

---

[5] According to Suszczyńska (1999), English speakers choose an expression of regret ("I'm sorry") routinely as an IFID rather than a more clearly performative offer of apology ("I apologize") or a request for forgiveness ("Please, forgive me"). The remainder of the apology in English is an expression of concern ("Everything OK?") and an offer of help. In addition, Suszczyńska argues that an explicit acceptance of responsibility is not common in an English apology.

is a possessive relational process and does not encode the force of a material, active process. The syntactical sentence pattern allows for some ambiguity in interpreting "have" as synonymous with "receive." This reading leads to the issue of request for clearance, which is not broached in the letter. The reference to the "emergency landing" preceding the phrase could already suggest that the formalities of requesting and waiting for clearance are less essential in these emergency circumstances. Thus, while the phrase could be read as an apology for "trespassing," one could also infer that clearance was perhaps requested and not given, or that there was simply no time for a request, given the emergency context. Clearly, agency is avoided by the letter writer's choice of a nominalized gerund. In conclusion, what the above speculation suggests is that the actual meaning of the Ambassador's letter is open to interpretation. The letter does not necessarily have to be interpreted as an apology, as was widely done in the media.

A fourth characteristic of the political apology, as indicated by Harris et al. (2006), lies in the response by the aggrieved party, which is expected to "initiate the process of negotiating absolution" (Robinson 2004: 292), but rarely offers an explicit form of absolution. Our media analysis also investigated this dimension of negotiation, which happened on a public level in the Chinese media. In short, absolution for the initial US expressions of regret was not given; on the contrary, Chinese voices demanded a more sincere demonstration of contrition. Absolution for the "sorry" expressed in the final letter was not explicitly offered, but action was taken in releasing the detained crew, which means the feelings expressed in the letter were officially accepted.

The cross-cultural aspect of apology behavior when a dispute between two nations is involved adds a further layer of complexity and meaning, such as in the present case study. Indeed, cultural differences in expectations contributed to the prolonged diplomatic standoff, but the culturally different interpretation of the ambiguous IFID "sorry" provided at the same time the magic key to its creative resolution. However, our analysis of the incident confirms the positions in Zhang (2001) and Gries and Peng (2002) that the standoff cannot be essentialized to merely cultural differences, since intricate power politics and strategic interests were at stake for both sides.

Besides the textual evidence of the components making up an apology, additional aspects of the psycho-social context can also serve as proof of the apologetic character, such as the effect on the audience, explicit comments by the speaker, hearer, or third parties, like the meta-discussion in the media. This in turn may lead to subsequent discussion, embedding the simple speech act into a larger discourse event. Indeed, journalists can have great influence as text producers and "ideological brokers" (Blommaert 1999) on how apologetic words are received. Jeffries (2007) addresses the question of "intention and sincerity" as a condition for success of the apology and argues that it is the way it sounds to the hearers that determines whether the speech act is counted as an apology. The apology is thus viewed as a reciprocal act and the nature of the politeness work is considered to be essentially negotiated. A similar attention to the role of the offended party in accepting/rejecting the apology as well as the co-production of national apologies by media texts is given in Yamazaki (2004).

13.4 Empirical Analysis: Metapragmatic Awareness of the Grammar and Semantics of Responsibility

The empirical analysis of the Chinese and American press narratives about the event is structurally divided into three parts: (1) the media outlets' contribution to the demand for a formal apology and the growth of public sentiment against the Other; (2) the media's anticipation of the final solution to the standoff through the US "letter of two very sorries"; and (3) the media's interpretation of the letter, thereby defining the success of the final speech act, which gave the green light for the release of the twenty-four US crew members.

The salience of metapragmatic attention to the force of the "apology" speech act raises the question about the contributive role of the press accounts in the final resolution of the standoff, be it by putting constraints on the decision makers in conceding to the other party, or in urging the authorities to take certain (verbal) actions. What captures the eye in the Chinese press coverage is the extensive reference to world opinion and global media supporting the Chinese stance in the dispute and thereby legitimating the demand for a US apology. These particular foreign press articles originated from media organizations across the globe. Not a single article adopting either a more balanced or a purely pro-US viewpoint found its way to the Chinese media. Knowing which nations are welcomed into the league of "China friends" and which ones belong to the category of "US foes" helps us to understand the particular choice of sources in the Chinese press. This strategy of a well-designed and ideologically influenced selection appears to be characteristic of Chinese discursive media practices (Lams 2019). A brief glance at the headlines cumulatively reveals a strategic selection of countries. Each of the three subdivisions in this analysis charts the media's meta-discussion about the apology in the Chinese and American press.

13.4.1 Press Accounts of the Chinese Public Demand for and the US Refusal of a Formal Apology

In the Chinese state-run press, one cannot miss the pattern of transitive syntactic structures placing the US in the semantic role of the perpetrator of actions with a negative connotation, implying intentionality (e.g., "ramming and destroying").[6] Pointing to the same mindset are the evaluative labels (e.g., "bandits") and adjectival descriptors for the US (e.g., "arrogant," "hegemonic"). Unquestioned meanings concerning the hegemonic character of US activities in the Pacific surface time and again. Angry Chinese citizens (at home and abroad) are quoted, many of them asserting that the initial expressions of US regret are not equivalent to an apology. On a daily basis, articles give the floor to foreign statesmen and media for accusatory speech acts against the US, and to direct admonitions to the US to change their hegemonic attitude and show humility in apologizing. To give a few examples, we refer to the *People's Daily* online version, which prints four articles on April 4, seven articles the next day, and eleven on April 6.[7]

Besides directives, the accounts are replete with deontic modality markers like "should," "must" in combination with "apologize," "bear full responsibility," "learn to be humble."

The same strategy holds for the headlines, in which China is put in the acting role of asserting authority ("urges," "demands"). In comparison with the other corpora investigated, the illocutionary force of admonitions stands out across the entire Chinese corpus. Modal epistemic adverbs, such as *dangran* [surely] stress the commonsensical and evidential nature of Chinese claims. These admonishments are premised on the assumption of US responsibility, before guilt was actually determined, and contribute to building up a general sense that a formal US apology is the only way this problem can be resolved.

The headline of the *China Daily* on April 5 allows the Chinese leader, Jiang Zemin, to take the moral high ground in calling on the US to apologize ("Jiang calls on US to apologize"). He is quoted as saying:

China has all along been dealing with the incident in a cool, responsible manner and with restraint, but the American side adopted an opposite attitude and methods. It has displayed an arrogant air, used lame arguments, confounded right and wrong and made groundless accusations against China.

These arguments set the overall tone for the legitimacy of the Chinese demand for an apology, which thus assumes a symbolic character to enhance the selfconfidence of the Chinese people, aggrieved by a century and a half of foreign aggression. Central in this discourse are the moral calls and exhortations, the accusatory diatribes against the hegemonic US, threatening to harm the

---

[6] A counter-screening phase of the Chinese corpus (looking for any counter-examples) revealed a 100% consistency in placing the US in the negative semantic role.

[7] Further illustrations are: "China has right to demand US apology for air collision: Syrian Daily," "Malaysian PM laments US spying on China," "Newspapers UAE, Spain, Indonesia blast US stance" (*China Daily*, April 5); "Hong Kong media point out: a US plane collides with our plane; hegemony exposed" (*Renminribao*, April 5, p.4); "Overseas Chinese make a statement and strongly condemn US hegemonic act" (*Renminribao*, April 5, p.4). "US uses cold war language in spy plane incident, Castro says" (*People's Daily online*, April 6).

Chinese principles of territorial sovereignty and national dignity. When Secretary of State Colin Powell expresses regret for what happened to the Chinese airplane and the pilot, the *RMRB* issues a significantly tiny report hidden among the larger adjacent reports on April 6 (p.4). The same strategy holds for the short article at the bottom of p.4 on April 11, in which Colin Powell "expressed US regrets" [the Chinese term used is *yihan*] "and apologies" [the Chinese lexical variant chosen is *daoqian*, carrying the connotation of apology, admission of wrongdoing, and expression of remorse] and "admitted violation of Chinese air space because of emergency." The lexical presupposition-carrier "admit" presupposes acceptance of guilt. Throughout the corpus up until the announcement of the US letter of regret, plenty of quotes by Chinese students and academics can be found that simple expressions of regret will not suffice. Yet, an in-depth metapragmatic discussion of the nuance in meaning between the various Chinese-language options to utter an apology is not found in the Chinese corpus.[8]

In the US papers, on the other hand, one can find an extensive meta-discussion of specific shades of meaning behind words like "regret" and "sorry" and the Chinese equivalents throughout the corpus. Some headlines already testify to this focus on semantics.[9] Both positions of Chinese and US authorities are quoted directly. The news articles do not easily give away a particular position, but the editorials reveal an anti-Chinese stance and plead for a more constructive approach emphasizing the need for fact-finding and sharing of information about the incident. In an op-ed article, the US crew is referred to as "pawns" or "hostages" in the standoff. It deems China's decision to detain the crew members as utterly offensive.[10] Washington's response to Chinese claims is viewed as more measured, although criticism is also leveled at Bush's "stern" admonitions to China, since they could have the unintended effect of limiting the time and diplomacy needed for a solution.[11]

The *International Herald Tribune* (*IHT*) mostly reprints articles from the *New York Times* (*NYT*) and the *Washington Post* (*WP*). A single article, written by its own staff and published on April 6 ("Bush offers regret for China's losses"), brings balanced quotes on the personal expression of regret by

---

[8] Quotes from interviews with Chinese students and academics on the semantic difference between apologies and expressions of regret are given in Western papers, e.g., *The Independent* "Regrets, they've had a few. But sorry? That's the one word both sides find hard to say" (April 10).

[9] In the *CCN* online articles, the following headlines show the metapragmatic attention given to the semantics of apologies: "David Ensor: Words do matter in US-China standoff" (April 9); "Sorry is nice, but not what China wants – Struggling over the wording" (April 10); the *International Herald Tribune* issues these headlines: "Regrets won't do, Chinese students assert" (April 7); "'Bao' or 'dao'? Seeking right 'sorry'" (April 10).

[10] "Time for diplomacy," op-ed article in the *NYT*, April 6.

[11] For example, "Time for diplomacy," op-ed article in the *NYT*, April 6.

President Bush and similar comments by Colin Powell. The newspaper is also attentive to what the Chinese media publish. A reference to a *China Daily* editorial in that same article paves the way for the US letter of apology of April 11. Two successive articles (April 7 "Regrets won't do, Chinese students assert"; April 10 "Angry litany pouring from Chinese people") devote ample attention to the Chinese reaction to the US regrets, quoting students who insist there cannot be a middle ground between the US "regret" and the "apology", insisted upon by the Chinese authorities. In these negative images, the Chinese students characterize the US as "a careless bully," "international policeman," "fond of war." An editorial from the *WP* reprinted in the *IHT* on April 11 and headlined "Beijing should relent" urges the Bush team to "stick to its refusal to deliver the freighted code words of apology that China would like to extract," as the demand is considered "unacceptable." These code words are in language-pragmatic terms the IFIDs discussed above.

In conclusion, it can be argued that in the days leading up to the "letter of regret," the Chinese papers contributed extensively to the debate as to whether a US apology was due, while giving hardly any room to the opposite voices, whereas the American news narratives reported positions of both sides and engaged in an in-depth meta-discussion of the semantics involved in English and Chinese ways of apologizing and expressing regret. It cannot be readily inferred that this discussion contributed to the final outcome, but it did prepare readers for the significance and repercussions of whatever formula was about to emerge. That the US papers also rallied around their own flag is evident in the anti-Chinese editorial stance, although criticism against the US administration's handling of the affair is not absent.

13.4.2 The Media's Anticipation of the "Two Very Sorries" Letter

The content and form of the US official letter was negotiated by the diplomatic corps of both countries behind closed doors. Eckholm (2001: 1) writes:

In the Friday briefing, the diplomats elaborated on the circumstances of the collision and its frantic aftermath, as well as the secret, day-and-night negotiations in Beijing and Washington that resulted in a contrite letter from the US in return for release of the crew.

Thus, a private circuit of talks existed alongside the public rhetoric conducted in the media by both parties. The two circuits, private and public, were held in parallel. While publicly the media of both protagonists reported positions oscillating between softening and hardening tones, with speech acts shifting between welcoming certain moves to issuing warnings and threats, behind-the-scenes diplomatic talks appeared to move steadily towards resolution. Menaces or intimidations revolve around the impact the incident may have on Sino–US relations and are usually uttered indirectly by means of conditional clauses. The following two examples illustrate this point for the US corpus: "If China then fails to do so, the consequences could shadow both nations for years to come."[12] "If we resolve this rather quickly, then hopefully it will not affect the overall relationship between the US and the PRC."[13] The admonitions from the Chinese side are articulated as follows: "The US should not make any erroneous calculation and continue to do anything that may lead to escalation and complication of the situation, he warned."[14] The only two news features detailing the private discussions, conducted in parallel to the saber-rattling discourse in the media, appear in an online *CNN* article ("Analysis: Behind the scenes in Beijing's corridors of power," April 11) by W.W.L. Lam, a veteran China analyst, and in a special article of the *Far Eastern Economic Review* by Ambassador Prueher's Special Assistant, J. Keefe (2002), who details, for example, how many hours it took before the last addition of the adverb "very" broke the ice. Lam reports that the tactics underlying President Jiang's so-called "diplomacy of apology" were inspired by a flexible approach under a veneer of toughness.[15] It cannot be claimed that the Chinese and US media directly contributed to the drafting of the letter, but they arguably helped build up the momentum leading to the positions adopted by both camps. Although the crafting of the final wording was devised by the diplomats in charge, not least both ambassadors with long-standing experience in US–China relations,[16] much of the wording had already been suggested and discussed in the US media prior to the letter's release.

In this phase of the standoff, the articles in the Chinese corpus hardly touch upon this parallel circuit of negotiations, whereas in the Western dataset, the diplomatic wheel of intensive talks is extensively discussed. The US papers anticipate the letter in detailed discussions about the shades of meaning of apology in both languages. An article in the *CNN* corpus on April 9 reports a proposal, suggested by one of the former Clinton advisors, to apologize only for the landing in Hainan without permission. On the next day a feature article

---

[12] *IHT*, "An overture to China," April 7–8, 2001, p.8.
[13] Secretary of State Colin Powell, quoted in Craig S. Smith; "US envoys meet crew of spy plane," *IHT*, April 4, p.1.
[14] Foreign Minister Tang Jiaxuan, quoted in Gang Ji, "Jiang calls on US to apologize," *CD*, April 5, www.chinadaily.net/hkedition.history/2001/04/05/d1-1.xy3.html, accessed on September 19, 2006, no longer retrievable).
[15] Lam argues that "Before leaving, President Jiang Zemin indicated to Vice President Hu Jintao and Foreign Minister Tang Jiaxuan that on the surface, Beijing should adopt a posture of no compromise on the issue of a full apology, but if Washington were willing to demonstrate sincerity and contrition, Beijing should leave a way out for Bush." (in "Analysis: Behind the scenes in Beijing's corridors of power," *CNN online*, April 11. http://edition.cnn.com/2001/WORLD/asiapcf/east/04/11/china.plane.wlam/index.html.
[16] According to Craig S. Smith, the Chinese Ambassador to the US, Yang Jiechi, was a former translator in the Foreign Ministry who worked on the intentionally ambiguous language of the three communiqués defining the US–China relationship ("Collision with China: The semantics; US and China look for a way to say 'sorry'," *NYT*, April 9).

chronicles the negotiation process over the precise wording and reports that both countries are working on the fourth draft of the letter. Again, all specifics of the possible wording are already laid out. As the Chinese language is seen to be a precise tongue ill-suited to diplomatic vagueness, translators reportedly "complain of the difficulty of using Chinese to portray English euphemisms and their calculated lack of meaning."[17] In a news report of *IHT*, Senator Warner is cited as saying that the letter would include expressions of regret, but no apology. Colin Powell gives a preview in commenting that the intensive negotiations exchange precise ideas on how to conclude the dispute. The metapragmatic attention to semantics is once again most salient in the article "'Bao' or 'Dao'? Seeking right sorry'" (*IHT*, April 10).

We can conclude that the method of finding a common understanding was extensively discussed in the US media but hardly mentioned in the Chinese text corpus. Most US reports hinted at the use of an official letter, some even discussed the number of drafts that led up to the final version. However, the eventual diplomatic solution, namely the approach of "one utterance, two interpretations" to the meaning of "sorry" via creative (mis)translation had not been predicted in the US media. The unbridgeable gap between the words "regret" and "apologize," so often discussed in the media, was eventually closed in the translation process in combination with the willingness of both sides to leave interpretive space to the other. The game played in the translation process is elaborated in the next subsection.

13.4.3 The Media's Interpretation of the "Two Very Sorries" Letter

The US issued an official English version of the letter presented to the Chinese Premier with the terms "sorry" clearly contextualized. Here are some extracts of the letter. The crucial parts are in **bold** [author's marks].

Both president Bush and Secretary of State Powell have **expressed their sincere regret** over your missing pilot and aircraft. Please convey to the Chinese people and to the family of pilot Wang Wei that **we are very sorry for their loss**.

Although the full picture of what transpired is still unclear, according to our information, our severely crippled aircraft made an emergency landing after following international emergency procedures. **We are very sorry the entering of** China's airspace **and the landing did not have verbal clearance**, but very pleased the crew landed safely.[18]

---

[17] *CNN online*, "Sorry is nice, but not what China wants," April 10.
[18] Ambassador Joseph W. Prueher's Letter to Foreign Minister Tang Jiaxuan," Beijing, China, April 11, 2011. Available at https://china.usc.edu/amb-prueher-foreign-minister-tang-ep-3-incident-2001. The Chinese version was accessed from www.usembassy-china.org.cn/press/release/2001/c/0113letter.html. The Chinese Foreign Ministry's translation of the letter was posted at www.fmprc.gov.cn/chn/ziliao/wzzt/2354/2355/2379/t111184.htm. These articles, unfortunately, are no longer retrievable.

The Chinese government first reported the US letter to the Chinese people in a press conference and on nationwide TV channels through a selection of quotes and paraphrases from the letter. In the press articles, crucial parts were edited out. These relied on the official translation by China's Foreign Ministry, which had been disseminated through the Chinese news agency Xinhua. The translation by the Chinese clearly chose lexicons in the Chinese language with the connotational value of an apology including assumption of responsibility, the very point the American authorities wanted to avoid. These terms differ from the Chinese translation offered by the US embassy, who had instantly released their Chinese version online. The official US translation of the letter into the Mandarin language used the following terms: *chengzhi de yihan* for the first expression of regret over the missing pilot and aircraft, *feichang wanxi* [in the sense of regret] for the first mentioning of sorry to the Chinese people and the pilot's family for their loss, and *feichang baoqian* [in the sense of a lighter apology] for the second "sorry" about the landing without verbal clearance. However, the translation by the Chinese Foreign Ministry, which was spread to the public via the official Chinese press agency Xinhua, used the terms with the stronger connotation. These were, in the same order *zhencheng de yihan*, *shenbiao qianyi* [deeply sorry in the sense of apology], *shenbiao qianyi*. Hence, the Chinese lexicons used in the American translation are weaker in illocutionary force than the Xinhua version. Where the Chinese interpreted the speech act as a real apology, the Americans insisted nothing much had changed in their stance. The latter simply repeated the expressions of regret for the missing pilot and added the phrase "very sorry that the entering of Chinese airspace and landing did not have verbal clearance." The possible alternative interpretation of the latter utterance in the sense of indirect criticism for not receiving clearance has been discussed earlier in this chapter. The Chinese media narratives, reporting the letter with indirect quotes or a paraphrase of the second "sorry" interpreted it unequivocally as a straight apology. Quite interestingly, while paraphrasing the statement, accounts differ in choice of material process verbs and adverbial qualifications, ranging from "sorry the plane landed without permission," to "sorry the plane violated Chinese airspace," and they prefer an active material process verb to the original relational process, thus placing more responsibility on the US. For example, in the article "US: we are 'very sorry'," published on April 12, the *CD* paraphrases the content of the letter in the following way: "He said on behalf of the US Government that they were very sorry for the **US plane entering** China's airspace and **landing** without verbal clearance."

As with the conclusions in the second subsection of this analysis, the Chinese papers do not bring up the semantic differences between the translations. The news of the letter is presented as a victory for the Chinese. In reporting the letter itself, it is said that the Americans offered their well-meant apologies for intruding on Chinese airspace and landing without verbal permission (*RMRB*, April 11). Selective quotes from the letter and interviews with Colin Powell enhance the impression the Chinese came out victorious in extracting an apology from the US. On April 11, the *RMRB* issues an article with the following headline "US Foreign Secretary recognizes a surveillance plane of the US army infringed Chinese territorial airspace" [author's translation]. Besides printing headlines such as "US spy plane did violate Chinese airspace: Powell" (April 11), the *PD* relays foreign media accounts with headlines such as "The side making mistake in collision apologizes: Laos" (*PD*, April 11). The presentation of the speech act as a real apology was to be expected, since an earlier report of the *RMRB* on April 11 had already (mis)translated Colin Powell's first use of the word "sorry" in an interview on April 8 into the term *daoqian*, which has an even stronger apologetic force with a connotation of admission of wrongdoing than the term *baoqian*, a slightly less formal apology that accepts responsibility. The focus in the Chinese press is on the humanitarian considerations for releasing the crew, and on appeals "to turn patriotic enthusiasm into strength to build a powerful nation" (*RMRB* Comment, April 12). In response to tough comments by the US after debriefing the US crew, the Foreign Ministry spokeswoman, Zhang Qiyue, accuses the US of neglecting the facts, reversing the truth and of shedding their responsibility.[19]

In the English-language *China Daily*, the emphasis is on the Chinese Foreign Minister's reaction to the letter, urging the US to take full responsibility, to provide a convincing explanation to the Chinese people, to stop reconnaissance activities, and to take actions to prevent recurrence. The ball is thus put in the US court.[20] In a *CD* commentary on April 11, "A step forward, no conclusion yet," the significance of the letter is explained as follows:

That the US government finally backed down from its aggressive no-apology stance, which had annoyed not only the Chinese but all upright people the world over, is certainly a welcome move toward the ultimate solution of the potentially explosive issue. That was the very least they should have done, and done earlier.

Negative portrayal of the Other pervades the entire corpus of Chinese texts and is also evident in this same article:

---

[19] *RMRB*, "Recent statements of US officials concerning the incident with two planes: Foreign Ministry Spokeswoman publishes her speech," April 16 (see also *PD*, "China refutes irresponsible comments of US side on collision incident," April 14).
[20] In the online *CD* article, "Breaking news: US says 'very sorry', 24 crew to leave China," part of the letter's content was first quoted indirectly. Not until the second half of the article did direct quotes appear. In the final version of the article, the direct quotes were deleted. Retrieved from www.chinadaily.net/cover/storydb/2001/04/11/mn.2brea.411.html; accessed on May 31, 2008, but no longer retrievable. A similar article, however, can be found at www.chinadaily.com.cn/en/doc/2001–04/12/content_51310.htm; accessed on October 23, 2021.

The difficulty of squeezing an expression of repentance from the US Government for its apparent wrong-doing in this case shows the magnitude of the US hegemony that is poisoning relations with many other countries besides China. [...] Neither intimidation nor condescension solves international conflicts. That the incident happened at all and became a damaging stalemate, was entirely because of US provocation and its subsequent unrepentance.

Disparaging comments about the US take precedence over a rational reflection on the various potential causes of the collision and on what factors precisely yielded the key to the détente.

Unlike the Chinese media approach, and also in line with the findings in the second subsection of the analysis, the US narratives again demonstrate substantial metapragmatic attention. They extensively discuss the semantic dimension of the letter on the macro-level of headlines, as well as in the body text itself.[21] The essence of what led to the resolution is widely discussed in the US sample. For example, the first report on the letter on *CNN* states that the negotiations boiled down to semantics and to nuances in translation and that, in the end, both claimed they had what they wanted. The perspectives of both sides get ample media mileage, but not without mentioning an interview with Colin Powell asserting "there was nothing to apologize for." *CNN* also features an analysis of how the Chinese propaganda campaign is alive and kicking in repeating Chinese media commentaries on how "the successful struggle against the US has again proven the ability of the Jiang-led party to take the long view, act wisely, and handle complicated situations." It also mentions how Chinese internet forums carry critical messages of the government for releasing the US crew without securing concrete concessions and points to the absence in the Chinese media of Colin Powell's subsequent remarks and of any metapragmatic discussions of the real significance of the letter.[22] In a survey of eleven days of behind-the-scenes decision making in Beijing corridors, Lam chronicles how President Jiang Zemin suggested Beijing should drop some hints to Washington on how to climb down without losing face. Alternative expressions would be offered to the Bush team to circumvent a full-fledged apology. The term *baoqian* is said to be considered by many Chinese to be just one rung down the philological ladder from apology, or *daoqian*.[23] The final solution is deemed a testimony to pragmatism for both sides, although the Chinese were reportedly "convinced they had dominated the negotiations from day one."

---

[21] Examples of headlines are: "Careful language breaks Washington-Beijing impasse" (*CNN*, April 11), "Precise language secures release of US spy plane crew: US-China standoff: a study in semantics" (*CNN*, April 12); "Chinese-US word game again helps to salve historic wounds" (*IHT*, April 12).

[22] "Propaganda campaign cranks up" (*CNN*, April 12).

[23] Interestingly, the same metaphor is used in *The Independent*, which prints an article on April 12 giving agency to the US in building a ladder for the Chinese to climb down ("Wording built a ladder for China to climb down").

Besides printing the original letter verbatim, much attention in the US press goes to official Chinese reactions and media comments as well as quotes from Chinese scholars and vox-pop interviews. The *IHT* editorials, reprinted from the *NYT* and the *WP*, call Beijing's approach needlessly confrontational at times, but argue that in the end both governments acted sensibly. A comment on April 14 finds the idea that a slow-moving, propeller-driven surveillance plane flying on autopilot rammed into a Chinese jet fighter ludicrous. But since Chinese leaders are seen to have "lacked the self-confidence to admit this," the Bush team is said to have "wisely found a way to apologize without really apologizing."[24] Clearly, most articles in the US press emphasize that the US letter expressed sorrow and regret but did not accept responsibility.

13.5 Discussion

This study shows how factual reality can adopt many faces in a reconstructed media reality. It primarily focused on the significance of the speech acts of apologizing and expressing regret, and on the role of the media in constructing, interpreting, and translating these verbal acts. The journey to arrive at mutually agreeable language was a long dialogical process trying to reconcile divergent national perspectives, while at the same time placating domestic sensitivities. These multiple constituencies make the process of apology-making quite challenging. In this case, the right balance had to be struck in a two-level game of making mutual concessions up to a point still palatable to the respective domestic hardliners (Yee 2004). Besides the interactive level occurring between the various versions of apology/expressions of regret and the response by the stakeholders, one cannot neglect the constitutive role of the media discourse leading up to and following the final US speech act.

Evidence of the evolutionary and negotiated nature of apologies is given by the various forms of the US expressions of regret over the eleven days' standoff, climaxing in the letter of two "very sorries." In the first few days after the collision, the absence of contrition from the US government occasioned in-depth discussion in the Chinese media, enlisting comments from domestic sources as well as foreign dignitaries siding with the Chinese. The components of what is counted as a speech act of apology (including showing remorse and using the IFID "apologize") are widely discussed in the Chinese media prior to the announcement of the decisive letter. In support of Jeffries' (2007) argument, there appears to be a clear agreement among civil society, including the media both in the US and China, on what constitutes an apology. Precise, culturally determined ideas circulate of what components are

---

[24] "Continue building bridges and Beijing regime will weaken" (*IHT*, April 14).

considered essential for the speech act to be counted as an acceptable apology in their respective discursive communities.

A perceived evasion of US responsibility is the main argument pervading most Chinese accounts of the incident. They all seem to reflect a clear set of cultural expectations as to what constitutes a valid apology as a formal speech act. As Harris et al. (2006) argue, it is precisely because the audience of the public apology does have a sense of what makes up an "unequivocal apology" that the discourse struggle is continued. In our case study, it is the Chinese sense of what a sincere apology should sound like and the American understanding of the repercussions of a formal apology, which protract the standoff. Additionally, the fact that the Chinese media keep insisting on some extra sign of remorse by the US, more explicit than a mere "regret," supports Jeffries' (2007) argument that sincerity is a condition for the success of the apology and that it is the way the apology sounds to the hearers which determines whether what is said is counted as an apology.

Domestication theory holds that in international news coverage, national media usually "rally around the flag." Our findings suggest that the media in the protagonist countries defended the official line, albeit to a lesser extent in the US media. Criticism of the Bush administration's handling of the affair, as well as overall balanced accounts giving both perspectives, appeared across the US corpus.

The actual key to the détente, namely the willingness of both sides to leave room for multiple interpretations and the acceptance of diverging translations of the "very sorry" letter, was devised behind closed diplomatic doors, but speculations about the possible wording of the letter abounded in all papers, except in the Chinese corpus. It is hard to determine to what extent the media contributed to breaking the impasse. Yet, the extensive discussion in editorials or via quotes in vox-pop interviews or comments from Chinese experts in US–China relations of what was deemed (im)possible, (un)acceptable, (un)advisable, or morally (in)appropriate and (un)fair, must have given some sort of indication to policymakers of the limits to any concessions/demands and the degree of flexibility in the semantic lines that had so far been drawn in the sand.

The question whether the actual letter was successful as a speech act of apology, thus enabling the reader to determine the victor in this duel, drew much metapragmatic attention in the US papers, but not in the Chinese press. The large majority of the US accounts lingered on the absence of the illocutionary force indicating advice (IFID) "apology" and the ensuing comments by Colin Powell that the letter was not an apology. Equal attention went to the overall claims in the Chinese media of gaining a victory by extracting an apology from the US. Given the extensive meta-discussion in the US papers on the interpretation of the letter, we can argue that journalists can have a powerful role as "ideological brokers" (Blommaert 1999), influencing the way the apologetic words are received. In the foreign press, the words of "apology" were mostly discounted as a mere smokescreen or a quasi-apology with just enough ambiguity to mollify public opinion. As much as the essence of the speech act was discussed in the US articles, as salient appears to be the absence of metapragmatic discussion about the letter in the Chinese narratives after April 10. The Chinese government clearly steered away from an in-depth language analysis after the announcement of the letter. This argument is supported by the reaction of the Foreign Ministry spokesman, Sun Yuxi, in answering a metapragmatic probe into the actual change in the US position during a press conference as follows: "it is up to you to interpret the changes." This brings the Chinese philosopher Chuang Tzu's words to mind: "Words are for catching ideas; once you've caught the idea, you can forget about the words." It appears that the Chinese government primarily wanted to instill the idea of victory in the minds of the Chinese people and then move the attention from the language issue away to "turn patriotic enthusiasm into strength to build a powerful nation" (Comment *RMRB*, April 12).

The US corpus, by contrast, indicates how most journalists interpreted the resolution to lie in the arduously negotiated language allowing China to assert it won a moral victory, while the US could say it simply expressed humanitarian sympathy and regret. The compromise phrasing of the letter was welcomed in most comments and editorials as a skillful piece of diplomacy or "a carefully choreographed game, by both, of propaganda blended with diplomacy."[25] The resolution was a "matter of what the 'US chose to say and China chose to hear',"[26] in other words "one utterance, variable interpretations," or what language pragmatics is all about.

References

Austin, John. 1962, 1975. *How to Do Things with Words*. Oxford: Oxford University Press.
Avruch, Kevin, and Zheng Wang. 2005. "Culture, Apology, and International Negotiation: The Case of the Sino-U.S. 'Spy Plan' Crisis." *International Negotiation* 10: 337–353.
Blommaert, Jan. 1999. *Language Ideological Debates*. Berlin: Mouton de Gruyter.
Brown, Penelope, and Stephen C. Levinson. 1987. *Politeness: Some Universals in Language Use*. Cambridge: Cambridge University Press.
Blum-Kulka, Shoshana, Juliane House, and Gabriele Kasper (Eds.). 1989. *Cross-Cultural Pragmatics: Requests and Apologies*. Norwood, NJ: Ablex.
Chang, Deng-ji. 2001. "從宏觀歷史視野解讀美「中」軍機碰撞事故— 一次對「現狀霸權」與「新興大國」共容性的考驗 [Interpreting/Decoding the

---

[25] *The Times*, "Stand-off: the American backlash that China should fear," Editorial, April 6, p.23.
[26] *WP*, "Resolving crisis was a matter of interpretation," April 12.

'Sino'-American EP3 Collision Incident from a Macro-Historical Point of View]." *Chinese Communist Party Studies* 27(5): 104–106.
Cohen, Raymond. 1997. *Negotiating Across Cultures: International Communication in an Interdependent World*. Rev. ed. Washington, DC: United States Institute of Peace Press.
Cummings, Louise. 2005. *Pragmatics: A Multidisciplinary Perspective*. Edinburgh: Edinburgh University Press.
Eckholm, Eric. 2001. "US Crew Destroyed Secrets, Aides Assert." *International Herald Tribune*, April 14–15, p. 1.
Ensor, David. 2001. "CNN Breaking News: China Promises Releases of U.S. Crew Members." *CNN* April 11. http://transcripts.cnn.com/TRANSCRIPTS/0104/11/bn.24.html.
Entman, Robert M. 1993. "Framing: Toward Clarification of a Fractured Paradigm." *Journal of Communication* 43(4): 51–58.
Gries, Peter H., and Kaiping Peng. 2002. "Culture Clash? Apologies East and West." *Journal of Contemporary China* 11(30): 173–178.
Harris, Sandra, Karen Grainger, and Louise Mullany. 2006. "The Pragmatics of Political Apologies." *Discourse & Society* 17(6): 715–737.
Hessler, Peter. 2006. *Oracle Bones: A Journey between China's Past and Present*. New York: Harper Collins.
Jeffries, Lesley. 2007. "Journalistic Constructions of Blair's 'Apology' for the Intelligence Leading to the Iraq War." In *Language in the Media, Representations, Identities, Ideologies*, ed. by Sally Johnson and Astrid Ensslin, 48–69. London: Continuum.
Keefe, John. 2002. "A Tale of 'Two Very Sorries' Redux." *Far Eastern Economic Review* 21(03): 30–33.
Lams, Lutgard. 2005. "Language and Politics in the Chinese English-Language Newspaper *The China Daily*." *The Stockholm Journal of East-Asian Studies* 15: 109–137.
Lams, Lutgard. 2010. "Linguistic Tools of Empowerment and Alienation in the Chinese Official Press." *Pragmatics* 20(3): 315–342.
Lams, Lutgard. 2019. "Ideological Patterns in Chinese State Media Narratives Concerning Issues of Security and Sovereignty." In *Routledge Handbook of Chinese Discourse Analysis*, ed. by Chris C. Shei, 444–457. Oxford: Routledge.
Leech, Geoffrey. 1983. *Principles of Pragmatics*. London: Longman.
Lewis, Margaret K. 2002. "An Analysis of State Responsibility for the Chinese–American Airplane Collision Incident." *The New York University Law Review* 77: 1404–1441.
Mills, Sara. 2003. *Gender and Politeness*. Cambridge: Cambridge University Press.
Olshtain, Elite, and Andrew Cohen. 1983. "Apology: A Speech Act Set." In *Sociolinguistics and Language Acquisition*, ed. by Nessa Wolfson and Elliot Judd, 18–35. Rowley, MA: Newbury House.
Pruitt, Dean, and Sung Hee Kim. 2004. *Social Conflict: Escalation, Stalemate, and Settlement*. 3rd ed. Boston, MA: McGraw Hill.
Robinson, Jeffrey D. 2004. "The Sequential Organization of 'Explicit' Apologies in Naturally Occurring English." *Research in Language and Social Interaction* 37(3): 291–330.

Scollon, Ron. 2000. "Generic Variability in News Stories in Chinese and English: A Contrastive Discourse Study of Five Days' Newspapers." *Journal of Pragmatics* 32(6): 761–791.
Searle, John R. 1969. *Speech Acts: An Essay in the Philosophy of Language.* Cambridge: Cambridge University Press.
Solomon, Richard H. 1999. *Chinese Negotiating Behavior: Pursuing Interests Through "Old Friends"* Washington, DC: United States Institute of Peace Press.
Suszczyńska, Małgorzata. 1999. "Apologizing in English, Polish and Hungarian: Different Languages, Different Strategies." *Journal of Pragmatics* 31: 1053–1065.
United Nations. 1982. *United Nations Convention on the Law of the Sea.* www.un.org/depts/los/convention_agreements/texts/unclos/unclos_e.pdf.
Yamazaki, Jane W. 2004. "Crafting the Apology: Japanese Apologies to South-Korea in 1990." *Asian Journal of Communication* 14(2): 156–173.
Yee, Albert S. 2004. "Semantic Ambiguity and Joint Deflections in the Hainan Negotiation." *China: An International Journal* 2(1): 53–82.
Yule, George. 1996. *Pragmatics.* Oxford: Oxford University Press.
Zhang, Hang. 2001. "Culture and Apology: The Hainan Island Incident." *World Englishes* 20(3): 383–391.

14 Constructing Identities in Crisis Situations
A Study of the "Volunteer" in the Spanish and English Press

María del Mar Sánchez Ramos

14.1 Introduction

The media are increasingly used as resources for studying how topics such as immigration (Blinder and Allen 2016; Taylor 2009), ideology (Vessey 2013), identity (Caballero-Mengibar 2015), and other social processes are represented (Branun and Charteris-Black 2015). These studies illustrate the potential of linguistic analysis in providing insight into various sociocultural phenomena. There is no doubt that the choice of language can shape public perception of a particular subject, with the result that the choice of linguistic mechanisms, such as the use of metaphor or lexical selection, is not neutral.

Emergency situations seem also to be frequent in our world. Governments and public institutions of the countries affected and the countries that offer help are well aware of the different needs (i.e., linguistic and cultural) associated with these situations. The United Nations Office for Disaster and Risk Reduction (2009) defines "crisis" as "[a] serious disruption of the functioning of a community or a society involving widespread human, material, economic or environmental losses, which exceeds the ability of the affected community or society to cope."[1] This definition, as Pena Díaz (2019) states, encompasses numerous crisis situations, including natural disasters, terrorist attacks, outbursts of violence, and any other situation requiring action by emergency services to ensure the safety of the population. Indeed, volunteers can cover different fields of action in emergency or crisis situations, and they are mostly related to communication tasks.

Communication is essential in crisis situations if messages are to be transmitted successfully. Such communication is not only necessary between peers and public organizations and administrations, but also with and between the

---

[1] *2009 UNISDR Terminology on Disaster Risk Reduction*, www.unisdr.org/files/7817_UNISDR TerminologyEnglish.pdf.

people affected by these situations (Pena Díaz 2019). In this context, communication is even more crucial in multilingual settings, where rapid, concise and immediate information may have to be given in different languages to mitigate the negative effects of an emergency.

Voluntary work is not an activity that has emerged recently (Robinson 2015). However, situations have arisen in the last few years that could be described as crisis or emergency situations, in response to which various non-governmental institutions (NGOs) and organizations have put forward the volunteer as their principal agent. The recent refugee crisis, also known as the European migrant crisis, started around 2015–2016 and has sparked episodes that have been captured in the press, for example. We should always be aware that a news item can have immediate repercussions. In this respect, its ultimate purpose, besides that of communicating information, is to attract an audience by focusing on a particular discourse. Consequently, a study of the discourses produced by the media can help us learn how an event or a group of social actors are represented or constructed.

The media (i.e., the written or digital press) are often analyzed through the prism of discourse analysis (DA), and more specifically through approaches known as Critical Discourse Analysis (CDA). These are qualitative approaches that clearly provide information about the symbolic load that the press constructs, while the press also reproduces ideologies among the dominant groups. These qualitative approaches make increasing use of quantitative methodologies such as corpus linguistics (CL), which analyzes large volumes of texts with tools that provide statistical information about the frequency of certain words or lexical and grammatical patterns. Although there are a considerable number of studies on the media and crisis situations, such as refugees, migrants and asylum seekers (Baker et al. 2013, 2008; Taylor 2014, 2009), this chapter concentrates on the under-represented figure of the volunteer. Using a corpus-assisted discourse (CADS) framework, we will examine media discourses of volunteering in the English and Spanish press during 2016 to 2019.

The chapter begins with a contextualization of the study by focusing attention on the third sector and the figure of the volunteer. Following a theoretical appraisal of these concepts, the quantitative and qualitative approaches underpinning this study are presented, namely CL and CADS. The methodological section describes the compilation of the corpus and the analytical techniques employed in the study. Following the analysis and discussion, the chapter concludes with a reflection on the results.

14.2 The Third Sector and Volunteering

The figure of the volunteer is closely related to the development of society (López Franco and Shahrokh 2015). Volunteering is also related to the concept of civil society, a concept defined by Ehrenberg (1999, 161) as "a sphere of mediating organizations between the individual and the state." Civil society, as Robinson (2015) also describes, displays a range of meanings and usually refers to the various non-government and non-profit organizations that address a variety of the needs of the different members of a community. Although volunteering action can take place in various sectors of the economy, research is generally focused on the so-called "third sector."

One of the first challenges of examining the third sector is to agree on a definition, since it varies according to the geographical area. As Eschweiler and Hulgård (2018) recognize, there are two lines of thought: on the one hand, a European conceptualization, in which the idea of the social economy is utilized; and on the other hand, an Anglo-American perspective, in which the term "third sector" is explicitly used (Defourny et al. 2016). This distinction is very much in line with the concept of social innovation to which Moulaert et al. (2018) refer. The third sector plays a major role in satisfying the social needs of the population in areas of action that are beyond the reach of public organizations and institutions.

As indicated in the exhaustive report by Enjolras et al. (2014, 4), in order to be considered part of the third sector, entities must:

1. have a legally binding social mission that may limit the surplus generated by their activities;
2. be prohibited from distributing any more than 50 percent of any profit they may earn to any stakeholders or investors; and
3. operate under a "capital lock" that requires that all retained profits must be used to support the organization or, in the case of its dissolution or conversion, to support another entity with a similar social purpose.

In a more recent work, Salamon and Sokolowski (2016) include within the third sector those organizations or institutions that meet the following requirements:

1. It is an organization, that is, institutionalized to some extent, though not necessarily legally registered or constituted.
2. It totally or significantly limits through some binding provision distributing any surplus generated from its activities to its directors, employees, investors, or others.
3. It is self-governing, that is, it is institutionally separate from government, is able to control its own general policies and transactions, and has the capacity to own assets, incur liabilities, or engage in transactions in its own right.

4. It is non-compulsory, that is, involving some meaningful degree of uncoerced free choice on the part of individuals working for, or participating in, its activities.
5. It is private, i.e., not controlled by government.

In the specific case of Spain, the data published by the PwC Foundation (2018) are extremely insightful:

The Third Sector's importance in Spain is borne out by the almost 30,000 organizations that make up the sector, the more than seven million people they attend to annually, the €10,500 million managed or the more than two million people, including volunteers and employees, who work daily in the fight against poverty and social exclusion. Particularly relevant is the Third Sector's role especially in hard times, for example, during the years of the economic crisis. During this period, sector organizations played an essential role in mitigating the undesirable effects of the crisis for the population.

Due in great part to a sense of engagement and responsibility, being part of society can reorient citizens about the notion of "the good citizen" and provide communities with a sense of cooperation and responsibility (Yap et al. 2011). This idea of being part of a community is seen as a means for citizens to overcome individualism and selfishness (Ehrenberg 1999, 233).

Volunteering usually relates to a non-remunerated activity, and also to the third sector and, more specifically, to non-governmental institutions. The term "volunteering," whose origins go back to the nineteenth century (Lough 2015), is complex, spanning different sectors and social classes. The motivations behind a volunteering activity can be equally diverse. Therefore, as in the case of the third sector, volunteering as a concept does not lend itself to a single conceptualization (Courtney 2002). According to the work conducted by Kelemen et al. (2017), there are three schools of thought that conceptualize volunteering: (1) based on the nature of the activities undertaken (active vs. passive; discretionary vs. compulsory); (2) based on the purpose of volunteering (e.g., for an organization, for a community); and (3) based on the duration of the volunteering activities (short or long periods).[2]

Various definitions can also be found for the term "volunteer." Jenner (1982, 30) defines a volunteer as "a person who, out of free will and without wages, works for a not-for-profit organization which is formally organized and has as its purpose service to someone or something other than its membership." Howards and Burns (2015, 12–14) define volunteers in accordance with the activity they perform and state that "[the volunteers are] well placed to respond

---

[2] It is beyond the scope of this chapter to elaborate on the various types of volunteering, so we refer the reader to the works by Rodell (2013), Holmes and Smith (2012), and Tomazos and Luke (2015).

to some of the big challenges of the new development landscape," as well as being entrusted with "navigation values that are embedded in power relations."

Different studies focus on the volunteer from different perspectives. As stated above, there are several conceptual research studies based on providing an adequate definition of the volunteer (Howards and Burns 2015). Other scholars, such as Robinson (2015) and Bartram (2017), are good examples of studies that depict the intrinsic motivation of the volunteer in society. Closely related to volunteering is the coined term "voluntourism," – a highly topical term that refers to a very specific type of volunteering practiced by young people – "a popular form of travel for young tourists in which adventure travel is paired with short-term 'volunteer' placements in host communities around the countries of the global South" (Calkin 2014, 30). Particularly interesting for this research is the paper presented by Yap et al. (2011), where attention is set on the role of refugees as volunteers. Other studies focus on volunteer translators and interpreters in crisis situations (Al-Shehari 2020), volunteers and their impact in NGOs (Kartika Dewi et al. 2019), or research on volunteering and self-identity (Grönlund 2011).

14.3 Corpus-Assisted Discourse Analysis

Corpora are an essential source for the quantitative analysis of language through specialized computer programs (e.g., AntConc, Wordsmith, Sketch Engine, or LancBox). However, these apparently quantitative data also allow room for another type of qualitative analysis in the form of collocations and concordances as examples of grammatical and lexical patterns, and their interpretation in discourse. As Jaworska states (2016): "insights derived from corpus research have increased our understanding of language use by providing empirical evidence for the existence of regularities and patterns that are not immediately visible to the naked eye." Corpus analysis tools usually provide information about word frequency, wordlists, so-called keywords, concordances and collocations. The first of these – frequency, makes reference to the number of items that appear in the corpus. What are known as frequency lists are usually generated and they can provide information about the words used most in the corpus, as well as where they are found there. Thus, with respect to the most frequent words, certain patterns in the regularity of their appearance in the text may be observed. Wordlists are "lists of corpus words in alphabetical or frequency order, upon which further data (such as keywords) may be generated" (Calzada Pérez 2017, 241). Next, keywords are the result of statistical comparison (e.g., log-likelihood or chi-square tests) between the terms in the wordlist and a reference corpus (Scott 2010), and they are usually words that denote the specificity of a corpus. Thirdly, there are concordances, through which words or groups of words selected in context can be studied. The word searched for appears in the middle and is known as a Key Word in Context (KWIC). Finally, there are functions for the analysis of collocations, defined by McEnery and Hardie (2012, 123) as "a co-occurrence pattern that exists between two items that frequently occur in proximity to one another – but not necessarily adjacently or, indeed, in any fixed order." Another definition that is considered to be very appropriate is that made by Stubbs (2001: 35), who states that collocations are not just lexical elements, but "are also widely shared within a speech community," and are associated with "nodes around which ideological battles are fought." Calzada Pérez points to other data of a more statistical nature (2017, 241):

1. corpus, text, and sentence (average) word length;
2. standardized type/token ratio (STTR): the ratio of the different words (i.e., types) in the corpus to the total number of words (tokens). STTR is normally calculated in sets of 1,000 words and then an average is established. It may be used to measure the degree of lexical variety in corpora. Consequently, STTR standard deviation (STTR SD) is a good indication the homogeneity/ heterogeneity of the lexis within each corpus.
3. significance (p-value) figures as measured by log-likelihood or chi-square.

The combination of the quantitative methods provided by corpora and the qualitative methods inherent in discourse analysis leads to mixed-method approaches such as CADS (Partington 2004; Partington et al. 2013). CADS-based methodology uses quantitative methods drawn from CL, as referred to earlier, which tie together with the qualitative techniques employed in DA. In this way, together with the data provided by the corpus analysis tools, such as wordlists or word frequency, a more qualitative reading of the texts can be monitored, with the aim of explaining the reasons behind these statistics. This explanation is frequently examined taking close account of the social, political and historical context (Partington 2014). Examples of research undertaken in CADS are extremely varied. There are studies that perform comparative studies from a diachronic point of view, as in the case of Calzada Pérez (2017). In this work, the author employs CADS as a methodology for comparing the original discourses of the European parliament in English and in translation. The use of CADS has also yielded results in the field of political discourse (Caballero-Mengibar 2015), the construction of nationalism and identity (Jaworska 2016; Vessey 2013, 2016), and discourse analysis in the press (Taylor 2009; Al Fajri 2019), in addition to the depiction of immigrants in the British and Italian press (Baker et al. 2013; Taylor 2014).

There are also authors who advocate the use of CL in CDA in order to provide greater objectivity (Taylor and Marchi 2018); these include Partington and Marchi (2015) and Partington et al. (2013). According to Taylor (2020, 21), this research is founded on the concept of similarity because "it involves the search for 'usuality' and repeated patterns of behaviour." Another example can be found in the words of Marchi and Taylor (2009), who state that CL is based on a descriptive study characterized by its objectivity and based on data, which leads to reliable and generalizable results, whereas CDA is an eminently qualitative approach grounded in a theory-driven framework and relying on samples selected subjectively, which lead to investigation that is also subjective. This is why the combination of CL and CDA can provide a line of investigation into a variety of social issues, such as ideology, political conflicts, immigrants and refugees or ethnic minorities. As a principal source of data, the media – the press, for example – are seen to be the main resource. The work of Baker et al. (2008) serves as one of the most representative examples; this influential piece of research combines CL and CDA. Both methodologies are employed to describe how the image of the so-called RASIM (refugees, asylum seekers, immigrants and migrants) was constructed in the British press during the period 1996–2005. These scholars offer a diachronic and synchronic study based on the analysis of frequencies, lexical patterns and concordances. Some of their most relevant results show that the British press tends to paint a negative picture of these groups. Scholars who have followed in the footsteps of Baker et al. (2008) are Taylor (2009) and, more recently, Blinder and Allen (2016).

As stated by (Robinson 2015), discourse is not only a reflection of society, but it also constructs the way people think and represent social practice. Analyzing how volunteering is represented in discourse (e.g., in the media) can give some insights into how it is discursively constructed and reflects the dominant discourse in a specific context such as crisis situations. With relation to the main theme of the current study, there are various studies about volunteers in their different conceptualizations. For example, Yap et al. (2011) investigate the representation of the refugee as a volunteer through discourse analysis. Similarly, Sin (2010) carries out a qualitative study of interviews with a group of young people on their volunteering trip to South Africa, with the aim of learning about the different motivations that led them to take this trip. Robinson (2015) also uses CDA to establish a discursive representation of the motivation and the ideology of a group of volunteers in the United Kingdom. As mentioned by Al Fajri (2019: 168) regarding CADS studies and the media, "what might be highlighted from these previous studies is that a range of corpus techniques can effectively assist (critical) discourse analysts to find patterns of particular grammatical and word choices that contribute to the representation of certain realities for the reader, suggesting that news represent particular ideologies."

Table 14.1 *VOLUNTEER-COR:*
A comparable corpus of volunteering in crisis situations

Corpus	Words
TheGuardian_EN	915,590
ElPais_ES	898,669

14.4 Methodology

Our research is based on the analysis of the VOLUNTEER-COR corpus, which is made up of newspaper articles about volunteering in the European migrant or refugee crisis published in *El País* (Spain) and *The Guardian* (United Kingdom) from 2016 to 2019. These newspapers are daily liberals – left-of-center-tendency newspapers. VOLUNTEER-COR consists of 1,200 articles with 1,814,259 words. The corpus was compiled semi-automatically using the database Lexis Nexis (see Table 14.1). Although the corpus was not compiled manually, the results obtained were carefully checked and revised in order to avoid inappropriate data, such as additional metadata or irrelevant information. It also has to be stated that this is a preliminary study, and the corpus is still being compiled.[3]

We used the *Sketch Engine* software for our analysis as it allows the creation of consistency lists to identify words that are shared across different texts and therefore the identification of keywords in each text to reveal repeated patterns. This software also provides the statistical functions needed for the analysis, such as the frequency of words.

The main analytic procedure is usually based on a keyword and collocational analysis. Keyword analysis is focused on words "which occur with unusual frequency in a given text ... by comparison with a reference corpus of some kind" (Scott 1997, 236). In this line, the way words are grouped provides representations of socioculturally significant concepts and helps identify discursive patterns. Although keyword analysis has certain limitations, it helps to introduce objectivity into the selection of discourse features for analysis (Robinson 2015). Regarding keyness, Baker et al. (2008, 278) define it "as the statistically significant higher frequency of particular words or clusters in the corpus under analysis in comparison with another corpus." High-frequency words will provide a clue about the semantic domains of the corpus. Examining and comparing the frequency lists or words will "reveal aspects of identity

---

[3] This research was carried out within the framework of the project Original, translated and interpreted representations of the refugee cris(e)s: methodological triangulation within corpus-based discourse studies (PID2019-108866RB-100), funded by the Spanish Ministry of Science and Innovation.

constructions" (Jaworska 2016). Also, keywords "may be shown to be indicative of the writer's position and identity, as well as the discourse community with its values and beliefs about the subject matter" (Bondi 2001, 7). Keyword analysis compares the corpus under study with a refence corpus in order to identify those words that are significantly more frequent in that corpus than in the reference corpus. By doing this, keywords are "items of unusual frequency in a given corpus" (Calzada Pérez 2017) and offer valuable information about the specificity of the corpus. In the analysis, we used the Bank of English (BoE) corpus and Corpus de Referencia del Español Actual (CREA) as our reference corpora for the English and Spanish sub-corpora respectively. Finally, collocation analysis is always crucial to understanding how words (here, volunteering in a crisis situation) are discursively constructed. Defined by McEnery and Wilson (1996, 123) as "a co-occurrence pattern that exists between two items that frequently occur in proximity to one another – but not necessarily adjacently or, indeed, in any fixed order," collocations can be used to reveal discursive patterns.

14.5 Analysis and Results

After comparing each of the corpora with a reference corpus (BoE for TheGuardian_EN and CREA for ElPais_ES corpus), we obtained two keyword lists. *Sketch Engine* ranks the keywords by their keyness score. As both generated keywords include thousands of keywords, we took into consideration the top fifty key keywords to focus our analysis (see Table 14.2). Our keyword analysis shows that the corpora (ElPais_ES) and (TheGuardian_EN) have great similarity in the most significant topics covered. The semantic areas covered by both corpora are: volunteering, immigration, refugees, disasters and crisis. For instance, ElPais_ES contains keywords such as *migrantes* [migrants], *voluntarios* [volunteers], *ONGs* [non-governmental organizations], *fronteras* [borders], *crisis* [crisis], *solidaridad* [solidarity], *España* [Spain], *país* [country], *Aquarius* and *internacional* [international]. TheGuardian_EN is focused on topics covered by the words 'volunteers,' 'refugees,' 'disasters,' 'immigration,' 'Brexit,' and 'crisis.'

As Baker (2010) explains, "a corpus assisted analysis of discourse is therefore reliant on qualitative methods of analysis as well as those that are more traditionally quantitative." The next step was thus to examine words that were identified as being quantitatively important in the texts and interpret them alongside the social and background events which could have influenced the patterns found in the data. As the study is aiming to elicit information about the identity construction of the volunteer, attention is focused on the lemma 'volunteer' (noun and adjective) in both corpora as it obtained a high frequency rank in the keyword analysis.

Regarding the collocational analysis, and to be as precise as possible, this research is narrowed down to a window of the five closest words (−5 to +5) to left and right of the node, that is, 'volunteer.' Collocation analysis provides information about the grammatical structure and the minimum occurrence of the collocates. A detailed collocation analysis of the lemma 'volunteer' reveals that volunteering is constructed as a helping activity in the comparable corpus, which draws on a humanitarian discourse. The volunteer is envisioned as a caring person who has a social responsibility (Yap et al. 2011). Using lexical items typically associated with community involvement and social responsibility, the volunteer is discursively constructed as a person who helps tackle a crisis or an emergency. Examples of humanitarian and social discourse can be found in both corpora. Regarding the English corpus (TheGuardian_EN) and the humanitarian discourse, it was observed that the lemma 'volunteer' is associated with some specific working groups (e.g., worker, teacher, interpreter, nurse, lawyer or police), which shows the wide range of groups of social workers involved in a crisis situation. Indeed, it also contributes to the visibility of the role of the volunteer. The lemma 'volunteer' is also the subject of action verbs such as 'help,' 'work,' 'attend,' 'provide,' 'bring,' 'give,' 'come' or 'commit' (see Table 14.2).

The Spanish corpus (ElPais_ES) also offers examples of the humanitarian and social discourse. In the first case, the lemma 'volunteer' is related to *abogados* [lawyers], *traductores* [translators], *intérpretes* [interpreters] or *policías* [police]. There are other examples that give a more specific picture of the volunteer as pertaining to different local communities, NGOs or institutions: volunteer *de la ONG*. The volunteer, in contrast with the English corpus, has also an identity and belongs to a geographical community (Noun + Adjective as modifier): *voluntarios andaluces, voluntarios jerezanos, voluntarios tarifeños* or *voluntarios de Tarifa*, referring to the different places volunteers are from. The humanitarian discourse is also constructed with grammatical patterns (subject + active verb), where the word 'volunteer' is the subject of verbs such as *asistir* [attend], *ayudar* [help], *dar* [give] or *proporcionar* [provide] (see Table 14.3).

Table 14.2 *Most frequent collocates for the lemma 'volunteer' (TheGuardian_EN)*

Collocates	Frequency	Mutual information score
work	54	12.34
help	45	12.21
thousands	40	11.32
group	35	11.15
gather	30	10.56
recruit	12	9.41
support	10	9.15
dozens	8	8.89

Table 14.3 *Most frequent collocates for the lemma 'volunteer'* (ElPais_ES)

Collocates	Frequency	Mutual information score
ayudan [help]	42	12.25
Miles [thousands]	36	11.70
solidaridad [solidarity]	22	11.50
denuncian [speak out]	15	11.34
dan alojamiento [give shelter]	20	10.12
arriesgan [risk]	12	9.76
activistas [activists]	10	9.56
luchan [struggle]	7	9.23

As mentioned before, a feature in both corpora is the pervasive use of terms closely connected to the humanitarian role played by volunteers in our society and exemplified in constructions such as:

1. Volunteers can help people stay in their homes, rather than be admitted to hospital [...].
2. The Red Cross has deployed hundreds of staff and volunteers to the area [...].

This finding reveals that, just as for the reference corpus, both the English and Spanish corpora draw on a humanitarian discourse of helping. The volunteer appears as a caring person who feels a social responsibility to help tackle a crisis or emergency.. However, and closely related to the new values of the volunteer as part of civil society (Robinson 2015), a close observation of the Spanish corpus shows there is a non-neutral discourse in line with the construction of volunteering as social change (Yap et al. 2011). This "politicized" discourse (Yap et al. 2011) is based upon the idea of the volunteer as "activist," that is, as a person who resists power and struggles against injustice. It is evident, however, that the Spanish media also empower the volunteer as a person who addresses injustices and wants to change society. Indeed, this "politicized" discourse gives volunteers the voice to exercise their power.

3. También los voluntarios son activistas, que intentan hacer de este mundo un mundo mejor. [The volunteers are also activists who try to make this world a better place]
4. Un grupo de voluntarios denuncia la situación actual de los refugiados. [A group of volunteers speak out against the current situation of the refugees]

5. Los grupos de voluntarios luchan por un mundo digno para la población migrante recién llegada. [A group of volunteers struggle for an equal world for the newly arrived migrant population]

We can see that there is a highly generalized discourse of the volunteer as a caring person revolving around a humanitarian role in both corpora. However, the construction of the volunteer as an activist and as a person able to change society is highlighted in the Spanish corpus. It is worth bearing in mind here that Spain is a country characterized by a high influx of immigrants. Also, the Spanish NGO called Open Arms took an important role during the European refugee crisis, which may explain the construction of the volunteer as an activist (Open Arms and Aquarius were among the top fifty keywords in the Spanish corpus).

14.6 Conclusion

The media have a direct influence on the social representation of different sectors and the way society today perceives reality. The present study sought to provide some exploratory research into how the English and Spanish press constructed the identity of the volunteer in one of the most serious crises or emergency situations of our century in Europe, the refugee crisis in the period 2016–2019. Unlike previous studies on refugees, migrants and asylum seekers that focus on the media representations of these groups of people or interventions from governments, NGOs, etc., this study concentrates its attention on volunteers – a group that has received little attention.

The study employed a CADS approach, and thus utilized both quantitative and qualitative analysis. The quantitative methods were applied to extract statistical data about the most frequent words (keywords) and collocations while the qualitative methods provided information to interpret the data, thereby revealing the discourse that the press constructs around the volunteer. In the study, the comparable corpus reveals similarities in the discursive constructions, where the volunteer acquires an identity and is depicted as involved in the crisis situation as a humanitarian agent. There is also a shift of discourse in the Spanish press, where the media empower the volunteer as an activist in crisis situations. In fact, as other studies have also revealed (Yap et al. 2011), the current study also supports the idea of the construction of the volunteer as part of the humanitarian discourse of "good citizen" and the "politicized" discourse of the volunteer as "activist."

By way of conclusion, this study contributes to the existing scholarship on the extremely important role of the media in the construction and representation of ideologies and identities of minorities. It also serves as a starting point for future research that will help to consolidate the results obtained, for example, through data triangulation with other qualitative techniques, such as ethnographic methods.

References

Al Fajri, Muchamad Sholakhuddub. 2019. "The Discursive Portrayals of Indonesian Muslims and Islam in the American Press: A Corpus-Assisted Discourse Analysis." *Indonesian Journal of Applied Linguistics* 9 no. 1: 167–176.

Al-Shehari, Khaled. 2020. "Crisis Translation in Yemen: Needs and Challenges of Volunteer Translators and Interpreters." In *Translation in Cascading Crisis*, ed. by Federico M. Federici and Sharon O'Brien, 25–45. London: Routledge.

Baker, Paul. 2010. *Sociolinguistics and Corpus Linguistics*. Edinburgh: Edinburgh University Press.

Baker, Paul, Costas Gabrielatos, Majid Khosravinik, Michal Krzyzanowski, Tony McEnery, and Ruth Wodak. 2008. "A Useful Methodological Synergy? Combining Critical Discourse Analysis and Corpus Linguistics to Examine Discourses of Refugees and Asylum Seekers in the UK Press." *Discourse & Society* 19, no. 3: 273–306.

Baker, Paul, Costas Gabrielatos, and Tony McEnery. 2013. "Sketching Muslims: A Corpus-Driven Analysis of Representations around the Word 'Muslim' in the British Press 1998–2009." *Applied Linguistics* 34, no. 3: 255–278.

Bartram, Clara. 2017. *Why Do People Volunteer? A Critical Study in Motivations of International Volunteers*. Ph.D. dissertation, University of Edinburgh.

Blinder, Scott, and William Allen. 2016 "Constructing Immigrants: Portrayals of Migrant Groups in British National Papers 2010–2012." *International Migration Review* 50, no. 1: 3–40.

Branun, Jens, and Jonathan Charteris-Black. 2015. "The Edward Snowden Affair: A Corpus Study of the British Press." *Discourse and Communication* 9, no. 2: 199–220.

Bondi, Marina. 2001. "Perspectives on Keywords and Keyness." *In Keyness in Texts*, ed. by Marina Bondi and Michael Scott, 1–18. Amsterdam: John Benjamins.

Caballero-Mengibar, Ana. 2015. "Critical Discourse Analysis in the Study of Representation, Identity Politics and Power Relations: A Multi-Method Approach." *Communication and Society* 28, no. 2: 39–54.

Calkin, Sydney. 2014. "Mind the 'Gap Year': A Critical Discourse Analysis of Volunteer Tourism Promotional Material." *Global Discourse. An Interdisciplinary Journal of Current Affairs and Applied Contemporary Thought* 4, no. 1: 20–43.

Calzada Pérez, María. 2017. "Corpus-Based Methods for Comparative Translation and Interpreting Studies: Mapping Differences and Similarities with Traditional and Innovative Tools." *Translation and Interpreting Studies* 12, no. 2: 231–252.

Courtney, Roger. 2002. *Strategic Management for Voluntary Nonprofit Organization*. London: Routledge.

Defourny, Jaques, Kristen Gronbjerg, Lucas Meijs, Marthe Nyssens, and Naoto Yamauchi. 2016. "Voluntas Symposium: Comments on Salamon and Sokolowski's Re-conceptualization of the Third Sector." *Voluntas: International Journal of Voluntary and Nonprofit Organizations* 27, no. 4: 1546–1561.

Ehrenberg, John. 1999. *Civil Society: The Critical History of an Idea*. New York: New York University Press.

Enjolras, Bernard, Lester Salamon, Karl Sivesind, and Annette Zimmer. 2014. *The Third Sector. A Renewable Resource for Europe*. Summary of Main Findings of The Third Sector Impact Project. Brussels, European Union, https://bit.ly/30ItfNt.

Eschweiler, Jennifer, and Lars Hulgård. 2018. *Channelling Solidarity: Inputs from Third Sector, Social Innovation and Co-Creation of Public Goods*. Report of the European Commission, https://bit.ly/3cwUbWe.

Grönlund, Henrietta. 2011. "Identity and Volunteering Intertwined: Reflections on the Values of Young Adults." *Voluntas: International Journal of Voluntary and Nonprofit Organizations* 22, no. 4: 852–874.

Holmes, Kristen, and Karen Smith. 2012. *Managing Volunteers in Tourism*. Oxford: Blackwell.

Howards, Jo, and Danny Burns. 2015. "Volunteering for Development within the New Ecosystem of International Development." *Institute of Development Studies (IDS) Bulletin* 46, no. 5: 5–16.

Jaworska, Sylvia. 2016. "Using a Corpus-Assisted Discourse Studies (CADS) Approach to Investigate Constructions of Identities in Media Reporting Surrounding Mega Sport Events: The Case of the London Olympics 2012." In *Critical Events Studies: Approaches to Research*, ed. by Ian Lamond and Louise Platt, 149–174. London: Palgrave Macmillan.

Jenner, Jessica. 1982. "Participation, Leadership, and the Role of Volunteerism among Selected Women Volunteers." *Journal of Voluntary Action Research* 11, no. 14: 27–38.

Kartika Dewi, Miranti, Melina Manochin, and Ataur Belal. 2019. "Marching with Volunteers: Their Role and Impact on Beneficiary Accountability in an Indonesian NGO." *Accounting, Auditing and Accountability Journal*, 32, no. 4: 1117–1145.

Kelemen, Mihaela, Anita Mangan, and Susa Moffat. 2017. "More than a 'Little Act of Kindness'? Towards a Typology of Volunteering as Unpaid Work." *Sociology* 51, no. 6: 1239–1256.

López Franco, Erika, and Thea Shahrokh. 2015. "The Changing Tides of Volunteering in Development: Discourse, Knowledge and Practice." *IDS Bulletin* 46, no. 5: 17–28.

Lough, Benjamin. 2015. "The Evolution of International Volunteering. United Nations Volunteer programme." Presentation at the *International Volunteer Service Exchange Conference*, October 12–13, Beijing, China. https://bit.ly/2Nj9JUL.

Marchi, Ana, and Charlotte Taylor. 2009. "If on a Winter's Night Two Researchers: A Challenge to Assumptions of Soundness of Interpretation." *Critical Approaches to Discourse Analysis across Disciplines (CADAAD) Journal* 3, no. 1: 1–20.

McEnery, Tony, and Andrew Wilson. 1996. *Corpus Linguistics*. Edinburgh: Edinburgh University Press.

McEnery, Tony, and Andrew Hardie. 2012. *Corpus Linguistics: Method, Theory and Practice*. Cambridge: Cambridge University Press.

Moulaert, Frank, Abid Mehmood, Diana MacCallum, and Bernhard Leubolt. 2018. *Social Innovation as a Trigger for Transformations: The Role of Research*. Brussels: Publication Office in Luxemburg (European Union), https://bit.ly/3eGFti4.

Partington, Alan. 2004. "Corpora and Discourse, a Most Congruous Beast." In *Corpora and Discourse*, ed. by Alan Partington, John Morley, and Louann Haarman, 9–18. Frankfurt: Peter Lang.

Partington, Alan. 2014. "Mind the Gaps: The Role of Corpus Linguistics in Researching Absences." *International Journal of Corpus Linguistics* 19, no. 1: 118–146.

Partington, Alan, and Ana Marchi. 2015. "Using Corpora in Discourse Analysis." In *The Cambridge Handbook of English Corpus Linguistics*, ed. by Douglas Biber and Randi Reppen, 216–234. Cambridge: Cambridge University Press.

Partington, Alan, Alison Duguid, and Charlotte Taylor. 2013. *Patterns and Meanings in Discourse: Theory and Practice in Corpus-Assisted Discourse Studies (CADS)*. Amsterdam: John Benjamins.

Pena Díaz, Carmen. 2019. "The Role of the Translator and the Interpreter in Terrorist Conflicts." In *Intercultural Crisis Communication Translation, Interpreting and Languages in Local Crises*, ed. by Charles Declercqu and Federico Federici, 63–80. London: Bloomsbury.

PwC Foundation. 2018. *A Close Look at the Third Sector in Spain: Challenges and Opportunities in a Changing Environment*. https://pwc.to/3tkGKPJ.

Robinson, David. 2015. *Local Heroes? A Critical Discourse Analysis of the Motivations and Ideologies Underpinning Community-Based Volunteering*. Doctoral thesis, University of Birmingham.

Rodell, Jessica. 2013. "Finding Meaning through Volunteering: Why Do Employees Volunteer and What Does It Mean for Their Jobs?" *Academy of Management Journal* 56, no. 5: 1274–1294.

Salamon, Lester, and Wojciech Sokolowski. 2016. *The Size and Scope of the European Third Sector*. Brussels: European Commission.

Scott, Mike. 1997. "PC Analysis of Key Words and Key Key Words." *System* 25, no. 2: 233–245.

Scott, Mike. 2010. "Problems in Investigating Keyness, or Clearing the Undergrowth and Marking Out Trails." In *Keyness in Texts*, ed. by Mike Scott and Marina Bondi, 43–58. Amsterdam: John Benjamins.

Sin, Harng. 2010. "Who Are We Responsible to? Locals' Tales of Volunteer Tourism." *Geoforum* 36, no. 3: 983–992.

Stubbs, Michael. 2001. *Words and Phrases: Studies in Lexical Semantics*. London: Blackwell.

Taylor, Charlotte. 2009. "The Representation of Immigrants in the Italian Press." *CIRCaP Occasional Papers* 21: 1–40.

Taylor, Charlotte. 2014. "Investigating the Representation of Migrants in the UK and Italian Press: A Cross-Linguistic Corpus-Assisted Discourse Analysis." *International Journal of Corpus Linguistics* 19, no. 3: 368–400.

Taylor, Charlotte. 2020. "Representing the Windrush Generation: Metaphor in Discourses Then and Now." *Critical Discourse Studies* 17, no. 1: 1–21.

Taylor, Charlotte, and Ana Marchi. 2018. *Corpus Approaches to Discourse: A Critical Review*. London: Routledge.

Tomazos, Konstantinos, and Sheila Luke. 2015. "Mega Sports Events Volunteering: Journeys with a Past, a Present and a Future." *Voluntas: International Journal of Voluntary and Nonprofit Organizations* 26, no. 4: 1337–1359.

Vessey, Rachelle. 2013. "Challenges in Cross-Linguistic Corpus Assisted Discourse Studies." *Corpora* 8, no. 1: 1–26.

Vessey, Rachelle. 2016. *Language and Canadian Media: Representations, Ideologies, Policies*. London: Palgrave Macmillan.

Yap, Su Yin, Angela Byrne, and Sarah Davidson. 2011. "From Refugee to Good Citizen: A Discourse Analysis of Volunteering." *Journal of Refugee Studies* 24, no. 1: 157–170.

Conclusion

Innocent Chiluwa

By analyzing news stories of old and more recent regional and global conflicts, the chapters in this book demonstrate how both mainstream and online media can be instrumental to either exacerbating conflicts or contributing to peaceful resolutions of conflicts. Some of the studies in the chapters are based on many years of research into the relationship between the media and conflict by the authors, who are themselves scholars and practitioners of linguistics and media studies. Hence, the research results presented in these chapters are the products of academic studies and funded projects by seasoned academics, professionals, and experts, as well as doctoral students.

Parts I and II present interesting and unique patterns of news presentations of conflicts from the print media (or the press) and radio and television, as well as online (new) media. These may be of special interest to students and scholars of print and electronic media. On the whole, there are nine chapters, out of a total of fourteen (excluding the introductory and concluding chapters), that are focused on the analysis of conflict and peace discourses in the print media. Two of these focus on electronic media and three on online/digital communication. What this suggests is that there is a lot more interest in research studies around print media, especially on media framing and representations of people, events, and situations, and the ideologies associated with such representations. This book does not provide a direct answer to why there are more studies that focus on print media. But it is important to note that print media data are more readily available than electronic data in some cases, which also may require some form of transcription. The few chapters on radio and TV have highlighted the possibilities of researching language patterns and resources in the electronic media and have arguably illustrated a "how to do" approach to researching news.

In some of the chapters (e.g., 7 and 9), the authors reflect on more practical observations and firsthand experiences of particular conflicts. This means that these chapters recount not only how journalists and political groups represent certain violent conflicts, but also how individuals respond to these conflicts as "citizen journalists" in reporting their own stories, or as participants in revolutionary actions such as protests or social collective actions. In this regard, chapter 9 is different from all the other chapters as it does not analyze news reports from news sources, but rather engages with social media and offline activism. One of the original objectives of this book was to include chapters that would demonstrate how citizen journalism and online activism might contribute to real conflicts or precipitate actions that may lead to social change, or alternatively contribute to the peaceful resolution of existing conflicts. Chapter 9 happens to fall within this objective. This chapter examines how real people – students in conflict with university authorities and the government – resisted what may be termed debilitating social and economic conditions in modern South Africa. Unfortunately, this is reminiscent of apartheid, and also shows how participants in the #FeesMustFall campaign applied social media to mobilize support for their cause.

This collection contributes to showcasing the interdisciplinary relationship and methodological synergy between linguistics, media studies, and international relations. thus far, not very many media scholars have applied themselves sufficiently to the methodological resources available in linguistics, such as discourse analysis, pragmatics, or stylistics in the analysis of data connected to conflict and peace. Conflict and peace studies are traditionally associated with academic disciplines such as international relations, law and social psychology. This book illustrates how methods in linguistics may be applied to study topics in international relations and related disciplines. Also, not many (new) scholars of linguistics and media studies are aware that topics that are generally known to belong to other social sciences, such as political science, psychology, and international relations, are of interest to linguistics, and neither do many media scholars understand the relationship – in terms of the methodology that exists between linguistics and media and communication studies. As a matter of fact, textual analysis, content analysis, genre analysis, and frame analysis (which are popular with communication and media researchers) are all types of discourse analysis – a branch of applied linguistics. Interestingly, linguistic scholars appear to have taken more advantage of the rich data in news reports to advance their studies on the functions of language in social research. As shown in the linguistic and media studies research literature highlighted below, and also in the introduction to this volume, linguistic approaches have been widely applied by language scholars to analyze media reports illustrating the roles of language in the representation of conflict and ideology.

Earlier works that applied linguistic and discourse analytical methods to study media stories have analyzed representations of minorities in conflict situations or the constructions of stereotypes associated with certain people. For instance, such studies have shown that persons and groups have been linked with particular patterns of behavior such as aggression, violence, terrorism, jihadism, or victimhood (see Chiluwa 2011). Such earlier findings have also revealed some negative representations of ethnic minority groups (Chiluwa

2011), Islam and Muslims (Ahmed and Matthes 2017, Awan and Rahman 2016; Baker 2014), immigrants (Caps 2018; Perez-Paredes et al. 2017), asylums seekers (Baker and McEnery 2005), and separatist groups (Chiluwa 2018). These studies associate these groups with violence, terrorism, and criminality. Van Dijk (1991) shows that "new racism" – a subtle form of discrimination among the Extreme Right – is prevalent in Europe and North America and that news in the press has done a great deal to contribute to the increasing practice of racial discrimination. Similarly, Polovina-Vukovic (2004) argues that the negative representation of social actors in the *Globe and Mail* during the break-up of the former Yugoslavia contributed to Western actions in the Balkans and Western acceptance of refugees. Perez-Paredes et al. (2017) argue that the negative representations of immigrants in the EU and British newspapers contribute to jeopardizing the integration of legal immigrants in EU countries, and negatively influence the attitudes of EU citizens and immigration policies toward them. Thus, it is quite easy to discern racism, intolerance, and prejudice in the discourse of representation in the press. The current volume has significantly added to these insightful efforts as they further illustrate how linguistic methods may be applied to media analysis, especially on the topic of conflict and peace.

It is clear therefore that media representations of sociocultural and political realities such as governance, conflict, gender asymmetry, and racism, among others, have received significant attention in research involving critical discourse studies. The qualitative (critical) discourse analysis employed in most of the chapters and the quantitative lexical analysis/corpus linguistics in chapters 3, 8 and 14 will be of great interest to students and researchers in linguistics, communication and media studies, international relations, and sociology. Some of the contributions, such as chapters 1, 5 and 7 combine both qualitative and quantitative approaches.

In terms of theory as highlighted in the Introduction, this book presents discourse analyses of media reports primarily showcasing the theoretical position that discourse is a social practice and that, unfortunately, the representations of the world illustrated in media texts are arbitrary. Media reports reflect media creations and lack the authority to be regarded as absolute truth (for example, see Ahmed Shalane's "Covering the War on Iraq: The Pragmatics of Framing and Visual Rhetoric" in Chapter 4). Critical Discourse Analysis, for example, is a critical scholarship that integrates both theory and practice to analyze how individuals and institutions use language in real-life situations, and also shows how the analyses of this *use* reveal different levels of subjectivity, ideology, polarization, and value judgments. The post-structuralist position on the analysis of discourse – that knowledge of the world should not be treated as objective truth (Laclau and Mouffe 1985), and the application of this theory to the analysis of media texts is a major contribution of this book.

In comparison to existing books on similar topics, and the gap this book attempts to fill, I dare say that this particular volume is unique in the sense that topics on conflict resolution are not common. Moreover, the application of linguistic approaches and methods to the study of vital topics in political science and international relations is also not widespread. However, scholars in linguistics and language studies are increasingly realizing how social research may benefit from approaches in linguistics and discourse analysis, as highlighted above. This book brings the best minds, as well as emerging scholars in discourse studies, to showcase how approaches in discourse analysis may advance research into the roles of the media in conflict studies and conflict resolution. Research into the causes of conflicts and conflict resolution remains a vital global security issue, and this makes this volume all the more timely.

So, we can ask, how does this volume stand out among other specific publications that are already on the market? One key edited volume on the subject of language and conflict is the *Routledge Handbook of Language in Conflict* (2019), edited by Matthew Evans, Lesley Jeffries and Jim O'Driscoll. In this book, the authors examine a range of linguistic approaches as a means of analyzing the nature of communication related to conflict. In it, they draw samples from real-life case studies of conflict from different geographic locations. But that volume does not include the functions and roles of the media in the mediation of conflict and peace as the current volume has done. A monograph by Cees J. Hamelink entitled *Media and Conflict: Escalating Evil* (Routledge, 2011) examines some identified negative roles of the media during conflict. It shows "how the media create anxiety, provide space for agitation, and disconnect people." Again, our current volume not only highlights war journalism, which these other books focus on, but also looks into how the media contribute to global peace processes. The publication that is arguably closest in nature to the current work is Judith Nijenhuis's position report (Radboud University, Nijmegen, 2014). It is called *Peace and War Frames in the Media Representations of the Libyan Civil War* and analyzes the role of war and peace journalism, with particular reference to the Libyan conflicts. Our current book examines conflict and peace reports on the Israeli–Palestinian conflicts, as well as conflicts in Iraq, Afghanistan, Nigeria, the USA, Northern Ireland, and Germany, etc.

Other published works on the subject of media and conflict are mostly research articles published in discourse and media journals; but again, these studies mainly analyze war journalism, rather than peace journalism.

While research into the roles of language in the mediation of conflict in a variety of social and cultural contexts is gradually gaining traction, the investigation of media representations of conflict, especially research on how the media may promote conflicts, has certainly come of age. However, studies of the potential and power of the media to contribute to peaceful and sustained resolution of conflicts are not yet widespread. This book opens up scholarly enquiry in this direction. Unfortunately, five chapter contributions in the book may not have been enough to inspire sufficient motivation and interest, but hopefully, what these authors have done in these short chapters constitutes a roadmap for future research.

References

Ahmed, Saifuddin and Matthes, Jorg. 2017. "Media Representation of Muslims and Islam from 2000 to 2015: A Meta-Analysis." *International Communication Gazette* 79(3), 219–244.

Awan, Imran and Rahman, Mohammed. 2016. "Portrayal of Muslims Following the Murders of Lee Rigby in Woolwich and Mohammed Saleem in Birmingham: a Content Analysis of UK Newspapers." *Journal of Muslim Minority Affairs* 36 (1), 16–31.

Baker, Paul. 2014. "Representations of Islam in British Broadsheet and Tabloid Newspapers 1999–2005." *Journal of Language and Politics* 9(2), 310–338.

Baker, Paul and McEnery, Tony. 2005. "A Corpus-Based Approach to Discourses of Refugees and Asylum Seekers in UN and Newspaper Texts." *Journal of Language and Politics* 4(2), 197–226.

Cap, Piotr. 2018. "From 'Cultural Unbelonging' to 'Terrorist Risk': Communicating Threat in the Polish Anti-Immigration Discourse." *Critical Discourse Studies* 15 (3), 285–302.

Chiluwa, Innocent. 2011. *Labeling and Ideology in the Press: A Critical Discourse Study of the Niger Delta Crisis*. Frankfurt: Peter Lang.

Chiluwa, Innocent. 2018. "A Nation Divided Against Itself: Biafra and the Conflicting Online Protest Discourses." *Discourse & Communication* 12(4), 357–381.

Laclau, Ernesto and Mouffe, Chantal. 1985. *Hegemony and Socialist Strategy. Towards a Radical Democratic Politics*. London: Verso.

Perez-Paredes Pascual, Jimenez, Pillar, and Hernandez, Purificacion Sanchez. 2017. "Constructing Immigrants in UK Legislation and Administration Informative Texts: A Corpus-Driven Study (2007–2011)." *Discourse & Society* 28(1), 81–103.

Polovina-Vukovic, Dragana. 2004. "The Representation of Social Actors in the *Globe* and *Mail* During the Break-up of the Former Yugoslavia." In L. Young and L. Harrison (Eds.), *Systemic-Functional Linguistics and Critical Discourse Analysis: Studies in Social Change*. London: Continuum, pp. 155–167.

Van Dijk, Teun. 1991. "The Interdisciplinary Study of News as Discourse." In K. Bruhn-Jensen and N. Jankowksi (Eds.), *Handbook of Qualitative Methods in Mass Communication Research*. London: Routledge, pp. 108–120.

Index

Abbas, Ali Ismaeel, 107, 108
act, perlocutionary, 306
actors, 70
admonition, 311, 312, 314
Afghanistan, 11, 195, 281, 291
    refugees, 281
    war, 281
Africa, 5
African Union (AU), 127
agenda(s), 93, 94, 95, 109, 111
    fifteen-point, 282
aggression, 69, 73. *See also* violence/violent
aḥādīth, 195, 198, 199, 202
air bases, operational, 281
aircraft, surveillance, 303
alarm, 2
Al Jazeera, 94, 96, 106, 109, 258, 266, 267, 268, 269, 270, 271, 272, 273
Al-Khansaa, 201
al-Qa'ida, 194, 195, 196, 199, 202, 205, 209, 210
Al-Shamika, 201
ambiguity, 308, 309, 321
Amharic, 196
annexation, 267, 268, 269, 271
apology, 300–321
    political, 307, 309
approaches, 2
Arab, 4
    nations, 281
Arabic, 196, 198, 200, 210
Aramaic, 196
army officers, 282
Army Public School, 282
assault, 96, 109
asylum seekers, 8
attacks, 71, 79, 83, 88, 90
attention, metapragmatic, 310
Austin, John, 306

Bajwa, Asim Major General, 290, 291
Balochistan conflict, 280

Banet-Weiser, Sarah, 24, 43
banned outfit, 283, 288, 290
baoqian, 316, 317, 318
BBC, 258, 266, 267, 268, 270, 271, 272, 273
belief systems, 279
Bender, Lynn Darrrell, 23
Bhutto, Benazir, 282
biases, 264, 266, 267, 268, 272, 278, 279, 280, 292
Black students, 214, 219, 220, 221, 222, 223, 224, 226, 227
blame
    attribution, 300, 301 (*see also* guilt attribution)
    avoidance, 301
Blight, James, 23, 43, 44
Bobby Sands, 165
Boko Haram, 71, 74, 88
    terrorism, 83
Brenner, Phillip, 20, 23, 43, 44
brutal killings, 90
Bush, President, 94, 111, 304, 312, 313, 315, 318, 319, 320
    rhetoric of, 105

Carter, Jimmy, 135
Castro, Max, 25
Castro, Soraya, 20
cattle, 71
CDA. *See* Critical Discourse Analysis (CDA)
CDS. *See* Critical Discourse Studies
channels, 5
Chechens, 291
China, government-sponsored media, 140–158
China Radio International, 142, 144–145, 147–154, 157–158
Christians, 83
chronic conflict, 280
civil war, 121
climate change, 71
CNN effect, 121
co-existence, 3

Index

Cold War, 279
Collins, John, 28
collision, 11
Colombian peace talks, 280
communication, 10
 tool, 278
concession, 305, 318, 319, 320
conditions, felicity, 306
condolences, 308
conflict(s), 1, 2, 3, 6, 69, 70, 74, 75, 76, 86, 87, 89, 162, 163, 164, 165, 167, 174, 182, 184, 187, 257, 258, 259, 260, 261, 262, 264, 265, 266, 267, 268, 270, 271, 272, 273
 escalation of, 280
 management, 305
 resolution, 1, 8, 12, 305
constitution, 284
constitutional rights, 6
constructive journalism, 142
content analysis, 10, 26
contention, 12
context, 2, 257, 258, 261, 266, 267, 268, 270, 273
contrition, 309, 314, 319
conversation analysis, 3, 4
corpus linguistics, 325
CRI. *See* China Radio International
criminal organization, 281
critical, 279, 280, 288, 290
critical analysis, 2, 3
critical discourse, 213
Critical Discourse Analysis (CDA), 3, 7, 10, 76, 199, 257, 258, 259, 260, 261, 262, 264, 279, 282, 325
Critical Discourse Studies, 140–141, 147–148, 157
Cuban American National Foundation (CANF), 25
Cuban exile community, 25
Cuban exiles in the United States, 39, 43
Cuban Missile Crisis, 23
Cuban people, 40
Cuban propaganda, 38
Cuban protesters, 39
Cuban style of deterrence, 23, 44
Cuba's communist economy, 37
Cuba's economy, 29
Cuba's political system, 29
Cultural-Historical and Activity Theory, 257, 259, 261, 262, 263, 273
cultural meanings of apologies, 305
cultural mindsets, 279
culture, 48–49, 54–57, 59, 63–65

Dabiq, 194, 195, 199, 200
Da'esh, 194, 195, 196, 199, 202, 205, 206, 209, 210
daoqian, 312, 317, 318
decolonization, 213, 216, 219, 221, 222, 228, 229
decolonized education, 215, 216
de-escalate, 280
delegitimation, 8
democratic, 69
Department of Higher Education, 215, 222
Diaz, Alan, 44
digital media, 8
diplomacy, 9, 38, 301, 312, 314, 321
discourse, 3, 257, 258, 259, 260, 261, 262, 263, 264, 265, 266, 267, 268, 271, 273
discourse, dialectical theory of, 259, 260
discourse analysis, 2, 3, 4, 26, 325
discrimination, 280
discursive, 278, 282, 286, 289, 293
displacement, 70, 71
dissident republican(ism), 162, 163, 165, 166, 167, 183, 188, 189
DPRK. *See* North Korea, media coverage of

Easter, 164, 167
economic sanctions, 38
EEZ, 303
elections, 257, 258, 266, 268, 269, 270, 272
embedded journalism, 279
embedded journalists, 279
emergency situations, 324
empirical studies, 2
environmental degradation, 71
EP-3, 300, 303
escalate conflicts, 280
ethnic, 2, 70
 minorities, 8
ethnocratic, 164
ethno-religious, 71
evaluations, 2
extremism, 195, 286

fallists, 223
Fanon, Frantz, 216, 220, 221, 222, 228, 229
farmer attacks, 75
farmer–herders crisis, 71
farmers, 70, 71, 73, 79, 82, 85, 86, 87, 90
 and herdsmen, 70
Federally Administered Tribal Area (FATA), 282, 291
#FeesMustFall, 213, 214, 216, 219, 220, 221, 222, 225, 226, 227, 228
Fidel Castro, 37, 40

Five Pillars, 202, 204, 209
force, illocutionary, 306, 308, 309, 310, 311, 316, 317, 320
frame analysis, 3
framing, 6, 93, 94, 95, 99, 101, 108, 111, 302
freedom, 6
free education, 215, 217, 220, 228
free expression, 6
Fulani, 70, 79
  herdsmen, 70, 73, 76, 79, 80, 82, 85, 88, 89
fundamentalism, 195

Gadhafi, Muammar, 120
Ghraib, 102, 106, 107, 108, 110
global conflicts, 8
Global War on Terror, 28
Glover, Ross, 28
Golden Exiles, 25
governments, 5
grammatical structure, 2
grazing rights, 71
Greiner, Guillermo, 25
Grounded Theory, 53
guerrilla warfare, 165
guilt attribution, 304, 305, 311, 312. *See also* blame attribution

Hainan, island, 300, 303, 304, 314
Haq, Samiul, 286, 287
headlines, 72, 73, 85
Hebrew, 196
hegemony, 9, 260
herdsmen, 70, 71, 73, 79, 83, 86, 87, 90
  farmers conflict, 74, 75
  killings, 75
heroism, 9
higher education, 213, 214, 215, 216, 217, 219, 222, 224
history, 257, 258, 261, 262, 263, 264, 266, 273
humanitarianism, 119
human rights abuses, 29, 42
Human Rights Watch (HRW), 288, 289, 290
humiliation, century, 305
hunger-strikes, 165
hyperbolic proportions, 24, 43

Ibrahim, 286
identity(ies), 3, 49, 53–54, 59, 61, 63–65, 70, 324
ideological functions, 73
ideology(ies), 3, 6, 76, 163, 164, 166, 171, 172, 174, 175, 176, 195, 196, 199, 324
IFID, 307, 308, 309, 319, 320
immigrants, 8
immigration, 324

independence, 6
in-group, 279, 292, 293
initiatives, 12
insecurity, 80
Inspire, 194, 195, 199
insurrection, 164
interest groups, 280
international diplomacy, 137
international human rights organisation, 288
International Monetary Funds (IMF), 120
international relations, 12
interpretations, 12
interpretations, two, 315
  different, 300
interpretive schemes, 48, 51, 53–59, 61–65
Inter Services Public Relations (ISPR), 290
Iraq, 195
  war, 279
Irish independence, 164
Irish peace process, 280
Irish Republican Prisoner Welfare Association (IRPWA), 167
ISIS, 52, 60–61
Islam, 9, 48–49, 54–58, 64–65, 195, 196, 197, 198, 199, 202, 206, 209
Islamic State, 55
Islamism, 195
Islamophobia, 48, 49
Israel, 11, 257, 259, 260, 261, 265, 266, 267, 268, 269, 270, 272, 273
  reasons for negotiating, 250, 252
  recognition of the PLO, 251
Israel–Palestine conflict, 11

Japan, media coverage of, 151–153
Jiang Zemin, President, 311, 314, 318
jihadism, 195
Jihadists, 88
Jorgensen, Marianne, 2
José Martí, 20
journalism, 1, 2, 6, 7, 11
journalists, 1, 2, 7

Karachi Airport, 282
keyword, 2
killer-herdsmen, 80, 82
killings, 70, 75
knowledge, 4
Kurd, 206

Laclau and Mouffe, 2
landing, emergency, 303, 308, 309, 315
language, 2
Lashkar-e-Jhangvi (LeJ), 288
leftist social ideology, 284

Index

legitimacy, 162, 170, 171, 172, 174, 188
letter
 of apology, 305, 313
 of two very sorries, 301, 310, 313–319
Letters to the editor, 41
lexical/lexicalization, 79, 278, 290, 292
Lexis Nexis, 125
liberation, 95, 96, 108, 109
Libya, 119
linguistics, 2, 4, 12
loyalist, 165, 183

magazines, 8
martyrdom, 6
mass media, 6
Mayer, William G., 26
McKee, Lyra, 162, 167, 174, 184
meanings, of apologies (cultural), 305
Mecca, 197, 203
media, 1, 5, 10, 47–49, 51, 55, 65, 69
 representation, 48–49
 role of, 301, 310, 319, 320
 studies, 8
mediation, 1, 6
mediators, 2
Medina, 197
memory discourses, 285
metaphors, 20, 26, 43
 David and Gulliver, 20
 parent child, 20
methodology, 9
Middle Belt region, 70
migration, 48–49, 59–60, 63
militant groups, 11
militant organization, 281
military, 8
Milwaukee Symphony, 28
Minister of Higher Education, 216
Miranshah, 286
model, 1
morphology, 196
movements, 213, 214, 215, 216, 217, 218, 219, 220, 221, 224, 225, 227, 228, 229
Mujahidin, 281
Muslims, 8, 47–51, 54–59, 61–62, 64–65

narratives, 124, 278
 victimization, 305
nationalism, 5
negotiation, 11, 12
 diplomatic, 304, 305, 309, 315
New Irish Republican Army (NIRA), 162, 166, 167, 187
news, 2, 73
 actors, 72
 coverage, 280
 discourses, 278, 279, 292
 headlines, 70, 74
 production of, 280
newspapers, 4, 7, 47, 51–52, 55, 70, 86
New York Times
 coverage, 238
 global importance, 237
Nigeria, 6, 70, 74, 76, 83, 89
Nigerian civil war, 71
Nigerian conflict situation, 90
Nigerian press, 70
Nigerians, 89
9/11 attacks, 21
non-violent conflict, 69
North America, 4
North Atlantic Treaty Organization (NATO), 119
Northern Ireland, 162, 163, 164, 165, 189
North Korea, media coverage of, 140–141, 147–151, 154–158
North Waziristan, 281, 282, 286, 290, 291, 293
NYT, 95, 96, 97, 102

Obama, Barack, 133
objective truth, 2
occupation, 264, 265, 268, 269, 270, 271, 272
open grazing system, 71
opinion, 9
Orientalism, 40, 44
orthodox extremists, 286
Oslo accord, 7
otherness, 48–50, 55–59, 63–64
out-group, 279
outlawed organisation, 286

Pakistan Air Force, 291
Pakistan ideology, 283
Pakistani government, 278, 283
Pakistan Muslim League-Nawaz (PML-N), 284, 287
Pakistan People's Party (PPP), 287
Palestine, 11, 257, 259, 260, 261, 264, 265, 266, 267, 269, 270, 272, 273
Palestinian–Israeli conflict, 280
Palestinian official negotiators
 concreteness, 250
 excluded from secret negotiations, 239
 occupied territories, 250
paucity, 280
peace, 4, 69, 70, 163, 164, 165
 activist, 10
 agreement, 11
 efforts, 2
 journalism, 6, 7, 293

peace (cont.)
  negotiations, 11
  processes, 6
  reporting, 1
  studies, 12
peace agreement, DoP
  delays before agreement, 244
  delays in implementation, 248
  first postponement, 247
  Israel-Syria negotiations, 243
  mutual recognition, 239, 242, 244
  powers, functional, 252
  secrecy, 237
  separation, 251, 252
  stalemate, in secret channel, 251
  vagueness, 242, 251
peace-building, 6, 12
peace conference for the Middle East
  Madrid Conference, 237
peace discourses, 7
  peace as partition, 252
  political, Israeli, 250
  political, Palestinian, 250
  social, 251
peaceful resolution, 11
Perez, Louis, 22, 43
performativity, 306
perspectives, 2
Peshawar, 286
Philippines' Mindanao conflict, 280
Phillips, Louise J., 2
photographs, 5, 6
pilot, EP-3, 308
Platt Amendment, 20
PLO
  excluded from official negotiations, 237, 250
  exiled, 250
  leadership, 250, 251
  recognition of Israel, 243
polarization, 28, 69, 279, 290, 292
Police Service of Northern Ireland (PSNI), 162, 163, 166, 167, 184, 185
politeness
  strategy, 308
  theories, 306
political science, 12
political violence, 162, 163, 170, 172, 173, 174, 184, 187, 189
portrayal, negative, 317
post-apartheid, 213, 220
post-structuralist, 2
Powell, Colin, Secretary of State, 303, 304, 312, 313, 314, 315, 317, 318, 320
pragmatic acts, 123
pragmatics, 8

cross-cultural, 305
language, 321
press, 74
system, 302
pressure groups, 278
propaganda, 5, 6, 96, 104, 318, 321
protests, 213, 214, 215, 216, 217, 219, 220, 221, 222, 223, 224, 225, 226, 227, 228, 229
Provisional Irish Republican Army (PIRA), 165, 166, 183
Prueher, Ambassador, 304, 314, 315
public diplomacy, 142–146, 158
public opinion, 2, 4, 122
Public Opinion Quarterly, 26
purview, 2

qianyi, 316
Quaid-e-Azam, 287
Qur'an, 194, 195, 197, 198, 202
Quraysh, 206

racism, anti-Muslim, 48–50, 54, 57–58, 64–65
radio, 7
Raqqa, 195
reconciliation, 12
refugees, 58–61, 63, 65
regret expression, 308, 312, 316. *See also* contrition; remorse expression
relations, 3
religious, 70
  extremism, 286
remorse expression, 312. *See also* contrition; regret expression
report, 2
representations, 2, 4, 6, 8, 70, 85, 86, 129
reprisal attacks, 71
republican(ism), 164, 165, 166, 175, 183, 184, 185, 186, 188, 189, 190
research, 11
  techniques, 3
resistance, 163, 166, 180, 182, 184, 185, 265, 270, 272
resolution, 2
Resolutions 338 and 242
  in the DoP, 251, 253
  in the *New York Times*, 244
responsibility, 1
Responsibility to Protect (R2P), 119
retaliatory attacks, 71
rhetoric, 93, 99, 101, 104, 107, 108, 111
rhetorical device, 287, 293
Rumiyah, 195
Rwanda, 5

Sabotage, 37
sacrifice, 6
Saddam, 101, 102, 105, 108
Said, Edward, 40
Saoradh, 162, 163, 166, 167, 174, 180
Sarkozy, Nicolas, 133
security, 11, 49, 53–54, 57–65
  agents, 90
  state, 50, 53–54, 63
semantic moves, 285, 290
semantics, 310, 312, 313, 314, 315, 318
sensationalize war, 280
sentiment, intensifiers, 304
Shah, Yousaf, 286
Sharia, 286, 287
Shari'ah, 195, 196, 207, 208, 209
Sharif, Nawaz Muhammad, 282, 286, 288, 289
Shi'a, 207
silent killings, 90
Sinn Féin, 164, 165
Snow, Nancy, 143, 158
social action, 4
social change, 213, 214, 216, 218, 219, 220, 221, 222, 224, 226, 228, 229
social cognition, 282
social group, 279, 289
socialist leftist agenda, 283
socially constituted ideology, 279
social media, 215, 216
social movements, 213, 214, 217, 218, 219, 224, 229
social security, 4
social world, 2
society, 257, 258, 260, 262
socio-cognitive approach, 282
Sociology of Knowledge Approach to Discourse (SKAD), 48, 50–51, 53, 65
solution-oriented, 1, 5
South Asia, 281
South China Sea, dispute, 145, 151–152
South Korea, media coverage of, 140–142, 148–151, 156–157
South Waziristan, 291
Soviet Army, 281
Soviet invasion, 279
Soviet Union, 281
Spain, separatist movement in, 280
speech acts, 123
speech act theory, 11, 305–310
standoff, diplomatic, 300, 303, 304, 308, 309, 310, 312, 314, 318, 319, 320. *See also* conflict; diplomacy
stereotypes, 9
  anti-Muslim, 48, 65
strategies, 213, 216, 222, 224, 225, 228

suffering, 94, 95, 98, 100, 101, 103, 104, 105, 107, 109, 110
sunnah, 195, 198, 209
Sunni, 207, 209
surah, 197
sustainable peace, 12
synergy, 8
syntactic structures, 72
systematic constructions, 70

Taliban, 11
  committee, 282
  good/bad, 290, 291
  insurgency, 281
  Mulish, 286
Tehreek-e-Taliban Pakistan (TTP), 281, 284, 286, 288
television, 4, 7
temporal words, 286
terrorism, 9, 47–48, 54–55, 57, 59–65, 73, 87, 163, 171, 176, 265, 266, 272
terrorism, Islamist, 47–49, 51–52, 60, 62, 64–65
terrorist groups, 284, 290
terrorist organization, 278, 281, 283, 284
terrorist threats, 9
textual functions, 73
textual macrostructure, 283
theories, 2, 3
third sector, 326
Tigrinya, 196
tool of communication, 278
trajectories, 9
transformation, 1
transitive verbs, 285
translation, creative, 315
tribal people, 282
The Troubles, 163, 165, 185

UNCLOS, 303
UNESCO, 12
United Nations Security Council (UNSC), 119
United States, government-sponsored media, 140–142, 144–148
United States Agency for Global Media, 146
United States embargo, 23
University of the Witwatersrand, 213, 214, 215, 222, 225
USA
  host of negotiations, 237
  superpower, 237
USAGM. *See* United States Agency for Global Media
US economy, 29
US embargo, 33, 38, 42, 43

US government, 281, 291
US propaganda, 38
utterance, one, 300, 315, 321
Uzbeks, 291

value systems, 279
van Dijk, Teun A., 278, 279, 280, 282, 293
vigilante militias, 70
violence/violent, 8, 47, 48, 51–52, 54–55, 59–61, 69, 70, 80, 213, 216, 219, 221, 222, 223, 225, 226, 227, 228. *See also* aggression
violent conflicts, 70
VOA. *See* Voice of America
Voice of America, 144–148, 154–158
volunteer/volunteerism/voluntary engagement, 12, 325
Vygotsky, 257, 262, 263, 264, 273

Wahhabi, 194
Wang, Wei, 303, 315
wanxi, 316

War of Independence, 164
war(s), 1, 2, 69, 70, 74
  journalism, 293
  policy, 4
  reporting, 2
  against terror, 281
waters, international, 303
Waziristan, 11
weaponry, 9
weapons of mass destruction (WMD), 279
West African fulanisation, 83
Western actors, 11
Western media, 279, 286
women, 100, 101, 102, 104, 106, 107, 110

Yezidi, 206, 207
Yi, Wang, 149–154
yihan, 312, 316
Yugoslavia, 5

Zarb e Azab, 278, 281, 282, 283, 290, 293
Zardari, Bilawal Bhutto, 287, 288

www.ingramcontent.com/pod-product-compliance
Ingram Content Group UK Ltd.
Pitfield, Milton Keynes, MK11 3LW, UK
UKHW031825020325
455765UK00012B/90